1 SAMUEL

1 SAMUEL

A CONCEPTUAL FEMINIST INTERPRETATION

Susanne Scholz

Fortress Press
Minneapolis

1 SAMUEL
A Conceptual Feminist Interpretation

30 29 28 27 26 25 1 2 3 4 5 6 7 8 9

Library of Congress Control Number: 2025937150 (print)

Cover image: Yehuda Levy-Aldema, *Seeing*, oil painting, by permission of the artist.
Cover design: Kris E. Miller

Print ISBN: 979-8-8898-3662-9
eBook ISBN: 979-8-8898-3663-6

To my mother,
Roswitha Scholz-Ardebili,
who would have loved a feminist interpretation of 1 Samuel,
instead of the phallogocentric reading she was taught,
back in ninth grade, in 1952

CONTENTS

ACKNOWLEDGMENTS

Sometimes unexpected experiences lead to researching new exegetical topics. I admit I never thought I would concern myself with one of the most evidently androcentric biblical books: 1 Samuel. But it did happen, and I am most grateful for the support received in various ways during the research, writing, and publishing process of this volume. A sabbatical leave at the École Biblique in East Jerusalem in the fall of 2018 allowed me to visit various archaeological locations traditionally identified with places mentioned in 1 Samuel. I acknowledge with profound gratitude Yehuda Levy-Aldema, with whom I have been in *havruta* conversations on Skype and Zoom for the past seven years. A former museum curator and an artist of exquisite abstract sculptures on the book of Genesis, he is also a certified Israeli tour guide. He had offered to show me various archaeological sites related to 1 Samuel. Yehuda knows his country and its history, traditions, and troubles inside out. I benefited enormously from his erudite guidance, and I treasure our friendship across our diverse social locations. He showed me places in his native land that I could have never seen without his professional and adept expertise. I also thank my Palestinian guide Hijazi Eid, the director of Hijazi Travels, who led me to archaeological sites on the West Bank that I could have never visited without his guidance. I will never forget how he, another Bedouin man, and I drove toward one of the military checkpoints that Palestinians are prohibited from crossing. Three Israeli soldiers checked their papers and my passport. The inevitable happened. Denied crossing the checkpoint, we were required to turn back and unable to continue our journey on 1 Samuel's itinerary. This checkpoint encounter gave me a tiny bit of a sense about the harassment Palestinians living on the West Bank experience daily. In different ways, both Yehuda and Hijazi made my effort of getting a geographical and geopolitical feel for the locations mentioned in 1 Samuel exceptionally memorable, and chapter 1 of this book owes a great deal to their guidance.

I also thank Dr. Craig C. Hill, a former dean of SMU's Perkins School of Theology. He supported my research stay at the École Biblique when a grant unexpectedly fell through. I am very grateful for the special support of this important trip that catapulted me into writing this conceptual feminist interpretation of 1 Samuel.

As the work began taking shape on my computer screen, other unexpected projects continuously interrupted the writing process. During another research leave in spring 2022, I again enjoyed uninterrupted writing time to work on the manuscript. I would like to thank the librarians of SMU's Bridwell Library for their reliable and calm support in finding this or that book in the stacks or for getting my interlibrary loans processed. I greatly appreciate the exquisite resources of this scholarly gem of a theological library and am privileged to have daily access to its tremendous resources.

Toward the end of the writing process and the beginning of the editorial refinements of the manuscript, I also benefited greatly from the loyal support and friendship of my Old Testament colleague Dr. Carol J. Dempsey, OP. Her collegial enthusiasm of and scholarly admiration for this manuscript gave me critical backing. Carol modeled feminist collegiality in the flesh, and her professional encouragement, solidarity, and friendship are a treasure. I also would like to thank other feminist and womanist colleagues, among them Drs. Linda Maloney, Cheryl Kirk-Duggans, and Valerie Bridgeman for their collegial cheer and support. I am grateful to Sue Burich, who quickly transformed the manuscript into a presentable Word file. Lorraine Keating's enduring help made it all happen when the situation seemed at a standstill. I am thrilled that my acquisition editor, Michael West of Fortress Press, expressed great interest in my work. What a blessing to have the support from like-minded colleagues. I appreciate the collective encouragement and passion that have heartened me to be my strident feminist self and never to give up.

Finally, I express my gratitude to my colleagues who accepted my invitation to write short pieces or whose excerpts from their published works are included in the sections titled "For Further Reflection" at the end of each chapter of this book. I thank the respective publishers for permitting me to reprint the excerpts. Thanks to my colleagues in the order of their work's appearance in the volume: Kevin M. McGeough, University of

Lethbridge, Canada; Carol J. Dempsey, OP, University of Portland, USA; Isam Shihada, Al Aqsa University, Gaza/Palestine; Aren M. Maeir, Bar-Ilan University, Israel; Yaron Peleg, University of Cambridge, UK; Helen Leneman, independent scholar and cantor, London, UK; Ken Stone, Chicago Theological Seminary, USA; the late Marc H. Ellis, Baylor University, USA; Silvia Schroer, University of Bern, Switzerland; Randall C. Bailey, Faulkner University, USA; Robert Drews, Vanderbilt University, USA; Serge Frolov, Southern Methodist University, USA; Harry A. Hoffner Jr., University of Chicago, USA; David A. Schones, Austin College, USA; David J. Zucker, rabbi and scholar, USA; Brian B. Schmidt, University of Michigan, USA; Rachel Ofer, Herzog College, Israel; J. Kabamba Kiboko, Forest Chapel United Methodist Church, Cincinnati, USA; Mary Chan; Shatha Almutawa, Willamette University, USA.

I wrote several chapters of this manuscript during the coronavirus pandemic, an extraordinary time in our lives. Entire countries experienced lockdowns. Our academic courses moved to digital delivery systems as the academic infrastructures turned increasingly digital. Conference travels basically ended for almost two years. The isolating time of those years made it easier to finish delinquent writing projects like this one. My exegetical work also reminded me again that it is good for humans to hang on to "old texts" like the Bible. Although we do not really know where they originated from, despite plentiful historiographical hypotheses by historical critics, 1 Samuel has been read for a very long time. In an era of extensive and existential changes in our world, I am glad to offer my conceptual feminist interpretation. Whether we are feminist or not, we ought to stay connected and wrestle with what previous generations transmitted to us. Let's make sure we pass on those texts to the next generation so that they, too, have something to contend with during difficult times. The point is not to agree, and certainly not to comply, with what earlier interpreters said about the Bible but to come up with our own (feminist) readings. In this spirit, I am offering my book as a continuation for worthwhile and hopefully never-ending exegetical conversations, and even debates, about biblical meanings in the world in which we live. Intellectual engagement is deeply sustaining to the human spirit and very much needed in societies that want us to have neither unmonetized nor uncontrollable critical thinking anymore.

ABBREVIATIONS

AASOR	*The Annual of the American Schools of Oriental Research*
AThR	*Anglican Theological Review*
AUSS	*Andrews University Seminary Studies*
BA	*The Biblical Archaeologist*
BAR	*Biblical Archaeology Review*
BAS	Biblical Archaeology Society
BASOR	*Bulletin of the American Schools of Oriental Research*
BDB	Brown, Francis, S. R. Driver, and Charles A. Briggs. *A Hebrew and English Lexicon of the Old Testament*
Bib	Biblica
BibInt	Biblical Interpretation Series
BW	Bible and Women
BWANT	*Beiträge zur Wissenschaft vom Alten und Neuen Testament*
BZAW	Beihefte zur Zeitschrift für die alttestamentliche Wissenschaft
CBQ	*Catholic Biblical Quarterly*
CH	*Church History*
CurBR	*Currents in Biblical Research*
FCB	*Feminist Companion to the Bible*
GBS	Guides to Biblical Scholarship
GTR	Gender, Theory, and Religion
HS	*Hebrew Studies*
IFT	Introductions in Feminist Theology
JANER	*Journal of Ancient Near Eastern Religions*
JBL	*Journal of Biblical Literature*
JBQ	*Jewish Bible Quarterly*
JFSR	*Journal of Feminist Studies in Religion*
JSOT	*Journal for the Study of the Old Testament*
JSOTSup	*Journal for the Study of the Old Testament Supplement series*
KJB	King James Bible

LHBOTS	The Library of Hebrew Bible / Old Testament Studies
LXX	*Septuagint*
NEA	*Near Eastern Archaeology*
NSKAT	Neuer Stuttgarter Kommentar, Altes Testament
OBT	Overtures to Biblical Theology
PEQ	*Palestine Exploration Quarterly*
PL	*Patrologia Latina*
PSB	*Princeton Seminary Bulletin*
RevExp	*Review & Expositor*
SBL	Society of Biblical Literature
SemeiaSt	Semeia Studies
SHBC	Smyth & Helwys Bible Commentary
SJOT	*Scandinavian Journal of the Old Testament*
SVTQ St.	*Vladimir's Theological Quarterly*
SymS	Symposium Series
TQ	*Theologische Quartalschrift*
USQR	*Union Seminary Quarterly Review*
VC	*Vigiliae Christianae*
Vg	*Vulgate*
VT	*Vetus Testamentum*
VTSup	Supplements to Vetus Testamentum
WBC	Word Biblical Commentary
WCS	Wisdom Commentary Series
ZAW	*Zeitschrift für die Alttestamentliche Wissenschaft*

INTRODUCTION

On a Conceptual Feminist Interpretation of 1 Samuel

> *I ask instead: What is the meaning of inventing, and then making assumptions and claims (about knowledge and authority) in connection with scriptures? What work do we make scriptures do for us—and to us? What cultural practices are involved? What power dynamics and issues are imbricated and structured and codified, and sometimes questioned and resisted, in connection with such practices? What fears and anxieties motor the practices and manage the resultant system?*
>
> —Vincent L. Wimbush, *Scripturalectics: The Management of Meaning*

THIS IS THE first feminist, genderqueer, and masculinity-oriented interpretation of the book of 1 Samuel. Of course, many feminist, genderqueer, and masculinity-oriented scholarly books and journal articles have been published since the emergence of gender-based scholarship on the Hebrew Bible in the 1970s. At the same time, many generic (i.e., phallogocentric, heteronormative, and misogynist) readings have been published. In other words, this is indeed a historic moment. Elaborating on this moment, my introductory comments address, first, why the time is now for a conceptual feminist reading of 1 Samuel; second, why the exegetical move beyond an essentializing focus on women matters; third, how the textual-linguistic character and source-critical composition of 1 Samuel support a conceptual feminist framework; and, finally, what the chapter outline is of this interpretation of 1 Samuel.

Why Now, and Why at All?

Since the emergence of feminist biblical scholarship in the early 1970s, feminist exegetes have taken on the arduous and joyous task of interpreting biblical texts with questions, concerns, and emphases not seen in the long interpretation history of the Bible. Sometimes individual Jewish and Christian women read their Bibles with protofeminist concerns in mind, namely, those concerns that existed prior to the nineteenth-century women's movement conjoining the abolitionist movement in the United States. For example, the German Christian mystic Hildegard von Bingen (1098–1179) emphasized the significance of Genesis 1:26–27 to support the idea that both women and men are created in the image of God in every regard. The extraordinarily independent Christian thinker, writer, and French woman Christine de Pizan (1364–1430) maintained, based on her reading of Genesis 1–2, that woman, like man, is not only created in God's image but also made of much better material than man. She is taken from human flesh, whereas man comes from soil. For this and several other reasons, de Pizan considered woman to be the culmination of divine creation. Many other activists who fought for women's suffrage and the abolition of slavery, such as the US-Americans Sojourner Truth and Elizabeth Cady Stanton, also interpreted the Bible in line with their sociopolitical causes. The nineteenth-century women's movement in the United States even produced the renowned Woman's Bible, edited by Cady Stanton and with contributions from numerous women writers and suffragists, though no Bible scholars.[1]

Yet only with the arrival of the feminist movement in the late 1960s and early 1970s did feminist Bible scholars, credentialed with doctorates in the various subfields of biblical studies, begin publishing explicitly feminist exegetical books and articles. Initially, their attention was drawn to individual female characters, including women in 1 Samuel such as Hannah, Michal, or Abigail, because after centuries of phallogocentric neglect,

1. For more details about these developments, see, e.g., Susanne Scholz, *Introducing the Women's Hebrew Bible: Feminism, Gender Justice, and the Study of the Old Testament*, 2nd ed. (London: Bloomsbury, 2017). See also Joy A. Schroeder and Marion Ann Taylor, *Voices Long Silenced: Women Biblical Interpreters Through the Centuries* (Louisville, KY: Westminster John Knox, 2022); Marion Ann Taylor, ed., *Handbook of Women Biblical Interpreters: A Historical and Biographical Guide* (Grand Rapids, MI: Baker Academic, 2012). For a critical analysis of Cady Stanton's anti-Semitic and racist viewpoints, see, e.g., Kyla Schuller, *The Trouble with White Women: A Counterhistory of Feminism* (New York: Bold Type Books, 2021).

feminist exegesis of the 1970s and 1980s was mainly interested in recovering women in the Bible. For instance, attention to female characters helped historical critic Carol L. Meyers to reconstruct women's lives in premonarchic Israel.[2] Literary feminist critic Esther Fuchs examined not the historical but the literary strategies pitting Hannah and her rival Peninnah against each other, as well as depicting the latter as the former's "evil victimizer."[3] Some feminist interpreters reclaimed certain women, such as Michal. Feminist interest in Abigail was halting at first,[4] but her verbal power and agency eventually attracted feminist exegetes.[5] All of these feminist readers recommended readerly resistance against androcentric conventions, embedded in the text, that present women primarily as mothers or wives.

Overall, the fragmented nature of women's stories and the general absence of their viewpoints in 1 Samuel did not produce a massive amount of feminist readings. The Catholic feminist Old Testament scholar Silvia Schroer at the University of Bern in Switzerland, known for her groundbreaking feminist exegesis in the German-speaking theological world,[6]

---

2. See the updated revision of Carol L. Meyers's 1988 book titled *Rediscovering Eve: Ancient Israelite Women in Context* (New York: Oxford University Press, 2013).

3. Esther Fuchs, *Sexual Politics in the Biblical Narrative: Reading the Hebrew Bible as a Woman*, JSOTSup 310 (Sheffield: Sheffield Academic, 2000), 156.

4. See, e.g., the comprehensive discussion by Lai Ling Elizabeth Ngan, "Class Privilege in Patriarchal Society: Women in First and Second Samuel," in *Feminist Interpretation of the Hebrew Bible in Retrospect: Biblical Books (vol. 1), Recent Research in Biblical Studies 5*, ed. Susanne Scholz (Sheffield: Sheffield Phoenix, 2013), 110–134.

5. See, e.g., L. Juliana M. Claassens, "An Abigail Optic: Agency, Resistance and Discernment in 1 Samuel 25," in *Feminist Frameworks and the Bible: Power, Ambiguity, and Intersectionality*, ed. L. Juliana M. Claassens and Carolyn J. Sharp, LHBOTS 630 (London: Bloomsbury T&T Clark, 2017), 21–38. See also Jo Ann Hackett, "1 and 2 Samuel," in *Women's Bible Commentary*, 3rd ed., ed. Carol A. Newsom, Sharon H. Ringe, and Jacqueline E. Lapsley (Louisville, KY: Westminster John Knox, 2012), 150–163; Luise Schottroff and Marie-Theres Wacker, eds., *Kompendium Feministische Bibelauslegung* (Gütersloh: Chr. Kaiser / GütersloherVerlagshaus, 1998), which has been translated into English: *Feminist Biblical Interpretation: A Compendium of Critical Commentary on the Books of the Bible and Related Literature* (Grand Rapids, MI: Eerdmans, 2012).

6. For instance, she has been the founder and chief editor of *lectio difficilior: European Electronic Journal for Feminist Exegesis*, http://www.lectio.unibe.ch/index.html.

published a one-volume commentary on 1 and 2 Samuel in 1992.[7] The work of this accomplished feminist exegete does not, however, offer feminist perspectives. Even Athalya Brenner's edited volume *Feminist Companion on Samuel and Kings* includes only four essays on 1 Samuel; three of them focus on Hannah, and a fourth essay discusses David and "his women."[8] In sum, it is high time for a feminist interpretation that engages 1 Samuel as a whole. I thus offer this volume with a certain degree of historical self-consciousness, trusting that my readers, feminist or not, will read this book with gracious understanding for the difficult road ahead.

Moving Beyond an Essentializing Focus on Women

This book expands the feminist interpretation from an essentializing focus on "women" to an intersectionally framed investigation of various gender issues. It is fair to ask why the exegetical move beyond an essentializing focus on women matters. In my conceptual feminist reading of 1 Samuel, gender issues are not limited to "women," although female characters will be discussed in chapter 5 of this book. I define gender broadly, and it includes the description of male characters or even geopolitical locations as markers of sexual difference.[9] The decades-old feminist insight that feminist work ought to shift beyond an essentializing focus on women goes back to Elisabeth Schüssler Fiorenza, a pioneering feminist Bible scholar of the Second Women's Movement that began in the 1970s. Schüssler Fiorenza noted already in 1983 that many mid-twentieth-century books on "women in the

7. Silvia Schroer, *Die Samuelbücher*, NSKAT 7 (Stuttgart: Verlag Katholisches Bibelwerk, 1992).

8. Athalya Brenner, ed., *Samuel and Kings: A Feminist Companion to the Bible*, FCB 5 (Sheffield: Sheffield Academic, 1994). The follow-up volume is also edited by Athalya Brenner and titled *Samuel and Kings: A Feminist Companion to the Bible*, FCB 7, 2nd series (Sheffield: Sheffield Academic, 2000). It includes only two essays on 1 Samuel; one discusses Saul, David, and Jonathan, and another focuses on Michal.

9. For what is by now a classic feminist philosophical analysis of gender that famously characterizes gender as a "performance," see Judith Butler, *Gender Trouble: Feminism and the Subversion of Identity*, Routledge Classics, 2nd ed. (New York: Routledge, 2006; originally published 1999).

Bible" existed since the early twentieth century and were primarily popular in religious-conservative circles that emphasized women's roles as mothers and family-oriented figures.[10] Schüssler Fiorenza observed that books "of so-called data and facts on 'Women in the Bible' . . . take the androcentric dynamics and reality constructions of patriarchal texts at face value."[11] A good example is Annie Russell Marble's 1923 volume, titled *Women of the Bible: Their Services in Home and State*, which includes a predictable array of patriarchal roles for women in chapters such as "The Hebrew Woman in Her Home," "Wives of the Bible: Some of Them Were Wise and Some Were Foolish," "Mothers in Israel," and "Women in Patriotic and Religious Service."[12]According to Schüssler Fiorenza, these kinds of books advance an apologetic hermeneutic that legitimizes "societal and ecclesiastical patriarchy and . . . women's 'divinely ordained place.'"[13] Identifying doctrinal truth in stories about biblical women, these and similar books turn the Bible into "an absolute oracle revealing timeless truth and definite answers to the questions and problems of all times."[14] Schüssler Fiorenza went even further in her daring analysis that sharply criticized essentializing readings of women in the Bible. She explained that these books often claim that even God wants women in roles assigned to them by patriarchal society and religion.

In contrast to these books and in accordance with Schüssler Fiorenza's insight, my conceptual feminist interpretation critically interrogates the conceptualization of "women in the Bible" by advancing an intersectional feminist, genderqueer, and masculinity-oriented approach. My reading does thus not reinforce exegetical complacency with the hegemonic status quo. Grounded in Deryn Guest's critique of essentialized gender notions, my interpretation aims to expose literary strategies of heteropatriarchy and "male dominance inherent in heterosexism,"[15] critically interrogating the

---

10. For more details, see my *Introducing the Women's Hebrew Bible*, 19–23.

11. Elisabeth Schüssler Fiorenza, *In Memory of Her: A Feminist Theological Reconstruction of Christian Origins* (New York: Crossroad, 1983), xxiii–xxiv, 30.

12. Annie Russell Marble, *Women of the Bible: Their Services in Home and State* (New York: The Century Company, 1923).

13. Marble, *Women of the Bible*, 7.

14. Marble, *Women of the Bible*, 5.

15. Deryn Guest, *When Deborah Met Jael: Lesbian Biblical Hermeneutics* (London: SCM Press, 2005), 46.

"heterocentric framework"[16]of depicting female characters as the negative foil of male characters. When female and male characters appear mainly as wife and husband or daughter and father, a heterosexist readerly imagination remains oblivious to this kind of hegemonic fantasy. Yet it needs to be uncovered even in stories that center on the power struggles among males because this kind of imagination advances a kyriarchal worldview. To critique such a worldview is at the heart of my conceptual feminist reading of 1 Samuel.

The rejection of an essentializing focus on women also implies that my approach takes seriously the interrelatedness of all structures of domination. As gender, misogyny, phallogocentrism, and heteronormativity do not appear in isolation, my reading connects these interrelated issues to other categories of identity, such as various forms of masculinity, ethnonationalism, religion, or geopolitics, to name the central ones in my approach to 1 Samuel. Biblical works of minoritized scholars affirm the need to produce intersectionally informed feminist exegesis.[17] For instance, Gale A. Yee problematizes the ethnic/racial identities of biblical readers when she wonders about her own "Asian Americanness, and how . . . this identity affect[s] my biblical interpretation."[18] Similarly, womanist exegetes Gay L. Byron and Vanessa Lovelace state that exegetical discourse needs to attend to "the multilayered and interlocking systems of oppression."[19] Accordingly, the Black women contributors in Byron and Lovelace's volume offer biblical meanings

16. Guest, *When Deborah Met Jael*, 107.

17. See, e.g., Tat-siong Benny Liew and Fernando F. Segovia, eds., *Reading Biblical Texts Together: Pursuing Minoritized Biblical Criticism*, SemeiaSt 98 (Atlanta: SBL Press, 2022); Randall C. Bailey, Tat-siong Benny Liew, and Fernando F. Segovia, eds., *They Were All Together in One Place? Toward Minority Biblical Criticism*, SemeiaSt 57 (Atlanta: SBL, 2009).

18. Gale A. Yee, "Yin/Yang Is Not Me: An Exploration into an Asian American Biblical Hermeneutics," in *Ways of Being, Ways of Reading: Asian American Biblical Interpretation*, ed. Mary F. Foskett and Jeffrey Kah-Jin Kuan (St. Louis: Chalice, 2006), 156.

19. Gay L. Byron and Vanessa Lovelace, "Introduction: Methods and the Making of Womanist Biblical Hermeneutics," in *Womanist Interpretations of the Bible: Expanding the Discourse*, ed. Gay L. Byron and Vanessa Lovelace, SemeiaSt 85 (Atlanta: SBL Press, 2016), 8.

in conversation with issues of African American cultures, politics, and various manifestations of sociopolitical, economic, or religious injustice. In general, then, womanist and other minoritized exegetes have developed exegesis within an intersectional framework. Delores S. Williams's reading of Hagar in Genesis 16 is perhaps the most well-known and one of the earliest intersectionally framed approaches. Her study highlights Hagar's story as shaped by the categories of gender, ethnicity, and class (female, Egyptian, enslaved/poor).[20]

In alignment with the hermeneutical insights of intersectional biblical hermeneutics, my conceptual feminist approach advances five thematic areas. They include the geopolitics of land and gender, the variously positioned male characters, the depicted governance model of the monarchy, the ethnonational stereotypes embedded in references to the (male) Philistines, and the inscription and erasure of female characters as mothers, wives, daughters, unnamed women, and witch. The next section explains how the textual-linguistic nature and source-critical composition of 1 Samuel support a specifically conceptual design.

Textual-Linguistic and Source-Critical Observations

A linear, sequential reading of 1 Samuel runs into manifold difficulties due to this biblical book's textual-linguistic character and source-critical composition. Scholars have long acknowledged that the book's Hebrew text is one of the most corrupt texts in the Bible. Many passages are unclear in the original Hebrew, and different manuscripts offer divergent texts. Text critics always wrestle with the problem of putting together a readable Hebrew text.[21] Interestingly, parallel reports in 1 Chronicles resolve many textual disorders of 1 Samuel by omission or modification. The Septuagint, too, makes many corrections, changes, and even eliminations that persuade some

20. Delores S. Williams, *Sisters in the Wilderness: The Challenge of Womanist God-Talk* (Maryknoll, NY: Orbis Books, 1993).

21. See, e.g., Philippe Hugo and Adrian Schenker, eds., *Archaeology of the Books of Samuel: The Entangling of the Textual and Literary History*, VTSup 132 (Leiden: Brill, 2010). For a recent text-critical study on 1 Samuel 17–18 in English, see Simeon Chavel and Jessie DeGrado, "Text- and Source-Criticism of 1 Samuel 17–18: A Complete Account," *VT* 70 (2020): 553–580.

source critics to prefer the Greek translation over the Masoretic Text.[22] Like the text of the Septuagint, the Qumran scrolls (discovered in the mid-twentieth century CE) include four scrolls of the book of Samuel, one of them dating to the third century BCE. This is about two hundred years later than the presumed Deuteronomistic edition of the Hebrew text, as source critics have dated the earliest literary traditions of Deuteronomy, Joshua, and Judges, as well as the books of Samuel and Kings, into the preexilic or exilic period of biblical history (seventh and sixth centuries BCE). Shimon Bar-Efrat explains that the Qumran fragments of 1 Samuel are often identical to the Septuagint, further convincing some text critics to favor the Greek text over the Masoretic Text.[23] Robert Alter offers a compelling example for the textual variants in the Septuagint and the Masoretic Text:

> Let me give one illustration of a moment in which it seemed to me that the case was fairly compelling for turning to a variant in the Septuagint. In 1 Samuel 14:18, Saul, at the head of his army, is wondering what course of action he should take against the Philistines. We are told, in the Masoretic Text (this rendering is quite literal), "And Saul said to Ahijah, 'Bring forth the Ark of God.' For the Ark of God on that day was, and the Israelites." It is immediately evident that the second sentence here is fragmentary, each of its two clauses breaking off abruptly, with the syntactic link between them unclear. An even greater perplexity is the presence of the Ark of God on the battlefield and its use (as the context makes clear) for inquiry of an oracle. After the earlier disaster in carrying the Ark to the front and after the lethal consequences of its return from Philistia to Israel, the people had firmly concluded that the

22. The Masoretic Text was produced by the Masoretes, Jewish scribes working from the end of the fifth through the tenth centuries CE. For a discussion of Greek and Hebrew texts of 1 Samuel, see, e.g., Jong-Hoon Kim, *Die hebräischen und griechischen Textformen der Samuel- und Königebücher: Studien zur Textgeschichte ausgehend von 2 Sam 15,1–19,9*, BZAW 394 (Berlin: De Gruyter, 2009).

23. Shimon Bar-Efrat, *Das Erste Buch Samuel: Ein narratologisch-philologischer Kommentar*, trans. Johannes Klein, BWANT 176 (Stuttgart: Verlag W. Kohlhammer, 2007), 29.

> dangerous Ark should be left at Kiriathjearim (1 Samuel 5), and the later narrative strongly implies that it remained ensconced there until the victorious David came to take it up to Jerusalem. There is, moreover, no indication elsewhere in the Bible that the Ark was ever used as an instrument of divination. The oracular device that was repeatedly employed was a cultic object called the ephod, and that is what appears in the Septuagint reading of this verse, which I decided to adopt: "And Saul said to Ahija, 'Bring forth the ephod.' For on that day he was bearing the ephod before the Israelites." Admittedly, there can be no certainty in such matters, but when the received text combines in a single verse a blatantly contradictory narrative datum and syntactic incoherence, it is not unreasonable to conclude that an ancient version free of both defects may reflect the original wording of the story.[24]

Textual incongruencies in the biblical Hebrew led translators to modify the wording in the target language, as is the case in the Septuagint here and elsewhere in the Hebrew Bible.

Other translations, such as the Targumim in Aramaic, the Peshitta in Syrian, or the Vetus Latina and Vulgate in Latin, show this kind and many different solutions, although text critics do not value them as much as the Septuagint. Nor does Flavius Josephus's first-century *Greek Antiquities of the Jews* solve the many textual-linguistic difficulties. Josephus embellished the biblical tales of 1 Samuel extensively, and so his work does not assist in the text-critical task of establishing a reliable text. Produced by the Masoretes, the Masoretic Text aims to offer an authoritative reading. Yet the Masoretic Text includes an unusually high number of *Qere*, from the Aramaic for "[what is] read," indicating how the text should be read or, more precisely, pronounced, over against the *Ketiv*, from the Aramaic for "[what is] written," indicating how the text is spelled (e.g., 1 Sam 5:6, 9, 12; 6:4, 5; 17:23; 20:14). As the Masoretic vocalization clarifies the meaning of the Hebrew consonants (*Ketiv*), it also highlights the textual difficulties. For instance,

24. Robert Alter, *The David Story: A Translation with Commentary of 1 and 2 Samuel* (New York: Norton, 1999), xvii.

in 1 Samuel 6:4, 5, the *Ketiv* has "golden boils" (עפלי זהב).The problem is that nobody knows what *'opalim* are. The Masoretes suggested in their *Qere* to read this Hebrew word as "golden *tumors*" (טחרי זהב), a completely new Hebrew word in the *Qere*. Many English translations render the Hebrew as "hemorrhoids," but interpreters are not sure what disease is afflicting the male Philistines at that point in the story.[25] The medical vocabulary thus varies in different translations.

The textual-linguistic corruption is not the only hurdle for interpreting 1 Samuel in a sequential fashion. Another exegetical feature, long recognized in the interpretation history, illustrates the difficulty of reading 1 Samuel sequentially. At issue is whether 1 Samuel ought to be read as an individual book in the canon. Historically, 1 Samuel has not always been considered as a single book because in earlier eras it was put together with 2 Samuel, 1 Kings, and 2 Kings. For instance, the Septuagint lists the four books as *ΒασιλειωηΑ*, *ΒασιλειωηΒ*, *ΒασιλειωηΓ*, and *ΒασιλειωηΔ*, traditionally translated into Latin as *Regnorum I–IV* (Kingdoms I–IV). Early Christian translators, such as Jerome, adopted this terminology and grouping. The fourfold division of contemporary Bibles (1 Samuel, 2 Samuel, 1 Kings, 2 Kings) goes back to the first *printed* Hebrew Bible of the Daniel Bomberg edition, published in Venice in 1517. Daniel Bomberg (1483–1549) was an important Christian printer of Hebrew books who employed Jewish scholars and rabbis.[26] For instance, he printed the first Mikraot Gedolot (rabbinic Bible) and the entire Babylonian Talmud. Interestingly, the first print edition of the Bible used Hebrew terminology for the four biblical books (שמואל א, שמואל ב, מלאכים א, מלאכים ב).

The separation of 1 Samuel from its larger canonical-literary context must thus be recognized as a late decision that disregarded the literary connections of 1 Samuel to what precedes this biblical book's first few chapters

25. For an accessible explanation of this particular *ketiv* and *qere* in 1 Samuel 5–6, see Zev Farber, "Unspoken Hemorrhoids: Making the Torah Reading Polite," *The Torah.com*, https://www.thetorah.com/article/unspoken-hemorrhoids-making-the-torah-reading-polite.

26. For more details on this historically important printer of the sixteenth century CE, see Abraham Habermann, "Bomberg, Daniel," in *Encyclopaedia Judaica*, ed. Michael Berenbaum and Fred Skolnik, 2nd ed. (Detroit: Macmillan, 2007), 5.

and what follows after its last chapter. Obvious examples are the early stories in 1 Samuel about the birth, adolescence, and work of Samuel, the judge, because these stories continue the storyline of the book of Judges. Similarly, chapter 31 does not complete 1 Samuel, but the storyline continues into the early chapters of 2 Samuel where the installation of David as the second king is reported, and David laments the death of Saul and Jonathan reported in 1 Samuel 31. Yet at the same time, the thirty-one chapters of 1 Samuel provide more than ample texts for my conceptual feminist reading, and so this treatment confines itself to 1 Samuel.

Yet there is another reason for limiting my reading to 1 Samuel only. David Jobling notes that analog or digital printing has contributed to the false readerly impression that 1 Samuel is an individual biblical book. He observes that economic decisions reign over the production process, as publishers aim to produce attractive books to make a living and often more than that.[27] Jobling explains:

> We write a lot of books whose topic, even whose title, is "1 Samuel." As we do so it is hard to avoid asserting at some level the rightness of beginning to read at 1 Samuel 1 and stopping at 1 Samuel 31. Many of these books are, like this one, constrained by being part of a series on the books of the Bible. There are, to be sure, works that take as their topic some literary object not coterminous with 1 Samuel, and so disturb our tendency to let canonical tradition decide into what bits we divide the Bible for the purpose of study. But I surmise that authors who let the canon define the scope of their book

---

27. Jobling does not include any evidence for his observations, but scholars outside of biblical studies address the general economics of publishing. On the contemporary economic situation of book publishing, see, e.g., Albert N. Greco, *The Economics of the Publishing and Information Industries: The Search for Yield in a Disintermediated World* (New York: Routledge, 2015). On pages 223–224, Greco states, "Book publishing is not rocket science; you do not have to know Ito calculus to understand this business. . . . Educational publishers must reevaluate their existing editorial operation to ascertain with more precision textbook needs in the next five years. . . . University presses will continue to experience serious declines in library purchases, their largest market."

> get more contracts, and sell more copies, than those who do not. The canonical books tend to define academic courses in theological schools or elsewhere, and a course on 1 Samuel will tend to favor as its textbooks those that are on 1 Samuel. So an industry develops that privileges books that take a biblical book as their topic. The implications of the canon extend even into economics![28]

Said differently, the biblical canon shapes economics, as readers desire a coherent reading experience of 1 Samuel. Yet the storyline that begins in Judges and continues with 2 Samuel is fragmentary, even choppy, repetitive, truncated, and convoluted. In my view, the conceptual feminist design of my reading brings thematic order to this biblical book's textual-literary disjointedness by limiting itself to the thirty-one chapters.

Perhaps even more significant is another observation that is focused on source criticism. Source critics have long identified multiple layers of textual traditions in 1 Samuel. Already in 1926, the Bible scholar Leonhard Rost (1896–1979) established that the Ark Narrative (1 Sam 4:1–7:1; 2 Sam 6) and the so-called Succession Narrative (2 Sam 9–20; 1 Kings 1–2) are two independent and early literary traditions that were secondarily added to a complex network of literary traditions constituting 1 and 2 Samuel.[29] Then in 1943, German Bible scholar Martin Noth (1902–1968) proposed what has become a famous source-critical construct. He located 1 Samuel within what he called the Deuteronomistic History.[30] This construct about

28. David Jobling, *1 Samuel* (Berit Olam; Collegeville, MN: Liturgical Press, 1998), 32–33.

29. Leonhard Rost, *Die Überlieferung von der Thronnachfolge Davids*, BWANT 42 (Stuttgart: Kohlhammer, 1926). For the English translation, see Leonhard Rost, *The Succession to the Throne of David*, trans. Michael D. Rutter and David M. Gunn, Historic Texts and Interpretations in Biblical Scholarship 1 (Sheffield: Almond Press, 1982).

30. Martin Noth, *Überlieferungsgeschichtliche Studien: Die sammelnden und bearbeitenden Geschichtswerke im Alten Testament*, 2nd ed. (Tübingen: Max Niemeyer Verlag, 1957). This is a reprint of the first edition of 1943. For a translation into English, see Martin Noth, *The Deuteronomistic History*, JSOTSup 15 (Sheffield: JSOT, 1981).

the literary origins of Deuteronomy, Joshua, Judges, and the books of Samuel and Kings has been modified, expanded, and even challenged ever since Noth articulated it.[31] For instance, already in 1953, George B. Caird explained in the influential *The Interpreter's Bible*[32] that 1 Samuel contains an "Early Source,"[33] a "Late Source,"[34] a "Deuteronomic Edition,"[35] and "Later Additions."[36] Although Caird's source-critical categories present a "maximalist" position that attributes large chunks of 1 Samuel to the "Early Source," Caird also recognized the book's literary complexity and disjointedness. It is thus fair to assert that a sequential interpretation of 1 Samuel is difficult to justify from a source-critical stance. This biblical book does not advance a linear storyline, given its double[37] or even triple[38] repetitions of similar, contrasting, or even entirely disconnected texts. Indeed, the leaky storyline preserves diverse, disconnected, and fragmentary textual traditions. My conceptual feminist approach respects these traditions, viewing them as an opportunity to create conceptually designed textual units that I interpret from a feminist, genderqueer, and masculinity-oriented hermeneutical perspective.

---

31. For a popularizing overview of the current scholarly situation on the Deuteronomistic History (DtrH), see, e.g., Brian Neil Peterson, *The Authors of the Deuteronomistic History: Locating a Tradition in Ancient Israel* (Minneapolis: Fortress, 2014).

32. See George B. Caird, "1 Samuel: Introduction and Exegesis," in *The Interpreter's Bible*, ed. George Arthur Buttrick, vol. 2 (New York: Abingdon, 1953), 856–865.

33. 1 Sam 4:1–7:1; 10:6, 10; 11:6; 9:1–10:16; 11; 13–14; 16:14–23; 17; 18:5, 6–16, 20–29a; 18:20–29a; 19:11–17; 21:1–9, 10; 22:1–23:13; 25:2–31:13.

34. 1 Sam 1; 2:11–26; 3:1–4:1a; 7:3–17; 8; 10:17c–27a; 12; 15:1–16:13; 17:12–31, 41, 48b, 50, 55–18:5, 10–11, 17–19; 19:1–10; 20:1–42; 23:14–24:22; 25:1

35. 1 Sam 14:47–51.

36. 1 Sam 2:1–10; 10:8; 13:7b–15a; 19:18–24; 21:10–15.

37. See, e.g., the repeated rejection of Eli's priestly lineage in 1 Sam 2:27–36 and 3:11–14 or the two explanations on the origins of the proverbial saying about Saul being among the prophets in 10:10–13 and 19:18–24. Also, David spares Saul twice in 23:19–24:22 and 26:1–25.

38. See, e.g., the three accounts of David's escape from Saul in 19:11–17, 18–24; 20:1–24.

My idea to organize 1 Samuel on the basis of a conceptual design is not entirely new, although the combination with feminist intersectional concerns has not been done before. Other recent commentators have also recognized the benefits of a conceptual design. For instance, Stephen B. Chapman relies on a christological framework to legitimize his reading of 1 Samuel from a theological stance. He organizes his reading according to the notion that Saul symbolically represents the crucified Christ, and David is "a type of Christ."[39] For different reasons and in a different way, David Jobling organizes his interpretation of 1 Samuel according to the concepts of class, gender, or race.[40] Interestingly, the feminist interpreter Jo Ann Hackett discusses female and some male characters, such as Hannah, David and Goliath, David and Jonathan, David and Saul, Michal, Ahinoam, and the woman of Endor, outside her otherwise sequentially organized, chapter-length reading of 1 and 2 Samuel that is part of the *Women's Bible Commentary*.[41]

In sum, 1 Samuel is not an internally coherent, linear, or sequential text. The literary stratification of the "imagining of history"[42] is unquestionably complicated, and it is debatable where the book begins and where it ends. Although 1 Samuel begins with the conception and birth narrative of the man whose name the book carries, the book stands indeed within a much larger literary "arc of biblical narrative that begins with the creation of the world."[43] Overall, then, the textual-linguistic character and source-critical observations, as well as the conceptual organization of recent readings, support a conceptual design, as I present it in this volume. To some readers, the design may seem innovative, but it is grounded in the textual, literary, and hermeneutical-theological peculiarities of this biblical book and its interpretation history. In my view, the "textual perplexities"[44] are remarkable

---

39. Stephen B. Chapman, *1 Samuel as Christian Scripture: A Theological Commentary* (Grand Rapids, MI: Eerdmans, 2016), 17–18, 35, 245–255 (quote on 246, 258).

40. Jobling, *1 Samuel.*

41. Hackett, "1 and 2 Samuel," 153–158.

42. Alter, *The David Story*, xvii.

43. Johanna W. H. Van Wijk-Bos, *The Road to Kingship: 1–2 Samuel*, A People and a Land, vol. 2 (Grand Rapids, MI: Eerdmans, 2020), ix.

44. Van Wijk-Bos, *The Road to Kingship*, xxiv.

enough to venture forth and read 1 Samuel on the basis of a conceptual feminist approach.

On the Chapter Outline

Although this book approaches the various literary units of 1 Samuel within a conceptual framework, the five chapters do not ignore the textual-literary sequence altogether. Accordingly, the first chapter begins with the book's initial verse (1 Sam 1:3), and the last chapter ends with almost the last chapter (chap. 28). Nevertheless, the structure of the five chapters does not always follow the textual sequence verse by verse, but each chapter features biblical texts related to the conceptual feminist issues under consideration.

Noticeably, the five areas critically interrogate the geopolitics of land and gender (chapter 1), variously positioned male characters (chapter 2), the discourse on the emerging monarchy (chapter 3), the ethnonational stereotypes embedded in rhetorical references to the (male) Philistines (chapter 4), and the erasure of female characters (chapter 5). Although other feminist interpreters highlight the few women of 1 Samuel in the attempt of recovering those characters from androcentric marginalization, most feminist recovery projects demonstrate the relative insignificance of female characters to the overall storyline.[45] My approach follows a different path. It exposes the gender-stereotypical ways of featuring women by mapping the female characters within the patriarchal roles in which they appear. Women are mothers, wives, and daughters; some of them are named, and others are unnamed. Only the woman of Endor stands possibly outside the phallogocentric imaginary. Yet perhaps her exceptional status merely affirms this pattern, and so her story, too, does not offer a glimpse beyond the predominantly patriarchal representation of female characters.

The five chapters offer wide-ranging insights into the hermeneutical, ethical, and exegetical issues of a conceptual feminist reading of 1 Samuel. The first chapter focuses on major geographical sites mentioned in 1 Samuel to illuminate the interaction of land and gender, with special attention to archaeology, including Tel Shiloh, 'Izbet Sartah, and Tel eṣ-Ṣâfi/Gath. As

45. For a comprehensive and concise survey of feminist recovery efforts of female characters in 1 Samuel, see Ngan, "Class Privilege in Patriarchal Society."

postcolonial feminist interpreters have convincingly maintained, gender is always linked to past and present geopolitics of the land.[46] Thus, this reading suggests that locations mentioned in 1 Samuel should be linked to geopolitical concerns related to today's Palestine and Israel. Since we always read in the present era in which we live, even when we claim to read the past, we ought to recognize contemporary geopolitical issues involved in reading the Bible, as Fernando F. Segovia explains so eloquently: "If critics are to deal with the intersecting nature of the crisis in the world system, they have no option but to examine and address such a crisis from a variety of perspectives, theorizing in the process their own locations in and perception of the world."[47] Said differently, the notion that biblical texts ought to be read as ancient literature is a modern construct. This construct allows contemporary readers to create interpretations that readers have classified as conveyors of historical information. Yet so-called ancient texts are always a contemporary construct of and about the imagined past, and so our readings are less about the past than about readers imagining texts as ancient memories. Exegetical urgency and epistemological integrity require that my reading, grounded in a conceptual framework, exposes unspoken assumptions on which interpreters rely in their readings of 1 Samuel as a historical source about ancient Israel.

This methodological insight is important. For instance, traveling the routes depicted in the tales of 1 Samuel is increasingly difficult, perhaps even impossible, depending on one's identification papers or passport. The Israeli military occupation of the West Bank and the Israeli closure of Gaza[48] make

---

46. See, e.g., Musa W. Dube, *Postcolonial Feminist Interpretation of the Bible* (St. Louis: Chalice, 2000); Caroline Vander Stichele and Todd C. Penner, eds., *Her Master's Tools? Feminist and Postcolonial Engagements of Historical-Critical Discourse*, Global Perspectives on Biblical Scholarship 9 (Atlanta: SBL, 2005). For a general and comprehensive overview of the field, see R. S. Sugirtharajah, ed., *The Oxford Handbook of Postcolonial Biblical Criticism*, Oxford Handbooks (Oxford: Oxford University Press, 2023).

47. Fernando F. Segovia, "Criticism in Critical Times: Reflections on Vision and Task," *JBL* 134 (2015): 25.

48. Gaza was closed from June 2007 to October 2023. Until 2011, Egypt kept restrictive policies at its Rafah crossing, and Israeli authorities almost completely closed the Gaza Strip, with a few exceptions. The political-military situation

a smooth and unhindered journey from Israel proper to the West Bank, and back, cumbersome and, in the case of Gaza, practically impossible. In fact, the war and destruction of Gaza since October 2023 will probably produce entirely new geopolitics for Gaza once the war will be over. Unfortunately, exegetes mention rarely, if ever, the geopolitical realities of today's so-called Holy Land, to use a Christian term that some consider more politically "neutral" than "Israel/Palestine" or "Israel and the Occupied Territories." Yet by referring to current conditions on the ground, the first chapter brings attention to the geopolitical reality of reading 1 Samuel today. Commenting on geography, archaeology, and gender, the first chapter highlights the movements of things and people that contemporary travelers cannot always duplicate due to current military-political conditions on the ground.

Another word of consideration about my book's insistence on reading 1 Samuel in front of the text, as part of the geopolitical here and now: If I had lived during any previous moment in time, such as during the Jordanian control of Jerusalem prior to 1967 or under Hadrian's closure of Jerusalem to Jews after the Bar Kokhba Revolt in 136 CE or under the Ottoman Empire's control of the Middle East from about 1516 to 1917 CE, my reading would have taken into account the respective geopolitical conditions of those time periods, similar to chapter 1's recognition of today's Israeli military occupation of the West Bank. That past and present exegesis has not been developed with the respective geopolitical sensibility in mind is, in my view, a loss for contemporary readers. I for one would have found it extremely interesting to learn how past readers related to the many geopolitical locations mentioned in 1 Samuel from the particular and unique viewpoints of past readers' time

---

changed dramatically in October 2023 after the Hamas attack in Israel proper on October 7, 2023, and the ensuing military response by Israel since October 14, 2023. For further information on the situation from 2007 to 2023, see, e.g., "Gaza: Israel's 'Open-Air Prison' at 15: Israel, Egypt Movement Restrictions Wreak Havoc on Palestinian Lives," *Human Rights Watch*, June 14, 2022: https://www.hrw.org/news/2022/06/14/gaza-israels-open-air-prison-15. For the genocidal war situation in Gaza since October 2023, triggered by the Hamas attack in Israel on October 7, 2023, see, e.g., this assessment by Oxfam and Human Rights Watch, "Israeli Forces' Conduct in Gaza," March 19, 2024, https://www.hrw.org/news/2024/03/19/israeli-forces-conduct-gaza.

and place. Perhaps in future decades and centuries, this or that exegete will look back to the geopolitical references of chapter 1 and be surprised how the situation has changed in light of future geopolitical conditions. Unfortunately, I did not have the benefit of learning from past readers how they thought about the many locations in relation to past geopolitical realities. Yet as the Israeli military occupation shapes today's access and movement from Israel proper into the West Bank and vice versa, the first chapter discusses central locations mentioned in 1 Samuel with the current geopolitical reality in mind.

Titled "Detailing the Geopolitics of Land and Gender," the first chapter examines several major geopolitical locations. One prominent location is Shiloh, mentioned in 1 Samuel 1:3. Another group of geographical locations pertains to the journey of the ark from Shiloh to Eben-ezer to Ashdod into the house of Dagon to Gath to Beth-Shemesh and finally to Kiriat-jearim (1 Sam 4–7). Another set of locations relates to David's journey as he escapes from Gibeah to Naioth in Ramah (1 Sam 19:18–24), from there to Nob, Gath, Adullam, and Mizpeh of Moab (1 Sam 20:1–22:23), from there to Keilah, the hill country of the wilderness of Ziph at Horesh, then into the wilderness of Maon, En-gedi (1 Sam 23–24), and eventually to the land of the Philistines, where David receives the gift of Ziklag (1 Sam 27). A feminist tracing of those itineraries benefits from understanding past and present geopolitics, as 1 Samuel includes famous, lesser-known, and even unknown places in today's Israel and Palestine. The itineraries teach that various gender-related dynamics, rarely put into words, reinforce hidden archaeological interests and geographical realities in the so-called Holy Land.

The second chapter, titled "Displaying the Masculinities of Major and Minor Male Characters," uncovers several constructs of hegemonic masculinity in 1 Samuel. As this biblical book is filled with male characters, nobody will contest that male elite hegemony permeates it. Three male characters (Samuel, Saul, and David) dominate the storyline, and other male figures play secondary and only supportive roles. Unsurprisingly, women perform only in secondary roles as male heroes prepare, advance, or even fail on their paths to the Israelite monarchy. The narrated attention is firmly focused on the three major characters, even when other interspersed accounts interrupt, confuse, or divert the readerly attention from them. A key question is whether a feminist deconstructive approach,[49] aiming to expose the hegemonic status of male characters, does not simultaneously assume and even accept their centrality, as it centers on the men's stories. As androcentric interpretations assume male hegemony, I suggest that feminist exegesis needs to critically assess male characters and their stories. Since androcentric readers do not explicitly scrutinize male dominance in the world within or behind the text, my feminist reading interrogates the hegemonic status of the male characters, especially in light of the relative absence of female characters. Accordingly, one section of the second chapter focuses on Samuel's murderous masculinity. Another section investigates Saul's failure to perform normative masculinity, and yet another section explores David's toxic masculinity. A final section analyzes the submissive masculinities of Jonathan, Abner, Elkanah, and Eli. As a whole, the chapter emphasizes the feminist need to account for the various masculinities depicted in 1 Samuel.

The third chapter, titled "Determining the Specter of Monarchy at the End of Democracy," takes a closer look at those riveting accounts that outline the move from the political system of the judges to the appearance of the Israelite monarchy. My interpretation recognizes that most biblical research has considered the transition from ancient Israel's "tribal organization"[50] to a monarchical system as largely inevitable. Many exegetes, preferring the monarchy to the "old order" of the "tribal confederacy,"[51] do not mention the authoritarian challenges of past or present monarchical systems. They accept the imagined governmental system of the biblical storyline even

49. For a comprehensive explanation of deconstruction in feminist biblical interpretation, see Susanne Scholz, "Tracing Difference, Power, and the Discourse of Gender: Deconstruction in Feminist Hebrew Bible Studies," in *Feminist Interpretation of the Hebrew Bible in Retrospect: Methods (vol. 3)*, ed. Susanne Scholz (Sheffield: Sheffield Phoenix, 2016), 199–222.

50. See, e.g., John Bright, *A History of Israel*, 3rd ed. (Philadelphia: Westminster, 1981), 182, who assumes ancient Israel was organized in twelve tribes. This view has been rejected in historical-critical research, such as in Niels Peter Lemche's scholarship; see, e.g., Niels Peter Lemche, *Back to Reason: Minimalism in Biblical Studies, Discourses in Ancient Near Eastern and Biblical Studies* (Sheffield: Equinox, 2022).

51. See, e.g., the classic volume by Bright, *A History of Israel*, 184, 186.

when the narrative presents God as resisting a monarchical system for biblical Israel, such as in 1 Samuel 8:7–9. In contrast, the third chapter explores the kyriarchal nature of the depicted monarchical system by interrogating the fusion of ethnoreligious, class-biased, and androcentric power in the biblical institution of the monarchy. The chapter also explores why so many exegetes take for granted the literary move from the institution of the judges to the installation of the first king. They read *with* the text, whereas my interpretation accentuates the violent, kyriarchal, and politically simplistic portrayals of the rise and fall of the first king and the rise of the second one. My exegetical focus on personalized, sexualized, and bloody kyriarchal power struggles reminds readers of the authoritarian political dynamics of the depicted emerging royal system. The aim is to encourage readers to resist rising authoritarianism even in our own time.[52] Two sections explore the stories in 1 Samuel about the ascending Israelite monarchy. One section highlights narratives on the rise and fall of the first Israelite king, Saul. Another section presents stories on the rise of the second Israelite king, David. As a whole, the third chapter warns against literalist or seemingly historicized readings that do not recognize the tales on the developing biblical monarchy as dangerous fantasies about an imagined future.

The fourth chapter, titled "Decolonizing Foreskin Talk About the Nation and the Philistines," examines the depictions of the (male) Philistines as the masculine Other nation in the land of Canaan. Focusing on the characterization of the Philistines as the major military opponent to be fought and defeated by the male Israelites, the chapter argues that the ethnonational binary is also always androcentrically envisioned. Accordingly, my feminist reading deconstructs the ethnonational assumptions embedded in the descriptions of the (male) Israelite-Philistine military encounters. Since the biblical discourse about the (male) Philistines constitutes a literary rhetorical effort of so-called nation-building grounded in colonizing phallogocentric strategies, the biblical texts position the (male) Philistines as the archenemies of the Israelites. Importantly, the interpretation of those texts illustrates

---

52. For a description of the political, economic, and social system emerging in our time, see, e.g., Yanis Varoufakis, "Techno-Feudalism Is Taking Over," *Project Syndicate*, June 28, 2021, https://www.project-syndicate.org/commentary/techno-feudalism-replacing-market-capitalism-by-yanis-varoufakis-2021-06.

the contemporary explosiveness of correlating the logic of ethnonationalism within the logic of phallogocentrism, as this kind of logic results in war, murder, and destruction. Four sections examine the ethnonational and phallogocentric references to (male) Philistines as Other. One section examines how 1 Samuel reduces (male) Philistines to the skin of the male reproductive organ. Another section, interpreting the Ark Narrative (1 Sam 4:1–7:1) as a literary construct, shows that the phallogocentric and ethnonational rhetoric depicts the male Philistines as the archenemies of the male Israelites. Yet another section focuses on a most famous Philistine character, Goliath of Gath, to uncover the andro-ethnonational dynamics of this famous warrior tale. Still another section explores the ethnosexist function of the Philistine king of Gath, Achish, serving as a stepping stone on David's path toward power and glory to become the second Israelite king. Overall, then, the chapter encourages readers to recognize the persistent ethnonational and phallogocentric characterization of the male Philistines as Other in 1 Samuel.

Finally, the fifth chapter, titled "Detecting the Erasure of Women and the Inscription of a Witch," exposes the erasure of female characters in 1 Samuel. Although some women do appear in this biblical book, they are not its protagonists. Showing up here and there, they again disappear quickly. Esther Fuchs explains that the mere recovery of erased female characters does not lead to their full inclusion even when they are inscribed in various roles prior to their erasure in biblical texts and interpretations.[53] This chapter takes seriously Fuchs's feminist-theoretical insight: The logic of inscription already entails the logic of erasure. Additionally, the cursory mention of women in 1 Samuel should not be misunderstood as a reflection of lived realities or as evidence of real people but always as phallogocentric fantasies. In this sense, the chapter seeks to uncover the phallogocentric need for erasing female characters and to connect this need to androcentric, heteronormative, patriarchal, and misogynist assumptions, conventions, and preferences of limiting women to roles accepted, and sometimes even respected, as mothers, daughters, and wives.

---

53. Esther Fuchs, "Prophecy and the Construction of Women: Inscription and Erasure," in *A Feminist Companion to Prophets and Daniel*, ed. Athalya Brenner, FCB 8, 2nd series (Sheffield: Sheffield Academic, 2001), 54–69.

Several sections illuminate the spectrum of female appearances in "classic" roles in 1 Samuel. Women are depicted as mothers, piously endorsing men or serving as cursed props and quiet devotees of men; they are wives, functioning as incidental embellishment of polygynous husbands; and they are named and unnamed daughters, appearing as royal bait or phallogocentric ciphers. Importantly, all women—named or unnamed—are largely insignificant to the androcentric, imperialist, and ethnonational struggles over geopolitical, social, and economic power, as structured by the elite phallogocentric imaginary. Interestingly and famously, one of the female characters is inscribed as a witch of a particular place, Endor.[54] Moreover, my analysis of this biblical book's female characters challenges another feminist viewpoint that regards women as playing a qualitatively "larger role"[55] in 1 Samuel than in many other parts of the Hebrew Bible. My interpretation disagrees with this viewpoint, showing that in 1 Samuel women only appear in a "conscripted look"[56] favored by the phallogocentric order. Whether the woman of Endor is an exception in this conscripted look is questionable, as a minimum.

In sum, all five chapters offer a comprehensive and detailed interpretation of 1 Samuel. Other exegetes might, will, and should emphasize different aspects. Ideally, future interpreters will find the broadly defined and expansively discussed issues helpful for their own readings. Standing in the long tradition of Bible readers is a great privilege and pleasure to me, although I also realize how difficult it is to read against hegemonically defined conventions of biblical exegesis. To know, deconstruct, and resist these conventions is crucial, but so is the engagement with the theoretical and exegetical insights from feminist, queer, womanist, masculinity, and otherwise-gendered scholarship in its intersectional dimensions. My hope is that my conceptual feminist approach offers new energy to those involved in the arduous work of eliminating gender injustice in its various manifestations in the Bible and in the world today.

---

54. For the cultural appropriation of the term *witch* as a positive classifier, see, e.g., Ethan Doyle White, "Wicca," *Encyclopedia Britannica*, https://www.britannica.com/topic/Wicca.

55. Hackett, "1 and 2 Samuel," 162.

56. Andrea Bachner, *The Mark of Theory: Inscriptive Figures, Poststructuralist Prehistories* (New York: Fordham University Press, 2018), 207.

1

DETAILING THE GEOPOLITICS OF LAND AND GENDER

The image of the traveler depends not on power, but on motion, on a willingness to go into different worlds, use different idioms, and understand a variety of disguises, masks, and rhetorics. Travelers must suspend the claim of customary routine in order to live in new rhythms and rituals. Most of all . . . the traveler crosses over, traverses territory, and abandons fixed positions, all the time.

—Edward Said, "Identity, Authority, and Freedom: The Potentate and the Traveler"

From Narrative Fiction to Archaeological Realities: An Introduction

Since the stories in 1 Samuel are not based on historically accurate or scientifically verifiable events,[1] the existence of many geographical sites related to those stories is striking even today. In contemporary Israel and Palestine, including in the militarily occupied West Bank and the closed and blocked Gaza Strip,[2] many places mentioned in the thirty-one chapters have received considerable archaeological attention once archaeology had become part of

1. For an introduction on the methodological debates about biblical historiography, see, e.g., Lester L. Grabbe, *Ancient Israel: What Do We Know and How Do We Know It?* rev. ed. (London: Bloomsbury T&T Clark, 2017).

2. For more details on the geopolitical, military situation of the Gaza Strip until October 2023, see, e.g., Al Mezan Center for Human Rights, "15 Years Too Long: A Factsheet on the Devastating Effects of Israel's Closure on the Gaza Strip," 2022, https://www.mezan.org/uploads/files/16551887811136.pdf; "Blockade of Gaza Strip," Britannica, https://www.britannica.com/place/Gaza-Strip/Blockade. The Egyptian border was closed from mid-2007 until 2011. In mid-2018, Israel

biblical studies at the end of the nineteenth century CE. One of the first biblical excavations was led by an aristocratic British woman, Lady Hester Lucy Stanhope (1776–1839). Excavating "the earth in search of hidden treasures,"[3] she was "the first person who ever intentionally excavated an ancient artifact in the Holy Land"[4] when she came to the ruins of Ashkelon in April 1815. The Ottoman authorities had allowed her to excavate the site. Yet only at the turn of the twentieth century did excavations become an established method to search for biblical evidence. By then, Lady Stanhope's pioneering efforts had been long forgotten in the male-dominated field of biblical studies.

Unsurprisingly, in the so-called Holy Land, every tel[5] has its own excavation story. Nowadays, many archaeological excavations are interrelated with governmental and financial support, often from Christian evangelical organizations or institutions of higher education (grant money), to cover the enormous expenses involved in digging up ancient stones and pottery buried in layers and layers of soil. Archaeology in Israel/Palestine is thus intimately related to the geopolitics of the era in which the excavation takes place. This dynamic also applies to the sites mentioned in 1 Samuel. For instance, Tel Shiloh, which is located on the West Bank about thirty-one kilometers north of Jerusalem or twenty-seven kilometers north of Ramallah, is a worship place mentioned in 1 Samuel 1:3 ("Now this man used to go up year by year from his town to worship and to sacrifice to [YHWH] at Shiloh, where the two sons of Eli, Hophni and Phinehas, were priests

---

began easing restrictions on its blockade. Since October 2023, the war in Gaza has changed everything in Gaza; see also footnote 48 in the introduction of this book.

3. Charles Lewis Meryon, *Travels of Lady Hester [Lucy] Stanhope Forming the Completion of Her Memoirs, Narrated by Her Physician*, vol. 1 (London: Henry Colburn, 1846), vi.

4. Neil Asher Silberman, "Restoring the Reputation of Lady Hester Lucy Stanhope: A Little-Known Episode in the Beginnings of Archaeology in the Holy Land," *BAR* 10 (1984): 68. He acknowledges her contribution to archaeological excavations when he states, "Lady Hester Lucy Stanhope's 1815 expedition to Ashkelon might be rightfully called the first modern excavation in the history of archaeological exploration of the Holy Land" (75).

5. A tel is a small hill or mound containing accumulated and stratified remnants of earlier human habitation.

of [YHWH]").[6] The archaeological site has become a major archaeological tourism park with an active excavation going on since 2017. The tel is also part of interesting political dynamics that do not belong to the margins of biblical interpretation. The mere mention of this site within the first story of 1 Samuel, centered on a classically androcentric quest for a son by the central female character of Hannah, is insufficient because of the postcolonial feminist insight that gender is always linked to a land's geopolitics.[7] Yet the geopolitics of Palestine and Israel has become so complicated due to the Israeli military occupation of the West Bank since 1967 that the routes mentioned in 1 Samuel are difficult to repeat today.

The postcolonial feminist hermeneutical insight that gender and land need to be analyzed together is the basis for this chapter's focus on several geographical references in a biblical book that is filled with traveling people and objects. Three main geopolitical considerations organize the reading. The first section refers to the archaeological significance of Tel Shiloh in the scholarly literature. The second section traces the journey of the ark from Shiloh to Ebenezer to Ashdod into the house of Dagon to Gath to Beth-Shemesh and finally to Kiriat-jearim (1 Sam 4–7), with interspersed references to gender and sexuality. The third section follows David, one of the major male characters, who escapes from Gibeah to Naioth in Ramah (1 Sam 19:18–24), and from there to Nob, Gath, Adullam, and Mizpeh of Moab (1 Sam 20:1–22:23), from there to Keilah, the hill country of the wilderness of Ziph at Horesh, then into the wilderness of Maon, En-gedi (1 Sam 23–24), and eventually to the land of the Philistines, where he is

6. Tony W. Cartledge explains that the pejorative names of Eli's sons hint at their corruption. He states, "Two of the most notable miscreants in Scripture are the sons of Eli, Hophni and Phinehas. Ancient readers, of course, would not have expected much from men with such names. 'Hophni' may be from the Egyptian word for 'toad.' In Hebrew, it is similar to a term describing the empty hollow of a hand. 'Phinehas' means 'brass lips'—an uninspiring name for one who is called to speak for God." See Tony W. Cartledge, *1 & 2 Samuel: Bible Commentary*, SHBC (Macon, GA: Smyth & Helwys, 2001), 51.

7. For a critical review of postcolonial feminist Bible readings, see, e.g., Susanne Scholz, "Postcolonial Biblical Criticism and Feminist Studies," in *The Oxford Handbook of Postcolonial Biblical Criticism*, ed. R. S. Sugirtharajah (Oxford: Oxford University Press, 2023), 623–646.

gifted the city of Ziklag (1 Sam 27). The interpretation centers on the depiction of the competitive masculinities attributed to the prominent male characters, David and Saul, in their epic physical and psychological struggle. This chapter's conclusion comments on the relationship between the narratives and the archaeological findings.

Uncovering Historical Literalism and Ethnonational Fundamentalism: About the Archaeological Development of Tel Shiloh as a Feminist Matter (1 Sam 1:3)

The archaeological site of Tel Shiloh is a much-visited tourism attraction in the militarily occupied West Bank today. For centuries, however, the location of biblical Shiloh, mentioned in 1 Samuel 1:3 as an Israelite worship destination, was uncertain.[8] An American biblical scholar, Edward Robinson (1794–1863), established the current location during his travels to Palestine in 1838. In his magnum opus, *Biblical Researches in Palestine, and in the Adjacent Regions: Journal of Travels in the Year 1838*, he mentions the difficulties of pinpointing the location of biblical Shiloh. He explains, "The crusaders . . . held the place [of Neve Samuel] to be also the Shiloh of Scriptures, or as Brocardus expresses it: 'Mount Shiloh, which is now called St. Samuel.' . . . From that time onward (1187) to the present day [1838], the natives [i.e., the local population] have known the place as Neby Samwil; while the monks and travelers have varied in describing it either as Shiloh or Ramah."[9] Said differently, the Palestinian population on the one hand and monks and travelers from the West on the other hand disagreed on the

8. Other references to Shiloh appear in 1 Sam 2:14; 3:21; 4:4; 14:3. Shiloh also appears in Josh 19:1 as the location where the Israelites set up the tent of meeting, in Josh 22:12 where the Israelites gather to make war against the Canaanites, and in Judg 21:12 when the young women of Jabesh-gilead are trafficked to Shiloh. The root of the name also appears in Gen 38:5, 11, 14 for the male son of Judah's first wife; his name is Shelah (in Hebrew: שֵׁלָה, or *request, petition*).

9. Edward Robinson, *Biblical Researches in Palestine, and in the Adjacent Regions: A Journal of Travels in the Year 1838*, vol. 1 (Boston: Crocker and Brewster, 1856), 459. Brocardus Jacopo Brocardo was an Italian Protestant convert and biblical interpreter who lived from approximately 1518 to 1594 CE. "Neby Samwil" means "Prophet Samuel."

geographical location of Shiloh until Robinson's travel memoirs settled the case in the 1830s. In fact, Robinson himself reidentified the current site as Shiloh on the basis of the description in Judges 21:19, "north of Bethel, on the east of the highway that goes up from Bethel to Shechem and south of Lebonah," and on the basis of Eusebius's description,[10] which places Shiloh twelve miles from Neapolis (or Shechem, which is today's Nablus, one of the largest Palestinian cities) in the district of Acrabatene, an area about nine miles eastward from Shechem.

In 1993, the Israeli archaeologist Israel Finkelstein does not mention the dispute about the location in the pre-nineteenth-century era when he explains, "The location of Shiloh was still known in the 14th century C.E. when the Jewish traveler Eshtori ha-Parchi found it in ruins. The modern identification of Kh. Seilun as ancient Shiloh was made without difficulty by Robinson during his journey in Palestine in 1838. . . . The Madaba Map also shows Shiloh to the southeast of Neapolis (Shechem). . . . The identification of Shiloh with Kh. Seilun was never challenged except for Richardson's proposal (1927) to locate it as Kt. Beit Sila southwest of Ramallah, a suggestion which was promptly dismissed by Albright (1927)."[11] Finkelstein's comment presents the geographical location of Tel Shiloh as known and self-evident since the fourteenth century, with a suggestion ("still known") of continuity before that. The reference also hints at a dispute over the site's location in the 1920s, settling it with the mention of a renowned early to mid-twentieth-century US-American Old Testament scholar, William F. Albright.

Interestingly, Finkelstein does not acknowledge the relative irrelevance of Shiloh during nineteenth-century Hebrew Bible studies. This significant point in the understanding of the first stage of Tel Shiloh's geopolitical development is, however, made by the Bible scholar Donald G. Schley. He clarifies in a study on the history and tradition of Tel Shiloh in biblical scholarship,

10. Eusebius of Caesarea (260/265–339 CE) was a Greek historian of Christianity.

11. Israel Finkelstein, ed., "Introduction," in *Shiloh: The Archaeology of a Biblical Site*, ed. Israel Finkelstein, Shlomo Bunimovitz, and Zvi Lederman, Monograph Series of the Institute of Archaeology Tel Aviv University 10 (Tel Aviv: Institute of Archaeology of Tel Aviv University, Publications Section, 1993), 1–3.

> Shiloh did not attract sufficient interest in scholarly circles to become the subject of a separate controversy. Instead, the question of Shiloh's status in Israel's early period nearly always arose in the context of the larger literary-critical and historical issues regarding the relationship of pentateuchal law to the narratives of the historical books, particularly as this problem related to the centralization of the cult. Consequently, scholarly opinion concerning Shiloh was usually formulated in treatments of these larger issues. Only Karl Heinrich Graf saw fit to prepare a separate treatment on Shiloh: in 1855 he published a little-known Latin monograph on the temple of Shiloh, which encompassed most of the major issues that subsequently occupied scholars with regard to Shiloh. Otherwise, Shiloh continued to play an *important tangential role* in the Old Testament [Christian] criticism of the nineteenth century.[12]

The general disregard of Tel Shiloh during the nineteenth century climaxed in the 1878 book *Geschichte Israels* (History of Ancient Israel), written by the German Bible scholar and linguist Julius Wellhausen (1844–1918).[13] Wellhausen's historical reconstruction severed the connection between the local sanctuary tradition of Shiloh, as assumed in 1 Samuel 1:3, and later stories about the building of the temple in Jerusalem. Accordingly, he located the tent-of-meeting tradition, first mentioned in Exodus 33:7, in which God appears in a tent outside the Israelite camp, as a later Shiloh tradition (e.g., 1 Sam 2:22) that, however, belonged historically in the sixth century BCE. Wellhausen mentioned that this tradition is modeled according to stories

---

12. Donald G. Schley, *Shiloh: A Biblical City in Tradition and History*, JSOTSup 63 (Sheffield: JSOT Press, 1989), 13; emphasis added.

13. Julius Wellhausen, *Geschichte Israels* (Berlin: G. Reimer, 1878). For a critical overview of Wellhausen's anti-Jewish exegetical assumptions, see, e.g., Stacy Davis, "Unapologetic Apologetics: Julius Wellhausen, Anti-Judaism, and Hebrew Bible Scholarship," *Religions* 12 (2021): 560, https://doi.org/10.3390/rel12080560. For a historical analysis of German Protestant and Jewish relationships in the latter part of the nineteenth century, see Christian Wiese, *Challenging Colonial Discourse: Jewish Studies and Protestant Theology in Wilhelmine Germany*, trans. Barbara Harshav and Christian Wiese, Studies in European Judaism 10 (Leiden: Brill, 2005).

about the Solomonic temple and thus ought to be viewed as entirely fictional. The literary argumentation is complicated, but, in a nutshell, Wellhausen maintained that "Shiloh could no longer be considered the pre-monarchic central holy place, since there had been no cultic centralization before the reign of [King] Josiah [640–609 BCE] and his reform [622 BCE; 2 Kings 22–23; 2 Chron 34–35]. The succession of central holy sites from Shiloh to Nob, to Gibeon, and finally to Jerusalem, was to be dismissed."[14] In other words, to Wellhausen, the narratives in which Shiloh plays a central role were written centuries later, and thus Wellhausen viewed them as insignificant literary evidence for the earlier era's historical reconstruction.

Toward the end of the nineteenth and into the early twentieth centuries, however, some scholars began contesting elements of Wellhausen's interpretation. Usually, their arguments depended heavily on theological-ecclesial conservatism. For instance, the German Old Testament scholar Rudolf Kittel (1853–1929), who had been the father of the Nazi theologian Gerhard Kittel (1888–1948), struggled mightily with Wellhausen's position that classified the system of so-called cultic services as a much later, sixth-century literary invention. Kittel, countering Wellhausen's source-critical assessment, claimed that Shiloh was "the center for and seat of the transmission of the true Yahwistic faith imparted to Israel by Moses,"[15] as described in the biblical texts. Like other opponents of the Wellhausen model, Kittel did not want to give up the idea that Shiloh had played a central role in "the emergence of the national consciousness [in ancient Israel], which had led to the creation of the monarchy."[16] Perhaps Kittel unconsciously modeled his historical speculations about Shiloh according to notions of the growing German national consciousness that had become prominent in German society in the so-called Wilhelmine era.[17]

---

14. Schley, *Shiloh*, 45.

15. Schley, *Shiloh*, 56.

16. Schley, *Shiloh*, 63.

17. For a historical assessment of German Protestant pietism on the developing German national consciousness that led to the German nation-state in 1871, see Hartmut Lehmann, "Pietism and Nationalism: The Relationship Between Protestant Revivalism and National Renewal in Nineteenth-Century Germany," *CH* 51 (1982): 39–53.

Similarly, archaeologists pursued the idea that biblical references to Shiloh were historically accurate. In 1922, a Danish team led the first archaeological excavation at the very location that Robinson identified almost one hundred years earlier as the site of Shiloh. Aage Schmidt inaugurated the excavation, and from 1922 to 1932 Hans Kjaer directed it. He received significant scholarly support from William F. Albright, who exclaimed in 1923, "Again we have archaeological confirmation of the statements of the Bible."[18] To these archaeologists and their supporters, archaeology offered a path to uphold biblical accuracy about Shiloh. Said differently, Northern European and US-American Christian historical critics started to challenge Julius Wellhausen, who argued against the Bible as a historically reliable document. Over time, a steadily increasing number of Christian apologetic voices defended the biblical record as the historiographical and archaeological quest for biblical accuracy grew stronger and louder during the twentieth century.

Importantly, Christian apologetic voices received mounting support from Jewish Bible scholars such as Yehezkel Kaufmann (1889–1963) and his student Menahem Haran (1924–2015). All of them rejected the Wellhausen model for various reasons, including its embedded anti-Jewish assumptions. For instance, Wellhausen suggested that the Priestly source of the Documentary Hypothesis expressed late, legalistic, and spiritually dead ideas flowing directly from the Babylonian exile of the sixth century BCE into what he called the "Spätjudentum" ("late" Judaism).[19] In contrast, Wellhausen's crit-

18. William F. Albright, "The Danish Excavations at Shiloh," *BASOR* 9 (1923): 11, https://www.journals.uchicago.edu/doi/pdfplus/10.2307/1355044. See also William F. Albright, "The Danish Excavations at Seilun: A Correction," *PEQ* 59 (1927): 157–158.

19. For a critical discussion on this anti-Jewish Christian nomenclature, see, e.g., Konrad Schmid, "The Interpretation of Second Temple Judaism as 'Spätjudentum' in Christian Biblical Scholarship," in *Confronting Antisemitism from the Perspectives of Christianity, Islam, and Judaism*, ed. Armin Lange, Kerstin Mayerhofer, Dina Porat, and Lawrence H. Schiffman, An End to Antisemitism, vol. 2 (Berlin: De Gruyter, 2020), 139–152. Also see the accessible discussion by Alan T. Levenson, "Was the Documentary Hypothesis Tainted by Wellhausen's Antisemitism?" *TheTorah.com*, 2021, https://thetorah.com/article/was-the-documentary-hypothesis-tainted-by-wellhausens-antisemitism.

ics sought to establish the antiquity of the Pentateuchal priestly source in the effort to affirm the historicity and ongoing religious viability of the Bible in general and of biblical references to Tel Shiloh in particular. As a result, the argument in favor of the historicity of the biblical accounts about Shiloh was also related to an implicit post-Shoah affirmation of the state of Israel. At the same time, historical and archaeological exegetes took for granted, or even endorsed, the geopolitical developments of their time, which usually included ignoring the plight of the Palestinian population in the land.

The acceptance of contemporary geopolitical developments has also played out at Tel Shiloh. After Israel Finkelstein excavated there during four seasons from 1981 to 1984, he positioned himself right of center.[20] His interpretation of the archaeological findings at Tel Shiloh neither rejects nor affirms the historicity of the biblical narratives of Shiloh. He offers an intellectual-exegetical compromise when he acknowledges, "If our theory as to the function of the Area C buildings is correct, then they are the only public buildings known so far in Iron Age I hill country sites. Scholarly opinion is divided between those who interpret 1 Sam 1 as evidence that a stone-built temple stood at Shiloh . . . and those who doubt the existence at Shiloh of a stone sanctuary. . . . The excavation results would *seem* to reinforce the former view."[21] In this comment Finkelstein suggests that a stone-built temple possibly stood at the site during the eleventh century BCE (Iron Age I). This early date seems atypical for Finkelstein. He mentions that his excavation at Tel Shiloh received financial support from various governmental and private organizations, institutions, and individuals invested in the historicity of the Bible, including the National Council for Research and Development (Israel), the Archaeological Staff Officer for Judaea and Samaria, and the Israeli settlement Binyamin Regional Council.[22] Could it be that Finkelstein offers his tentative scholarly support for the biblicist view that a stone-built

20. Finkelstein is sometimes called a "centrist"; see, e.g., Hershel Shanks, "A 'Centrist' at the Center of Controversy: BAR Interviews Israel Finkelstein," *BAR* 28 (November/December 2002), https://library.biblicalarchaeology.org/article/a-centrist-at-the-center-of-controversy/.

21. Finkelstein, "Introduction," 385; emphasis added.

22. Finkelstein, "Introduction," xi.

temple existed at Tel Shiloh during premonarchic times (Iron Age I) in a nod of recognition toward his funders' religious or national interests?

His dating effort might also have related to larger societal developments in Israel's politics on the West Bank. Finkelstein's archaeological work at Tel Shiloh took place in the early 1980s after the Israeli military started occupying the West Bank in 1967 and before the first Intifada occurred in 1987. During that time, Israelis were able to travel to and within the West Bank relatively easily and safely, allowing Israeli academics to engage in archaeological research there. Finkelstein's excavation of Tel Shiloh was part of this research wave. As the report of the human rights groups Emek Shaveh and Yesh Din explains, "Archaeological activity reached a peak in the second decade of the Occupation, between 1977 and 1987, during the golden age of the Israeli settlement policy. . . . The occupation of the West Bank in 1967 had a substantial impact on the status of Israeli archaeology, fed by Israel's already existing perception that archaeology can provide proof of the Jewish people's historic connection to sites in the Occupied Territories."[23] Perhaps intellectual-political pressures contributed to Finkelstein affirming the "Jewish people's historic connections" to Tel Shiloh. Not wanting to disappoint his financial and institutional supporters with a position that would question or even reject the historical reliability of biblical Shiloh, he upheld the destruction of ancient Shiloh in Iron Age I. His interpretation of the archaeological artifacts of Tel Shiloh thus affirms, even if hesitantly, the *Israelite* nature of Shiloh in the eleventh century BCE, in accordance with the Danish archaeologist Kjaer and his US-American supporter, Albright.[24]

---

23. Ziv Stahl, Emek Shaveh, and Yesh Din, "Appropriating the Past: Israel's Archaeological Practices in the West Bank," December 2017, 23, https://emekshaveh.org/en/wp-content/uploads/2017/12/Menachsim-Eng-Web.pdf.

24. Finkelstein, "Introduction," 389: "The results of the recent excavations lay this problem to rest. First and foremost, Iron Age I Shiloh was destroyed in a great conflagration whose traces were clearly visible everywhere in Area C as well as in Area E and possibly in the burnt silos of Area D. . . . Furthermore, it is now clear that the site was not occupied in the early phases of the Iron Age II, that in the late-Iron Age II it was a tiny, insignificant settlement, and that this late-Iron II site was not destroyed by fire but was apparently gradually abandoned. The ceramic evidence that Shiloh was already abandoned at the end of the 11th century B.C.E. also rules out the theory that the site emerged as a sanctuary of national importance

Figure 1.1. Flags of the tower at Tel Shiloh, photo taken on October 10, 2018. Copyright 2018 Susanne Scholz.

Today the political dynamics of Tel Shiloh's archaeology have turned even further toward the religious-right spectrum, as an Israeli ethnonational and Christian fundamentalist alliance defines the ongoing archaeological and tourist developments of Tel Shiloh. This new archaeological moment began in the mid-1970s, when Israeli settlers established the settlement of Shilo

---

only in the days of Saul. Finally, dump Debris 623 which seems to date slightly later than the Area C pillared buildings . . . may hint that for a short time after the destruction of Iron I Shiloh people from the vicinity continued to bring offerings to the ruined site, a practice which somewhat resembles the Late Bronze Age activity at Shiloh." In the previous explanations, Finkelstein states that "the 1929 excavations, that revealed an Iron I destruction layer, led Kjaer . . . and Albright to suggest that the site was indeed destroyed by the Philistines following the defeat of the Israelites at the battle of Even-ezer" (p. 388). Although Finkelstein does not go so far as to assert the specifics of Shiloh's destruction, he concurs with both Kjaer and Albright that Shiloh was destroyed at the end of Iron Age I.

on the land of the Palestinian village called Qaryut.[25] With governmental support from Israeli politicians, such as then Minister of Agriculture Ariel Sharon and Defense Minister Ezer Weizman, and bilateral support from representatives of the Labor and Likud Parties in Israel, the establishment of the settlement of Shilo was justified under the pretext of archaeological excavations.[26] The originally illegal settlement grew into a small town, and in 1979 the state of Israel legally recognized the small village of about 4,100 religious Israeli settlers. The settlement is currently under the jurisdiction of the Mateh Binyamin Regional Council, whose flags are proudly flown at Tel Shiloh. That the state of Israel considers the archaeological site as part of Jewish heritage has certainly contributed to the speed with which the settlement was legally recognized only a few years after it had been illegally built.

Nowadays, the settler council and the private nonprofit organization Mishkan Shiloh, rather than Israel's Nature and Parks Authority, manage and run the archaeological site, although Tel Shiloh was part of Palestinian-owned land and Palestinians were barred from entering the archaeological site prior to 2016.[27] The right-wing agenda of the archaeological presentation has received impressive international political support. For instance, in March 2019, Israeli Prime Minister Benjamin Netanyahu, the former Arkansas governor Mike Huckabee, and the chair of the Binyamin Regional Council, Yisrael Gantz, visited Tel Shiloh, at which time Netanyahu called the site Israel's "first capital."[28] Netanyahu's terminology is identical to the phrase used by Tel Shiloh's site director, Lilyan Zaitman. In 2019, she characterized Tel

25. For a detailed profile of Qaryut village since 1969, see, e.g., the report prepared by the Applied Research Institute in Jerusalem (ARIJ), "Qaryut Village Profile (Including Jalud Locality)," http://vprofile.arij.org/nablus/pdfs/vprofile/Qaryut_vp_en.pdf. The ARIJ is a Palestinian NGO founded in 1990 with its main office in Bethlehem on the West Bank.

26. Shaveh and Din, "Appropriating the Past," 20.

27. See Ilan Ben Zion, "Ancient West Bank Site Draws Christians, and Controversy," *Arab News Pakistan*, March 29, 2019, http://www.arabnews.pk/node/1473241/middle-east. Since 2016, Palestinians are allowed to enter Tel Shiloh.

28. Emily Jones, "'I Am Very Excited to Be Here': Netanyahu, Huckabee Tour Ancient Shilo," *CBNNews*, March 20, 2019, https://www1.cbn.com/cbnnews/israel/2019/march/i-am-very-excited-to-be-here-netanyahu-huckabee-tour-ancient-shilo-nbsp.

Shiloh as "the first capital city of the Jewish people before Jerusalem."[29] The strengthening of the archaeological connection between biblical Shiloh and the modern settlement of Shilo continues unabatedly. In 2010, an archaeological excavation was carried out by the Archaeological Staff Officer for Judea and Samaria in the IDF Civilian Administration Antiquities Unit and the Binyamin local authority (the Israeli settlement regional organization) and by the University of Ariel, an Israeli public university founded in 1982 that is located in the urban Israeli settlement of Ariel on the West Bank.[30]

The site has also received serious evangelical Christian interest. Since 2017, a team of Christian-right archaeologists from the United States has begun excavating several areas of Tel Shiloh with the stated goal of determining the location of the biblical tabernacle.[31] Scott Stripling serves as the director of excavations at Shiloh for the Associates for Biblical Research (ABR), a nonprofit Christian organization founded in Philadelphia in 1969.[32] The ABR, defending the Bible's historical accuracy, characterizes itself as "a Christian apologetics ministry dedicated to demonstrating the historical reliability of the Bible through archaeological and biblical research."[33] The organization supports "original field research, including

29. Ben Zion, "Ancient West Bank Site."

30. Gil Ronen, "Digging Up Shiloh," *Israel National News*, July 28, 2010, www.israelnationalnews.com/News/News.aspx/138836. See also Shaveh and Din, "Appropriating the Past," 32: "Subsequently, in 2010, excavations were resumed by the SOA in cooperation with the Mateh Binyamin Regional Council and Ariel University."

31. Amanda Borschel-Dan, "With Bibles and Shovels, Search for Biblical Tabernacle Gathers Pace at Shiloh," *Times of Israel*, July 17, 2017, https://www.timesofisrael.com/with-bibles-and-shovels-a-search-for-the-biblical-tabernacle-gathers-pace-at-shiloh/.

32. The following website provides information on the 2020 tax-filing information of ABR: https://www.causeiq.com/organizations/associates-for-biblical-research,420947695/. According to the latest available online information from June 2020, ABR received $344,989 in total grants, contributions, etc. in the reporting years, which includes a grant in the amount of $40,000 from the Azb Foundation in 2019. For this foundation, see https://www.causeiq.com/organizations/azb-foundation,472394448/. Further details on the Azb Foundation are not available to me.

33. See https://www.believerstewardship.org/ministry-spotlight-associates-biblical-research/.

archaeological excavations to determine the location of specific biblical sites and events, especially sites dismissed as folk legends by the world of critical scholars."[34] The ABR also maintains that it "address[es] critical scholarship in the realms of science, theology, and biblical studies, establishing the factual and historical truth of Scripture"[35] with the goal "to resolve apparent conflicts between the findings of archaeology and science, and the Bible." Thus, the ABR, classifying the Bible as "infallible, inerrant and authoritative,"[36] hopes to make "biblical truth applicable and useful to all believers in Jesus Christ."[37]

In short, the Christian-right belief in the literal-historical accuracy of the Bible drives this organization's activities. As Stripling is closely affiliated with this Christian-right organization, the ABR has sponsored his excavation at Tel Shiloh since 2017. In 2018, the Assemblies of God's Center for Holy Land Studies joined the effort.[38] The Christian-right excavation team obtained an official Israeli permit to conduct the excavation at Tel Shiloh. Since Stripling has yet to publish a scholarly report on the several seasons of excavating at Tel Shiloh, and since he has yet to disclose his financial ties to the settler organization, Mishkan Shiloh, that supervises Tel Shiloh, it is impossible to know how US-American fundamentalist Christians have sustained a multiyear US-American and privately funded archaeological excavation on the West Bank.

The 2017 report by Emek Shaveh and Yesh Din characterizes the current archaeological plans for Tel Shiloh as the culmination of one hundred years of archaeological excavations at the site. The report was published just prior to Stripling's first season at Tel Shiloh, perhaps indicating that the Israeli human rights group was unaware of the imminent Christian archaeological activity. The report explains:

> The authorities' conduct regarding the antiquity site at Tel Shiloh-Khirbet Seilun illustrates how archaeology serves to

34. See https://biblearchaeology.org/about/.
35. See https://biblearchaeology.org/about/.
36. See https://biblearchaeology.org/about/.
37. See https://biblearchaeology.org/about/.
38. See https://news.ag.org/en/News/CHLS-Joins-ABR-in-Historic-Dig-at-Shiloh.

> achieve political and settlement-friendly goals: the inclusion of the site in the jurisdiction area of the settlement of Shiloh; the transfer of its management to the Regional Council and then to the Association; the narrative highlighted at the site; the pronouncement of the site as a national heritage site; and of course the extraordinary and grandiose development plan. All these are aimed at creating a major attraction in the West Bank for a large number of visitors from Israel and the world, and to embolden a narrative which strengthens the bond between Israel and the Jewish people to the stretch of land in which the site is situated.[39]

Clearly, then, the archaeological excavations at Tel Shiloh are not academically innocent projects but serve sociopolitical and economic goals of the Israeli military occupation. Although the Israeli report does not mention the impending archaeological excavation of summer 2017, it refers to the big tourism plans for Tel Shiloh that regional and national Israeli governmental agencies and councils approved. US-American Christian tourists will probably be bused to Tel Shiloh on Highway 5, the so-called Trans-Samaria Highway, to learn about biblical Shiloh as Israel's first capital, detached from the geopolitical and military realities of the West Bank. The tourist developments that have been undertaken at Tel Shiloh will strengthen the bonds not only between Israel and the Jewish people but also between Israel and Christians around the globe. Such work will deepen the assumed historical truth of the Bible, adding weight to archaeological findings as scientific evidence of Shiloh's status as Israel's first capital. The Christian-right agenda could not have found more fertile ground than at Tel Shiloh. Whenever the goal is to prove the literal historicity of the Hebrew Bible with archaeology and religious fervor, the Christian right is already there.

To read 1 Samuel 1:3 without these geopolitical-archaeological developments in mind is to misunderstand both fundamentalist and liberal Bible readers. Both believe that the Bible would be irrelevant if biblical

---

39. Shaveh and Din, "Appropriating the Past," 38.

Shiloh could not be proven to have been a worship site during the eleventh century BCE. A literalist reference to Hannah as an infertile woman, yearning for motherhood, is the customary one-sentence summary of this story, especially to those readers for whom everything depends on the historicity of Shiloh as the tabernacle site during the presumed era of the biblical judges (usually dated around the eleventh century BCE). Even today, then, the ongoing archaeological excavation at Tel Shiloh serves an ideologically right-wing purpose. With so much evidence above the ground at Tel Shiloh, feminist readers need to understand these dynamics so they do not fall prey to the misleading ethnonational and religious fundamentalist presentations at the site.

Exposing Phallic Supremacist Ideology in Crude Sexual Allusions to Male Groins: About the Ark's Journey from Shiloh to Ebenezer, Ashdod's House of Dagon, Gath, Beth-Shemesh, and to Kiriat-jearim (1 Sam 4:1–7:1)

The journey of the ark narrated in 1 Samuel 4:1–7:1 could not easily be replicated in today's Israel/Palestine. Current travels depend on who is on the journey and where the location is. A West Bank Palestinian traveler would run into serious difficulties because Israeli military checkpoints would prevent this traveler from entering Highway 5 to drive west after leaving Shiloh on Route 60 and Highway Route 505. At the very latest, a West Bank Palestinian would be prohibited from crossing the Kafr Kassem Checkpoint into Israel proper.[40] This traveler would be unable to reach the ark's next stop at biblical Ebenezer, located five kilometers south of the ancient path along the north-south Via Maris, an ancient route connecting the regions north of

40. For a list of West Bank roads on which Palestinian vehicles are completely prohibited to drive, see https://www.btselem.org/freedom_of_movement/forbidden_roads and also https://en.wikipedia.org/wiki/Highway_5_(Israel%E2%80%93Palestine). For a map of West Bank checkpoints, see https://en.wikipedia.org/wiki/File:West_Bank_Access_Restrictions.pdf.

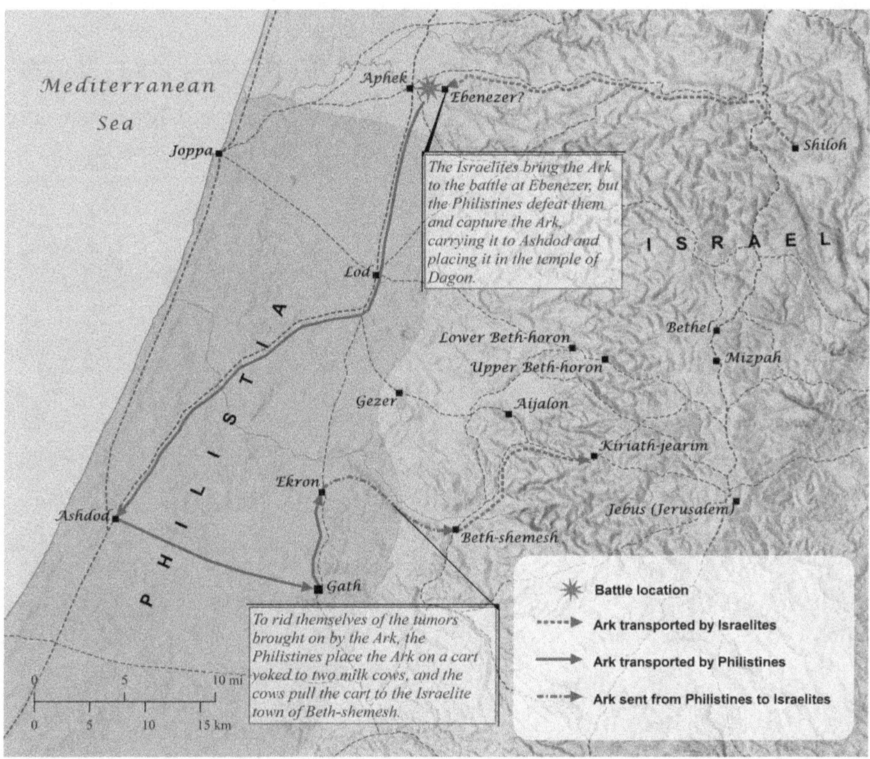

Figure 1.2. The Ark of the Covenant captured and returned. Bible Mapper Atlas.

Israel (Mesopotamia, Asia Minor, and Syria) to the south (Egypt).[41] Archaeologists identified biblical Ebenezer with the ruins of ʻIzbet Sartah, a small Iron Age settlement on the hills close to the ancient city of Aphek (Antipatris). The site is mentioned in 1 Samuel 4:1–11, a report on the battle during which the (male) Philistine warriors defeat the (male) Israelite warriors and capture the ark.

41. For additional information on the Via Maris, see https://en.wikipedia.org/wiki/Via_Maris.

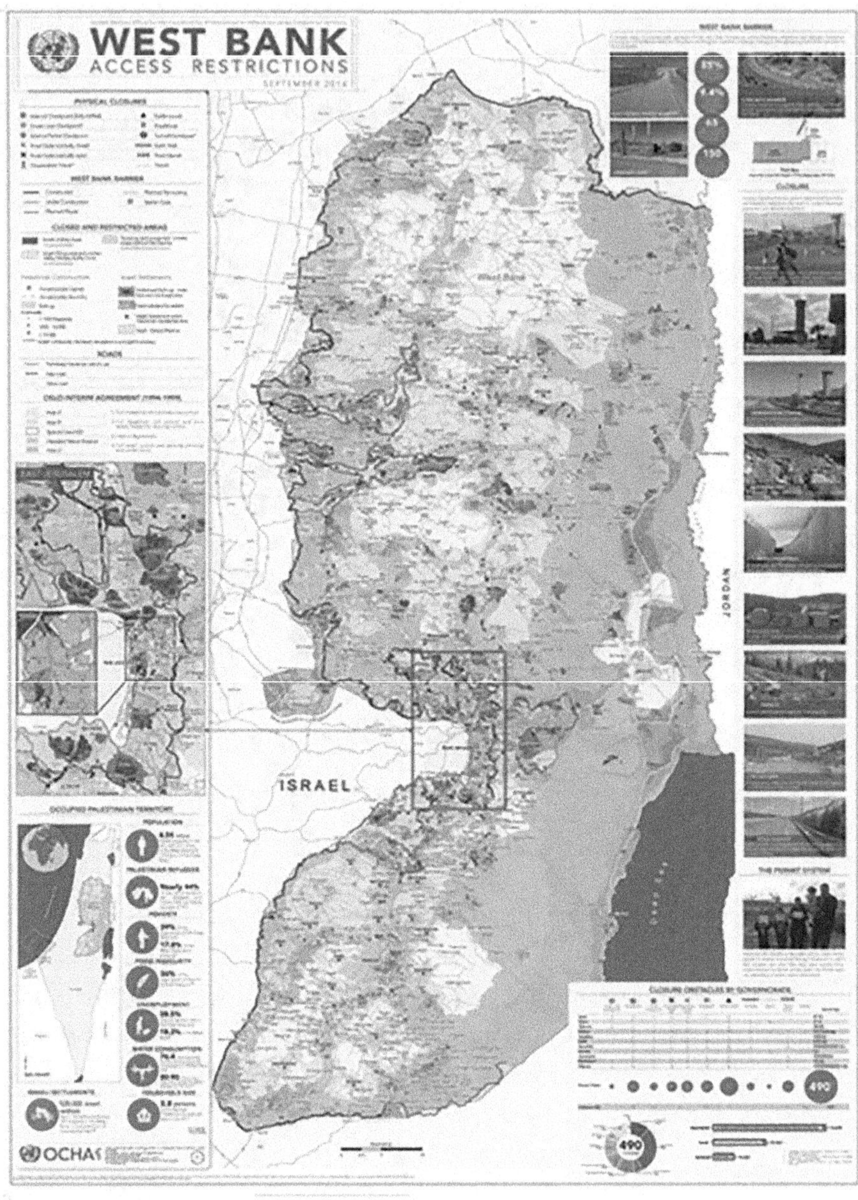

Figure 1.3. The West Bank, with checkpoints. May 2023. Used by permission of the UN Office of Coordinated Humanitarian Affairs.[42]

42. Map by United Nations OCHA oPt, https://www.ochaopt.org/sites/default/files/westbank_a0_25_06_2020_final.pdf.

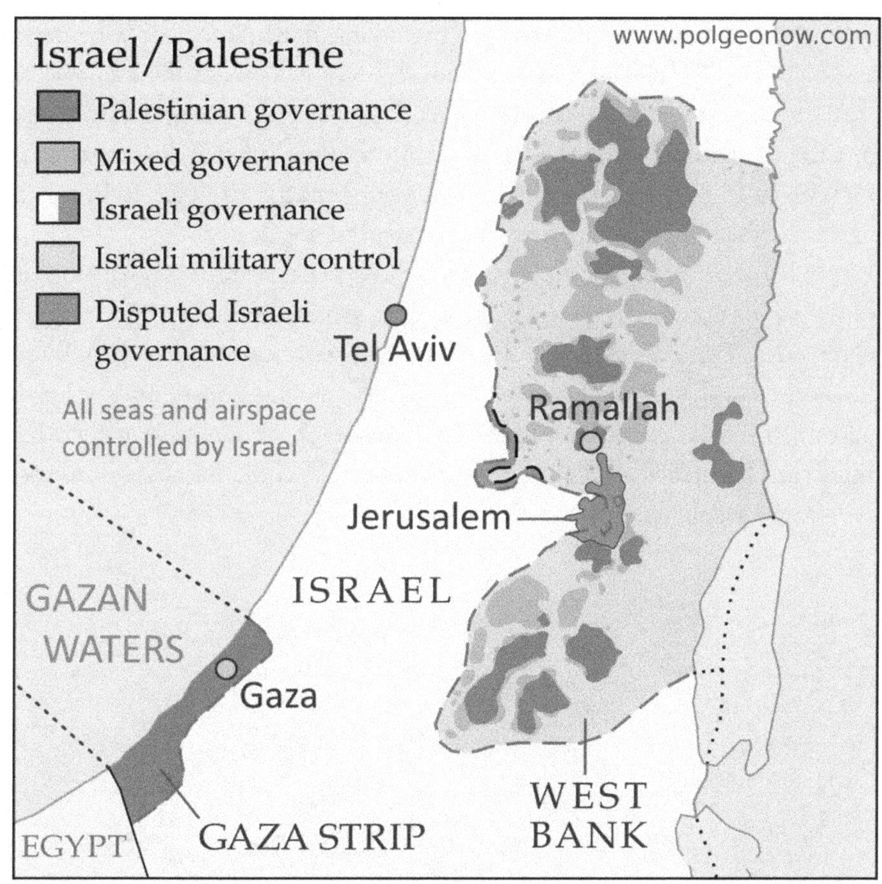

Figure 1.4. Israel/Palestine map. Used by permission of Evan Centanni.[43]

"In those days the Philistines mustered for war against Israel, and Israel went out to battle against them; they encamped at Ebenezer, and the Philistines encamped at Aphek" (1 Sam 4:1b). The Israelites lost the battle even after they decided to get the ark "[to] save us from the power of our enemies" (v. 3b). The ark arrives promptly, with Hophni and Phinehas, the two sons of Eli, the priest of Shiloh (v. 4). The celebratory shouts of the Israelite men are so loud that the Philistines fear they will lose the next battle just as the Egyptians had lost their battle against their "gods" (v. 8). The Philistines encourage each

43. Map by Evan Centanni, all rights reserved, https://www.polgeonow.com /2017/12/jerusalem-israel-capital-recognition.html.

other with the following expression of hegemonic masculinity: "Take courage, and be men, O Philistines, in order not to become slaves to the Hebrews as they have been to you; be men and fight" (v. 9). They win the next battle, capture the ark, and kill thirty thousand Israelite foot soldiers as well as the sons of Eli (vv. 10–11). The verse assumes a phallic supremacist ideology: To be a man means subjugating other men; to fail as a man means death.

Phallic references shine through the entire passage that archaeological explanations do not always mention, despite some interesting archaeological discoveries. The archaeological site of 'Izbet Sartah, identified as the biblical Ebenezer, can be reached by walking in between the houses on the north part of Rosh-Ha'ayin. North of the location beyond Highway 5 is the Afek Industrial Park. A visit requires a knowledgeable guide because no tourist signs facilitate the path to the top of the hill.

Figure 1.5. Aerial view of the site of 'Izbet Sartah from Eben Ezer (Izbet Zarta). Used by permission of BibleWalks.[44]

44. From "Eben Ezer (Izbet Zarta)," *BibleWalks*, https://www.biblewalks.com/ebenezer.

Once there, a panel in Ivrit (modern Hebrew) explains the significance of the site: "The 'Izbet Sartah site was discovered in 1973 when the Tel Aviv University Archeology Institute conducted a scientific survey at the area of Tel Afek. During the four excavation seasons between 1976 and 1978, the archaeologists found a small village with three stages of settlement. Each of the settlement stages seemed to end with the quiet and orderly departure of the residents. There is no sign of a sudden or violent destruction of the houses" (my translation of the Hebrew). Moshe Kochavi, directing the excavation from 1976 to 1978, found an important piece of pottery with ancient letters on it, the famous ostracon of 'Izbet Sartah.[45] Kochavi identified the letters as part of the alphabet in ancient Hebrew script and the site with Ebenezer of 1 Samuel 4:1.[46]

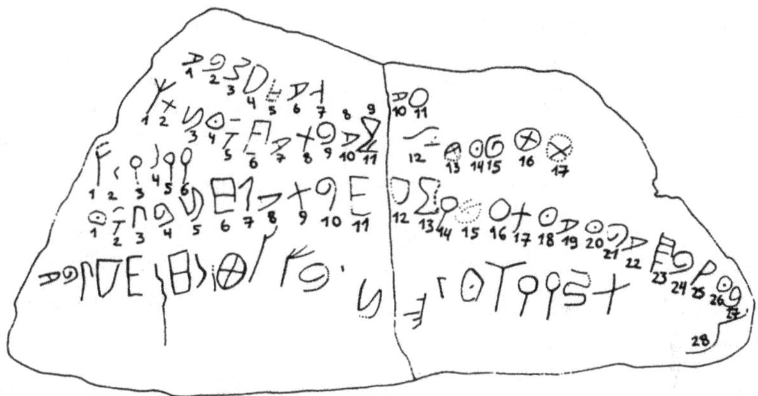

Figure 1.6. 'Izbet Sartah ostracon. From Benjamin Sass, *The Genesis of the Alphabet and Its Development in the Second Millennium B.C.* (Ägypten und Altes Testament 13; Wiesbaden: Harrassowitz, 1988). Used by permission of the author.[47]

45. For a discussion of scholarly translations of the ostracon, see Lawrence J. Mykytiuk, "Is Hophni in the 'Izbet Sartah Ostracon?," *AUSS* 36 (1998): 69–80. He states toward the end of his essay, "The present degree of knowledge of second-millennium B.C.E. Northwest-Semitic inscriptions does not permit us to *demonstrate* it to be anything more than a five-line penmanship exercise written by someone practicing the Proto-Canaanite alphabet" (80; emphasis in the original).

46. Moshe Kochavi, "An Ostracon of the Period of the Judges from 'Izbet Sartah," *Tel Aviv: Journal of the Institute of Archaeology of Tel Aviv University* 4 (1977): 1–13.

47. Benjamin Sass, *The Genesis of the Alphabet and Its Development in the Second Millennium B.C.*, Ägypten und Altes Testament 13 (Wiesbaden: Harrassowitz, 1988).

Among the archaeological findings are a four-room house, a few smaller buildings, and various stone-lined silos, "collared-rim" *pithoi* (i.e., large terracotta storage containers), and two sherds that, fitted together, form an ostracon with five lines of letters. Yet the text on this ostracon does not prove the historicity of the biblical account despite some efforts by the director of the excavation and other Bible scholars.[48] Since the biblical narrative reports the battle of Ebenezer as a huge loss to the Israelite soldiers, with thirty-five thousand of them lost in battle and the Philistines capturing the ark, perhaps unsurprisingly the archaeological location has remained of marginal interest to today's travelers.

The tale about the defeat of the Israelite men is part of the Deuteronomistic historical imagination that reads like the beginning of a *Saturday Night Live* episode. Dotted with crude sexual allusions, the story mentions how the Philistines capture the ark and bring it to Ashdod, placing it into the temple of Dagon. Twice the Philistine god is said to have fallen on his face to the ground (5:3–4). The second time the narrative mentions that both of Dagon's hands (ידיו) are cut off, and the Philistine deity lies face down. Because "hand" (יד) is a Hebrew euphemism for penis, the scene refers to the deity's dismemberment. The Philistine deity is dismembered where it hurts most in the male imagination: in the groin (1 Sam 5:4). As Ken Stone puts it, the Philistine deity is "symbolically castrated" rather than "symbolically raped."[49] An etymological explanation in 1 Samuel 5:5 states, "This is why the priests of Dagon and all who enter the house of Dagon do not step on the threshold of Dagon in Ashdod to this day." The reference "to this day" indicates perhaps that this text comes from the early Hellenistic era[50] because, according to 1 Maccabees 10:83 and 11:4, the temple of Dagon existed in Ashdod during the Maccabean period (167–37 BCE). Yet here in 1 Samuel 5:3–4, the Deuteronomistic imaginary claims that due to the

48. Moshe Kochavi dated the archaeological findings into the era of the biblical judges. For a translation of the ostracon in line with 1 Sam 4:1, see William H. Shea, "The Ṣarṭah Ostracon," *AUSS* 28 (1990): 59–86. To prove the historicity of the Ark Narrative in 1 Sam 4:1–7:1 is foremost on the mind of this Bible scholar.

49. Ken Stone, "1 and 2 Samuel," in *Queer Bible Commentary*, ed. Deryn Guest, Robert E. Goss, Mona West, and Thomas Bohache (London: SCM Press, 2006), 205.

50. For dating the Hebrew Bible into the Hellenistic era, see, e.g., Niels Peter Lemche, *Ancient Israel: A New History of Israel*, 2nd ed. (London: T&T Clark, 2015).

Figure 1.7. An excavated area of ʻIzbet Sartah. Copyright 2018 Susanne Scholz.

threat of castration, or perhaps even emasculation, the Philistine priests avoid the location of defeat. Interestingly, archaeologists have not discovered any archaeological remnants of a temple in Ashdod.[51]

More importantly, the classification of Dagon as a Philistine deity is historically incorrect. Dagon was a West Semitic god of crop fertility throughout the ancient Near East, popular from southern Mesopotamia to the upper Euphrates and not exclusive to the Philistines.[52] The biblical narrative is a polemic reference to the fictional nemesis of biblical Israel. During the late Bronze Age (approximately 3300–1200 BCE), the deity's temple was in Ashdod, a complex cultural and commercial center in Canaan. The Ark Narrative remembers the city as such but with a twist. Accordingly, not only does the Philistine deity succumb to the power of the ark, but the people of Ashdod are also next in line of defeat

51. Jeffrey P. Emanuel, "'Dagon Our God': Iron I Philistine Cult in Text and Archaeology," *JANER* 16 (2016): 22–66.

52. See, e.g., "Dagan," *Britannica*, https://www.britannica.com/topic/Dagan.

(1 Sam 5:6–8). Like a comedy show, the story moves further below the beltline. After God wins the contest against Dagon, the narrative describes how God attacks the inhabitants of Ashdod, striking them with *'opalim* (5:6, 9, 12, עפלים). Nobody knows this word's meaning. Translations often insinuate that the disease refers to tumors or hemorrhoids, later made into golden casts as payments given to the Israelites, appeasing them for having captured the ark (6:4, 5, 11). In any case, the Israelite deity emerges as a male hegemon destroying the feminized Canaanite deity and bringing dis-ease to male Canaanite groins.

Recent discoveries support Aren Maeir's interpretation of the meaning of *'opalim* (עפלים). In 2004, his archaeological team found phallic-looking ceramic vessels in the stratum of the late ninth to early eighth centuries BCE (Iron Age II) at Tel eṣ-Ṣâfi/Gath, located halfway between Jerusalem and Ashkelon and attributed to the Philistine cultural realm.[53] Maeir explains that "the presence of phallic-shaped vessels in a well-defined Iron Age context associated with Philistine culture is a clear indication of the symbolic significance that such vessels had in the Philistine worldview."[54] Since Philistine foreskins also play a central role later when Saul is asking David to bring him such trophies as a required dowry to marry his daughter Michal (1 Sam 18:25), perhaps already in this earlier satire, here in 1 Samuel 5, "the Philistines were struck in a very painful and awkward place, which presents the Philistines in a rather ridiculous light in the Ark Narrative."[55]

In sum, the noun *'opalim* עפלים might euphemistically refer to the male sexual organ, the penis, afflicted by a serious discomfort or illness. The story incorporates the phallic reference to ridicule the Philistine enemy. They are hit at their most vulnerable body part representing their masculinity. According to this interpretation, the Philistines are not "real men" after all (1 Sam 4:9).

---

53. For an accessible online article on this archaeological excavation taking place since 2013, see Stuart Thornton, "Tell eṣ-Ṣâfi/Gath Excavations," *National Geographic Society*, May 20, 2022, https://education.nationalgeographic.org/resource/case-study-tell-es-safigath-excavations. For Aren Maeir's blog, visit https://gath.wordpress.com/.

54. Aren M. Maeir, ed., "Chapter 1: Introduction," in *Tell eṣ-Ṣâfi I: The 1996–2005 Seasons*, Ägypten und Altes Testament 69 (Wiesbaden: Harrassowitz, 2012), 29.

55. Maeir, "Chapter 1: Introduction," 30.

Figure 1.8. In-situ *ʿopalîm* found at Tel eṣ-Ṣâfi/Gath. Used by permission of Aren M. Maeir.[56]

56. Maeir, "A New Interpretation of the Term *ʿopalim*." Permission for photos granted by Aren M. Maeir.

In contrast to the polemic references in 1 Samuel, modern Ashdod pales. Established in Israel on the sand hills near the site of the ancient city ruins in 1956, today's beach town is the sixth largest city in Israel and an important regional industrial center. The city is the home of the largest Moroccan Jewish community in Israel, the largest Karaite Jewish community in Israel, and the largest Georgian-Russian Jewish community in the world. The site of ancient Ashdod was excavated in nine seasons between 1962 and 1972, and Tel Ashdod goes back to the seventeenth century BCE. In Joshua 15:47, Moses, following God's commandment, gives Ashdod to the tribe of Judah. Yet in 1 Samuel, the city is in the hands of the Philistines, whose imagined suffering groins must have delighted Israelite listeners, as it would tickle today's comedy-show audiences.

The reported kick into the male Philistine groins ensures that the ark moves from city to city. Nobody wants the holy container. For seven months the Philistines move the ark from Ashdod to Ekron (5:10), where it creates a "deathly panic" among the Philistine population (5:11) and more עפלים for those who did not die (5:12). Eventually, the Philistines send back the ark to the Israelites of Beth-Shemesh (6:9, 12, 13), paying their dues in golden עפלים (6:17) on behalf of Ashdod, Gaza, Ashkelon, Gath, and Ekron.

Since, for unknown reasons, not every Israelite, such as "the descendants of Jeconiah" (6:19), welcomes the ark in Beth-Shemesh, God kills seventy of them. Thereupon the citizens of Beth-Shemesh send off the ark to Kiriath-jearim. Comedy turns into a threatening tale to readers identifying with the Israelites, as this story does not describe full victory for the Israelites. The remaining people of Beth-Shemesh cannot get the ark out of town fast enough and to Kiriath-jearim, where the ark stays for twenty years (7:2). No further health issues are reported.

In sum, this tale is filled with crude sexual jokes that entertain any audience, as sooner or later people do not worry anymore who is winning or losing. They enjoy the jokes in which Philistine and Israelite men are killed for being on God's wrong side. Yet these kinds of jokes also reinforce ethnonational supremacy based on unquestioned phallogocentrism. The jokes focus on male Philistine failure, including male Philistine groins, although some male Israelites are not spared either. Only one female Israelite character appears; she is the priest Eli's daughter-in-law, who dies in childbirth (4:19–22) after she dutifully announces the absence of God as the male

Philistines capture the ark.[57] In this ethnocentrist and heterosexist story, the male deity threatens both Philistine and Israelite men with a phallic disease. To highlight these ideological markers is the best feminist guarantee not to fall prey to jokes that assume Israelite male supremacy and Philistine male incompetence.

Watching a Mel Gibson Drama of Male Bonding: About David's Flight from Saul's Murderous Intent (1 Sam 19:18–24; 20:1–22:23; 23–24; 27)

Another major travel story appears in 1 Samuel. This time it is an escape story in which a young man runs for his life from an older man. One is an emerging king; the other is the sitting king ready to kill the young man over political power and status. The pursued man is David, and the pursuer is King Saul. The starting point is a town in the West Bank, at King Saul's palace in Gibeah. William F. Albright was the first Bible scholar to excavate at the site, from 1922 to 1923.[58] Most late nineteenth- and twentieth-century archaeologists identified Gibeah with Tel el-Fûl near Beith Hanina, a Palestinian neighborhood in East Jerusalem on the road to Ramallah. Only in the twenty-first century was this identification challenged. In 1967, King Hussein of Jordan started building a palace there, as Jordan ruled over the West Bank until the Six-Day War ended its territorial rule in the same year. The Israeli victory led to the Israeli military occupation of the West Bank. With the building of the Separation Wall in the early twenty-first century CE, Beith Hanina has been divided into two villages: Al-Jadida (the new village) and Al-Balad (the old village). In 1978, Nancy L. Lapp noted that "the identification of Tell el-Fûl with Gibeah of Saul has again been questioned" and that "in many respects this is justified, and advances in archeology and

57. For a more detailed discussion on the role of Eli's daughter-in-law in this story, see chaps. 4 and 5 of this book.

58. William F. Albright, *Excavations and Results at Tell el-Fûl (Gibeah of Saul)*, AASOR, vol. 4 (New Haven, CT: Yale University Press, 1924). For a discussion of the various arguments that Albright and other biblical archaeologists made to identify Tel el-Fûl with Gibeah and the counterarguments by Israel Finkelstein challenging this identification, see Horton Harris, "Albright's Identification of Gibeah with Tell el-Fûl," *PEQ* 146 (2014): 17–30.

Figure 1.9. The reconstructed palace of biblical Gibeah. Photo by Tai Pinchevsky, https://commons.wikimedia.org/w/index.php?title=File:ארמון_חוסיין,_תל_אל_פול.jpg&oldid=908147433.

textual criticism demand renewed consideration."[59] In 2011, Israel Finkelstein rejected the idea that, based on the archaeological record, Tel el-Fûl is the location of Saul's Gibeah. He proposes the possibility that Tel el-Fûl is identical with the "late monarchic Perath/Parah and Hellenistic Phirathon"[60] and the biblical Gibeah with Geba.

Yet regardless of Gibeah being identical with Tel el-Fûl, Gibeah has an illustrious place in biblical storytelling. Allotted to the tribe of Benjamin in Joshua 18:28, Gibeah is the location of a most gruesome tale. In Judges 19:25, the men of this town gang-rape the male Levite's woman (פילגש).[61] Afterward the male Levite cuts her into twelve pieces (Judg 19:29)

59. Nancy L. Lapp, "The Third Campaign at Tell el-Fûl: The Excavations of 1964," *AASOR* 45 (1978): 15–16.

60. Israel Finkelstein, "Tell el-Fûl Revisited: The Assyrian and Hellenistic Periods (with a New Identification)," *PEQ* 143 (2011): 116.

61. For an explanation on the Hebrew term פילגש typically translated as "concubine," see my entry in the section "For Further Reflection" on pages 122–123 in chap. 2.

and distributes all twelve body parts among the tribes of Israel. The outrage of eleven tribes leads to their fight against the Benjaminites, of whom they kill in battle "twenty-five thousand one hundred men" (Judg 20:35). To avoid the extinction of the remaining Benjaminite men, the other tribes allow the Benjaminite men to sexually traffic four hundred young women from Jabesh-gilead (Judg 21:12) and another two hundred women from Shiloh (Judg 21:23–24). In the biblical imagination, the Benjaminite men and their location of Gibeah emerge as gruesome references to gang rape and murder. Another reference to Gibeah appears in 1 Samuel 10:1. The verse reports that the prophet and judge Samuel anoints Saul as the first king of Israel, who will reign in Gibeah for twenty-two years.

In short, the mention of Gibeah puts feminist readers on high alert because the place stirs up stories of gang rape and sex trafficking as well as tales of the first biblical king, Saul. He is an authoritarian, militaristic, and murderous leader who takes his own life in battle after he makes a final statement about the Philistine warriors. When Saul orders his arms-bearer, he reduces the Philistines to their foreskins (הערלים): "Draw your sword and thrust me through with it, so that these uncircumcised (הערלים, literally *foreskins*) may not come and thrust me through and make sport of me" (1 Sam 31:4). In other words, the mention of Gibeah alludes to an authoritarian governing structure that is based on ethnonational and phallogocentric storytelling about rape, war, and murder. One could, in fact, argue that the monarchical system deepens othering dynamics in the story and in the world. The third chapter of this book elaborates on some of these dynamics. Suffice it to mention here Samuel's speech in which he points to the economic demands and class-stratified requirements of the future king (1 Sam 8:11–18). At stake are always power, status, and control over material resources, land, and people.

Yet the story world of 1 Samuel leaves Gibeah behind when young David escapes the king's murderous intentions. Three main characters shape the storytelling; as 1 Samuel 19:1 states, "Saul spoke with his son Jonathan and with all his servants about killing David. But Saul's son Jonathan took great delight in David." Both Jonathan, the son of the king, and Michal, one of Saul's daughters who marries David in 18:27, help David escape from the king. Saul had already become suspicious and jealous of David (18:9) after the women's victory song depicts David as the more successful man: "Saul has killed his thousands and David his ten thousands" (18:7). Another verse makes even clearer Saul's feelings toward David: "Saul was still more afraid of David. So Saul was David's enemy from that time forward" (18:29). The king fears the competition from the young man and aims to get rid of his likely successor, while the king's son Jonathan, the king's daughter Michal, all of Saul's servants, and all of Israel and Judah love David (18:3, 16, 22, 28). Saul thus repeatedly tries to kill David with his spear (18:11; 19:10), but David escapes successfully (19:18; see also 19:10).

When Saul plans to murder David a fourth time (19:11; see also 18:11, 25; 19:10), Michal warns her husband to escape (19:12). She tricks her father, as Rachel deceives her father, Laban (Gen 31:34–35), with a "household god" (תרפים). Michal gathers some goat hair and covers it with clothes to make it look like a human body (19:13). The sham figure in the bed gives David time to escape from Saul, who does not immediately recognize the deception. Once he does, he accuses his daughter of lying, but she lies again, saying, "[David] said to me, 'Let me go; why should I kill you?'" (19:17). The second sentence, "why should I kill you," states literally in Hebrew, "Why should I cause you to die?" (למה אמיתך). In other words, Michal gives her father the impression she had no other option but to help David because he threatened to kill her if she refused. Due to his wife's help, David escapes from Gibeah to Ramah, where Samuel the prophet resides. Both move on to Naioth for unknown reasons, perhaps to put further distance between them and Saul (19:18). When Saul hears about David's whereabouts, he sends three groups of messengers after him, all of whom engage in the activity of prophesying (נבא 19:20, 21). When Saul himself makes his way to Naioth, the same happens to him: "He, too, stripped off his clothes, and he, too, fell into a frenzy before Samuel. He lay naked all that day and all that night" (19:24). In this passage, prophecy means getting naked and lying on the ground day and night: "Therefore it is said, 'Is Saul also among the [male] prophets?'" (19:24; see also 10:12 but without a reference to Saul being naked).

Although Esther Fuchs in her seminal feminist study on female biblical prophecy does not refer to this male performance of the prophetic, a feminist interpreter ought to ask if this story presents yet another articulation of the "andro-theistic infrastructure of monotheistic ideology" in which male prophecy is "the core and culmination of the monotheistic paradigm."[62] Provocatively, Fuchs, a radical feminist Jewish-Israeli and US-American exegete, posits that biblical prophecy is always depicted as a male activity in the monotheistic discourse of the Hebrew Bible. This discourse mentions five named and unnamed female characters as "[female] prophets" (נביאה),[63] simultaneously inscribing and erasing them as authoritative and respectable prophets. To Fuchs, biblical texts present only male prophets as adequate conversation partners for the male deity; women are not part of the andro-theistic speeches. Fuchs's exegetical, hermeneutical, and theological critique urges feminist and nonfeminist readers alike to consider why prophecy appears only as male activity. The naked royal (male) messengers and the naked king lie in the streets for days and nights without an apparent purpose, yet readers accept these male characters as prophets.

Interestingly, these male vagabonds are not the only ones depicted as nude male prophets. Isaiah, the prophet, is instructed to walk naked and barefoot through the streets of Jerusalem for three years. His nudity receives a purpose; it is "a sign and a portent against Egypt and Cush" (Isa 20:3). Another prophet who promises to go barefoot and naked is Micah, as he announces that he will lament and wail (Mic 1:8). Of course, nowadays, prophets and nonprophets alike, of any gender, would be fined, arrested, or both if they acted in "open and gross lewdness and lascivious behavior" in the United States.[64] The depiction of naked Saul as a (male) prophet is thus puzzling. No purpose is mentioned. Still, readers accept his characterization as a prophet, even if his actual words are not reported and he is depicted as a mere (male) drunk in the streets.

---

62. For the full argument, see Esther Fuchs, "Prophecy and the Construction of Women: Inscription and Erasure," in *A Feminist Companion to Prophets and Daniel*, ed. Athalya Brenner, FCB 8, 2nd series (Sheffield: Sheffield Academic, 2001), 54–69.

63. The five female prophets are Miriam (Exod 15:20), Deborah (Judg 4:4), Huldah (2 Kgs 22:14), Noadiah (Neh 6:14), and the nameless woman of Isaiah (Isa 8:3).

64. See, e.g., the US-American legal advice page here: https://www.hg.org/legal-articles/nudity-and-public-decency-laws-in-america-31193.

The Deuteronomistic references to male prophecy are indicated throughout by the Hebrew masculine verbal forms. As Saul acts like a male prophet, he forgets to murder David. It is as if becoming a male prophet causes divinely induced amnesia. Perhaps this depiction of being a male prophet is indeed based on an exilic or even postexilic projection that imagines the era of the first Israelite king as not yet being bogged down by geopolitical catastrophes like the Babylonian exile. Hence, this fragmentary story reads like a literary fantasy about a time when male prophesy was a regular occurrence that meant lying around nude for days on end and even included King Saul forgetting why he went to Ramah in the first place.

Meanwhile 1 Samuel presents David as not forgetting to run from the king. The story of an older and more powerful man who tries to prevent a young male competitor's political ascendancy focuses on the younger man's relationship with the older man's son (20:1–42). The triangular male relationship involves Saul, David, and Jonathan and leads to the eventual downfall of father and son. Before David flees from Saul, he listens to Jonathan, who "love[s] him as his own soul" (18:3) and "love[s] him as he love[s] his own life" (20:17). These articulations of love by another man have always intrigued queer and nonqueer interpreters alike. Some interpreters dismiss Jonathan's love as nonreciprocal. Jonathan's love ensures David's survival, but David never expresses his love to Jonathan or anybody else. For instance, Shimon Bar-Efrat thinks that the narrator emphasizes Jonathan's love, depicting it as the main force behind his actions, whereas the same cannot be said about David.[65] Even queer Bible scholar Ken Stone is ambivalent about Jonathan and David's relationship because "it may also be anachronistic . . . to assume that the deep affection Jonathan and David clearly have for one another in the text would automatically signify a sexual relationship in the ancient world."[66] Yet this story about life and death

65. Shimon Bar-Efrat, *Das Erste Buch Samuel: Ein narratologisch-philologischer Kommentar*, BWANT 176 (Stuttgart: Verlag W. Kohlhammer, 1996), 276.

66. Stone, "1 and 2 Samuel," 207–208. When the root *love* appears in other passages referring to heterosexual relationships, such as Gen 24:67; 29:20; 34:3; Ruth 4:15; Hos 3:1, or even 1 Sam 18:20, the distinction between physical and platonic love is not made. The uninhibited articulation of Jonathan's love for David

depicts an intense relationship between the two younger men, including symbolic expressions of loyalty and commitment, when Jonathan hands over his robe and armor, sword, bow, and even his belt to David, perhaps as a sign of giving up his inherited right to be the next king (18:4; 20:12–17; 20:41). In this sense, the royal son defers to the other man who is running for his life. They develop an intricate strategy that requires David to sit in hiding behind a rock while Jonathan shoots an arrow with code words. This strategy ensures that David knows he needs to escape and never to return to the palace (20:18–42).

The escape story thus continues, moving farther and farther away from Saul and his palace in Gibeah. David's next stop is Nob, where the priest Ahimelech trembles when he sees him (21:1). David lies about his true motives for visiting the priest. He wants to get supplies, including Goliath's sword, to be equipped with a weapon (21:2–9). Then David runs to Gath, where the Philistine King Achish rules (21:10–15). This story, too, involves only men, except when women and mothers appear to support male characters or when female characters are reduced to their genitals. For instance, Saul curses his son Jonathan when he realizes his son betrayed him. Asking a rhetorical question embedded in the curse, Saul insults his son. The king's curse reduces his son's mother to her genitals, usually translated as "nakedness" (ערוה), as Saul angrily parallelizes Jonathan's "shame" (בשת) to

makes even the most progressive scholar hesitant to accept its validity. Thus, Stone's insistence on the likely absence of "sexual intercourse" between Jonathan and David illustrates the contemporary popular fallacy of defining sex as love when sex has mostly very little to do with love but with physiological or psychological needs, urges, or even demands. Of course, sometimes sex also expresses love, and love can find expression in sex. David's lament over Jonathan's death is as powerfully touching as it can ever be imagined between two people, whether their love is heterosexual, queer, or "whatever" (2 Sam 1:26). At the same time, his speech could also be politically motivated, as interpreters maintain when they focus on the possibilities of David's duplicity. As interpreters always observe, David is the only character who never is said to love anybody. For a historical-critical discussion, see Susan Ackerman, *When Heroes Love: The Ambiguity of Eros in the Stories of Gilgamesh and David*, (GTR (New York: Columbia University Press, 2005).

the “shame” of his mother’s “nakedness” (ערות).[67] Saul asks, “Do I not know that you have chosen the son of Jesse to your own shame and to the shame of your mother’s nakedness?” (20:30). Saul condemns Jonathan for his “shameful” behavior, as he compares Jonathan with his mother’s genitals (“nakedness”). In another passage, women appear as figures from whom religiously proper-behaving men need to stay away (21:4–5). The priest Ahimelech asks David if he and his men “have kept themselves from women” (21:4) before he is willing to hand over to the visitor “holy bread” (לחם קדש) and several tools of war. All these references keep women on the margins, whereas men are depicted as helping (21:6, 9), admiring (21:11), betraying (21:7; 22:9, 18), or even killing each other. Saul tries to kill his son (20:33), whereas David murders not only other men (22:11–19) but also “women, children and infants, oxen, donkeys, and sheep” (22:19; see also 15:3). These are brutal, violent, and merciless narratives about men fighting for power, status, betrayal, love, and death. At the end, only one man remains alive, while his persecutor and the persecutor’s son are dead (31:8). Surprisingly, Mel Gibson, the movie director, who has been so captivated by visually depicting bloody macho-violence, has yet to make a film about this gory drama about competition, jealousy, and even love and death among powerful warrior men.

According to 1 Samuel 21:10, David flees next to the Philistine town of Gath. Since the slaves of King Achish, or, according to the NRSV, his “servants” (21:11, עבדים), greet the Israelite man’s arrival with the recognition of his superior military prowess (“Saul has killed his thousands and David his ten thousands,” 21:11) and as “the king of the land” (v. 11), David fears to be harmed by the Philistine king. After all, David is in enemy territory, and so he pretends to be cognitively challenged (21:13). His ruse works, and the Philistine ruler and his men dismiss him as one of the many “madmen” (משגעים) unworthy of their attention (21:15).

A comment about the location of Gath is in order. Archaeologists locate the Philistine city-state of Gath as Tel eṣ-Ṣâfi. The site is located on the southern banks of Wadi ʿAjjur and twenty-two miles northwest of Hebron in the West Bank. As the Israel Defense Forces (IDF) expelled the Palestinian population from the land during the 1948 Arab-Israeli war, the

---

67. For a discussion on the Hebrew term ערוה, see the section “For Further Reflection” in chap. 5.

Palestinian village of Tel eṣ-Ṣâfi, nestled at the northwest side of the upper tel, was abandoned on July 9, 1948.[68]

Already the first excavation, directed by the British archaeologist Frederick J. Bliss and assisted by the field director R. A. Stewart Macalister in 1899, demonstrated that an archaeological identification of Tel eṣ-Ṣâfi (Tel Tsafit) with the biblical town of Gath is impossible.[69] Yet, by then, the antiquity of the site was presumed because the settlement stones go back to the Early Bronze Age. In his report during the first season of 1899, Bliss wrote:

> The question may now be asked: what light [has] our investigation thrown on the identification of Tell eṣ-Ṣâfi with Gath? This identification was originally advanced purely on the grounds of the importance and position of the site, no determination having been made of its antiquity. . . . We have proved the existence of a city built in pre-Israelite times, and probably fortified during the Jewish period. . . . Our proof thus is negative: nothing has been found to show that Tell eṣ-Ṣâfi cannot be Gath. Positive proof cannot be expected short of the discovery of inscriptions. That the tell contains such records is quite within the range of possibilities. That these may be found by us is a desire felt, I am sure, by all the readers of these lines.[70]

Bliss was honest in his remarks. He hoped for archaeological proof that would affirm the biblical identity of the site as Gath. Yet he also acknowledged that he had not yet found such proof in the ground. As the antiquity of the archaeological findings is impressive, the desire to identify the site with Gath continues.

But even the current archaeological excavation, directed by Aren M. Maeir of Bar-Ilan University in Jerusalem and begun in 1996, has yet to find

68. Liora Kolska Horwitz, Rona Winter-Livneh, and Aren M. Maeir, "'The Archaeological Picture Went Blank': Historical Archaeology and GIS analysis of the Landscape of the Palestinian Village of Tell eṣ-Ṣâfi," *NEA* 81 (2018): 85.

69. For some details about the archaeological history of this tel, see, e.g., Rona S. Avissar Lewis and Aren M. Maeir, "New Insights into Bliss and Macalister's Excavations at Tell eṣ-Ṣâfi/Gath," *NEA* 80 (2017): 241–243.

70. Quoted in Lewis and Maeir, "New Insights," 242.

conclusive epigraphic evidence to match the site with biblical Gath. Maeir and his team assert that such an identification is still "possible."[71] Digging for archaeological artifacts on this huge tel that was continuously inhabited since the Chalcolithic era (late fourth to third millennium BCE), Maeir believes the site is the biblical Gath.[72] Other archaeologists are less optimistic. For instance, Israel Finkelstein finds such an identification unlikely because "the notion of historical writing in the tenth century BCE is highly unlikely."[73] Accordingly, the story of David escaping to Gath is at best written from the so-called Deuteronomistic theological and political perspective that always defames the Philistines. The story does not reflect Gath during the time of Saul (Iron Age I), as biblical scholars such as Albright assumed, and it is better dated into the seventh century BCE. Even the archaeological record gives only scant evidence of tenth-century occupancy. According to Finkelstein, the "seventh-century" story would explain how Ziklag, a city mentioned in 1 Samuel 27, became a Judahite town, "or even better [the story] claims Ziklag for Judah."[74] In this fictional account, the Philistine monarch, Achish of Gath, gives Ziklag to David (27:6). Later, Deuteronomistic writers invented the story to justify ownership of a piece of land that was originally seen as belonging to the more powerful ethnic group, the Philistines.

Since David is afraid to be found out by the Philistine king in 1 Samuel 21:10–15, he also runs away from Gath. Perhaps he even fears extradition to the Israelite king, Saul, from whom David has been running since he left the Israelite king's palace in Gibeah (19:12). After leaving the city of Gath, David ends up at the cave of Adullam (22:1), which today is in hiking distance of the Separation Wall and the West Bank. Often considered

---

71. Yigal Levin, "Gath of the Philistines in the Bible and on the Ground: The Historical Geography of Tell eṣ-Ṣâfi/Gath," *NEA* 80 (2017): 238. For a recent comprehensive report on the first decade of excavations, see Aren M. Maeir, ed., *Tell eṣ-Ṣâfi/Gath I: The 1996–2005 Seasons, vol. 1: Text, vol. 2: Plates*, Ägypten und Altes Testament 69 (Wiesbaden: Harrassowitz, 2016).

72. Aren M. Maeir, "The Tell eṣ-Ṣâfi/Gath Archaeological Project: Overview," *NEA* 80 (2017): 213.

73. Israel Finkelstein, "The Philistines in the Bible: A Late-Monarchic Perspective," *JSOT* 27 (2002): 132. See also much earlier Volkmar Fritz, "Where Is David's Ziklag?," *BAR* 19 (1993): 58–61, 76.

74. Finkelstein, "The Philistines in the Bible," 136.

Figure 1.10. Aerial view of archaeological findings at Tel eṣ-Ṣâfi/ Gath. Photo by Ori, https://commons.wikimedia.org/w/index.php?curid=8945813.

to be identical with Tell Sheikh Madkhur (*Khirbet 'Eîd el Mieh*), Adullam overlooks the Elah valley that touches the Green Line between Israel and the West Bank. The site is located south of Beit Shemesh and can be reached by driving through a little agricultural village, the Moshav of Aderet, to reach the "Adullam Grove Nature Reserve." David escapes to the cave of Adullam, and "everyone [כל־איש, literally *every man*] who was in distress, and everyone [כל־איש, literally *every man*] who was in debt, and everyone [כל־איש, literally *every man*] who was discontented gathered to him, and he became captain over them. Those who were with him numbered about four hundred" (ארבע מאות איש, literally, *four hundred men*, 22:2). A gang of distressed, indebted, and discontented men gather under their leader, David. Far from power and prestige, the remote location—borderland between Israel proper and the West Bank divided by the Separation Wall—makes Adullam a perfect hideaway even today.

Figure 1.11. View toward the West Bank and the Separation Wall. Copyright 2018 Susanne Scholz.

David's wilderness escape continues. He leaves Adullam to go to Moab (22:3), which is part of contemporary Jordan. Nowadays, only people classified as "foreigners" (with a visa) or "diplomats" are allowed to cross the Allenby / King Hussein Bridge (Allenby Border Terminal); Israelis can cross the border two hours north at the Jordan River Crossing in Irbid / Beit She'an or south at the Wadi Araba Crossing in Aqaba/Eilat. Yet in the biblical narrative, border controls do not exist. In 1 Samuel 22:5a, a prophet named Gad advises David to return to Judah, and so David goes to the forest of Hereth (22:5b), a location perhaps near today's Hebron in the West Bank. In the biblical narrative, David and his six hundred men move on to Keilah, located in biblical Judah, on the contemporary West Bank. The site is in ruins today, known as Khirbet Qeila and close to the Palestinian village of Qila, eleven kilometers northwest of Hebron. In the narrative, the warriors help the inhabitants of Keilah by fighting against the Philistines (23:1–12), but then they move into the wilderness of Ziph, located southeast of Hebron, to

Figure 1.12. A cave at Adullam. Copyright 2018 Susanne Scholz.

escape Saul's attention (23:13), as "Saul sought him every day, but [YHWH] did not give him into his hand" (23:14). Even Jonathan comes to see David in the wilderness and swears his loyalty when David will be king (23:17–18). When even the royal son in line to be the next king abandons his future to a man on the run, readers know who the hero is in this male-bonding escape narrative. As David runs from the wilderness of Maon (23:24–26), Saul almost catches him (23:28). Yet David again escapes, this time to En-gedi at the Dead Sea (23:29), where he could have killed Saul for the first time but instead cuts off only a corner of Saul's coat (24:5). Many interpreters suggest that this symbolic act indicates Saul's failing royal power, a development that Saul himself later acknowledges. When David calls Saul outside the cave, the dramatic dialogue between the two men results in Saul's acknowledgment that David will surely become the next king (24:20). Saul even asks for David's commitment to keep Saul's descendants and Saul's own name alive (24:21). David swears to do both, and then they depart, each traveling on their respective road (24:22).

Yet betrayal is permanent in this escape drama over political supremacy and male hegemonic domination of the royal older male by the young royal-aspiring male. Masculinity, intersected with class status, appears to be the prerequisite for the execution of power and status. The dynamic turns on a whim. For instance, before David spares the life of his relentless pursuer a second time, Saul learns from the Ziphites that David is roaming the deserted hills of Judah, hiding on the hill of Hachilah (26:1). As Saul goes after David, the young man has yet another opportunity to kill the king. But again he refrains from killing Saul (26:6–12) because "[YHWH] forbid that I should raise my hand against [YHWH's] anointed" (26:11). After a detailed explanation to his commander, Abishai, as to why he will not kill the king (26:6–12), David humiliates Saul's army commander Abner (14:50)[75] by asking him, "Are you not a man?" (הלוא־איש אתה 26:15). Manliness is at the core of the encounters of attempted murder, rejected assassination attempts, and verbal insults that hint at the future of this or that macho man. In the case of Abner, not only does David challenge his manliness for having failed to protect the king, but Abner's loyalty and masculine viability also become dubious, hinting at his downfall later (2 Sam 3:27).

As betrayal continues, David emerges as a shrewd political leader. He does not trust Saul's praises and apologies (1 Sam 26:17–25) and instead decides (27:1) to seek safety where before he had been afraid. In 1 Samuel 27:1 David recognizes that the only way to permanently escape from Saul is to live in the land of the Philistines. He, his six hundred men, all their families, and David's two wives, Ahinoam of Jezreel and Abigail of Carmel, arrive before King Achish of Gath in 1 Samuel 27:2–3. The king does not allow him to live in Gath, giving him one of the country towns, Ziklag (27:6), where, as the narrative reports, the escapees live for the next sixteen months (27:7). During that time, David raids neighboring peoples, such as the Geshurites, Girzites, and Amalekites, "leaving neither men nor women alive" (27:9; see 27:8–11). Interestingly, the Philistine king comes to trust David, thinking, "He has made himself utterly abhorrent to his people Israel; therefore he shall always be my servant" (27:12). A murderous macho-male

75. In 1 Chr 8:29–33, the genealogy implies that Abner is Saul's uncle.

warrior, just like Mel Gibson depicts men in his movies, David exercises his killer instinct, murdering all civilians and even fooling the Philistine king. David is determined, decisive, and never hesitant to take what he wants or to take back what is his, whether power, status, women, or the sword of Goliath. Reported in 1 Samuel 30, his last battle against the Amalekites is again victorious. David and his six hundred men successfully avenge the Amalekite destruction of Ziklag. Afterward David even sends off some of the booty as a gift to his friends, the elders of Judah (30:26), who live in all the places "where David and his men had roamed" (30:30). David is shrewdly planning for his political future, which is further narrated in 2 Samuel.

For now (1 Sam 30:26), he is back in the destroyed city of Ziklag, which archaeologists struggle to identify. In the narrative, Ziklag is yet another fringe location in the middle of nowhere, perhaps northeast of Beer-sheba and south-southeast of Gaza City.[76] It is a location in Israel proper today, where dust and endless flat land make any road seem long and dangerous to a car's tires. In October 2018, I visited Tel Sera' (Tell esh-Shari'ah), sometimes identified with Ziklag.[77] As I approached the site while driving on a dirt road in the middle of a hot and dry October day, a Bedouin man shepherded his sheep, with the help of a dog and a donkey, across the barren and dusty fields. It was a sight straight from the movies. These are the hinterlands of any country, including contemporary Israel, far from the centers of power. The biblical narrative places David there as the hunted future king, escaping

---

76. For a recent international Israeli and Australian archaeological collaboration that identifies Ziklag with Khirbet el Ra'i, see, e.g., "Biblical Town of Ziklag May Have Been Discovered," *BAS*, July 27, 2019, https://www.biblicalarchaeology.org/daily/biblical-town-of-ziklag-may-have-been-discovered/; Ruth Schuster and Nir Hasson, "Biblical Town of Ziklag May Have Been Discovered," *Haaretz*, https://www.biblicalarchaeology.org/daily/biblical-town-of-ziklag-may-have-been-discovered/; Ruth Schuster and Nir Hasson, "Biblical City of Ziklag Where Philistines Gave Refuge to David Found, Researchers Claim," *Haaretz*, July 8, 2019, https://www.haaretz.com/archaeology/.premium.MAGAZINE-biblical-city-where-philistines-gave-refuge-to-david-found-researchers-claim-1.7455800.

77. Eliezer Oren, "Ziklag: A Biblical City on the Edge of the Negev," *BA* 45 (1982): 155–166; Oded Browski, "The Biblical Identity of Tel Halif," *BA* 51 (1988): 21–27.

Figure 1.13. Shepherd on the way to Tel Sara'. Copyright 2018 Susanne Scholz.

the king of Israel, Saul, while the Philistine king of Gath believes David will never return home because of his murderous expeditions. David's future is arrested, as he becomes a killing machine in 1 Samuel, but in 2 Samuel this violent warrior man will become the second king of biblical Israel.

Between Narrative Fiction and Archaeology: Concluding Comments on the Geopolitics of Land and Gender in 1 Samuel

As the biblical tales mention famous, lesser-known, and even unknown places in today's Palestine and Israel, feminist interest in the gender aspects of 1 Samuel needs to be connected to past and present geopolitics. Archaeological excavations at some of the central places indicate the long-lasting scholarly attraction to the era labeled as the United Monarchy. This era is depicted in biblical narratives when they mention northern Israel and southern Judah

Figure 1.14. Tel Sara'. Copyright 2018 Susanne Scholz.

as being ruled by the first three kings, Saul, David, and Solomon. That we can still visit many of the sites suggests to some readers that the tales are somehow historically "true." Nothing could be further from the truth. People have lived in the land of Palestine/Israel since the Early Bronze Age, but the archaeological remains do not prove the historicity of the biblical stories.

In certain cases, the archaeological witness is propped up to signal direct connections between 1 Samuel and the ancient stones or ostraca found in the ground, such as in the case of Tel Shiloh or 'Izbet Sartah.[78] Serious ideological, political, and financial commitments invite such speculative links even when the scholarly analysis does not unequivocally sustain them. In other geographical locations, archaeological findings prove the existence

78. For a detailed discussion of current efforts of "propping up" the archaeological site of Tel Shiloh, see, e.g., Susanne Scholz, "The Disneyfication of Shiloh: Biblical Historiography and Archaeology as Methodological Regimes of Military Occupation," *SJOT* 36 (2022): 112–137.

of human habitation, sometimes since the Chalcolithic Age (late fourth to third millennium BCE), such as at Tel eṣ-Ṣâfi (Tel Tsafit/Gath). Still other sites, such as Ziklag, are not backed up by any archaeological record. It is no simple task to correlate the fictional biblical accounts to archaeological sites, also considering the militarized geopolitics of today's land. The Israeli military occupation of the West Bank makes every historiographical effort politically charged and contested for or against a different political arrangement. Most archaeological sites thus represent veiled geopolitical, religious, ethnic, intellectual-scholarly, and academic-institutional outlooks that lead to preferential investment in one but not another site.

Concealed archaeological interests are compounded by gender-related dynamics rarely put into words. One such dynamic concerns the fact that most archaeologists digging for archaeological artifacts at geographical locations mentioned in 1 Samuel are male academics. Many of them teach at Israeli universities, and often they collaborate with other mostly male scholars from European, North American, or Australian universities. They constitute an international bunch of mostly male researchers, although volunteers on excavations include many female students. The gender bias in ancient Near Eastern archaeology is deep and long-standing. Lady Hester Stanhope from the early nineteenth century was a pioneering female aristocratic British archaeologist, although her work did not create an immediate path for women in the field.[79] Should feminist Bible interpreters be surprised that tourist plaques at Tel Shiloh or Tel eṣ-Ṣâfi (Tel Tsafit) pursue androcentric ways of telling the biblical journeys in which Saul, David, or Samuel are the major figures? As archaeologists and site curators take for granted androcentric ideologies, male ethnoreligious supremacy in biblical depictions of male bonding is naturalized and normalized. That women serve as props in the competition for power, status, and prestige among the male characters appears only on the sidelines of what is perceived as the more important quest for archaeological evidence. The Disney-like presentation of the first

---

79. For an appreciative tribute to women in biblical archaeology, see, e.g., Kristine Henriksen Garroway, "Digging Up the Past: The History of Women Archaeologists in the Society of Biblical Literature," *lectio difficilior*, January 2020, https://lectio.unibe.ch/en/archive/kristine-henriksen-garroway-digging-up-the-past-the-history-of-women-archaeologists-in-the-society-of-biblical-literature.html.

chapters of 1 Samuel in the tourism film at Tel Shiloh exemplifies this trend to an extent not seen on any other archaeological site in Palestine and Israel, except at the City of David in Jerusalem.

In sum, this chapter exposes some of the geopolitical and gendered assumptions of past and present approaches, including in archaeological excavations, to 1 Samuel. The question is not "Did the stories really happen?" but "How are the geopolitical, sociocultural, and religious-cultural dynamics depicted in stories that feature central travel destinations (i.e., Tel Shiloh), traveling objects (i.e., the ark of the covenant), and escaping subjects (i.e., David)?" This feminist interpretation also acknowledges that today's travelers run into considerable geopolitical difficulties if they want to trace this biblical book's numerous geographical locations and destinations, although some of them, such as Shiloh or Gath, are exquisite archaeological tourism sites with a plethora of archaeological and ideological possibilities, while others, such as ʿIzbet Sartah, Tel el-Fûl (Gibeah), or the mysterious Ziklag, depend on a visitor's imagination. The related problem of masculine hegemony in the depictions of the main characters and their triangulation is the topic of the next chapter.

For Further Reflection

1. Kevin M. McGeough, "About Lady Hester Stanhope (1779–1839)," in *The Ancient Near East in the Nineteenth Century: Appreciations and Appropriations (vol. 1: Claiming and Conquering)*, Hebrew Bible Monographs 67 (Sheffield: Sheffield Phoenix, 2015), 328–330.

   Yet even before tourism to the Middle East had become common, women were able to play a role in the development of the field. One of the most interesting of these figures, who played a dubious role in the development of Syro-Palestinian archaeology, was Lady Hester Stanhope (1776–1839). She can be said to have conducted the first archaeological excavation in what is now Israel at the coastal site of Ashkelon. Lady Hester was the granddaughter of William Pitt the Elder and the niece of William Pitt the Younger, who held the office of prime minister twice. As an unmarried man, Pitt needed a hostess for his household, so his niece moved in with him to assume those duties during his second term in office (1804–1806). After his death, she received a pension from the British government, which provided her with some degree of independence. Silberman notes that her personality made her numerous enemies while head of Pitt's household, and, after his death, she found herself without supporters in London society. Romantic disappointment and the death of her brother in the Napoleonic wars further led her to give up London and move to Asia Minor.

Lady Hester's travels to Syria-Palestine are extremely interesting, and her unusual encounters cannot really be taken as normative for the period, other than to point to the eclectic nature of Near Eastern travel before the advent of middle-class tourism. According to Silberman, she was inspired to visit the Holy Land by an inmate of the insane asylum of Bedlam who told her that he had seen her future as the queen of the Jews, and that she would lead the Jews back to the Holy Land. En route to the Orient, at Athens, she visited Lord Byron. Her ship wrecked in Rhodes, where she was forced to borrow Turkish clothing, and it was at that point that she started wearing the clothing of Ottoman men (specifically choosing not to borrow typical Ottoman women's clothing). This remained her standard practice while in the Middle East. Once in the Holy Land, she met Burckhardt in Nazareth, who convinced her to further explore the region.

After visiting Palmyra, a location that had been thought too dangerous for Europeans to visit, Lady Hester gained the affection of local Bedouin. She settled on the coast of Syria, where all sorts of visitors came to see her. Among these visitors were Franciscan monks who gave her what was purported to be a medieval map indicating the location of buried gold at the site of Ashkelon. Lady Hester travelled to Ashkelon, having gotten permission to excavate the site from the sultan in Constantinople. Once at Ashkelon, and accompanied by a representative of the sultan, she commenced her excavations. There she did not find gold but did find a seven-foot-tall Roman statue in marble. Once it became clear that there was no gold, rather than collect the antiquities, she had the statue destroyed and cast into the sea. Silberman explains that this rather curious choice was rooted in her desire not to encourage the plundering of Holy Land sites by Europeans in order to fill museums. Having visited Athens and aware of the controversy associated with the Elgin Marbles, Lady Hester, who by this time was quite quick to temper and on bad terms with the British consulate, chose to make her public statement about European antiquities collecting through this act of vandalism. Thus ended the first excavation in Palestine and Lady Hester's archaeological career. She spent the last twenty years of her life in seclusion in Lebanon, although Tuchman notes that Lady Hester became something of a tourist attraction herself for European travelers.[80]

2. Carol J. Dempsey, OP, "Nakedness in 1 Samuel 19:18–24." Used by permission of the author.

Three textual issues affect the exegesis of 1 Samuel 19:18–24. The first issue is the translation of the Hebrew word גם. BDB offers several possibilities: "also," "even," "yea," "but," "though," and "even though." The word גם occurs seven times in the MT of 1 Samuel 19:18–24, specifically in verses 20, 21 (2x), 22, 23, and 24a (2x). In verses 21 and 22 (2x), it appears as גם-המה. NRSV translates all three occurrences as "*they also*." In verses 22, 23, and 24 (2x), גם appears as גם-המה. The NRSV translates the phase as "then *he himself*" in verse 22. In verse 23, the NRSV bypasses the phrase altogether to state "and the spirit of God came upon him." The NRSV translation of the phrase in verse 24a, however, is intriguing: "*He, too,* stripped off his clothes, and he, too, fell into a frenzy before Samuel." Significant here is the first part of the sentence that uses גם. Nowhere in 1 Samuel 19:18–24, either in the MT or in the NRSV, is a statement that the messengers stripped off their clothes and were naked. Thus, verse 24a with the double use of גם-הוא should read, "He *even* stripped off his clothes and he *also* fell into a frenzy." Verses 20 and 21 indicate that Saul's messengers fell into a frenzy, and now Saul does too.

The second issue centers on the word "naked" in verse 24b and its use in the NRSV. Having stripped off his clothes (v. 24a), Saul is

80. Barbara W. Tuchman, *Bible and Sword: England and Palestine from the Bronze Age to Balfour* (New York: Ballantine Books, 1984 [1956]), 168.

now naked: "He lay naked all that day and all that night." The root for "naked" in verse 24b is ערום. Interestingly, Genesis 2:25; 3:10; Isaiah 20:2–4; Micah 1:8; Ezekiel 16:7; Hosea 2:3; and Job 22:6 use the same root, but "naked" has many interpretations. For example, in Genesis 2:25, being naked appears in the creation story and indicates human physicality. In Genesis 3:10, nakedness occurs in the garden story where two humans eat a forbidden fruit. Nakedness becomes associated with not only human growth in awareness (v. 7) but also fear and the act of hiding. Commentator Mark Smith suggests that nakedness symbolizes vulnerability (see Smith, "Genesis," *The New Jerome Biblical Commentary*, 209); Richard Clifford, SJ, proposes that the man and woman's realization of their nakedness is the awakening of their sexuality, and so "they hurriedly cover themselves" (see Clifford, "Genesis," *The Paulist Biblical Commentary*, 19). In Isaiah 20:2–4 the character Isaiah walks barefoot and naked (vv. 2–3) as a sign of condemnation. Exiles walk "naked and barefoot, with buttocks uncovered" (v. 4) as a sign of shame. Likewise, the character Micah walks "barefoot and naked," an image that feminist interpreter Julia O'Brien refrains from commenting on. Ezekiel 16:7 and Hosea 2:3 focus on nakedness and the female body. In Ezekiel 16:7, the naked female body is the object of divine disdain; female sexuality is objectified. In Hosea 2:3 a woman's body is threatened with horrific sexual violence while experiencing disdain by a deity who warns her that she will be stripped naked and her body exposed "as in the day she was born." Nakedness, then, is associated with abuse and disdain, especially with respect to women's bodies. In the *Women's Bible Commentary* (2012), Gale Yee also offers no comment on nakedness in relation to female objectification, disdain, and abuse, except to say that the threats are aimed to get the woman to forsake her promiscuity (302). Finally, in Job 22:6, nakedness is the result of an injustice allegedly done by Job who "stripped the naked of their clothing."

In short, the idea of "nakedness" has many possibilities. Do we read frenzied Saul stripping off his clothes and lying naked all day and all night as an expression of vulnerability? Or do we hear resonances of sexual violence in Saul stripping off his clothes, prophesying before Samuel, and lying naked for an unspecified amount of time? Or do we find in this description hints of rape fantasies about Saul in relation to David? After all, Saul and David are enemies by now, and Saul even wants to kill David (1 Sam 18:10–16; 20:1). Curiously, the roots of both "strip," פשט, and "naked," ערום, appear in 1 Samuel 19:24b–c, as they do in the rape poem of Hosea 2:3.

The third issue pertains to the question in verse 24c where גם appears for the last time in verses 18–24: "Therefore it is said, "Is Saul *also* among the prophets?" The same question and wording occur in 1 Samuel 10:11, asked by the people after they saw Saul in a prophetic frenzy, prophesizing with the prophets. In the context of 1 Samuel 19:18–24, a different, more dubious tone could occur if גם were translated "even": Is Saul *even* among the prophets? In sum, this verse invites, first, a reflection on a pronoun (גם) to figure out whether Saul is classified *as* a prophet or as *being with* some prophets; second, the mention of the king as being naked (ערום) resonates with other important references to nakedness in the biblical canon, possibly even hinting at a male-on-male rape fantasy.

3. Isam Shihada, "The Gaza Strip: The People Deserve a Better Life" (Al Aqsa University, Gaza/Palestine, written in 2019). Used by permission of the author.

   Gaza, a narrow wedge of land on the eastern Mediterranean, is barely forty kilometers long and approximately ten kilometers wide. Most people in Gaza live in densely packed and low concrete tower blocks, and many areas in the city are severely damaged because of past fights between Hamas and Israel. Immediately after Hamas took power in 2007, Israel moved to isolate the militant group by restricting the flow of goods and people through Gaza, limiting access to the sea, and collaborating with Egypt to enforce a blockade. At the same time, Hamas had been in a near-constant dispute with the Palestinian Authority (PA) government based in the West Bank, prompting the PA to limit financial transfers to Gaza. Moreover, in 2017, the PA had asked Israel to reduce the supply of electricity. The United Nations Country Team in the occupied Palestinian territory released an incisive report on Gaza in 2012,[81] focusing on the humanitarian impact of Israel's ten-year blockade of the Gaza Strip and the internal political divisions among Palestinians. However, its report findings are bleak: Gaza's impoverishment is entirely the product of human decisions, and not the result of circumstances beyond human control.

Background to the Gaza Strip Crisis

The year 2007 was ground zero for Gaza. In July of that year, Israel imposed a comprehensive blockade on the Strip and declared it to be an "enemy entity." Life in Gaza was extremely difficult even before 2007, and now it is even more harsh and unrelenting. According to the report from the United Nations (UN), between 2006 and 2016, Gaza's real gross domestic product per capita declined by 5.3 percent, while it grew in the occupied West Bank by 48.5 percent. The rate of poverty increased from 30 percent of the Gazan population in 2004 to around 40 percent. Gaza suffers from one of the highest unemployment rates in the world, which was at 41 percent by the end of 2016. Over 60 percent of Gazans between the ages of twenty and twenty-four are without work, and the unemployment rate for women increased sharply from 35 percent to 64 percent between 2006 and 2016. More than 60 percent of the population in 2017 was either partly or wholly dependent on humanitarian assistance.

When it comes to education, if you were a professor of English literature and gender studies at Al Aqsa University, you would not be surprised to learn that some students are unable to attend class because they do not have enough money to travel from different parts of the Gaza Strip to the university. Due to the high unemployment rate in Gaza and the reduction in salaries paid by the PA, students are unable to pay their fees and receive their graduation certificates. Even professors have been paid half of their salaries by the PA since March 2017 as a punitive measure taken to pressure Hamas to relinquish the

81. United Nations Country Team in Palestine, "Gaza in 2020—A Liveable Place?" August 27, 2012, https://reliefweb.int/report/occupied-palestinian-territory/gaza-2020-liveable-place.

Gaza Strip, a step that has left a deep economic, social, and psychological impact on all sectors of life in the area.

In the Gaza Strip thousands of students graduate from Palestinian universities annually, and yet they do not find jobs because there is no marketplace after the complete destruction caused by the permanent siege and frequent wars in the Gaza Strip in 2008, 2012, 2014, and 2018. You will not be surprised when you find a doctor or an engineer working as a taxi driver or a waiter in a restaurant. Most qualified graduates work in low-skilled jobs because there is simply no work available. For example, at Al Aqsa University, new faculty members have not been recruited since 2007 because of the poor economic situation and the low budgets suffered by the Palestinian universities, which rely primarily on tuition fees.

Moreover, professors and students are unable to travel to pursue higher education abroad because of the closure of the borders by Israel and Egypt. In order to travel, agents have to be paid 2,000 dollars on the border as coordination to agents in order to travel. You can imagine how much you have to pay when you have a family of five! Yet without paying the thousands of dollars, you will stagnate in the Gaza Strip. People who are on the waiting list to travel have to wait for several years before they can leave, unless they pay thousands of dollars to quicken the process. This may explain how the suffering of Gazans is exploited and made perpetual by the parties that control the borders, making it a lucrative business. Therefore, poor people, who constitute the majority of the Gazan population, are unable to travel at all, and the sick may wither because they cannot afford to receive treatment.

Furthermore, Gazans have been experiencing severe shortages of electricity, a crisis that has been ongoing since 2007. The immediate cause of the crisis lies in the dispute between the PA and Hamas over the fuel tax due to the Palestinian division in 2007. This disagreement prompted the PA to request that Israel reduce the 120MW in power it sold daily to approximately 70MW, and Israel complied. A second source of electricity is Gaza's sole power plant, which can produce only 50–55MW daily and was badly damaged by Israeli bombings in 2006 and 2014. Moreover, Israel has restricted the exchange of replacement parts for the power plant into Gaza. The social consequences of this extraordinary power crisis are severe. Households without access to generators or solar panels—which is most of Gaza—have between four and six hours of electricity at the best of times, followed by twelve to sixteen hours of blackout. Hospitals must rely on overextended generators and have to ration power, and workplaces shutter due to power blackouts. More than 100 million liters of untreated sewage spill daily into the Mediterranean Sea, fouling beaches and fishing grounds. Food must be bought daily and consumed quickly; otherwise, it will spoil.[82] Without electricity, life is literally paralyzed at all levels in Gaza. The only resort for Gazans is to buy generators and solar panels, which are resources only wealthy families can afford. For example, some poor families make use of candles for light, which can result in tragic accidents such as the burning of their children and houses.[83]

When it comes to fresh water, Gaza's two million citizens rely on coastal aquifers as their primary source. Although, 95 percent of this water is not safe to drink because of the intrusion of the seawater polluted by sewage. According to the UN report on the Gaza Strip, only 10 percent of the population has access to adequate drinking water.[84] Most Gazans have access to water for only eight hours every four days. Therefore, people have to buy trucked-in fresh water, which is fifteen to twenty times more expensive than network water. The poor and vulnerable in Gaza are the ones most affected since they cannot afford this basic necessity.

---

82. Michael Lynk, "How Gaza Was Made into an Unlivable Place," *Al Jazeera*, July 24, 2017, https://www.aljazeera.com/indepth/opinion/2017/07/gaza-unlivable-place-170723091946355.html.

83. Rami Almeghari, "Three Children Burn to Death as Candles Replace Lights in Besieged Gaza," *Electronic Intifada*, April 10, 2012, https://electronicintifada.net/content/three-children-burn-death-candles-replace-lights-besieged-gaza/11147.

84. Lisa Schlein, "UN Says Gaza Could Become Uninhabitable by 2020," *Voice of America*, September 13, 2018, https://www.voanews.com/a/un-says-gaza-could-become-uninhabitable-by-2020/4569898.html.

Gaza's economic trajectory over the past decade is a strong indicator of the ongoing de-development in the Gaza Strip. When it comes to infrastructure and economic projects in the area, Israel controls what exits and enters Gaza. The average number of goods exiting Gaza in 2017 was one-third of what was allowed in 2007. Gaza's traditional economic sectors are withering; agriculture, tourism, fishing, and manufacturing have all declined. The principal source of growth, tragically, has come from the reconstruction of the Palestinian neighborhoods, which were destroyed and erased during the three wars launched by Israel in the Gaza Strip in the past ten years. Throughout these wars, 500,000 people were displaced in the Strip; 20,000 homes, 148 schools, and 15 hospitals were either completely or partially destroyed.[85]

There is no doubt that the Palestinian factional split[86] in 2007 has exacerbated the unbearable conditions imposed by the Israelis, as Hamas and Fatah fight over who will pay for services in Gaza, which continues to make life more miserable. The split within the Palestinian civil service reduced the capacity of local institutions in Gaza to deliver basic services, respond to emergencies, and enforce the rules of law, increasing the population's hardships.[87] Since 2007, disputes over the funding and taxing of fuel, as well as the collection of payments from electricity consumers, undermined the functioning of Gaza's sole power plant. Medical services in Gaza have been severely affected by the power cuts and the reduction in the budget allocated by the PA Ministry of Health. To cope with the lack of power,

---

85. Eyad El Baba, "Gaza Could Become Uninhabitable in Less than Five Years Due to Ongoing 'De-development'—UN Report," *UN News*, September 1, 2015, https://news.un.org/en/story/2015/09/507762-gaza-could-become-uninhabitable-less-five-years-due-ongoing-de-development-un.

86. Bernard Gwertzman, "The Tragedy of Palestinian Divisions," *Council on Foreign Relations*, October 28, 2009, https://www.cfr.org/interview/tragedy-palestinian-divisions.

87. OCHA, "The Humanitarian Impact of the Internal Palestinian Divide on the Gaza Strip," June 23, 2017, https://www.ochaopt.org/content/humanitarian-impact-internal-palestinian-divide-gaza-strip-june-2017.

hospitals are postponing elective surgeries, discharging patients prematurely, and reducing the cleaning and sterilizing of medical facilities. Following the Hamas takeover, key donors reduced and/or conditioned their funding for humanitarian and development projects in Gaza. This contributed to the channeling of assistance toward areas and institutions free of Hamas control rather than to where assistance is most needed. Knowing that salaries paid by the PA are the backbone of the already staggering economy of the Gaza Strip, the PA forced thousands of its military and civil employees into early retirement in order to isolate Hamas and dry up financial resources and revenues coming into the Gaza Strip, which in turn paralyzes the economy of Gaza completely. Therefore, several big stores and businesses are being closed, and thousands of business owners are either in debt or in prison because they are unable to pay their bank loans. Due to salary cuts, Gazans are unable to access services for their basic needs such as food, education, and health services.[88]

Mechanism of Survival in the Gaza Strip

Israel controls every aspect of life in the Gaza Strip and is unwilling to assume responsibility for the brutal consequences resulting from the hermetic siege it has imposed on the Strip since 2007. The Israeli imposed closure has wreaked havoc on the Gaza Strip's infrastructure, natural resources, economy, education, and social life. Factory equipment and raw materials are banned, and power shortages make production extremely expensive. Universities are isolated from the cosmopolitan exchange that is their lifeblood. Families are separated, and patients struggle to gain access to adequate health care.[89] The blockade enforced by Israel is a collective punishment of innocent people who live in the Gaza Strip and deserve to experience a life of dignity and freedom. Caging two million people, half of them

---

88. Nidal Al-Mughrabi, "Anger as Palestinian Authority Cuts Gaza Salaries and Pays Late," *Reuters*, May 3, 2018, https://www.reuters.com/article/us-palestinians-gaza-salaries/anger-as-palestinian-authority-cuts-gaza-salaries-and-pays-late-idUSKBN1I41LM.

89. Sari Bashi, "Can Gaza Survive?," *Jacobin*, April 25, 2018, https://www.jacobin mag.com/2018/04/gaza-strip-palestine-israel-occupation-blockade.

children, to live in unbearable human conditions for more than ten years is a crime against humanity and a gross violation of international law. The claim that the Israeli-imposed closure of the Gaza Strip is due to security reasons makes one wonder whether the three destructive wars launched in the Gaza Strip and permanent sufferings make the country and its people safe!

On the contrary, peace based on justice, instead of denial, can help both Palestinians and Israelis thrive and prosper. Gazans are aware that the hermetic siege of the Gaza Strip is meant to rob them of life. Palestinians are politically aware that isolating the Gaza Strip from the West Bank and Jerusalem is an ongoing strategic plan to sabotage any potential dream they might have of establishing a viable Palestinian state in the West Bank and the Gaza Strip with East Jerusalem as its capital. They are also cognizant that the Israeli measures of confiscating lands, isolating main cities through the use of checkpoints, building settlements all over the West Bank, separating Jerusalem by building a separation wall,[90] besieging the Gaza Strip, and watching its people (mainly children) slowly die make life unbearable for the inhabitants and are steps to evacuate Palestinians and force them either to leave their homes for Arab countries or to immigrate to Europe.

Palestinians have no choice but to perish eternally or survive in their homeland. Therefore, you find that life and death run in parallel in the Palestinian territories. Palestinians have to continue with their lives, create a future for their children, and build what Israelis destroy daily, despite the restrictions, pain, death, bombings, and fear they see in the eyes of their children. As a Palestinian who fortunately escaped death more than once during the past three wars in the Gaza Strip and as a former "scholar at risk" hosted by Southern Methodist University in 2010, I know that the road to freedom and dignity is long and littered with pain until we can live as free and prosperous

90. Netta Ahituv, "15 Years of Separation: The Palestinians Cut Off from Jerusalem by the Wall," *Haaretz*, March 10, 2018, https://www.haaretz.com/israel-news/.premium.MAGAZINE-15-years-of-separation-palestinians-cut-off-from-jerusalem-by-a-wall-1.5888001.

humans in our independent Palestinian state. Out of this deep conviction stems our mechanism of survival, courage, endurance, and hope at all moments in our daily lives.

The Role of the International Community

The Palestinian people in the Gaza Strip call on the international community to help lift the Israeli-imposed siege and make life for Gazans easier in terms of daily living, education, health services, safety, and free travel. The UN report from 2012 that detailed the sufferings of the Palestinian people in the Gaza Strip is a reminder for the international community that Israel remains the occupying power in Gaza as it controls its land, sea, and air borders, even if it no longer has "boots on the ground." The report also emphasizes that the numerous restrictions imposed by Israel on both movements of people and goods into and out of Gaza impede the enjoyment of a range of human rights, such as the right to freedom of movement, health, education, work, adequate standards of living, and social life. Since 2007, Gaza has endured a downward spiral of de-development, while the people of Gaza are trapped in a cycle of humanitarian need and perpetual aid dependency. Unless Gaza is saved, it will become more isolated, desperate, and prone to devastating conflicts and a flattened economy. Should this happen, the hope for political reconciliation among Palestinians and an enduring peace between Israel and Palestine will become more elusive.

4. Susanne Scholz, "Slave and Slavery in Biblical Hebrew."
   "And the servants [עבדים] of Achish said unto him, Is not this David the king of the land? did they not sing one to another of him in dances, saying, Saul hath slain his thousands, and David his ten thousands?" (1 Sam 21:11, KJB)

   Biblical Hebrew has only one noun for the English terms of "slave" and "servant." The noun is עבד in the masculine singular and עבדה in the feminine singular. The BDB offers both English nouns, "slave" and "servant," for the one Hebrew noun, without any differentiation.[91]

91. *BDB*, 713.

Translators have thus always been put in the precarious position to decide when to use which of the two English nouns that have different connotations in English.

Interestingly, the Oxford English Dictionary (OED; www.oed.com) differentiates the meaning of "servant" from "slave." For the noun "servant," the OED offers three succinct meanings that, however, also become increasingly amorphous and similar to the meaning of "slave." The first meaning defines a servant as "a person who is engaged to attend or wait upon, or to obey the directions and meet the needs of, a particular person, or to perform specified tasks or functions in a particular household or establishment (whether owned by a particular person or not); a person who is in service of another . . . ; or of a household, an attendant." The second meaning defines a servant "in religious contexts: a person who serves or is devoted to God/or any supernatural being." The third meaning defines a servant as "a person who is in bondage to another, a slave."

The noun "slave" also receives three meanings. The first meaning defines slave as "[a] person who has the (legal) status of being the property of another, has no personal freedom or rights, and is used as forced labour or as an unpaid servant; an enslaved person." The second meaning of slave refers to "[a] person who submits in a servile manner to the authority or direction of another or others; a submissive or devoted servant; a person who works very hard without proper remuneration or appreciation." The second meaning also receives a figurative sense when it is defined as "*[a] person* who or thing which is completely under the control or domination *of,* or subject *to*, a specified influence." Finally, a third meaning suggests that "slave" refers to "[a] person who plays the submissive role in bondage, domination, sadomasochism, or similar sexual activities." Unsurprisingly, this latter, sexualized meaning appeared for first time in writing only in 1901 whereas the first meaning goes back to a thirteenth-century English document.

The question, then, is whether biblical Hebrew has a specific meaning for "slave." The scholarly literature struggles with this question. A standard academic biblical dictionary, *The Theological*

Dictionary of the Old Testament, offers a predictably ambiguous explanation that indicates the general hesitation for a direct, clear-cut, and blunt acknowledgment about the exploitative and oppressive power and class dynamics involved when a person is classified as a slave in human history. The dictionary entry states: "The Subst. *'ebed* refers to a person who is subordinated to someone else. This subordination can manifest itself in various ways, however, and *'ebed* accordingly can have different meanings: slave, servant, subject, official, vassal, or 'servant' or follower of a particular god."[92]

In sum, readers have to stop and think how to translate the Hebrew noun. They have to ask themselves whether they are attempting to avoid the harshness of exploitation and oppression that the noun "slave" signifies, especially in a former slave country like the United States. When readers consult a Bible translation they always need to consider if translators "soften the blow" when they render the Hebrew noun as "servant," as most English translators have done since the time of the King James Bible in the seventeenth century CE.

5. Aren M. Maeir, "What Are the *'opalim*?" excerpt from "A New Interpretation of the Term *'opalim* (עפלים) in the Light of Recent Archaeological Finds from Philistia," *JSOT* 32 (2007): 30–32, 28.

[On] the question of the identification and interpretation of the term *'opalim*, . . . I would like to suggest an interpretation along the lines that it refers to the male sexual organ, both in the case of a body part that was afflicted during the "Philistine Plague" and that which is said to be imitated in gold in 1 Sam 6.5, 11.

Admittedly, interpreting the term *'opalim* as referring to the male sexual organ is somewhat problematic, since this is not the word used for this organ in other instances, either in Hebrew or in other Semitic languages. On the other hand, however, the alternative

92. G. Johannes Botterweck, Helmer Ringgren, and Heinz-Josef Fabry, eds., *Theological Dictionary of the Old Testament*, vol. 10, trans. Douglas W. Stott (Grand Rapids, MI: Eerdmans, 1999), 387.

interpretations (e.g., "swellings") do not have many comparanda either. In addition, the cognate word *'pl* (*ophel*) has a meaning of high, lofty, raised, etc., which would fit well as a euphemistic reference to the male sexual organ.

I believe that this interpretation can be supported by additional arguments. One is that Saul's daring David to bring him Philistine foreskins is not only related to the fact that the Philistines were considered an uncircumcised people but was meant literally, "to hit the Philistines below the belt," as well as being a pejorative statement about their cultic practice. Needless to say, if this interpretation is correct, the Philistines were struck in a very painful and awkward place, which presents the Philistines in a rather ridiculous light in the ark narrative.

This is supported by the archaeological evidence as well. In addition to the above-mentioned separate groups of well-dated and well-provenienced phallic-shaped objects found in Philistine contexts at Ashkelon and Tell eṣ-Ṣâfi/Gath, various phallic-shaped vessels and *ex-votos* (and/or depictions of these) are known from sundry cultic contexts in the early Greek world. Examples of this are seen from at least one Bronze Age Aegean context from the Graeco-Roman cult of Asklepius, as well as in the rites pertaining to the Cypriote Aphrodite at Alt-Paphos (Rantidi forest).

To this one can add that in the Graeco-Roman cult of Kybele, a central element of the ritual was the self-castration of the *galloi* priests, re-enacting the castration and death of Attis, Kybele's lover. This is of considerable interest, since Singer (1992, 2000) has quite convincingly argued that Dagon, the main deity of the Philistines, is to be associated with Kybele (identifying Dagon as a female deity), and that this deity was brought by the Philistines to Canaan from the Aegean and/or Anatolian milieu. In turn, Kybele is at times identified with Aphrodite, whose relevance to this issue is mentioned above. This being so, the possibility of a similar Philistine cultic praxis is not hard to imagine. Thus, it appears that the two groups of phallic-shaped objects from Ashkelon and Tell eṣ-Ṣâfi/Gath would best be understood in this light, as ex-voto or cultic objects relating to the male sexual organ.

The reference in 1 Samuel 5.6 to golden *'opalim* clearly indicates a recognizable object. Interpreting these as golden replicas of "swellings" (haemorrhoids) is somewhat problematic, since it is difficult to imagine how such an "object" would be depicted, not to mention that none of the various known Philistine cult-related objects fit such an interpretation. On the other hand, understanding the *'opalim* as related to the male sexual organ and the golden *'opalim* as being an imitation thereof has, as we have seen, excellent parallels in the archaeological record.

To sum up, I suggest that the term *'opalim* mentioned in the ark narrative in 1 Samuel 5 and 6 is a euphemistic reference to the Philistine male sexual organ that was afflicted in some manner by the "Philistine Plague," causing much discomfort—and ridicule—for the Philistines. In an attempt to alleviate this malady (using a sympathetic ritual, possibly similar to the copper snake ritual depicted in Num 21.4–9), they fabricated golden *'opalim*, which are to be understood as golden *ex-votos* in the shape of phalli. It would appear, then, that the biblical writer had a clear image and knowledge of this aspect of Iron Age Philistine cult and beliefs and incorporated it quite harmoniously, if somewhat humorously, into the ark narrative.

2

DISPLAYING THE MASCULINITIES OF MAJOR AND MINOR MALE CHARACTERS

> *Masculinity scholars reveal the ways in which the male body has been posited as both object and site for the exercise of power and to explore the implications of this for the subjectivities of men. It needs to be asked why some male bodies are invested with more visibility and power than others and how natural knowledge is deployed in the construction of differences between the sexes.*
>
> —Alan Petersen, "Research on Men and Masculinities: Some Implications of Recent Theory for Future Work"

Uncovering Hegemonic and Subservient Masculinities: An Introduction

Naturalized masculinities permeate many, if not all, biblical books, but the storyline of 1 Samuel makes escaping this pervasive bias particularly difficult. Although Barbara Pini and Bob Pease correctly state that "seeking to broaden feminist research methodology to encapsulate the study of men and masculinities is a risky venture for feminists, not least because it risks diluting the politics and practices of feminist research,"[1] this biblical book leaves feminist exegetes no option but to take a closer look at the major and minor male characters appearing in such abundance. Three male characters dominate; several others play secondary roles that ensure the main male characters shine even more brightly. As the narratives depict the emergence, successes, dangers, and casualties of hegemonic masculinity on its path to the Israelite

1. Barbara Pini and Bob Pease, "Gendering Methodologies in the Study of Men and Masculinities," in *Men, Masculinities and Methodologies*, ed. Barbara Pini and Bob Pease, Genders and Sexualities in the Social Sciences (Houndsmills: Palgrave Macmillan UK, 2013), 8.

monarchy, women either play subordinated roles or are entirely absent. At best, they assist in bringing the important men to prominence, after which they disappear again. The literary attention thus remains firmly pointed toward the three major male leaders, Samuel, Saul, and David, even when other interspersed accounts interrupt, confuse, or divert readers from the fragmented stories. Accordingly, any feminist interpretation is challenged to avoid reinforcing the hegemonic masculinity of Samuel, Saul, and David or the subservient masculinity of the minor male characters of Jonathan, Abner, Elkanah, and Eli. Perhaps all that can be done is to expose this dominant feature in the portrayal of these characters.

A feminist deconstructive approach uncovers the various masculinities of the major and minor male figures and the book's overall emphasis on elite hegemonic masculinities. The question is whether a feminist reading, aiming to expose the hegemonic status of the male characters, does not simultaneously assume or even reinforce their centrality. But what would be the alternative? Some radical feminist thinkers and theologians, such as Mary Daly, advise not reading the book at all. I do not think her position is a helpful option here. Addressing rather than refusing to deal with a problem is the better move. Yet the interpretations of this chapter also hold the feminist quandary in mind, as they interrogate, expose, and dismantle the elite hegemonic masculinities of Samuel, Saul, and David. The goal is neither a recovery nor a rejection project but the persistent critical reflection on elite hegemonic masculinities. Such a reflection recognizes the prevalence of hegemonic masculinities even today despite some women occupying some previously male-only positions. Gender essentialism that identifies gender roles with biological or ontological-philosophical markers must be dismantled under all circumstances, regardless of the gender identity of the occupant, but especially if the actions reinforce naturalized masculinity.

This chapter follows male characters according to their appearance in the book. As any feminist interpretation faces the problem of not reinforcing the hegemonic masculinity of Samuel, Saul, and David, the chapter exposes the portrayals of the male characters. Accordingly, the first section focuses on the stories of Samuel. The second section deals with the tales about Saul. The third section interprets David's narratives. The fourth section concentrates on four minor male characters (Jonathan, Abner, Elkanah, and Eli) whose subservient masculinities strengthen the dominance of the major male figures (Samuel, Saul, David). A conclusion summarizes key insights of the feminist exegetical effort to interrogate the variously depicted masculinities.

Like Mother, Like Son: An Interrogation into Samuel's Murderous Masculinity

Not many characters in the Bible receive a full-blown description of their lives from birth to death, but the male figure Samuel is one of those few characters. His biography even runs from his prenatal life to his postmortem appearance. The narrative begins with a detailed depiction of his mother's procreative difficulties (1:1–9). It mentions his birth (1:20), his calling by God, his extraordinary upbringing in the temple at Shiloh (1:21–28; 2:1, 18–21; 3:1–21), his speeches and important accomplishments (7:3–17; 8; 9:14–26; 10:1–8, 17–27; 12:1–25; 15:10–35; 16:1–13), his death and burial location (25:1), and even his appearance after death (28). Samuel is famous for appointing the first and second kings of biblical Israel, Saul and David, and for his unforgiving words of divine rejection to the first king (15:10–35). After condemning King Saul and the king of the Amalekites with a misogynist curse and then murdering the latter (15:33), Samuel never sees Saul again, although Samuel is said to have mourned the king's fate (15:35). Samuel is also mentioned in 1 Chronicles 9:22; 11:3; 26:28; Psalm 99:6; and Jeremiah 15:1. Yet despite the impressive attention to Samuel's life, biographical details are missing. For instance, the story does not even mention his wife, although the couple's sons, Joel and Abijah, become judges over Israel and are reportedly corrupt (8:1–3), similar to the sons of Eli, the priest (2:12–17, 22; 3:13) under whose guidance Samuel grows up (2:11, 18; 3:1). In short, the biographical details focus on his professional life as a prophet, judge, and priest.

Samuel has always attracted the attention of white male Western scholars. Although some of them observe that Samuel has not received as much scholarly attention as he should have,[2] many exegetes recognize the diffi-

2. See, e.g., Mark Leuchter, *Samuel and the Shaping of Tradition*, Biblical Refigurations (Oxford: Oxford University Press, 2013), 1: "The latter [Samuel] has not received the attention he deserves."

culties of recovering the historical figure underneath the highly ideological depictions. For instance, Joseph Blenkinsopp states how impossible it is to "say anything about Samuel as a historical figure" because of the heavy theological interpretation of his story.[3] Other interpreters emphasize that the royal literary agenda shapes the depiction of this biblical character, whether both emerged simultaneously, as Frank Moore Cross asserted in 1973,[4] or whether hegemonic monarchical interests influenced the portrayal of Samuel as a literary character in exclusive service of the royal agenda.[5] A few interpreters, however, do not relinquish their quest for the historical Samuel. Mark Leuchter speculates, "Samuel's literary liminality is the end result of pre-literary oral traditions about his leadership as deriving from liminal status."[6] Leuchter also recognizes the "mythic archetype" that is embodied in the description of Samuel as a "divine warrior" who "confront[s] and defeat[s] cosmic challenges."[7] To Leuchter, Samuel is a figure like Moses whose "sacral authority" symbolizes "the sanctity of liminality in Israelite imagination."[8] Said differently, some white male interpreters view Samuel as the unrecognized yet obviously desirable warrior hero, a prophet and judge at the dawn of the Israelite monarchy. To them, Samuel is on par with other luminary figures such as Moses or David, eminent masculine warrior heroes.

Many white male exegetes give Samuel a reputable place in the biblical shrine of holy men, warriors, prophets, judges, and priests. Those exegetes believe Samuel seemingly lacks, though deserves, this reputation in the cultural-religious imagination of the Bible. None of them, however, comments on the significance of gender in the biblical characterization. His masculinity does not matter to those interpreters, although gender plays a considerable role in Samuel's story. Gendered problems already haunt his parents before his conception. His father, Elkanah, is a bigamist who loves his childless

---

3. Joseph Blenkinsopp, *A History of Prophecy in Israel*, rev. ed. (Louisville, KY: Westminster John Knox, 1996), 52.

4. Frank Moore Cross, *Canaanite Myth and Hebrew Epic* (Cambridge: Harvard University Press, 1973), 223.

5. For an outline of this exegetical situation, see Leuchter, *Samuel*, 2–4.

6. Leuchter, *Samuel*, 7.

7. Leuchter, *Samuel*, 7.

8. Leuchter, *Samuel*, 7.

wife, Hannah, more than his other wife, Peninnah, with whom he has several daughters and sons (1:2). Samuel's mother, Hannah, accepts the patriarchal convictions of her society and thus ignores her husband's urging that he be more to her "than ten sons" (1:8). In her relentless quest to become pregnant ("So it went on year by year"; 1:7), she prays at the temple of Shiloh for a "male child," literally for "a seed of men" (זרע אנשים).

This is an unusual expression, and the famous Jewish medieval interpreter Rashi (1040–1105 CE) explains that the phrase refers to Hannah praying for a righteous and important man, based on 1 Kings 2:32 and Deuteronomy 1:13.[9] Hannah even promises to Eli the priest that she will give the child away as a "nazirite" (1:11),[10] and she does so after Samuel is weaned (1:24). When she brings the toddler to Eli, she does not even allow the priest to respond to her speech (1:26–27), so intent is she on leaving her child at the temple.

The references to the gender troubles of Samuel's parents do not stop with the marital and procreative lives of his father, mother, or stepmother. As Samuel is growing up at the temple "to minister to [YHWH]" (2:11), he is in the same house with Eli's two sons, who are "sons of worthlessness" or "wickedness" (2:12; NRSV),[11] who steal from the worshipping people, and who rape women at the temple entrance (2:22). Although Eli scorns his sons (2:23–25), asking, "Why do you do such things? For I hear of your evil dealings from all these people" (v. 23), he receives no answer, only a statement that "they would not listen to the voice of their father, for it was the will of [YHWH] to kill them" (2:25). Samuel grows up in this tension-filled

9. 1 Kgs 2:32: "[YHWH] will bring back his [Joab's] bloody deeds on his [Joab's] own head because, without the knowledge of my father David, he attacked and killed with the sword two men more righteous and better than he: Abner son of Ner, commander of the army of Israel, and Amasa son of Jether, commander of the army of Judah." Deut 1:13: "Choose for each of your tribes individuals who are wise, discerning, and reputable, and I will make them your leaders."

10. According to Num 6, a nazirite is a "holy" woman or man voluntarily taking a vow to live a life consecrated to God, abstaining from alcohol, leaving the hair uncut, and avoiding contact with corpses.

11. The 1989 NRSV is quoted here because, unfortunately, the NRSVue uses the old-fashioned translation of "scoundrel" for בני בליעל, thus eliminating the gendered connotation although the term refers to two males here.

environment. Liked by both God and the people (2:26), he develops into a dependable prophet (3:20). The tensions of his childhood haunt him, however, coming back in the actions of his own sons. They take bribes as judges over Israel (8:3), and silence prevails about their mother. No verse mentions Samuel's wife or wives, as the story is quiet about Samuel's love or marital life. Androcentric assumptions about masculinity make such information irrelevant about this male character whose career shapes the storytelling.

As professional accomplishments matter exclusively in the story's depictions of Samuel, only his speeches and activities with the emerging kings, Saul and David, feature prominently. That Samuel also turns into a murderer when he kills the Amalekite king, Agag, whose mother Samuel curses before he kills Agag (15:33), seems strangely unimportant to many phallogocentric readers. They emphasize that Samuel appoints and rejects kings and that God tells him what to do in visions and dreams. In the various stories in which he plays a prominent role, Samuel is a man who obeys God's commandments, and he requests the same from people and kings. When they fail, he turns away from them, perhaps mourning over the loss, as he does after he turns away from Saul (15:31, 35). Yet, in the end, Samuel is a man who does not cherish relationships. He makes sure he does the right thing ordered by God. He also establishes that no complaints are made about him (e.g., 12:2–3). He does not even want to come back as a ghost, putting himself first as he chides Saul, "Why have you disturbed me by bringing me up?" (28:15). The story depicts Samuel as a macho Israelite prophet who does not care for people, whether in his private or in his professional life. His main purpose is to speak for God, as Samuel embodies and lives out the bargain his mother made with God (1:11).

Not all interpreters agree with this assessment of Samuel, whose parental abandonment and early gender troubles of living in a bigamist household turn him into a God-obsessed character. Marti J. Steussy puts Samuel's authoritarian, threatening, even violent and warrior-like qualities on God, as he empathizes that Samuel's difficult upbringing points to the "dissonance between Lord and Samuel."[12] Steussy also characterizes Samuel's

12. Marti J. Steussy, *Samuel and His God*, Studies on Personalities of the Old Testament (Columbia: University of South Carolina Press, 2010), 97.

murder of the king of the Amalekites, Agag, as resulting from his feelings of frustration and helplessness in his interactions with God. Suggesting that Samuel "lost confidence in his intercessory power," Steussy believes that "at some subliminal level, although probably not consciously, [Samuel] may even feel that the one who deserves hewing is Lord."[13] Accordingly, Steussy views Samuel's murder as an act of "repentance."[14] Perhaps predictably, this highly sympathetic reading disregards Samuel's masculinity despite his open aggression and murderous violence. Yet those are typical expressions of toxic masculinity reinforcing the hegemonic dominance of men. It affords them to limit expressions of emotions, except in aggressive and violent ways.[15] To sympathize with Samuel is thus a dangerous move, but Steussy's reading is unaware of this danger, as it ignores and even excuses Samuel's violence and murder. Steussy's cautionary note that readers should not submit to "Samuel's view of God"[16] indicates a subtle critique, although Steussy's reading does not critically wrestle with Samuel's murderous masculinity.

Rather than ignoring Samuel's violence and murder, I view Samuel as a gender-disturbed man. The narrative portrays him as growing up in a patriarchal setting at the sanctuary of Shiloh, where Eli's sons disregard God, steal from people as a matter of fact (2:12–17), and publicly rape women at the religious site: "They laid the women who served at the door of the [tabernacle]" (2:22, שׁכב את).

Moreover, Samuel's biological parents live with great tension before he is born. His father is married to two women who barely speak with each other (1:2). His mother brushes off her husband's efforts trying to ease her away from her obsession of becoming pregnant (1:8). She even promises God that she will donate her future child to the temple if she gets pregnant with a son (1:11). Samuel's own sons—Joel and Abijah—are corrupt judges (8:2–3), and, like his religious teacher, Samuel is unable to change their ways, nor does he try (in contrast to Eli; see 2:23–25). Samuel's devotion is to God alone, who calls him as a young boy (3:1–19). Accordingly,

13. Steussy, *Samuel and His God*, 90.

14. Steussy, *Samuel and His God*.

15. For a discussion of toxic masculinity, see, e.g., Jeremy D. Posadas, "Teaching the Cause of Rape Culture: Toxic Masculinity," *JFSR* 33 (2017): 177–179.

16. Posadas, "Teaching the Cause," 101.

Samuel adheres to a binary way of thinking: One is either for or against God (12:13–15, 20–25). Samuel also seems oddly disconnected from other people, although he mourns the demise of the first king he appoints (15:35).

Said differently, this is a story of a professional male worker whose private life is largely irrelevant to the storyline. That he worries about himself above all, even when he appears as a ghost from the dead, should not be surprising (12:1–3; 28:15). The anointer of two kings (10:1–8; 16:1–13) thinks only about himself and, as the messenger of good and bad news, obeys only God. He is the firstborn son of his mother, a woman who listens only to God and ignores her husband and priest (1:15–16) to pursue her desperate goal of becoming a mother of a son. I regard Samuel as an unsympathetic, yet necessary, major male figure in these narratives that are primarily focused on the establishment of the first Israelite king.

A Tragic Hero, Simple Incompetence, or an Image of the Crucified Christ? A Reading of Saul's Masculinity of Failure

The plain introduction of the first Israelite king is remarkable to readers looking for gender in 1 Samuel. Most outstanding is the lack of interrogating the fact that the first royal leader must be of the *male* gender. Saul belongs to the smallest Israelite tribe—he is a Benjaminite (9:21). He comes from an explicitly misogynistic heritage, as illustrated in the story of the gang-raped woman in Gibeah, the *pilegeš* (פילגש), conventionally translated as "concubine," a term connoting Orientalist fantasies about harems, illicit prostitution, and extramarital affairs.[17]

The narratives in Judges 19–21 report not only the gang rape of a woman called פילגש but also the ensuing murder of many other women and men as well as the sex trafficking of over six hundred young women by the surviving Benjaminite men to ensure tribal survival (Judg 21:10–12, 20–24). The Benjaminite men, with the complicity of the other tribes, commit sexual violence and murder when "there was no king in Israel" (Judg 21:25). Ironically, the first Israelite king comes from the same tribe.

---

17. For the pervasiveness of Orientalist ideas in biblical scholarship, see Edward W. Said, *Orientalism* (New York: Vintage Books, 1978).

In other words, the narrative alludes to the past of the first Israelite king's tribal heritage by highlighting his physical appearance and material status as a wealthy son (1 Sam 9:1). Saul the Benjaminite is a handsome, tall, young man (9:2; 10:23). The story takes his masculinity for granted, as it naturalizes his gender as a given. The story presupposes male royal leadership, neither interrogating nor challenging this assumption's inherent androcentrism. As the narrative presents male judges, male prophets, and kings as the norm, men appoint and battle each other because appointment, succession, and defeat of male leaders occur among men only. Unsurprisingly, then, women characters are almost entirely absent, although binary gender dynamics always prevail. For instance, fathers determine the lineage of the first Israelite king: the son of Kish, who is the "son of Abiel son of Zeror son of Becorath son of Aphiah" (9:1). Girls appear only as guides to the young male, Saul, as they direct the future king to the man, Samuel, who is in charge (9:11–13). The young women, drawing water at the well, are there only to tell clumsy Saul where to find the man who will change the boy's destiny (9:12–13).

Accordingly, then, readers of Saul's story do not usually interrogate the king's gender. As they rehearse the narrative, they ignore the implications of his masculinity even when they refer to him as a "man." To many interpreters, other aspects of this biblical character stand out. For instance, the literary critic Northrop Frye maintains that the first king of ancient Israel is "the one great tragic hero of the Bible" who is "a doomed man."[18] His story is like the story of Macbeth, ending in rejection, defeat, and death. Johanna W. H. Van Wijk-Bos also assumes royal leadership to be male. She classifies the donkey-searching boy as "a handsome man of Benjamin,"[19] not commenting any further why it matters that the story depicts Saul as "a handsome man." Instead, she focuses on the gender of the donkeys (9:3–10:16), speculating, "It is possible that in the donkeys, we encounter the first group on the lookout for something, since a herd of female donkeys, 'jennies,' is usually led by a male, 'jack.' While the jennies look for their jack, Saul and his lad look

18. Northrop Frye, *The Great Code: The Bible and Literature*, ed. Alvin A. Lee (Toronto: University of Toronto Press, 2007), 181.

19. Johanna W. H. Van Wijk-Bos, *The Road to Kingship: 1–2 Samuel*, A People and a Land, vol. 2 (Grand Rapids, MI: Eerdmans, 2020), 75.

in vain for the animals, crossing and recrossing the difficult terrain of the hill country of Ephraim."[20] Van Wijk-Bos sees in the female donkeys a feminizing hint about Saul, who is as lost as the female donkeys looking for the leading "jack," or Samuel. Comparing Saul to a female donkey looking for the male leader, this interpreter feminizes the future king. To her, he searches in the wrong direction and finds the "man of God" only because of his male assistant. Had Saul been alone, leaderless like the donkeys after which he searches, the search would have ended unsuccessfully.

Van Wijk-Bos also compares the donkeys to the Israelite people searching for a leader and desiring to be brought under his control.[21] Van Wijk-Bos does not reflect on this sexist assumption, as her interpretation affirms that Saul is an improbable candidate for the Israelite monarchy. He is merely a "passive participant, receiving news and food, the spirit of Adonai, and a trance-like state, being turned into another man (10:6)."[22] Both the future king and his people act like females presumably lost without a male leader. The feminizing trope insinuates Saul's guaranteed demise as the first Israelite king, who resembles leaders in Judges more than a competent king. He also withholds crucial information from his unnamed uncle when Saul states the donkeys are already found (10:14–16). Male authority figures abound in 1 Samuel, but, according to Van Wijk-Bos, Saul is not one of them because he is depicted like a woman.

Although other interpretations do not compare Saul to female animals, they also do not consider his masculinity. For instance, Robert Alter sympathizes with young Saul, uncertain about what to do and how to respond to his encounters (10:5, 7). Young Saul wants to return when the donkeys have apparently disappeared, and so Alter writes about 1 Samuel 9:6, "Saul's utterance reveals him as a young man uncertain about pursuing his way, and quite concerned about his father. This concern . . . is touching, and suggests that the young Saul is a sensitive person—an attribute that will be woefully submerged by his experience of political power."[23] To Alter, Saul's

20. Van Wijk-Bos, *Road to Kingship*, 76.

21. Van Wijk-Bos, *Road to Kingship*, 84.

22. Van Wijk-Bos, *Road to Kingship*, 82.

23. Robert Alter, *The David Story: A Translation with Commentary of 1 and 2 Samuel* (New York: Norton, 1999), 47.

uncertainty stands in sharp contrast to Samuel's leadership. The "farm boy" encounters the "man of God," Samuel, who is also "a seer" (9:9). The future king bumbles along and follows the leadership of "a slave" who is his "assistant" (9:10).[24] In Alter's retelling, Saul becomes violent far too easily, a character trait connecting him to his ancestors. In 11:7, Saul hacks a yoke of oxen into pieces and sends them through the territory of Israel, just like the Levite man dismembering the woman into twelve pieces and sending them around. To Alter, Saul's action is "an explicit repetition of the dismemberment of the concubine" in Judges 19, though the allusion is ambiguous.[25] Saul resembles "Mafia capos,"[26] coercing the other tribes into submission to follow him into war against the Philistines.

In short, Alter agrees that the hesitant and timid Saul grows into a threatening king. He is in charge, even magnanimous now (11:13), and later ruthless against those he suspects of disloyalty. When Samuel turns away from the king, his move signifies divine rejection (15:23, 31). According to Alter, God's response to rejecting Saul is far stronger than Samuel's mourning. The same verb (רחם *rḥm*) describes God's dramatic emotional state, as God regrets Saul's royal appointment (15:35) in the same way as God regrets the creation of humanity (Gen 6:7). To Alter, the depiction of Saul as an incompetent king leads to God's reaction of enormous proportion. Should readers be surprised that the hesitant boy becomes a king who maims and kills his enemies (11; 13:47–52; 15:1–9; 22:6–23) and eventually dies by suicide in battle (31:4), after which his head is displayed among the Philistines to dishonor the dead king (31:9–13)? That this kind of king presents a toxic, yet failed, version of masculinity remains unsaid in Alter's reading and many others. Failing, Saul dies by suicide in 31:4, but before killing himself, he kills many other men in battle. He is a killer, a warrior, a man fully living out his toxic masculinity, but he is a failure. Interpreters, however, do not mention Saul's dysfunctional masculinity, characterizing him as a "tragic hero."

One interpretation stands out due to the retrograde effort of developing a christological reading of the first Israelite king. Following the early

24. Alter, *The David Story*, 48.
25. Alter, *The David Story*, 62.
26. Alter, *The David Story*, 62.

to mid-twentieth-century Protestant theologian Karl Barth, Stephen B. Chapman employs a christological approach to depict the rejected king as a representative of the crucified Christ and the second king, David, as a representative of the resurrected Christ.[27] The christological framework enables Chapman to contrast Saul, the rejected king, to David, the chosen one, and to simultaneously claim both characters as essential to "find[ing] their fulfillment in Jesus Christ."[28] Since both characters are "a type of Christ,"[29] both are necessary because both symbolize humanity and human powerlessness in relation to God. According to Chapman, human "reflexes are always those of Saul,"[30] and so Chapman strongly identifies with him. Claiming that humans, "we," are like Saul, Chapman believes that "we" need to strive to be like David. Chapman explains, "Saul was not rejected because he was big, but because the value he placed on size prevented him from rightly appraising God. Likewise David was not chosen because he was small or young, but because he relied on God and struggled to live faithfully for God in the world. His physical stature simply helped him to 'size up' God's reality more readily."[31] In this reading, then, both Saul and David teach Christians how to appropriately respond to God. As Chapman puts it, "But another response to a keener awareness of our human limitations can be a renewed sense of trust in the mysterious operation of God to effect good ends."[32] Saul is a model for Christians because his story helps them recognize that they, too, need to become more faithful.

I identify two problems in this kind of reading. First, as Chapman's christological interpretation aims to develop readerly piety and trust in God, it ignores the fact that Saul is a *male* character. A male character like Saul is a model for all of humanity in Chapman's reading, as if all of humanity had the same problems of hubris and failure like Saul. In my view, this christological projection is also problematic because

---

27. Stephen B. Chapman, *1 Samuel as Christian Scripture: A Theological Commentary* (Grand Rapids, MI: Eerdmans, 2016).

28. Chapman, *1 Samuel*, 253.

29. Chapman, *1 Samuel*, 246.

30. Chapman, *1 Samuel*, 260.

31. Chapman, *1 Samuel*, 259.

32. Chapman, *1 Samuel*, 260.

christological readings always smack of an anti-Jewish hermeneutic that Christian readers of the post-Holocaust era need to eliminate from their theological repertoire.

Second, 1 Samuel contains only fragmentary storytelling, making coherent character depictions difficult. For instance, the signs of royal promise that Samuel gives to young Saul in 10:2–6 are still in effect in chapter 13, which reports the so-called first rejection of Saul as the Israelite king. In 11:12–15 (see the previous attempt in 10:17–24), Samuel anoints Saul as a king after Saul's successful battle against the Ammonites in 11:1–11. These stories, probably combined by various redactors, tell of Saul's prowess as a warrior leader and king. His is toxic masculinity in action, fighting and killing as he moves around. The divine rejections in 1 Samuel 13 and 14, as articulated by the male sage Samuel, who anointed him previously, are thus confusing and unexpected. Although Saul performs as a macho leader, certain story fragments reject the brutalizing leadership of the first king. According to David Jobling, the rejection of Saul is rooted in his personal failure to move into the future as a king who is not stuck in the past of the judges. Saul's problem is that he is "ambiguous" about "kingship" and the responsibilities and duties it brings to him and the people.[33]

Saul's ambiguity about being appointed a king appears in two rejection scenes. In the first rejection scene of 13:8–12, Saul acts entirely on his own, which Samuel articulates as the cause for the divine rejection (13:13–14). In the second rejection scene of 1 Samuel 15, Saul craves Samuel's advice (15:25, 30). According to Jobling, the transition from the period of the judges to the kingship is difficult for Saul. He acts independently while also yearning for Samuel's mentorship. Psychologically stuck, he must be rejected as the king. Jobling states, "While he lives, the transition does not really happen. Saul cannot make it happen. He is willing to submit to the laws of the old order, and so he does not bring in a new one."[34] Because he is psychologically stuck, Saul does not perform his masculinity in line with

---

33. David Jobling, *1 Samuel*, Berit Olam (Collegeville, MN: Liturgical Press, 1998), 85.

34. Jobling, *1 Samuel*, 87.

phallogocentric expectations. His diminished status as a warrior is reinforced in the comment that he has "just one woman (14:50),"[35] indicating that "real" men have several wives. No wonder, then, that the king is depicted with a masculinity of failure and dies by suicide during a battle he loses against the Philistines (31:1–13). Rejected by his mentor and by God, he chooses death, and his body is desecrated by the Philistine victors (31:9–10). This is a gruesome end of a mighty warrior, and his death signifies toxic masculinity brought to its logical conclusion. Accordingly, Saul is a character neither to admire nor to correlate with a messianic identity. He is a male leader, the first Israelite king of the biblical narrative, failing miserably in reigning by violence and bloodshed.

Loved by Women, Men, and God: A Study of David's Toxic Warrior Masculinity

Without the first king, there would not have been a second one. One male leader follows the next, regardless of failures or successes, and so 1 Samuel presents Saul and David as dependent on each other. David Jobling observes this dynamic when he states, "Each incident in David's career is expressed in terms of his rivalry with Saul."[36] The first king fights and kills in war, and the second king does, too, but better. Unlike Saul, David does not even need armor in battle, winning in his regular clothes against Goliath and frustrating Saul's attempt to claim credit for the offered armor (17:38–39). David is the preferred man, against whom Saul is powerless. The women sing his praises: "Saul has killed his thousands and David his ten thousands" (18:7), a saying later remembered even by Philistine warrior commanders (29:5). Then there is Saul's daughter, Michal, who loves David before she is married to him (18:20, 28). Because of her love, she helps her husband to escape her father's plan to murder him (19:11–17), although she comes to despise him later (2 Sam 6:20; 1 Chron 15:29).

35. Jobling, *1 Samuel*, 88.
36. Jobling, *1 Samuel*, 91.

Yet the harmonious[37] beginning (1 Sam 16:14–23) during which Saul "loved [David] greatly" (16:21) does not last. Saul's love turns to vicious jealousy as he repeatedly attempts to murder his competitor, though unsuccessfully (18:11, 25; 19:10, 11). Saul's hatred makes him pursue David all over the land, but he always fails. In contrast, David has two opportunities to kill Saul but does not take advantage of either of them. Twice he does not eliminate the threatening competitor (24; 26). Unhesitatingly killing his enemies (e.g., 17:51; 27:8–12), David refrains from killing the elder king. Martial prowess, shrewdness, and prudence characterize the second king, while the first king lacks perspective. Saul is shown as repeatedly ignorant. For instance, he asks twice about David's identity (16:14–23; 17:55–58), and David could have killed him twice (24:3–22; 26:6–12). In contrast, David is confident about having God on his side (16:13, 18; 17:37; 18:12; 26:23; 30:6, 17), while Saul knows he does not (13:13–14; 15:23; 18:12; 30:15).

David's tale does not begin like Samuel's story with his conception or birth. Instead, David enters the narrative during Samuel's quest to anoint the next king (16:1–13). Samuel finds David in Bethlehem after God tells Samuel to "invite Jesse [David's father] to the sacrifice, and I will show you what you shall do; and you shall anoint for me the one whom I name to you" (16:3). The chosen one is no macho man but the youngest son, who is not even at home when Samuel is looking for the future king. Away herding sheep (16:11), he finally comes home: "Now he was ruddy [as in redheaded] and had beautiful eyes and was handsome" (16:12). Another handsome man will become the second king. Yet his installation is reported only in 2 Samuel 2:1–7. The narratives in 1 Samuel, focusing on dangerous power struggles and competition, depict the rivalry between the first king and his successor.

37. Alter, *Ancient Israel*, 90

Figure 2.1. *David,* by Michelangelo (1501–1504). Accademia di Belle Arti, Florence, Italy. Wikimedia Commons.

How shall we interpret the love, jealousy, and murderous hatred that surround David in 1 Samuel? Randall C. Bailey sees in the references of love and desire possibilities for a homoerotic reading. Pervaded queer love flows among the three major male characters, Samuel, Saul, and David.[38] While Michal, the king's daughter, loves (אהב) David (18:20, 28), and the servants also love (אהב; see also 18:16) him (18:22), Saul pretends to lust (חפץ) for him (18:22). Yet David, not responding to expressions of love, aims for "upward mobility."[39] Meanwhile, Saul hides his emotions when he attempts to trick David into being killed by the Philistines (18:25). Saul asks his future son-in-law for one hundred Philistine foreskins, so "seducing" David into military conflict. The image of David as a warrior, however, shields readers from recognizing the sexualized depiction of the Philistine enemies. Some interpreters recognize that the repeated references to the Philistine warriors as "foreskins" are filled with "phallic connotations."[40] The depiction of Saul and David entangles both men into kinky Philistine foreskin talk, a sexually perverted narrative strategy that identifies the other ethnic men by their genitalia.

The "warrior eroticism"[41] appears in the context of an androcentric power struggle between two *male* characters in which Saul is asking David for one hundred Philistine foreskins as a wedding gift (מהר dowry). Some readers rush to explain that the collection of enemy foreskins was not a military habit in ancient Israel.[42] Although the request may have *intended* to depict the enemy as emasculated warriors,[43] most readers do not consider the marriage gift that the king demands from his future son-in-law as particularly kinky. Regardless, Saul and David seem obsessed with male Philistine

---

38. Randall C. Bailey, "Reading Backwards: A Narrative Technique for the Queering of David, Saul, and Samuel," in *The Fate of King David: The Past and Present of a Biblical Icon*, ed. Tod Linafelt, Claudia V. Camp, and Timothy Beal, LHBOTS 500 (New York: T&T Clark, 2010), 66–81.

39. Jobling, *1 Samuel*, 152.

40. Ken Stone, "1 and 2 Samuel," in *The Queer Bible Commentary*, ed. Deryn Guest, Robert E. Goss, Mona West, and Thomas Bohache (London: SCM Press, 2006), 204.

41. Stone, "1 and 2 Samuel," 207.

42. Alter, *The David Story*, 116.

43. Stone, "1 and 2 Samuel," 204. The intentional meanings of this or other biblical texts are impossible to ascertain, although biblical scholars have surely tried in the last few centuries.

genitals, playing out their power struggle over dead men's foreskins (see also 2 Sam 3:14).

Predictably, David beats Saul's demand even in this case. He sends two hundred foreskins, at least according to the Hebrew text, while the Septuagint gives the requested number of one hundred. Bailey considers the possibility that "Saul knew that David was 'into' foreskins."[44] He even imagines David as counting: "76, 77, 78. What's that you are asking? Darn, I lost count. I'll have to start all over. Now, y'all be quiet now. One, two, three."[45] As Saul perhaps knows about David's desire, Saul pretends to lust (חפץ) for David (18:22), like Shechem lusts (חפץ) for Dinah (Gen 34:19), or the soldier lusts (חפץ) for a sex-trafficked woman (Deut 21:14), or the king in the book of Esther lusts (חפץ) for young women (Esth 2:14). The same is also true for the king's son, Jonathan, who is lusting (חפץ) for David (19:1; see also 18:1). Bailey asserts, "There is . . . evidence for the claim of a homoerotic reading to the engagement between David and Saul around the bride price of Philistine foreskins."[46]

In short, the first and second kings emerge as a male couple homoerotically entangled over power. The stories spice up their power struggle by mentioning dead men's foreskins (18:25, 27; see also 2 Sam 3:14), by referencing Saul's unsuccessful attempts to murder David (18:11, 25; 19:10; 24:2; 26:2), and by depicting David's refusal to kill Saul (24:4–7; 26:10–12). Keeping readers tensed up over male genitals and various murder attempts, the plot reads like a psycho-thriller. Unrequited love, an unusual desire for foreskins, and murderous hatred and fear build up tension-filled action tales in which David's internal thoughts remain hidden. For instance, Alter observes that in 20:1, David's speech follows "the pattern of occluding the personal side of David."[47] For instance, David's "oaths of innocence"[48] do not articulate his internal thought, as he "leaves his real motives uncertain" (see 18:15, 18).[49] Eventually, however, the first king acknowledges

44. Bailey, "Reading Backwards," 75.

45. Bailey, "Reading Backwards," 75.

46. Bailey, "Reading Backwards," 76.

47. Alter, *The David Story*, 123.

48. Alter, *The David Story*, 123.

49. Alter, *The David Story*, 114, 115.

defeat to David when Saul explains in 24:20, "Now I know that you shall surely be king and that the kingdom of Israel shall be established in your hand." The rivalry between the two warrior males is over, and the elder king will die by suicide while losing yet another battle against the Philistine army on Mount Gilboa (31:4). Saul's three sons, Jonathan, Abinadab, and Malchishua, are also killed there, wiping out almost the entire male lineage of the first king (31:2).[50]

While the rivalry between Saul and David ends victoriously for the younger man, David receives divine approval, strength, and love throughout 1 Samuel (e.g., 30:6). He wins the battle against an Amalekite militia of male warriors who destroy the city of Ziklag, the city previously given to him by the Philistine king Achish of Gath (27:6). The Amalekite militia captures the women, sons, and daughters of Ziklag (30:3), including David's two wives, Ahinoam and Abigail (30:5). A half-dead Egyptian man whom the militia left behind (30:11–12) gives David and his warriors the necessary information to rescue the captured people, David's two wives, and "all the flocks and herds" (30:18–20). Nothing and nobody stand in the way of David's success. Sending gifts and bribes to various towns in Judah (30:26–31), David also ensures the support of his royal leadership. The narrative presents him as a shrewd and honest leader who diligently works on his success and claims divine blessing (30:23). Later, the same people of Judah anoint David as the second king (2 Sam 2:4). The stories of 1 Samuel always emphasize that David's success comes from God (13:14; 16:13; 17:26, 45; 18:28) even when David, trying to impress Philistine leaders and kings, kills women and men and steals "the sheep, the oxen, the donkeys, the camels, and the clothing" (27:9, 11).

Masculine warrior behavior and love of the people are not the only reasons for David's rise, success, and anointment to royal leadership in 1 Samuel. Most importantly, David is a "man after [Yahweh's] own heart" (13:14), and he is also a confident recipient of divine support (17:26, 37,

50. It is unclear how many sons Saul had according to 1 Samuel. In 14:49, his sons are listed as Jonathan, Ishvi, and Malchishua. Yet in 31:2, the sons mentioned are Jonathan, Abinadab, and Malchishua. In 2 Sam 2:8, another son emerges: Ish-baal. In 1 Chr 8:33 and 1 Chr 9:39, four sons are listed: Jonathan, Malchishua, Abinadab, and Esh-baal.

45–47; 26:19–20, 23–24). Ralph W. Klein argues that Deuteronomistic historians advance their political agenda by depicting the second king as chosen by God and loved by many people. Klein views the narrative as composed by "the king's defenders in the royal court"[51] as he asserts, "David is the man who has a heart after Yahweh's own heart, demonstrated by his continual practice of inquiring of Yahweh and then declaring his trust in Yahweh."[52] David's "religious fervor" illustrates how to have faith "even after the construction of the Second Temple."[53] Consequently, David succeeds wherever Saul fails. For instance, David defeats the Amalekites (30:17–20) and shares the success with his countrymen. Klein, enamored with David's "heroism, his equity, and his generosity,"[54] states, "The narrator clearly sees David's successes as Yahweh's own deed. . . . David's successful campaign [against the Amalekites] just before Saul's final failure portrays him with characteristics and actions fit for a king who was proceeding with oracular guidance."[55] Forgotten are David's less heroic deeds, such as killing everybody—women, children, and men (17:51; 18:7, 27; 27:9; 29:5). David murders anybody, whether a warrior such as Goliath, a couple of Philistine warriors, innocent civilians, or even children. In short, Klein ignores David's murderous violence in the effort to highlight David's leadership qualities. Success of the male leader makes him and other interpreters forget about the violence and aggression so characteristic of David's toxic warrior masculinity.

Some exegetes explain that the theological interests of the Deuteronomistic writers are the reason for the positive depiction of David. Those writers composed narratives to teach audiences how to become better followers of God. This historical-literary speculative explanation, however, avoids the obvious question: What kind of authors would depict God as choosing a man who kills, bribes, maims, steals, fights for the opposite side, is a polygamist, uses people to his political advantage, and is a ruthless warrior

51. Ralph W. Klein, *1 Samuel*, WBC 10, 2nd ed. (Nashville: Thomas Nelson, 2008), l.

52. Klein, *1 Samuel*, 1.

53. Klein, *1 Samuel*, 1.

54. Klein, *1 Samuel*, 285.

55. Klein, *1 Samuel*, 285.

politician? Obviously, David is not a particularly sympathetic character despite the emphasis that everybody, even God, loves him. One interpreter, Rainer Kessler, observes that the tales raise the theodicy question. He wonders why Saul, coming from a wealthy family with impressive pedigree, fails, whereas David, a militia leader who works for Israel's enemies and turns into a murderer and rapist, establishes a royal dynasty lasting for generations.[56] To Kessler, the biblical writers, answering this perplexing question, depict David as divinely chosen. Kessler notes, "To them, not inner-worldly causalities and not accidental events determine the course of history but only the will of God."[57]

I find this theo-historical explanation difficult because it suggests that God loves only some people. They succeed, as others fail, because God makes it so. Such reasoning about success and failure advances retribution theology; it assumes good deeds will be rewarded and bad things will find punishment. Justifying the sociopolitical status quo, such a theology sides with the powerful. Yet Kessler is also right. The narratives depict God in this way. Endorsing David over Saul, they propagate the establishment of David's kyriarchal hegemony in biblical Israel (8:22). If feminist readers accept retribution theology, they will be left to read with the literary moves that present the alpha male David as chosen by God. Such a theological message about the toxic warrior masculinity of David, however, cannot model past or present faith in God. Rather, this message illustrates what happens when toxic warrior masculinity comes to power, seeking out battles, bloodshed, and hatred. Jealousy and violent competition dominate even when the male hero refrains from killing his opponent. A feminist reading needs to expose this kind of masculinity in the tales of David's rise to power (1 Sam 16–2; Sam 10) because feminism cannot approve of this devastating expression of masculinity.

---

56. Rainer Kessler, *Samuel: Priester und Richter, Königsmacher und Prophet*, Biblische Gestalten 18 (Leipzig: Evangelische Verlagsanstalt, 2008), 143: "Nicht innerweltliche Kausalitäten und nicht der Zufall bestimmen für sie den Verlauf der Geschichte, sondern letztlich der Wille Gottes."

57. Kessler, *Samuel*, 144.

Minor Male Characters: An Analysis of the Submissive Masculinity of Jonathan, Abner, Elkanah, and Eli

The book of 1 Samuel features not only the three major characters of Samuel, Saul, and David. The thirty-one chapters also include four minor male characters that enhance the prominence of the three major male figures. Among the minor male characters are, in the order of their significance, Jonathan, one of Saul's three sons (13:2, 16–22; 14; 18:1–4; 19:1–7; 20; 23:15–18; 31:2, 12); Abner, the commander of Saul's army (14:50–51; 17:55, 57; 20:25; 26:5, 7, 14, 15); Elkanah, husband of Hannah and father of Samuel (1–2); and Eli, the priest of the sanctuary at Shiloh (1–4). These four male characters are of different significance in the tales in which they appear. Mostly disconnected from each other, the four male characters always endorse one or another major male character. Some of the minor characters also reappear in 2 Samuel. One character, Jonathan, receives a famous postmortem lament song by David in 2 Samuel 2:17–27. Yet another figure, Abner, gains literary significance in 2 Samuel 1–3 as the military opponent to David's kingship. Two additional minor characters, Elkanah and Eli, appear only in 1 Samuel.

The most significant character is Jonathan, Saul's son, who appears as "Jonathan in Gibeah of Benjamin" (13:2) when he defeats "the garrison of the Philistines that was at Geba" (13:3). Jonathan's military success is swiftly declared as Saul's success (13:4). Jonathan's mention collapses into Saul's character, as if Jonathan were identical with Saul and any military success by anybody in the king's army equals the king's success. Preparing together for battle, as if of one mind, father and son share and hold sword and spear for all the people (13:15–22). The narrative does not indicate that Jonathan, recognized as Saul's son only in 13:16, resents the dominance of his father, the king. At this moment of the story, the son is one with his royal father without holding any reported grudges. The literary arrangement between the king and his son idealizes Jonathan's loyalty to his father, indicating the paternal superiority over the son.

Yet the idealized portrayal between father and son changes dramatically when the narrative moves toward its goal, namely, the installation of David as the second king. The changed relationship between father and son becomes manifest in the next battle against the Philistines at Michmash (14). Jonathan goes into battle without informing his father, who stays near Gibeah under a pomegranate tree with six hundred male warriors (14:1). Together with "the young man who carried his armor" (14:1), Jonathan tricks the Philistine warriors into defeat (14:13–15) and then tells his unnamed armor-carrying companion to go to the outpost of "these foreskins" (14:6 הערילים האלה).

Interpreters usually ignore this crude language. For instance, Chapman does not mention the genital characteristic of the Philistine men, highlighting instead Jonathan's religious outlook, his "firm understanding of God's freedom to act."[58] Chapman also recognizes this attitude in Jonathan's arms-bearer (14:7), though it is absent in Saul.[59] Differently, Van Wijk-Bos considers the reference to the Philistines as foreskins "assuredly not a complimentary label,"[60] although it is the usual word for Philistine men in Judges and 1 Samuel (e.g., Judg 14:3; 15:18; 1 Sam 14:6; 17:26, 36; 31:4). Stone observes that the reference to the Philistines by their male organs classifies them "as improper examples of manhood," and so the conflict between Israelite and Philistine males should be read as a struggle over who is manlier: "Israelite or Philistine, circumcised or uncircumcised."[61] The previous call of a Philistine commander illustrates the competition: "Take courage, and be *men* [והיו לאנשים], O Philistines, in order not to become slaves to the Hebrews as they have been to you; be *men* [והייתם לאנשים] and fight" (4:9; emphasis added). Failure to fight or to win means to be unmanly, emasculated, and subjugated. To the male Philistines, the removal of their foreskins would signify the termination of Philistine manhood.

The sexual connotation of the passage (14:1–23) that depicts Jonathan as an independent, perceptive, and victorious warrior against Philistine troops also shines through in the plan of uncovering "ourselves to them" (14:8 ונגלינו) and in the Philistine response. Seeing the two Israelite men "uncovering" or "exposing" themselves, the Philistine men exclaim, "Look, Hebrews are coming out of the holes (החרים) where they have hidden themselves" (14:11). In Song of Songs 5:4, the Hebrew noun חר is euphemistically used for *vagina*; elsewhere the noun refers to an eye socket (Zach

58. Chapman, *1 Samuel*, 130.
59. Chapman, *1 Samuel*, 131.
60. Van Wijk-Bos, *Road to Kingship*, 104.
61. Stone, "1 and 2 Samuel," 204.

14:12) or an animal shelter or a cave (e.g., Nah 2:13), which is also the usual translation of 1 Samuel 14:11. Yet in the literary context in which Philistine men are reduced to their foreskins, a sexualized connotation of the Israelite men as "uncovering" (גלה) or even "exposing" themselves by coming out of "vaginas" better captures the story's crude heterosexist humor with homoerotic tendencies. The tale depicts the royal son, together with his young male companion, as emerging from the motherly womb, a cave. They expose themselves sexually, perhaps to entice their foreskinned opponents who underestimate them as acting "womanly." Meanwhile Jonathan fights "on his hands and feet" (14:13), killing any Philistine coming his way. Images of sexualized violence make Jonathan a victorious fighter (14:14) despite the help he receives from his father and "all the people" (14:20 כל־העם). His victory is a win for all of Israel (14:23), and so the literary, though temporary, separation between royal son and royal father has begun.

The separation is most explicitly depicted in 1 Samuel 20, where Jonathan and David decide how to let David know about Saul's ongoing hostility. From the start of their conversation, Jonathan expresses his solidarity: "Far from it! You shall not die. My father does nothing great or small without disclosing it to me, and why should my father hide this thing (את הדבר הזה) from me? Never" (20:2). To help David, he is ready to betray his father, the king. Jonathan's position is clear, while David's motivation remains ambiguous. David calls himself Jonathan's "servant" (20:8 עבד), a striking word choice in light of Jonathan's expression of love in verses 12–17. Commentators often mention Jonathan's love for David, who loves the future king "as he loved his own life" (20:17), already stated in 18:1, 3 and 19:1. Jobling even classifies their relationship "as analogous to a marriage agreement."[62] Jonathan's submission to David's royal leadership is also mentioned in 18:4, where he takes off various royal indicators from his uniform, such as his robes, weapons, and even his belt, handing them over to David (18:4). The son of the first king, Jonathan, makes David the royal successor.

The question is whether Jonathan's love represents a form of "warrior eroticism" that appears elsewhere in ancient Near Eastern literature. If so, his life would perhaps turn any queer reading of this tale into an "anachronistic"

62. Jobling, *1 Samuel*, 163.

fantasy.[63] Or does the lamentation of David in 2 Samuel 1:19–27 indicate David's "affectionate and emotionally intimate" companionship with Jonathan, which contemporary readers justifiably classify as gay love between Jonathan and David?[64] Where else do two male characters express their love (אהבה) for each other in such unambiguous terms? After all, David's poem includes a powerful expression of love to the dead friend as "more wonderful than the love of women" (2 Sam 1:26). Jobling suggests that David turns Jonathan into "a better woman than David's women."[65] Perhaps Jobling tries too hard to find fault with David as an exploiter of the people who love him. Still, Jonathan is obviously only a minor character in this tale about the struggles over male hegemonic leadership. Even his father, Saul, distances himself from the son who betrays him. He shames Jonathan in crude, sexist language for being a mama's boy (20:30) because Jonathan acts against his father. Yet when the son fights and dies next to his father, the son is again aligned with his father (1 Sam 31). The phallogocentric logic of the narrative requires his death. Jonathan must die in battle, together with his father and his two brothers, Abinadab and Malchishua (31:2), because patriarchy is built on the heteronormative order in which men love and marry women. In sum, Jonathan is a necessary, though marginal, literary figure that enables the narrative to move smoothly from the first to the second king.

Three other male characters—Abner, Elkanah, and Eli—play important, though minor, roles. Like Jonathan, the three characters support in secondary roles the dominant characters of Samuel, Saul, and David. They move the plot toward the first Israelite monarchy and the rise of the second king. Hegemonic masculinity depends on subservient male characters to emphasize the literary patterns of murderous (Samuel), failing (Saul), and toxic warrior (David) hegemonic masculinity. In the case of Abner, the story introduces him for the first time in 14:50 as part of Saul's family, including three of his sons (v. 49), his two daughters (v. 49), his wife (v. 50), and his father (v. 51). In verse 50, the name is spelled "Abiner" in Hebrew but appears elsewhere as "Abner" (14:51; 17:55, 57; 20:25; 26:5, 7, 14;

63. Stone, "1 and 2 Samuel," 207.

64. Stone, "1 and 2 Samuel," 208.

65. Jobling, *1 Samuel*, 162.

2 Sam 2:89; 3:27). It is grammatically unclear in 14:50 whether Abner is Saul's uncle or whether Abner's father, Ner, is Saul's uncle. As Ralph Klein observes, "Note that the word uncle in 14:50 may have either Ner or Abner as its antecedent. No certain decision seems possible."[66] Abner, who serves as Saul's commander in chief (see also 17:55), works closely with the king in all matters, whether in identifying young David (see the duplication of Saul meeting David in 17:55–58; cf. 16:14–23) or eating dinner at the royal table (20:25).

A key moment for Abner appears in 1 Samuel 26, the second story about David sparing Saul's life. Abner appears in 26:5, 7, 14, 15 as Saul's protective army commander who fails to protect the king. Sparing the king's life, David takes the king's weapon while Abner and his army men sleep next to the king (26:7, 9). Later, David mocks Abner's manliness when he asks, "Are you not a man? (הלוא איש אתה) Who is like you in Israel? Why then have you not kept watch over your lord the king? For one of the people came in to destroy your lord the king" (26:15). Competition and disdain saturate David's rhetorical questions. Abner's deep loyalty to Saul contrasts with David's contempt for both the king and his army commander. Later in 2 Samuel 1–3, Abner gains literary significance as the military opponent to David's kingship. He also betrays Saul's surviving son, Ishbaal, and is then murdered by Joab, David's nephew and military commander (2 Sam 3:27, 30).[67] His support of a failing hegemonic male character, Saul, and his royal house (2 Sam 2:8–10) leads to his demise.

Another minor male character is part of the narrative primarily to support a major male character. This man, Elkanah, the father of Samuel, appears first in the story about the transition from Israelite male judges to Israelite kings in 1:1. Coming from a long lineage of fathers, Elkanah is a weak character in comparison to his wife, Hannah. He is a bigamist (1:4) with a large family, although his preferred wife is said to be infertile. He speaks only twice in the drama about Hannah's desperate quest to become pregnant and to give birth to a son. In two short responses (1:8, 23), Elkanah

---

66. Klein, *1 Samuel*, 142.

67. Joab is first mentioned in 1 Sam 26:6 as Abishai's brother and son of David's sister, Zeruiah; see 1 Chr 2:16.

tries to comfort and accommodate his wife. In verse 8 he is asking Hannah, "Am I not more to you than ten sons," and in verse 23 he affirms her decision: "Do what seems best to you." Feminist interpreters are conflicted about his question in verse 8. Jo Ann Hackett suggests that Elkanah's encouragement of the weeping Hannah over her lack of children is "hardly that of a patriarch who can see value in women only as childbearers."[68] To Hackett, he finds his love far more important than progeny. Hackett, however, also notes that Elkanah already has several children from his other wife, Peninnah, and so his lack of understanding Hannah's despair could also be interpreted as insensitive.

In my view, his response needs to be read with a grain of salt. The presumably generous and benevolent depiction of the bigamist husband stands in line with patriarchal interests that present women as clamoring for societal recognition through motherhood. In this way, Hannah's predicament is similar to Sarah's or Rachel's situations (Gen 11:30; 30:2), complying with patriarchal standards that define women's worthiness through motherhood. All these female characters attempt to gain societal recognition by giving birth to a son. The husband gains from his wife's single-minded focus on motherhood. Elkanah also accommodates Hannah's oath to give her son, Samuel, to the priest (1:23). Like other patriarchs before him, Elkanah tells her, "Do what seems best to you; wait until you have weaned him; only, may [YHWH] establish your word" (1:23). His compliance recollects Abraham, who submits to Sarah (Gen 16:6), or Jacob's nonverbal compliance in sleeping with whatever woman is in his bed (Gen 30:4, 9, 16). Like them, Elkanah submits to his wife while his patriarchal privileges remain intact. Together with Hannah, he brings the boy to the priest (2:11; see also 1:28), and he is the one receiving further fertility blessings from the priest (2:20). He has three more sons and two daughters with Hannah (2:21). His role as a minor male character ensures that Samuel, a major male character, appears in the logical sequence within the storyline.

---

68. Jo Ann Hackett, "1 and 2 Samuel," in *Women's Bible Commentary*, ed. Carol A. Newsom, Sharon H. Ringe, and Jacqueline E. Lapsley, 3rd ed. (Louisville, KY: Westminster John Knox, 2012), 154.

Finally, there is the minor male character of Eli, the priest of the sanctuary at Shiloh (1:3), whose two sons, Hophni and Phinehas, give him much trouble (22:12–17, 22–25, 34; 4:4, 11, 12–18). His sons "lay" (שכב את), or rather rape, women at the entrance of the temple (2:22), disregard their father's reprimand (2:23–25), become a "sign" to him via their deaths (2:34), and later die during or after a battle against the Philistines (4:11).[69] When their father learns about their deaths and the capture of the ark, Eli falls backward from his seat and dies instantly (4:18). Eli's sons are depicted as the opposite from the priest. They are evil, and he naively expects an honest response from them (2:23–25). The father needs to hear the truth about his sons and his lineage from "a man of God" (2:27–36), stating in verses 31–32, "See, a time is coming when I will cut off your strength and the strength of your ancestor's family. No one in your family shall ever live to old age." Nevertheless, Eli also raises a "trustworthy prophet" (3:20), Samuel, who will become Eli's successor. As a minor character, then, Eli serves as a transitional link from the former era of the judges to prepare the path for Samuel as a major male leader helping to implement the Israelite monarchy. As Samuel becomes the next link in this transition, other characters related to Eli die, whether they are Eli's sons or the pregnant daughter-in-law, the wife of Phinehas (4:19–22). All of them make room for the major male characters, Samuel, Saul, and David, highlighting who the "real men" are in this tale about the violent succession struggles over the emerging Israelite monarchy.

The Display of Hegemonic and Subservient Masculinities as a Feminist Concern: Concluding Comments

As this chapter depicts various masculinities in 1 Samuel, the focus has been on the three major and four minor male characters. Taking seriously the warning that a focus on the study of men and masculinities poses a risk to feminist exegesis, my interpretation does not aim to reinforce the relentless centrality of men in 1 Samuel. Rather, my goal has been to outline and reflect on the hegemonic masculinities portrayed in this biblical book and to expose rather than reinforce their literary pervasiveness. The analysis produces four versions

69. Also see the discussion on this story in chaps. 1 and 5 of this book.

of masculinities. The chapter discusses Samuel's murderous masculinity and its connections to his gender troubles, as they appear in the relationship of his parents, in his mother's obsession for a son, and in the brief mention of his sons. The chapter also describes Saul's masculinity of failure despite the early promises of his selection as the first Israelite king. The chapter outlines David's toxic warrior masculinity that seems attractive not only to other male or female characters in the narrative but also to interpreters throughout the ages. Finally, the chapter presents the submissive masculinities of four minor male characters—Jonathan, Abner, Elkanah, and Eli—in the order of these characters' significance. Their subservience to the elite hegemonic masculinities of Samuel, Saul, and David ensures not only the marginality of the four minor men but also their literary necessity. The minor male figures guarantee the smooth transitioning from judge to first king to second king.

The chapter demonstrates that the major and minor men depend on each other in the plot development, regardless of the fragmentary and often disconnected nature of their stories. Without the reliable appearance of the minor men, the stories of Samuel, Saul, and David would lack literary depth or substance. Sometimes the sexualized, heterosexist, or homoerotic entanglements among the various male characters include salacious, even crude, and always tension-filled stories. Even God, the ultimate male hegemon of 1 Samuel, appears intertwined in the tales about male competition, jealousy, warring, murder, and death. The narratives about the early Israelite monarchy present God as preferring David's toxic warrior masculinity over Saul's masculinity of failure. Yet feminist readers reject such a theological projection as offensive. The preference of David's toxic warrior masculinity is idolatrous and always requires bloodshed, hatred, violent competition, and war. In short, the various forms of masculinity must be exposed for their ethically, politically, and theologically dangerous endorsement of hegemonic masculinity. The men in 1 Samuel are not characters to be admired, emulated, or adored. They should never be excused, as interpreters have done over the ages when they classify Saul as a tragic hero or as simply incompetent. Similarly, Samuel's murder usually remains marginalized, and David is admired secretly as a womanizer and openly as a successful warrior king. These warrior heroes are despicable killers, sexist and misogynist male characters whom feminist readers need to reject.

In conclusion, feminist readers must recognize that silence and praise are dangerous responses to the male characters of 1 Samuel. Their masculinities injure the emotional, psychological, or mental constellations not only of males but also of women. We have to become conscious of these phallogocentric dynamics and then develop creative possibilities for the changed construction and performance of masculinities today. The next chapter exposes further as deeply troubling the fusion of ethnoreligious, class, and androcentric power in the tales about the emerging Israelite monarchy. As the narratives, favoring toxic masculinity in their various constellations, merge with the imaginary of a monarchical system, 1 Samuel must be recognized as theo-politically tendentious literature. Heavy emphasis on exclusively male leadership thus presents a rather troubling exegetical situation for feminist readers.

For Further Reflection

1. Yaron Peleg, "David, Jonathan, and the Biblical Politics of Gender," from "Love at First Sight? David, Jonathan, and the Biblical Politics of Gender," *JSOT* 30 (2005): 176, 187, 188–189.

   Several elements, then, which lend themselves to reading Jonathan as homosexual also lend themselves to reading him as a "woman." The first is Jonathan's sudden and complete infatuation with David, his subsequent courtship of him, and David's own admission of the depth and extent of his to Jonathan at his death (נפל אתה אהבתך לי מאהבת נשים, "wonderful was thy love to me, passing the love of women"). The second is the subtle analogy that is made between Jonathan and his sister Michal. Both siblings fall in love with David suddenly and passionately, but their affection is seldom returned, if at all. A third element arises from the paradoxical nature of the previous two: Why should the royal siblings develop such deep passion for such an inexpedient alliance? Moreover, military exploits replace previous descriptions of the military heroism of Jonathan (e.g., 1 Sam. 14), who is now relegated to a passive place around his father's table in the palace. . . .

   Then, just as Jonathan is given feminine characteristics, David is given masculine ones. The military exploits of David replace those of Jonathan, who is now relegated to a passive place around his father's table in the palace. David's virility is constantly stressed, first through his association with four different women (Michal, Merab, Abigail, and Ahinoam), but especially through the dowry he is asked to deliver Saul for his daughter Michal: the foreskins of one hundred Philistines. Before the deadline expires, David delivers not one, but two hundred foreskins, proving his manhood beyond doubt, literally and figuratively. . . .

Since the frequent reference, manipulation, and substitution of gender roles in this story draws attention to their very existence and carries a clear sexual meaning, it is not surprising that David and Jonathan were and still are read as lovers. But it seems to me that for the writer or editor of the story it was not the possibility of sex between the two men that mattered as much as their confusion of gender roles. Indeed, most of the differences between the two men play on the differences between the sexes. . . . For the most part, Jonathan is placed in the inferior and subservient role of a woman, whereas David assumes the superior and dominant role of a man. This is precisely one of the main difficulties in regarding the two men as same-sex lovers. While the traditional hierarchy of same-sex relationship usually stipulated that an older and socially superior man assumed the active role in a relationship, socially and sexually, the instability of the active-passive dichotomy and the shifting assignments of gender roles throughout the story obscure such a reading. Jonathan is seeking David's emotional support as well as his physical protection, despite the fact that he may be older, that he is more experienced, and that he is socially superior to David. Jonathan's portrayal may therefore be understood as mainly a means to an end, a literary construction of a political one. The unusual way it is done here is by casting the connection between the two men in the mold of relationship between a man and woman. Paradoxically, this untraditional casting of a traditional relationship seems to me to undermine rather than promote the potential for a homoerotic reading.

2. "Musical Portrayals of Michal in Love" by Helen Leneman, London, UK. Used by permission of the author.

Depiction of emotions was seldom of interest to biblical writers, but it is often the primary focus of composers and their librettists. This essay examines four musical settings of David's story, chosen because of the extent of their focus on Michal. Michal's small role in 1 and 2 Samuel is greatly expanded in many librettos. Though her love for David is mentioned in only two biblical verses (1 Sam 18:20, 28), it becomes central to the plot in many librettos. And contrary to the biblical story, her love is reciprocated. Every musical work is unique, but David never sings arias about his love for Michal; his love is suggested only in their duets, which were a necessary component of any musical work. There is often more music and text for David in regard to Jonathan, but that is another essay. In most biblical narratives, including this one, men's political considerations are the main concern, while Michal is known only for whom she loves. This dynamic perpetuates the familiar stereotype of men being motivated by ambition and women by their feelings.[70] In musical works, however, both express their love for each other in duets, although Michal (being a woman) is still the more emotional and expressive character.

Many musical works, particularly operas, alter the biblical plot sequence. For example, Carl Nielsen (Danish, 1865–1931), in his opera *Saul of David* (1902), includes the David–Goliath encounter in a lengthy scene that opens act 2. When the curtain rises, Saul appears on the throne, flanked by David and Michal. This scene is completely out of sequence. David has not met Michal when he offers to fight Goliath, and he has yet to become resident in Saul's palace. Although Michal is not depicted in Nielsen's opera as a particularly multidimensional character, Michal emerges as a passionate and determined woman. David's feelings for Michal are not evident until later in the opera.

In their first love duet in Nielsen's opera, Michal's music evokes great passion. For example, she sings, "David, my beloved," twice, on two descending octave leaps, which vividly depicts her great passion

70. J. Cheryl Exum, *Fragmented Women: Feminist (Sub)versions of Biblical Narratives*, Cornerstones, 2nd ed. (London: Bloomsbury T&T Clark, 2015), 22.

for David. When David goes off to battle, Michal kneels at Saul's feet and begs him not to let David go, because she "has given her soul into his hands." Her line is sustained, soft, and heartfelt. Saul, listening to the warriors' repeated calls to battle, is in a similar situation to Michal: both have little or no textual autonomy from David. In addition, this libretto goes beyond references to just Song of Songs. When Saul later joins the hands of David and Michal, the chorus equates David's love for Michal with that of Isaac for Rebecca or Jacob for Rachel, keeping his love in a biblical frame. An extensive duet that appears much later in the same opera is probably the most passionate and Wagnerian musical depiction of their love to be found in music, leaving no room for doubt of a great and reciprocal love between the two characters. But apart from these duets, David's feelings for Michal are not obvious.

In another musical genre—an oratorio (unstaged, unlike opera)—almost two hundred years earlier, George Frideric Handel's (German-British, 1685–1759) oratorio *Saul* (1738) presents Michal as proclaiming her love for David to a flowery accompaniment. A sweet and pastoral-sounding love duet follows. After Michal and David each sing their individual parts, their voices unite and interweave in perfect harmony, trilling and singing cadenzas. There is more sweetness than passion here, but that is the nature of Handel's music. Once again, the love duet implies mutual feelings. There could not be a love duet in any musical setting if only one of the two characters was in love. But these are standard set pieces, not altering the fact that David does not speak of his love for Michal elsewhere in the musical works. Michal does, however, talk to her friends about her love for David in several musical works, illustrating the same imbalance found in the biblical narrative.

A similar imbalance appears in other musical interpretations. In Ferdinand Hiller's (German, 1811–1885) oratorio *Saul* (1858), Michal sings a lengthy aria in which she declares her love for David. Her words either come from the Song of Songs or they are paraphrases of similar verses. Clarinets introduce the expressive and lyrical melody before Michal sings it. Although her song is a love song, the use of a minor tonality adds an underlying wistful quality. Moments like this illustrate the power of music to surpass the spoken word.

Different from Handel's and Hiller's works, some composers feature David's attraction to Michal more than in the biblical account. For instance, in C. Hubert H. Parry's (English, 1848–1918) oratorio *King Saul* (1894), David sings verses from the Song of Songs, such as "Rise up my love, my fair one, and come" (Song 2:10), to which Michal responds with other verses from the Song of Songs. The voices overlap constantly in this opening section. One voice enters while the other is sustaining a high note, showing eagerness and excitement. Much of the music lies in the high range for both voices to convey ardor. The fact that the text for their love duets is the Song of Songs not only places their love in a biblical realm but also depersonalizes them, thus equating them with the lovers who proclaim those verses.

Love duets between David and Michal are part of every oratorio and opera that include Michal.[71] Love duets by definition are emotionally expressive pieces of music. A good example is the very lengthy love duet in Parry's oratorio, which would certainly be the highlight of any performance. Yet one wonders how a biblically literate audience would consider a love duet at odds with the biblical story when the latter never even suggests David loving Michal. Perhaps Parry perceived the biblical depiction as judgment on David's inadequate character, and so he wrote the duet to remedy the biblical portrayal of David. Parry also must have known that an audience always expects a good love duet. After hearing such passionate declarations of love, audiences would not remember the details of the biblical account or doubt their memory of the biblical tale. The use of the Song of Songs also might distract listeners, as the inclusion of verses from this biblical book are common to biblical oratorios that include love duets. The librettists wanted to maintain an appropriately "biblical" feel,

71. Helen Leneman, *Love, Lust, and Lunacy: The Stories of Saul and David in Music*, Bible in the Modern World 29 (Sheffield: Sheffield Phoenix, 2010). My study discusses fifteen musical settings in great detail.

and so they either wrote original lyrics or borrowed from the Song of Songs, the quintessential biblical expression of love and passion.

The early twentieth-century work by Charles Hutchinson Gabriel (American, 1856–1932) is a rare exception. In his work, *Saul, King of Israel: A Dramatic Cantata* (1901), a short oratorio, Michal wishes that David would share her feelings. She begs God to shield David from the enemy. The absence of a clearly reciprocal love relationship is a major difference from all other musical treatments of Michal and David. The reason for this change is perhaps the desire to make David a "man of God" who cannot be in a normal romantic relationship. Elsewhere the libretto suggests that Michal has a child with David, but the child does not necessarily indicate a love relationship. The casting of Michal as an alto also makes her less appealing as a love interest than a usual soprano, perhaps portraying her as an older woman. But voice casting is more important in staged opera.

As oratorios, cantatas, and operas invent words of love between Michal and David to varying degrees, they also exclude a biblical incident from the musical depictions of the two characters. Rarely or never represented in musical settings is Michal helping David escape when she puts *teraphim* under the blanket on David's bed to fool Saul's guards (1 Sam 19:11–17). Notably in the biblical story, David does not utter a word of gratitude or farewell to her. Robert Alter wonders if this "asymmetrical presentation of the two characters" merely suggests David's hurried escape.[72]

In sum, Michal and David sing about their love in music, but David's responses to Michal are seldom heard in the Bible. Outside of love duets, which are conventional and integral parts of vocal music, many oratorios and operas do not express David's emotions for Michal. Thus, many later writers and composers created expressions of great and reciprocal love between the two characters, even if these expressions are limited to set pieces like love duets. Through the power

72. Robert Alter, *Ancient Israel: The Former Prophets: Joshua, Judges, Samuel and Kings—A Translation with Commentary* (New York: Norton, 2013), 353.

of music, then, both Michal and David come to life vibrantly and momentarily in these duets.

3. Ken Stone, "Queer Readings of David and Jonathan." Used by permission of the author.

With the emergence of queer readings of the Bible, David's lament "over Saul and his son Jonathan" (2 Sam 1:17) has received much attention for its inclusion of the line "your love to me was wonderful, passing the love of women" (1:26). Traditionally, biblical scholars have interpreted this verse by emphasizing the ancient use of the vocabulary of "love" to describe political relationships. The fact that the relationship between Jonathan and David does have political implications is clear from, among other textual features, Jonathan's acknowledgment to David, while making a "covenant" or "treaty" with him (1 Sam 23:18), that David will be king and Jonathan will be his "second" (1 Sam 23:17). Saul also observes angrily that his son's relationship with David will have consequences for Jonathan and his "kingdom" (1 Sam 20:31). In spite of the fact that they do not always involve eroticism or reference queer studies, traditional interpretations of this relationship in terms of ancient political relations and the vocabulary of love do have some usefulness for queer reading. They underscore the political nature of sex and gender over the course of history even as they demonstrate that the particular meaning of "love" is not universal but rather has specific connotations in different historical and cultural circumstances.

But might a queer reading of David and Jonathan go further than this? The language used for their relationship has proven to be tantalizing for later readers who find here hints of intimacy. David's reference to "your love" and David's comparison between Jonathan's love and "the love of women" in 2 Samuel 1:26 follows several references in 1 Samuel to Jonathan's "love" for (1 Sam 18:1–4; 20:17), "delight in" (1 Sam 19:1), and close relationship to (1 Sam 20:30–42; 23:18) David. They "kiss" and "weep" with one another (1 Sam 20:41). The emphasis on their affection for one another seems to go beyond what we might expect from the register of ancient covenantal and dynastic politics. Moreover, Saul's outburst against Jonathan in 1 Samuel 20:30

makes use of rhetoric about his "mother's nakedness" that arguably places Jonathan's favor for David in a sexual frame. Some scholars[73] therefore read the story in terms of a "warrior eroticism" comparable to that which is associated with some accounts of ancient Sparta.

An alternative way of understanding the story's language of male affection is offered by the gay classicist and queer theorist David M. Halperin. Though not focused on the Bible, Halperin includes the story of David and Jonathan among several ancient traditions that he glosses with the phrase "heroes and their pals," including traditions about Gilgamesh and Enkidu, and Achilles and Patroclus. Halperin points out that in these traditions we see representations of male homosocial friendship that are sometimes spoken about in conjugal or sexual language. Ancient depictions of close affection between males draws on this language of sexual relations as well as kinship relations, whether or not the friendship is sexual in our sense of that term.

The use of kinship relations as a framework for interpreting the relationship between Jonathan and David has been noted as well by biblical scholars who compare and contrast the characterization of Jonathan with the characterization of Michal, the sister of Jonathan who also loves David (1 Sam 18:20; 18:28) and becomes his first wife. The conclusions drawn from these comparisons are not always identical. For example, David Jobling argues that Jonathan and Michal share narrative roles (such as helping David escape from Saul), while Adele Berlin suggests instead that "characteristics normally associated with males are attached to Michal, and those usually perceived as feminine are linked with Jonathan."[74] Jennings characterizes Michal's love for David as having "played second fiddle to David's erotic relationships to Saul and Jonathan,"[75] relationships that Jennings interprets sexually. As different as these interpretations are, they

73. E.g., Theodore W. Jennings Jr., "YHWH as Erastes," in *Queer Commentary and the Hebrew Bible*, ed. Ken Stone, JSOTSup 334 (Sheffield: Sheffield Academic, 2001), 26–74.

74. Adele Berlin, *Poetics and Interpretation of Biblical Narrative* (Sheffield: Almond Press, 1983), 24. See also Jobling, *1 Samuel*, 162.

75. Jennings, "YHWH as Erastes," 51.

underscore the fact that Jonathan's literary characterization involves a certain amount of gender reversal, blurring, or transgression, accomplished through comparisons with his sister Michal.

Susan Ackerman brings together many of these dynamics in a compelling interpretation that highlights the ambiguity of gender performance and homoeroticism in the story of David and Jonathan. Ackerman also understands Jonathan to serve "metaphorically" as a kind of "wife" for David, a role his sister Michal fills "legally."[76] Although the hints of homoeroticism in the story are for Ackerman too numerous to be accidental, the story retains a certain "ambiguity" about eroticism that succeeds in feminizing Jonathan without absolutely accusing David of transgressing the prohibition against male intercourse that, in Leviticus 20:13, condemns both active and passive partners. As a consequence, the storyline subordinates Jonathan to David and thereby legitimizes David's royal position. On this reading, the political connotations of love do not provide an alternative explanation for homoerotic language. Rather, the ambiguity of the erotic language contributes to the story's political effects.

These examples and others show that there is not a single queer reading of the story of David and Jonathan. Rather than trying to determine the nature of their relationship with certainty, Anthony Heacock therefore argues that all such readings are influenced by the cultural contexts of readers. Thus he utilizes queer theories and modern accounts of gay male friendships as resources for the story's interpretation in our own world. The point here is not to romanticize David and Jonathan as biblical models for modern gay love. After all, as comparisons between Jonathan and Michal show, the story rests on a series of assumptions about male dominance in the context of royal hierarchies. By highlighting the instability of sexual and gender meanings even within the story of David and Jonathan, however, queer readings of it explore possibilities for reimagining the books of Samuel in new, and more complex, ways.

---

76. Susan Ackerman, *When Heroes Love: The Ambiguity of Eros in the Stories of Gilgamesh and David*, GTR (New York: Columbia University Press, 2005), 178.

4. Marc H. Ellis, "On Samuel and Saul" (1 Sam. 19:18–24). Used by permission of the author.

So you asked for a poem
On Samuel and Saul
The plot to kill David
That ends in party time
Handwriting on the wall?

Instead
Saul and David
Naked and drunk
Prophesied mightily all night
Under the Mediterranean moon

What could this mean, you asked
As if a simple Jew would know
Who was Saul
Prophet or King?

But I was thinking Samuel
Israel's demand for an earthly King
I know where that leads
This way and that
Through history

And now we're all here
With nowhere else to go
Israel's chariots fly over Palestine
Our flag waves
Our army grows

Permanent it is
Occupation for hire
Samuel knew it all
(Un)ethical fire

The Other Nations
We have become
As Samuel foretold
Our mission is finished
Ethics on hold

Shall we turn
Shall we fold?

5. Susanne Scholz, "Concubine," *Bible Odyssey*, https://www.bibleodyssey.org/people/related-articles/concubine/.
"I am only a Benjaminite, from the least of the tribes of Israel, and my family is the humblest of all families of the tribe of Benjamin. Why then have you spoken to me in this way?" (1 Sam 9:21; NRSVue)

Contemporary feminist scholars argue convincingly that the meaning of the Hebrew noun פילגש, which is usually translated as "concubine," is actually much more complicated than this rather inadequate English translation suggests. Dictionaries of Biblical Hebrew indicate uncertainty about the noun's origins. Usually, the noun is correlated with the Greek παλλάκ and the Latin *pellex*, both translated as "concubine." This term comes from the Latin feminine noun "concubina" derived from *concumbere*, which means "to lie with, to lie together, to cohabit." Some researchers mention the Middle Assyrian Law 41A as a proof that in the ancient Near East concubines were not married to the man with whom they slept but that a ceremony existed to make her his wife. The English word "concubine" is an anachronistic word for the biblical פילגש because the English word is attested for the first time only in the thirteenth century CE. English Bible translations, beginning with the King James Version, have habitually used concubine to translate פילגש for a Hebrew term of unclear meaning. In the process they have introduced into the text assumptions that devalue women (androcentrism) and make the Near East seem exotic (a process called orientalism). However, the highly respected Hebrew-English lexicon, edited by Francis Brown, S. R. Driver, and Charles A.

Briggs, observes that the Greek noun "probably" means "young girl." The Hebrew noun פילגש can then refer to a sexual relationship between an adult man and a young girl who is perhaps not even sexually mature.

Besides the factor of age, another important element in the translation of פילגש must be recognized. Several biblical texts suggest that a פילגש grows up to become an enslaved woman with no other function but to sexually please her master and produce his children. An obvious example is the story about David's ten פילגשים (2 Sam 15:16) who were slaves serving the king's sexual and progeny needs. The women were also raped by the king's son as a challenge to royal authority (see also 2 Sam 3:6–11; 1 Kgs 2:13–25).

The most explicit reference to a פילגש as a slave appears in the story of Bilhah. In Gen 29:29, Bilhah is Rachel's slave (שפחה; see also Gen 30:3–4, 7; 35:25; 46:25) and Gen 37:2 lists her and Zilpah as "the women [נשים, sing. אשה] of his [Joseph's] father." Yet in Gen 35:22 she is "the [פילגש] of his [Reuben's] father," and Reuben rapes his aunt's enslaved woman, Bilhah. Interestingly, in 1 Chr 7:13 Bilhah is neither Rachel's nor Jacob's possession. There she belongs to her sons, who are identified as "the descendants of Bilhah." These biblical texts about Bilhah's status and ownership hint at the complicated linguistic and historical situation reflected in the Hebrew term פילגש.

In sum, the translation of פילגש as "concubine" hides a complicated translation history that has been flavored by orientalist and androcentric assumptions. For sure, the classification of פילגש as a prostitute is linguistically, historically, and culturally inadequate. In addition, the classification of the male פילגשים in Ezek 23:20 as "paramours" also relies on antiquated English terminology. Most importantly, the translation of פילגש as "concubine" ignores aspects of age and social status in the biblical use of the Hebrew noun. It is urgent from an etymological, exegetical, and ethical perspective to establish the meaning of פילגש as a girl who grows up in involuntary sexual bondage. The noun must be translated as "(mostly) a sexually trafficked girl in life-time sexual bondage to produce progeny to her master."

6. Susanne Scholz, "Reading שכב את as Rape Terminology in 1 Samuel 2:22."
   "[T]hey raped (שכב את) the women at the door of the tabernacle" (1 Sam 2:22).

Why should we translate the Hebrew verb שכב as "to rape" but not as "to sleep with" or "to lie with" as the NRSVue does ("they lay with the women who served at the entrance to the tent of meeting")? The verb itself (שכב) means literally "to sleep." As usual, the New Living Translation abandons a literal rendering altogether when it translates the verb in this problematic fashion: "his sons were seducing [שכב] the young women." At stake is the translation of the particle את that follows the verb. The particle can function either as an object marker of the sentence, in this case "the women," or as the preposition "with." Translators who translate in a rape-prone fashion cannot fathom the sons of a priest raping women at the tabernacle's entrance, and so they choose to translate the particle as the preposition "with." In their mind, this translation insinuates mutual consent, as the sons sleep or lie "with" the women.

Yet in many biblical rape texts the translation of שכב את as "to sleep/lie with" is highly problematic because it hides the possibility of sexual violence. One such example is the rape of Dinah in Genesis 34:2 where the sexual violence is expressed in the increasing explicitness of the three verbs following each other: take, sleep/lie, rape (לקח, שכב את, ענה pi'el). There, Shechem does not sleep or lie "with" Dinah but he "rapes" her. Another clear-cut case is in 2 Samuel 13:14, where the narrative reports Amnon as overpowering (חזק) and raping (ענה pi'el) Tamar and "laying" (שכב את) her.

Another unknown case of rape that uses the verb שכב את is Genesis 35:22a. There, Judah rapes Bilhah, who is characterized as a פילגש (Orientalist translation of "concubine") and who was Rachel's slave, אמה, often translated as "maidservant." The power differential between Judah, the son of Leah, and Bilhah is obvious. To communicate her powerlessness as an enslaved woman in the family of Jacob,

Rachel, and Leah, the verb of Genesis 35:22a must be translated as "he [Judah] raped Bilhah" to express the implied sexual violence.

Finally, interpreters never hesitate to consider the activity going on between Lot and his two daughters in the cave as rape although here too translators do not usually render the verb שׁכב את as "to rape." The very verb appears in Genesis 19:33: "she lay with her father" (NRSV). However, whether a daughter ever rapes her father is a highly questionable proposition that some feminist interpreters emphasize on the basis of social science and related feminist hermeneutical considerations. Perhaps one needs to read this rape story as a successful obfuscation by a father who blames his daughters for the events in the cave in order to distract from his criminal behavior.

In short, the translation of 1 Samuel 2:22 as a reference to the sons of Eli raping the women at the tabernacle's entrance is a linguistically, hermeneutically, and ethically valid and even necessary interpretation. Eliminating rape-prone terminology, this translation uncovers the implied sexual violence. The explicit verb "to rape" ensures that contemporary readers understand the evil nature of Eli's sons who serve as priests at the tabernacle.

3

DETERMINING THE SPECTER OF MONARCHY AT THE END OF DEMOCRACY

If democracy is about participating in self-government, its first requirement is a supportive culture, a complex of beliefs, values, and practices that nurture equality, cooperation, and freedom. . . . Under nondemocratic forms of government, where the people are politically excluded as a matter of principle, lying is typically done by the sovereign or its agents, usually in order to mislead those presumed to be enemies or rivals of the sovereign.

—Sheldon S. Wolin, *Democracy Incorporated: Managed Democracy and the Specter of Inverted Totalitarianism*

Reading About Kingship Stories in the Twenty-First Century: An Introduction

THE NARRATIVES OF 1 Samuel are renowned not only for the many geographical references or the famous male characters but also for the riveting accounts about the emerging Israelite monarchy. In the first seven chapters, the political system of the judges still appears in seamless continuation of the book of Judges. Yet already the book of Judges lets readers know of the political troubles embedded in the tribal system: "In those days there was no king in Israel; all the people did what was right in their own eyes" (Judg 21:25; see also 17:6; 18:1; 19:1). The book of 1 Samuel begins with the same system that changes only in 1 Samuel 8. An aging Samuel appoints his sons Joel and Abijah as judges over Israel (8:1). Readers know already that Eli's sons are "worthless sons" (בני בליעל, 2:12), and the next verses confirm that they are corrupt, take bribes, and subvert justice (8:3). The political system has been broken for some time, but now even "the elders of Israel" (8:4) demand change from Samuel. They ask for a king.

Many interpreters endorse the monarchical system, mainly because the text tells them so. For instance, twentieth-century John Bright accepts as a given the transition from biblical Israel's "tribal organization" to a monarchical system.[1] Biblical historians explain that monarchies had been in place in ancient Near Eastern cities and regions "from time immemorial,"[2] given that monarchies have military and sociopolitical advantages over differently organized groups such as loose tribal confederations. Usually, those historians also mention biblical verses (e.g., Judg 8:22–23) that criticize hereditary monarchical rule as preserved memories of ancient Israel's rejection of a monarchical system.

Interpreters, however, do not always problematize the succession from the system of the judges to a monarchy. Accordingly, the kyriarchal character of the monarchical system depicted in 1 Samuel remains unexplored in biblical scholarship. Even in his admission that "in our enlightened, liberal-democratic and largely secular world" few are "interested in such a thing," namely, stories about the biblical monarchy, Joseph Blenkinsopp does not acknowledge that democratic societies must reject monarchies or "monocratic" governments.[3] In fact, he explains that "the institution of the monarchy" served people well for "millennia" and that knowledge of this institution might help contemporary people, who take for granted "our own Western, liberal-democratic institutions," to assess "the broader range of possibilities which a knowledge of the past affords."[4] He also claims, "No one will lightly advocate a return to absolutist monocratic government, but history teaches that there is often a price to be paid for attributing absolute validity to our current political institutions."[5] In his view, the history lesson is that governmental systems, including democracies in the West, are transitory. Blenkinsopp recognizes that the monarchical system is a prominent, long-lasting,

---

1. John Bright, *A History of Israel*, Westminster Aids to the Study of the Scriptures, 3rd ed. (Philadelphia: Westminster, 1981), 182.

2. So Martin Noth, *The History of Israel*, trans. P. R. Ackroyd, 2nd ed., Harper Theological Library (New York: Harper & Row, 1960), 164.

3. Joseph Blenkinsopp, *David Remembered: Kingship and National Identity in Ancient Israel* (Grand Rapids, MI: Eerdmans, 2013), 3.

4. Blenkinsopp, *David Remembered*, 4.

5. Blenkinsopp, *David Remembered*, 4.

and still available political system. In this sense, he speaks positively about the monarchical political system, a stunning position for a US-American Bible scholar.

Yet the unchallenged acceptance of biblical monarchy as the next logical step of the political order for biblical Israel, as presented in 1 Samuel, should be probed in a feminist commentary. In fact, the fusion of ethnoreligious, class, and androcentric power in the biblical institution of the monarchy requires critical interrogation. The question is why interpreters have taken for granted the narrated move from the institution of the judges to the installation of the first king. I think the developing kyriarchal order is presented as the only available political system because "the Bible tells it so." Thus, many contemporary interpreters simply accept the quest for an Israelite monarchical system as the logical next step in biblical Israel's development. They also do not mention other political systems, as ethnoreligious and gender assumptions tend to intellectually and exegetically limit interpreters. Following the storyline, they directly or indirectly approve of the monarchy as inevitable. Of course, they also do not consider the installation of a queen as a possibility, neither within the narrative nor in interpretations developed throughout the ages, although several queens, such as Jezebel (1 Kgs 16:31; 18:19–19:3; 21:5–6; 2 Kgs 9:30–27) or Athaliah (2 Kgs 11:1–3), appear in biblical literature.

In short, although today's commentators live in vastly different political systems, they do not offer constructive criticism of the Israelite monarchy as a political system. They do not usually critically remark on the leadership model as being almost exclusively male and of a single ethnoreligious background. Interpreters accept as a given that the model presupposes a king who represents the top of the political inner-ethnic Israelite hierarchy despite some ethnic confusion in the lineage, such as Saul's ancestors who were (male) Benjaminites sex-trafficking Canaanite women (Judg 21), or David's Moabite connections to Ruth and Lot's daughters (Gen 19:30–38). One thing thus seems obvious. The first two kings come from wealthy fathers, although their outstanding features are physical. Saul is particularly tall (10:23), and David is handsome (16:12). In 1 Samuel, the possibility of a tall or beautiful woman as the first or second royal leader is nonexistent in the minds of past and present exegetes.

At the same time, a feminist interpretation should not simply bemoan the absence of women in kyriarchal leadership roles. The mere inclusion of queens holds no promise for readers raised in a democratic system because the inclusion of women in an unjust political system merely guarantees the continuation of sociopolitical, economic, and cultural-religious oppression. This is a dilemma for liberal feminist interpreters striving to include women into kyriarchal political structures. As I am writing what appears to be at the end of Western democratic societies, I am not content to speak approvingly of a first, second, or even third queen. My interpretation aims to expose the inherent political limitations of any monarchical system, whether female or male or whether it appears in the Bible or elsewhere. As Western democratic societies struggle, the danger is that they move into autocratic or monocratic forms of governance, perhaps even into a biotechnofeudal order.[6] Feminist readers ought to worry about 1 Samuel depicting a monarchical system as the best, though contested, form of political governance that is even approved by God.

As contemporary political and economic thinkers observe that Western societies have entered a fragile democratic, increasingly authoritarian order,[7] a feminist commentary cannot review the stories about the developing Israelite monarchy without critical interrogation. As Yanis Varoufakis, an economist and former finance minister of Greece, explains, we have already left the neoliberal capitalist order since 2008 and have now begun to live in a technofeudalist order.[8] He asserts, "The democracy we have is simply a piece of propaganda. We have an oligarchy with elections and the elections

---

6. For a fascinating elaboration on biotechnofeudalism, see, e.g., Yanis Varoufakis, *Another Now: Dispatches from an Alternative Present* (London: Bodley Head, 2020).

7. See, e.g., Henry A. Giroux, *Race, Politics, and Pandemic Pedagogy: Education in a Time of Crisis* (London: Bloomsbury Academic, 2021).

8. For his explanations of this shift, see, e.g., Yanis Varoufakis, "Capitalism Has Become 'Techno-Feudalism,'" *Al Jazeera*, February 19, 2021, https://www.aljazeera.com/program/upfront/2021/2/19/yanis-varoufakis-capitalism-has-become-techno. See also his extensive analysis in *Technofeudalism: What Killed Capitalism* (Brooklyn, NY: Melville House, 2024).

are bought by the oligarchy."[9] In light of this geopolitical, economic, and cultural reality, this commentary exposes the early expressions of the biblical monarchical order as an inherently kyriarchal, ethnonational project that contradicts the feminist imaginary. Accordingly, this interpretation deconstructs the royal order of 1 Samuel as oppressive, androcentric, and ethnonationalist; it rejects a romanticized portrayal of the biblical monarchy. Saul and David cannot be admired as early role models for a political institution that has profoundly shaped not only the biblical imagination but also societies historically shaped by the Bible. In this way, the monarchical tales of 1 Samuel turn into teachable moments for the need to depart from authoritarian, or even royally ruled, societies. They ought to be read as warning tales to turn toward the only political alternative that positions people as viable political forces to shape and control their own lives and society: a democratic order. How fragile and even unwanted democratic freedom and autonomy are becomes apparent when we read 1 Samuel with a focus on the depicted shift toward the monarchical system.

In sum, this chapter discusses the difficulties and challenges that biblical monarchical politics involve from the start. Two sections structure the discussion. The first section discusses the stories on the rise and fall of the first Israelite king, Saul. The second section investigates the legends of the rise of the second Israelite king, David. A conclusion ponders engaging 1 Samuel at the end of the Western democratic order today.

On the Rise and Fall of the First Israelite Monarch

When the elders of Israel ask Samuel for political change by implementing a king (8:4–5), literary-theological caution for a monarchical political structure constitutes the core of Samuel's response. The key phrase "like other nations" (8:5, 20) suggests that according to the narrative, the tribal system is unique in the ancient Near Eastern world, and the Israelite elders and people hope to become like other nations by installing a king.

---

9. Alice Flanagan, "Techno-Feudalism and the End of Capitalism," April 30, 2021, https://nowthenmagazine.com/articles/yanis-varoufakis-techno-feudalism-and-the-end-of-capitalism.

Martin Noth explains that "Saul's elevation to the monarchy was [caused by] the growing power of the Philistines, who were attempting to gain absolute control over the whole country."[10] Noth believes that (male) Philistine military threats, attacks, and successes made it necessary for the Israelites to centrally organize themselves, and the stories of 1 Samuel 8–15 present legends and memories of this process. Since Saul proves himself successful in battle against the Ammonites (chaps. 11; 15), the Philistines (chaps. 13; 14), and other nations such as the Moabites (14:47–48), he becomes the royal candidate. This explanation about the need for the Israelite monarchical system offers a historical fantasy that justifies the authoritarian system as caused by the ethnic Other. The ethnic Other is, however, an invention of biblical storytelling. At best, therefore, Noth's explanation is moot, telling us more about this Bible scholar's political assumptions than what really happened in the era mentioned in 1 Samuel.

Three Legends About the Establishment of the Monarchy

In 1 Samuel 8–11, three legends depict how the monarchical government is established in biblical Israel. One legend (chap. 8) focuses on the elders of Israel telling Samuel that he is old now and his sons are unacceptable judges, and so they want a king like other nations (8:5). Samuel does not like what he hears. He prays, and God tells him to "listen to the voice of the people" (8:7) and to "listen to their voice and set a king over them" (8:22). God also advises Samuel not to take the request personally because the people do not reject him. They reject God, "as they have done to me from the day I brought them up out of Egypt to this day" (8:8). God advises Samuel to warn the people what it would mean to have a king ruling over them (8:9). Samuel then portrays a bleak picture (8:10–12) in which gender and class stereotypes prevail. The king "will take your sons and appoint them to his chariots and to be his horsemen, and to run before his chariots, and he will appoint for himself commanders of thousands and commanders of fifties" (8:11–12); additionally, the king "will take your daughters to be perfumers and cooks and bakers" (8:13). Samuel also notes that the king "will take your male and female slaves . . . and you shall be his slaves" (8:16, 17). Aggressive

10. Noth, *History of Israel*, 165.

class oppression is assumed after the installation of the monarchical system. Yet the people do not listen to Samuel's warning; they want to "be like other nations" (8:20). Accordingly, the monarchy comes into being because of the people's desire to fit into their geopolitical context. Because other nations have kings, the Israelites also want a king, and so they affirm their desire "that our king may govern us and go out before us and fight our battles" (8:20).

Two other legends focus on the election of the first king (1 Sam 9–10; 11).[11] As a queen is never considered as an option, these stories imagine the future monarch as male. Yet in the first legend (chaps. 9–10), the first king comes from a grim ethnic background. As a Benjaminite, Saul belongs to a tribe whose previous generation of male members gang-raped a *pilegeš* (פילגשׁ) of "a certain Levite" (Judg 19:1). The term *pilegeš* is usually translated as *concubine*, a term connoting Orientalist fantasies about harems and illicit prostitution and extramarital affairs.[12] The other Israelite tribes almost murder all the Benjaminites as punishment (Judg 20). Only six hundred male Benjaminites survive the revenge murder because they are allowed to sex-traffic several hundreds of young women from Jabesh-gilead and Shiloh (Judg 21). Yet the first king is also class privileged; he is the son of "a man of wealth," Kish (Sam 9:1 גבור חיל). Saul meets Samuel when Saul is sent out to capture his father's escaped donkeys (9:3–10). He undertakes the search for the animals with "one of the young men" (9:3), a phrase sometimes translated as "one of the servants" (את־אחד מהנערים) because the male noun נער can also euphemistically refer to a male servant. Another binary gender

11. Robert Alter succinctly summarizes the literary situation when he explains that there is a "triple story of Saul's dedication as king. First there was the clandestine anointment, with no publicly visible consequences. Then there was the tribal assembly at Mizpah in which a reluctant Saul was chosen by lot and proclaimed king. After that event, however, he appears to have returned for the time being to private life. Now, following his signal success in mustering the tribes and defeating Ammon, Samuel calls for a new assembly to reconfirm Saul's standing as king, which will then be seen in subsequent episodes manifested in the institutions and power of a regular court." See Robert Alter, *The Hebrew Bible: A Translation with Commentary, vol. 2: Prophets: Nevi'im* (New York: Norton, 2019), 218.

12. See the essay on "Concubine" (פילגשׁ) in "For Further Reflection" in chap. 2, pp. 122–123.

reference appears that distinguishes the young men from "some young women" (9:11 נערות). They direct the young men toward the town where Samuel stays "before he goes up to the shrine to eat" (9:13). A male and several female servants play a significant role in young Saul not getting lost during his search, symbolizing his path of becoming the first monarch in biblical Israel.

In the story, God informs Samuel to look out for "a man [איש] from the land of Benjamin" (9:16) whom Samuel should anoint as the "ruler (נגיד) over my people Israel" (9:16). Again, though this time put into the divine mouth, the male gender is spelled out. The leader is a man (איש) and not a woman (אשה). The purpose of this newly appointed male ruler is to "save my people from the hand of the [male] Philistines" (9:16). The noun *ruler* (נגיד) is different from the Hebrew noun *king* (מלך). As a generic norm, the noun *ruler* does not indicate monarchical power because a ruler is less permanent than a king, although readers learn in 1 Samuel that even this idea is fallible. As Saul becomes the king, he nevertheless is quickly removed from the throne, even by his own hands, a shocking end for any king and certainly for the first Israelite king.

The legend explains that God sets up the new leader to eliminate "the suffering of my people" (9:16), just like the "judges" are appointed by God to eliminate Israel's suffering from oppression by the Moabites, the Philistines, the Canaanites, the Midianites, or the Ammonites. For instance, in Judges 2:15–16, readers learn that "they [the Israelites] were in great distress. Then [YHWH] raised up judges who delivered them out of the power of those who plundered them" (see also Judg 3:8, 15; 4:3; 6:6–8; 10:10). When Samuel meets Saul, he instructs him "to go up before me to the shrine," eat with him, spend the night there, and not to worry about the donkeys anymore (1 Sam 9:17–21). They eat together (9:22–24), but what the meal exactly consists of is only ambiguously mentioned in verse 24: "the upper thigh and that which is on it" (את־השוק והעליה; my translation). The Hebrew noun for thigh, שוק, refers to the lower or upper leg of people or animals, often the thigh (e.g., Exod 29:27; Deut 28:35; Song 5:15). In Isaiah 47:2–3, Babylon is personified as a raped woman with uncovered legs (שוק) and genitals (*genitals*: ערותך; *shame*: חרפתך). Read in this literary context of vocabulary about genitalia, the detailed reference to the piece of meat in 1 Samuel 9:24 has a sexualized connotation.

A closer look at the description of the dinner leg indicates that the leg has yet another intriguing attribute. The cook gives Samuel a piece of meat "and that which is on it" (והעליה; my translation). This phrase supports the observation that more than a carnivorous meal is at play here. This piece of meat has a sexualized connotation, although to many interpreters, the prepositional phrase makes little sense. They either ignore it or explain why they do not translate it. For instance, Robert Alter states, "The text here seems clearly defective at two different points. The phrase 'lifted up the thigh' is followed by an anomalously ungrammatical form of 'and that which is on it' (*wehe'aleyha*). It seems best to delete this word, as does the Septuagint."[13] Although Alter finds the phrase *and that which is on it* "ungrammatical," he is correct that the phrase is awkward. The piece of thigh meat includes something that is on top of it or attached to it. The text explains that the cook prepared this "special" meal, described only by ambiguous terminology, for the special guest. The expression (והעליה) consists of a conjunction, definite article, and a preposition (*on*, על) with a suffix in the third-person feminine singular (translated as *it*). The suffix refers to the feminine Hebrew noun *thigh*. The piece of thigh meat includes an even higher part above and is connected to it, euphemistically left unspecified. What could be on the thigh? Does the indirect reference perhaps suggest that the piece of meat includes the genitals of the animal as a weird sort of delicacy in preparation for an even weirder situation following the meal in verse 25? In my reading, this second legend of the election of biblical Israel's first king hints at future problems integral to monarchical power: sexual abuse and violence of all sorts.

The story reports that after the meal, the two men visit a shrine and then return to town. Both end up on the rooftop of a house, either talking or making a bed, as the Septuagint suggests. The text states in 1 Samuel 9:25–26, "When they came down from the shrine into the town, a bed was spread for Saul on the roof, and he lay down to sleep. Then at the break of dawn Samuel called to Saul upon the roof . . . and both he and Samuel went out into the street." The strangely ambiguous scene hints at the possibility

13. Alter, *The Hebrew Bible*, 209.

that the seer and the future ruler spend the night in the same house, perhaps together on the rooftop, because they also get up early together in verse 26. The crucial phrase of this verse states in Hebrew, "They arose early" (וישכמו), that the NRSVue translation omits, following the shortened Greek translation. The situation is so murky and suggestive that Johanna W. H. Van Wijk-Bos, finding verses 24–25 "enigmatic," recognizes that any translation is only "an educated guess."[14] She also mentions that other interpreters classify the text as "garbled."[15] In my view, they miss the possibility of a homoerotic encounter between Samuel and Saul. As the encounter remains in the literary shadows of the text, the question is what it would mean if the aging judge had sex with the future king of Israel. I suggest that such an encounter should only be classified as a male-on-male rape scene because Saul is still underage, and the power differential between him and Samuel is enormous.

Yet the story presses on. In the morning, the two men leave town, and Samuel tells Saul to send off the "young man" (נער) because he wants to tell Saul "the word of God" in private (9:27). Eventually, Samuel kisses (נשק) and anoints Saul as the "ruler" (נגיד) over Israel (10:1). The kiss could be fatherly or passionate, and, in regard to my reading of the nightly scene, ought to be seen as reprehensible due to its pedophiliac implication. Few interpreters, if any, however, have considered this exegetical direction. That Saul will be the future king is foremost on their minds, and so, for instance, the renowned medieval midrash Tanchuma stresses, after a consideration of the various possibilities, that the kiss is one of homage.[16]

---

14. Johanna W. H. Van Wijk-Bos, *The Road to Kingship: 1–2 Samuel*, A People and a Land, vol. 2 (Grand Rapids, MI: Eerdmans, 2020), 81.

15. Van Wijk-Bos, *The Road to Kingship*, 81.

16. See Midrash Tanchuma, Shemot 28:2: "Have kissed each other (Ps. 85:11) tells us that he kissed him. Our rabbis teach us that all but three kinds of kisses are frivolous. Those not frivolous are the kiss of parting, the kiss of homage, (and) the kiss of reunion. How do we know about the kiss of parting? From the fact that it is written: And Orpah kissed her mother-in-law (Ruth 1:14); the kiss of homage we know from what is written: Then Samuel took the vial of oil, poured it upon his head, and kissed him (I Sam. 10:1); we know about the kiss of reunion because it is written: And he went, and met him in the mountain of God and kissed him (Exod 2:27)."

A detailed report follows, elaborating on whom Saul will encounter and what he is to do after the departure (10:1–8). His future activity includes prophesying during a meeting with "a band of prophets" (10:5 המה מתנבאים), and so it happens (10:9–16).

I want to mention an interesting grammatical side note on a gender aspect found in 1 Samuel 10:10: "and the spirit of God possessed him" (ותצלח עליו רוח אלהים). At stake is the verb that is often translated as "possessed" (NRSVue) or "take possession of" (REB). The verb goes back to the Hebrew root צלח. In this verse, צלח is in the qal stem and in the third-person feminine singular governed by the feminine singular noun *spirit* (רוח). The scholarly biblical Hebrew-English dictionary by Francis Brown, S. R. Driver, and Charles A. Briggs suggests that the Syriac meaning of this root is "cleave, penetrate, advance" (BDB, 852). This meaning surprises because the translation of "penetrate" has a heterosexual connotation by which the feminine spirit "penetrates" the future male king, enabling him to prophesy (נבא). The connotation of a "penetrating" feminine spirit puts the prophesizing king into the receiving position. The feminine spirit takes him over, perhaps a foreshadowing of his body being pierced with nails near Astarte's temple in Beth-shan (31:10).

When Saul returns home, he keeps his encounter with Samuel to himself, not telling his uncle about "the matter of the kingship" (10:16). To Alter, Saul's "studied reticence confirms the clandestine character of his anointment,"[17] and to Van Wijk-Bos, Saul's "brevity and secrecy add to the mysterious nature of the scene."[18] In my view, Saul is on a search for donkeys, but instead of finding them, he is found by Samuel, who sexually molests or even rapes him during the night, and in the morning Samuel secretly anoints Saul. This creepy story teaches that monarchical power and control come at a high price.

The role of the donkeys has attracted additional attention from Van Wijk-Bos. She thinks the entire scene of Saul searching for his father's donkeys signifies the quest of the people searching for a leader. Proposing a heterosexist reason, Van Wijk-Bos explains that the herd of female donkeys

---

17. Alter, *The Hebrew Bible*, 214.

18. Van Wijk-Bos, *The Road to Kingship*, 84.

is looking for "a male 'jack.'" She writes, "While the jennies look for their jack, Saul and his lad are looking in vain for the animals" but find "a man of God."[19] This heterosexist image of the donkeys looking for a male donkey turns into a homoerotic image in which Saul is the female donkey finding the male "jack," Samuel. While Van Wijk-Bos does not make this analogy explicit, the male-on-male homoerotic, and possibly sexually violent, encounter between Samuel and Saul ends Saul's search for the donkeys (10:14). The search also leads to Saul's secret status as the first king. The public announcement of Saul's royal status, identified by lot (10:21), appears only a few verses later (10:20–26), indicating that the secret nature of Samuel and Saul's meeting lasts only one night. On the next day, Samuel announces that the shy boy (10:22 "See, he has hidden himself among the baggage"), the tall Saul (10:23), is the Israelite king. The story ends with an explicit critique of the monarchy as "some worthless fellows" ask, "How can this one (זה) rescue (ישע) us?" (10:27; my translation). The ambivalence about the monarchical system is thus inherent in this narrative, especially in light of the possibility that it includes a rape scene between the judge and the future king. Whether or not this scene is a later addition, the final verse contributes to the creepiness of this entire development because the rhetorical question of the "worthless" or even "wicked" (בליעל) men is correct. A king does not rescue anybody, but he exploits, uses, and sends to war; a king rules over his people.

Yet another legend (1 Sam 11) depicts Saul's appointment as the king, or, rather, as Stephen B. Chapman notes, "He is styled as something like a local chief, residing in his own fiefdom."[20] In fact, Saul appears to be in close contact with the people even before he is officially made a king in verse 15. He is depicted as "a heroic, divinely authorized warrior after the fashion of the judges,"[21] who defeats the Ammonites under the leadership of King Nahash and then is made king "before YHWH in Gilgal" (11:15). The tale has four stages. The first stage in verses 1–3 describes how King Nahash threatens the people of Jabesh-gilead by gouging out their right eyes,

19. Van Wijk-Bos, *The Road to Kingship*, 76.

20. . Stephen B. Chapman, *1 Samuel as Christian Scripture: A Theological Commentary* (Grand Rapids, MI: Eerdmans, 2016), 115.

21. Chapman, *1 Samuel*, 115.

a strange detail, and how a messenger from the people reports the matter to Saul in Gibeah. According to Alter, this story preserves "some special kinship between them [the people of Jabesh-gilead] and Saul's tribe."[22] Their kinship goes back to their refusal to battle the tribe of Benjamin in Judges 20. The second stage depicts the reaction of Saul and the Israelites (vv. 4–7). The third stage outlines Saul's successful strategy and battle against the Ammonites (vv. 8–13). The fourth stage mentions Saul's appointment as king over Israel in Gilgal (vv. 14–15). In verse 14, the verb "renew" (חדש) refers to the kingdom, but in verse 15, much more happens than mere renewal. The whole people of Gilgal elect Saul as their king because he protects them and fights their battle, actions the people expect from their king (8:20). Apparently, they do not have to pay a price for this kind of leadership, in contrast to Samuel's warnings in the first legend (8:11–12).

The three stories about Saul becoming the first Israelite king offer three different, though not necessarily contrasting, traditions on what it means to be ruled by a king. The first legend in 1 Samuel 8 paints a dire picture of the monarchy. The decision for this governmental form is put squarely on the people's back, although monarchs have claimed divine authority and justification for the ages. The second legend in 1 Samuel 9–10 shows a young boy unable to find the lost donkeys and then ending up in a questionable overnight situation with the man who is going to anoint him as the first king. The third legend in 1 Samuel 11 depicts Saul as a mature warrior and leader of the people over whom he will rule and who will make him king.

Stories on Saul's Fall from Power

After three legends on the rise of the first Israelite monarch, three stories report Saul's fall from power: Two tales (1 Sam 13; 15) depict Saul's divine rejection, and a third legend (1 Sam 31) describes his suicide. Again, these stories about Saul's ongoing and ultimate failure as the first Israelite king indicate to this feminist reader that a monarchical system is fraught with problems. Authoritarian, monocratic, or even monarchical, not to mention feudal, systems must be rejected, especially if the king is getting increasingly more disturbed, as in the case of Saul, but also when successful royal leaders

22. Alter, *The Hebrew Bible*, 216.

are in power. Any centralized system of power is undesirable even when the people ask for this kind of system. Inherent suspicion and critique of such a system ought to be the first order of business.

The first rejection story centers on a battle (chap. 13) in which Saul and his son, Jonathan, defeat the Philistine warriors. Jonathan defeats the Philistines at Geba (13:3), and Saul claims his son's success as his own (13:3–4). Yet when the Israelites appear to be losing yet another battle against the Philistine soldiers and hide in caves, holes, tombs, and cisterns (13:6), Saul is in Gilgal waiting for Samuel's arrival and support of the ongoing battle against the Philistine fighters at Michmash (13:5). The Israelite men become so afraid when they see the enormous number of Philistine troops that they run away (13:6–7). After seven days, however, Samuel still has not arrived. As Saul offers several sacrifices, among them one burnt offering and offerings of well-being (13:9), Samuel appears. He reprimands the king, "What have you done?" (13:11). Accusing Saul of having "done foolishly" (13:13), Samuel tells Saul that his lack of keeping God's commandments means that his kingdom will not last forever. Since Saul did not wait for Samuel's arrival, offering a burnt offering without him (13:9), Samuel informs Saul that God has already found "a man after God's own heart" to rule over God's people (13:14). After the devasting reprimand, Samuel leaves Gilgal while Saul, Jonathan, and the army of six hundred Israelite men prepare their battle equipment. Since they do not have any smith to sharpen their weapons, they go down to the Philistines for assistance (13:22). What a strange piece of information! The opponents of the Israelite warriors help sharpen their weapons. The ensuing battle is complicated and led by Jonathan with a trick.[23] Jonathan wins with the help of Saul and other Israelites "who previously had been with the Philistines" (14:21). In 14:23, readers learn that "YHWH gave Israel the victory that day," although Samuel earlier mentioned that God has rejected this king (13:14).

The story further elaborates on Saul's desperation to stand in God's good graces. For instance, Saul forbids his soldiers to eat honey for unknown reasons, but Jonathan eats some honey (14:24–35). As Saul prays to God

23. For details on how Jonathan tricks the Philistines, see chap. 2 of this book on pp. 104–107.

in the presence of a priest (14:36–37) for advice on his next battle against the Philistines, God does not answer. When Saul reaches out to God again (14:41), he eventually recognizes that Jonathan disobeyed his command. Thereupon Saul threatens his son with death (14:44), but the people defend the son and oppose the king, saying, "Shall Jonathan die, who has accomplished this great victory in Israel? Far from it! As YHWH lives, not one hair of his head shall fall to the ground, for he has worked with God today" (14:45). This fragmentary tale foreshadows the ongoing troubles not only between father and son (e.g., 20:30) but also for Jonathan. Ultimately, he is killed in the battle against the Philistine soldiers at Mount Gilboa, during which his father commits suicide (see 31:2, 4, 8–13). In 1 Samuel 14, the Israelite men defend Jonathan, and, importantly, Saul does not retort. Instead, he even withdraws from any further battle, as verse 46 states: "Then Saul withdrew from pursuing the Philistines, and the Philistines went to their own place." Hopelessness in his ability to do right by God surrounds this biblical character said to have been rejected by God.

Next, a brief report (14:47–51) depicts the king's increasing desperation. The fragment summarizes Saul's successful battles "against Moab, against the Ammonites, against Edom, against the kings of Zobah, and against the Philistines" (14:47). He also "struck down the Amalekites and rescued Israel out of the hands of those who plundered them" (14:48). The verses indicate that Saul fulfills the desire of his people, protecting them and battling against their enemies. The passage notes that Saul has three sons, Jonathan, Ishvi, and Malchishua; two daughters, Merab and Michal; a wife, Ahinoam; and Abner, his cousin (or uncle?) and commander (14:49–51). The feminist takeaway of this short piece of information is that even a failing king like Saul continues battling his enemies while he is the head of a large family. The chances for a peaceful family life are, however, slim for any king and especially for Saul, who is so busy scheming to kill competitors like David and fighting Philistine warriors. In my view, we need to picture the royal children and his wife struggling to get his attention because the king is trying so hard to stay in power and gain back God's favor.

A second full-blown rejection story of Saul appears in 1 Samuel 15. Disconnected from the previous chapter, the tale presents Samuel as again talking to Saul. Samuel stresses that God sent him to anoint Saul to the monarchy (15:1). Samuel reports that God orders Saul to go and "utterly destroy" (חרם hiphil) the people of Amalek, to kill "both man and woman, child and infant, ox and sheep, camel and donkey" (v. 3). Meanwhile God speaks in the "ferocious imperative" of a prophet.[24] Yet the verse disturbs because it presents God as commanding the murder of innocent people. The only way out of this theological dilemma requires emphasizing that Samuel puts these words into God's mouth. Like any authoritarian, war-mongering politician, Samuel seeks to justify murder, war, and bloodshed with reference to a higher authority. Reading this verse as Samuel's speech and not as divine words is the only hermeneutical maneuver to avoid a theological crisis moment.

That in 1 Samuel 15:3 women are mentioned next to men, children, and animals leads commentator David Jobling to make an important statement. He explains that in all these wars, imagined and executed by men, women are always the ones dying (see also 22:19; 27:9, 11). They are the pawns of male transaction and male imagination. Women are also married against their will (e.g., 17:25), are made childless (15:33), are turned into "property" of the male victors in war (e.g., Judg 5:30), or are killed in war (15:3; 22:19; 27:9, 11).[25] The gruesome command given by Samuel and classified as the words of God prompts Saul to gather 200,000 soldiers (15:4) and tell the Kenites to leave the Amalekites (15:6). In the ensuing battle, Saul captures the Amalekite king, Agag, and he and his soldiers kill all the other Amalekites (15:9). Saul and the people, however, spare "the best of the sheep and of the cattle and of the fatted calves, and the lambs, and all that was valuable" (15:9). They keep the spoils of war and also spare King Agag. Jobling is thus appalled about this passage that presents women as well as men, children, and animals as divinely instructed victims of war.

The theo-ethical unacceptability of this passage goes even further. The keeping of the spoils, but not the killing of all these people, leads to Saul's explicit divine rejection: "The word of [YHWH] came to Samuel: 'I regret that I made Saul king, for he has turned back from following me and has not carried out my commands'" (15:10–11). According to Samuel's vision,

---

24. Alter, *The Hebrew Bible*, 234.

25. See David Jobling, *1 Samuel*, Berit Olam (Collegeville, MN: Liturgical Press, 1998), 179.

God determines that Saul did wrong by keeping the material goods for himself. The verb "I regret" (נחמתי) appears several times in the Hebrew Bible, most profoundly in Genesis 6:7, where it expresses God's extreme sorrow over having made human beings, and then the flood comes. Impressively, then, Samuel's regret echoes God's earlier dramatic regret that leads to the narrated destruction of the earth and its inhabitants. That Samuel is angry and cries out to God all night long (15:11) indicates that in the biblical imagination the regret is mostly Samuel's. Alter, however, believes Samuel's cry is "wonderfully unspecified, or perhaps overdetermined" because Samuel is "incensed" with everybody: with Saul, with the people who force Samuel to approve of "this whole distasteful monarchic business," and with God for asking Samuel to listen to the Israelites.[26] The problem with God commanding the murder of every human and animal remains, however, unresolved in this reading. Perhaps the command must squarely be placed into Samuel's mouth to escape the theodicy question.

The biblical tale continues with a detailed interaction between Saul and Samuel in which Samuel articulates what he believes is the divine verdict. On the next day, Saul submissively greets Samuel, telling him, "I have carried out the command of YHWH" (15:13). Yet in Samuel's view, the opposite occurred. Instead of killing all the Amalekites and all the animals, Saul disobeyed the divine command (15:17–19). When Saul attempts to defend his actions (15:19–21), Samuel refuses to listen. He condemns the king as a rebellious and stubborn sinner whom God rejects absolutely (15:22–23). Saul tries again to defend himself by accepting his wrongdoings (15:24–25), yet Samuel accuses him of having rejected God (15:26). As Samuel leaves, the desperate king grabs his robe, tearing off a piece (15:27), another symbolic move indicating the end of Saul's reign. Readers know Saul cannot win his disagreement over the divine decision.

The drama is complete when Samuel exclaims that Saul has lost the kingdom on this day and that God will not change God's mind on the matter (15:28–29). Saul acknowledges his guilt a second time (15:30), yet Samuel "abandons" Saul; he does not "return to" Saul, as Alter suggests.[27]

---

26. Alter, *The Hebrew Bible*, 235–236.
27. Alter, *The Hebrew Bible*, 238.

Samuel "turns back from" Saul, and so the king prays alone to God (15:31; my translation). At that moment, instead of killing Saul, Samuel "ritually butchers"[28] the Amalekite king, Agag, by cutting him into pieces near or on the altar of God in Gilgal (15:33). After abandoning Saul, Samuel butchers the Amalekite king. Is his extreme violence an indirect expression of his violent feelings about Saul, and so Agag receives the sword as the scapegoat for Samuel's disappointment about Saul's future? The gruesome act is part of the general murderous and ethno-royal violence permeating this rejection story. The Israelite king survives the rejection at first, but his separation from Samuel is complete by the legend's end (15:34–35). God's regret (נחם) for having made Saul king seals the rejection (15:35). Importantly, the reported regret is not over having established the monarchy but over having selected this particular king.

This biblical passage, especially 1 Samuel 15:3, in which Samuel calls Saul to genocidal murder of the Amalekites ("Now go and attack Amalek, and utterly destroy all that they have; do not spare them, but kill both man and woman, child and infant, ox and sheep, camel and donkey"), has gained renewed international attention after the Israeli prime minister Benjamin Netanyahu compared the biblical Amalekites to Hamas. Quoting from Deuteronomy 25:17, Netanyahu told Israelis in a televised statement on October 28, 2023: "Citizens of Israel, yesterday evening, additional ground forces of ours entered the gates of Gaza, at the doorstep of the fortress of evil. This is the second stage of the war, the goals of which are clear: Destroying Hamas's military and governing capabilities, and bringing the captives back home. . . . 'Remember what Amalek did to you' (Deuteronomy 25:17). We remember and we fight."[29] International reactions to this biblical reference were immediate and numerous. A professor of religion and philosophy, Motti Inbari, explained that the Israeli prime minister's quote from the Bible is disconcerting because Israel is a secular state and any "language of holy wars" means the state is "fighting in the name of God" and "when you are fighting in the name of God, it is a total war until a total victory of the God

28. Alter, *The Hebrew Bible*, 239.

29. For a transcript of Netanyahu's speech, see the Israeli Ministry of Foreign Affairs, "Statement by PM Netanyahu," October 28, 2023, https://www.gov.il/en/pages/statement-by-pm-netanyahu-28-oct-2023.

of Israel over the God of the enemy, even though it's the same God in that context."[30] Another Jewish Studies professor, Joshua Shanes, also mentioned that during most of Jewish history references to Amalek have been interpreted "metaphorically . . . as a call to stamp out evil inclinations within ourselves."[31] The literalism in Netanyahu's identification of Hamas with Amalek thus modifies the moral wrestling with the difficult call to kill all Amalekites in 1 Samuel 15, as well as in Deuteronomy 25:17–19 and Exodus 17:14, as if to justify military Israeli power and destruction in Gaza today. Some organizations even accused Netanyahu of "genocidal intentions" due to the biblical quote, as other Israeli politicians also stated that "there are no innocent civilians in Gaza."[32] The call to genocidal murder of the Amalekites in 1 Samuel 15:3 (and also later in 1 Samuel 27:8–9) has thus gained unexpected contemporary prominence. Many non-Jewish orthodox interpreters did not even know about the long-standing references to Amalek within the Jewish right. The genocidal war in Gaza since October 2023 has made these references suddenly highly scandalous and widely known.

The last moment in the life of the first Israelite king arrives when Saul commits suicide in 1 Samuel 31, the final tale about Saul's fall from power and divine grace. The suicide communicates his ultimate demise. Rejected by God, Saul kills himself in battle against the Philistines after his three sons are already dead and he lies wounded on the ground (31:1–4). Reducing the Philistine warriors to their male genitals, as Saul refers to them as "these

30. "Netanyahu's References to Violent Biblical Passages Raise Alarm Among Critics," *npr*, November 7, 2023, https://www.npr.org/2023/11/07/1211133201/netanyahus-references-to-violent-biblical-passages-raise-alarm-among-critics.

31. Noah Lanard, "The Dangerous History Behind Netanyahu's Amalek Rhetoric," *Mother Jones*, November 3, 2023, https://www.motherjones.com/politics/2023/11/benjamin-netanyahu-amalek-israel-palestine-gaza-saul-samuel-old-testament/.

32. Brett Wilkins, "Netanyahu Accused of 'Genocidal Intentions' in Gaza After 'Holy Mission' Speech," *Common Dreams*, October 30, 2023,: https://www.commondreams.org/news/netanyahu-genocide. Such a comparison is not entirely new, as earlier generations of rabbis called even Yasser Arafat "the Amalek and Hitler of our generation," see Elliott Horowitz, *Reckless Rites: Purim and the Legacy of Jewish Violence* (Princeton: Princeton University Press, 2018), 3.

uncircumcised" (הערלים האלה v. 4; see also 14:6; 17:4, 36; 2 Sam 1:20),[33] the Israelite king chooses to die by his own hands. He fears what the Philistine warriors would do to him if they found him. The vocabulary is ambiguous, connoting Saul's fears of being pierced (דקר) and sexually violated or gang-raped like the *pilegeš* in Judges 19:25 (התעלל). Saul prefers to die rather than being gang-raped and throws himself onto his sword. His arms-bearer does the same after refusing to kill his master (31:5). When the Philistine men find the dead men the next day (31:8), they mutilate the king's body (31:9) and bring his armor to the temple of Astarte, a Canaanite goddess.

The reference to the goddess Astarte and her temple offers an interesting gender aspect to the king's suicide. The female goddess, absorbing the king's body and his armor, seems more powerful than the Israelite god. Johanna H. Stuckey characterizes Astarte as "Baal's other self" when she elaborates on the significance of Astarte in the ancient Near Eastern world, stating:

> Another equally important goddess from the ancient Levant was Astarte. Her name was written as Athtart, *'ttrt*, and appears forty-six times in Ugaritic texts, but relatively rarely in the mythic material. These texts hold the goddess up as a model of beauty and usually associate her closely with Baal, often designating her "Name-of-Baal" or . . . "Baal's Other Self." When she speaks, it is to support Baal. At least five times the mythic texts pair her with Anat, perhaps an indication that the two goddesses were already beginning to meld into one another. Nevertheless, her name occurs quite often in the cultic material, which makes clear that she had an important, if not central place in ritual and sacrifice. To date, no scholar has identified any of the many female images from Ugarit as undoubtedly representing Astarte. Though a deity of note at Ugarit in the Bronze Age, Astarte was to become a much more significant goddess in the ancient Levant of later periods.[34]

---

33. See also the discussion on the references to male Philistines as "foreskins" as part of the ethnonational discourse of 1 Samuel in chap. 4, pp. 165–170.

34. Johanna H. Stuckey, "The Great Goddesses of the Levant," *Journal of the Society for the Study of Egyptian Antiquities* 30 (2003): 131.

This goddess is popular in ancient Near Eastern traditions, appearing many times in Ugaritic texts that are often read to decipher ancient historical realities and viewpoints beyond information gleaned from the biblical literature.

Moreover, the mention of the king's armor in a Philistine temple horrifies even contemporary readers who may still sympathize with Saul. Rejected by God, the first king of Israel has lost all power, signified by his armor in front of the famous goddess. Saul's body hangs with the "other" gods after the Philistines attach his and his sons' bodies to the wall of Beth-shan (31:10). According to this horrid tale, the men of Jabesh-gilead hear of the desecration and decide to take the bodies down from the wall during the night (31:12). They later bury the bones in Jabesh (31:13). When the male monarch and his male descendants are dead, the first effort of establishing the Israelite monarchy is over.

Yet, surprisingly, in 2 Samuel 1:14, the first king remains "[YHWH's] anointed" in the eyes of David, even after Saul's gruesome demise. The various legends and traditions conflate, diverge, and leave ambiguous how to evaluate the first Israelite king. The monarchical system itself, however, remains intact. Predictably, this king and most future monarchs are male, with a few exceptional queens who do not fare well (e.g., Jezebel in 1 Kgs 16:31; 18:19–19:3; 21:5–6; 2 Kgs 9:30–37; Athaliah in 2 Kgs 11:1–3). The dispute in these legends is only over who is a bad or a good king. Unfortunately, a people-centered or even democratic political system remains outside the scope of this biblical book.

On the Rise of the Second Monarch

Interwoven with the legends on the rise and fall of the first king are stories about the rise of the second king, who is the most famous and beloved king in Judaism and Christianity. The tales of David's monarchy continue in 2 Samuel, and thus 1 and 2 Samuel are classified as one book in the early canonical tradition. Again, all of the legends assume the continuation of the monarchical system, with the next leader not being a queen but again a king. The stories describe how David is anointed as a king (1 Sam 16:13; 2 Sam 2:4; 5:4–5). They focus on the power struggles between him and Saul, who tries to kill David three times (1 Sam 18:10–11, 20–25; 19:10); David spares Saul's life twice (24:1–7; 26). Legends about David's monarchical rule appear only in 2 Samuel, outside the purview of this interpretation. In 1 Samuel, double and even triple stories recount the difficult, painful, and violent process of David's rise to power after the first king rules as a divinely rejected king. The book ends with the death of Saul, paving the way for David to become the next king in 2 Samuel.

Legends About the Anointment of the Second King

Unlike the decision to set up a monarchical order told in the legends about Saul's rise as the first king, stories about David's rise put the candidate's choice squarely on God's metaphorical shoulders. God reminds the still-grieving Samuel that the rejection of Saul is complete and that God already has another man in mind (literally, "sees," ראה) as the next king (16:2). Under the pretense of a "sacrifice to [YHWH]" (16:2), God instructs Samuel to go to Jesse in Bethlehem and await further directions there (16:2–-3). The elders of the city tremble in fear or even terror (חרד) when they meet Samuel, as they probably know of the estrangement between him and the current king. The religious ritual serves as a pretext (16:5) for Samuel to calm the people and to invite Jesse and his sons. Instead of relying on a lot, as in Saul's election (11:20–24), and entirely foregoing the promised sacrifice, Samuel has Jesse's sons parade one by one in front of him (16:6–10). The scene is male homocentric, as no mother or daughters are mentioned. God instructs Samuel to not look at the appearance or height of the boys to determine which boy is the anointed one (16:7). Randall C. Bailey identifies a "cover up translation" in 16:11, which literally means "Have the young boys finished?"[35] Bailey notes that most English interpreters translate the question as "Are all your sons here?" In his view, most scholars "obfuscate" the sexual connotation of the scene. In his reading of this moment, Samuel is disappointed because he cannot accomplish his mission because "the parade [of the boys] has ended."[36]

35. Randall C. Bailey, "Reading Backwards: A Narrative Technique for the Queering of David, Saul, and Samuel," in *The Fate of King David: The Past and Present of a Biblical Icon*, ed. Tod Linafelt, Claudia V. Camp, and Timothy Beal, LHBOTS 500 (New York: T&T Clark, 2010), 78.

36. Bailey, "Reading Backwards," 78.

The homoerotic connotation becomes even more dramatic. When Samuel sees David, who is the youngest son, he is described as red-haired or "ruddy" (אדמוני) with beautiful eyes and all-around handsome (16:12). Despite God's earlier caution to look at people's interior only, even God "jumps in and says: 'That's him!'"[37] similar to Samuel seeing Saul in 9:17. Bailey chastises God's superficial attitude in David's case because, "given the unethical behavior of David in subsequent chapters, it must be the physical to which YHWH responds and not the interior."[38] Read from a feminist perspective, the legend depicts God as homoerotically interested in David, similar perhaps to Samuel being interested in Saul during the murky pre-anointment scene in 9:25–27. Like Saul, David experiences "the spirit of [YHWH]" as "rushing into" (תצלח) or, according to the Syriac, even "penetrating" the newly anointed king.[39] The Syriac translation suggests an explicitly homoerotic meaning of the male God's involvement in David's process of becoming the second king. David's monarchy receives divine approval, as God is highly interested in this divinely and "clandestine[ly]"[40] appointed king. The scene illustrates what Ken Stone calls the persistent "warrior eroticism" in the books of Samuel.[41]

As God is attracted to David, Saul is also drawn to David, as depicted in one of the two legends (16:14–23; 17:12–15, 57–58) that report David encountering King Saul. In 16:14–23, the depressed king is attracted to (מצא חן) young David and his lyre music (vv. 21, 22), so much so that he makes the young man his arms-bearer (v. 21). The story presents an intimate portrayal of the two men, in sharp contrast to later stories in which Saul attempts to kill David (18:10–11, 20–25; 19:10). In this first legend about Saul meeting David, the king falls in love with the handsome man (16:21,

37. Bailey, "Reading Backwards," 78.

38. Bailey, "Reading Backwards," 78.

39. See Francis Brown with the cooperation of S. R. Driver and Charles A. Briggs, eds., *The New Brown, Driver, and Briggs Hebrew and English Lexicon of the Old Testament* (6743 צלח) (Grand Rapids, MI: Baker, 1907 and 1981), 852.

40. See Alter, *The Hebrew Bible*, 241.

41. Ken Stone, "1 and 2 Samuel," in *The Queer Bible Commentary*, ed. Deryn Guest, Robert E. Goss, Mona West, and Thomas Bohache (London: SCM Press, 2006), 207.

22), as his son Jonathan will later (18:1, 3; 19:1; 20:17) and everybody else, too, including the Israelite people (18:16) and Michal (18:20). The complex relationship of the two men also shines through other scenes. For instance, David's lyre-playing can be read as involving more than just music-making. Bailey suggests that David's hand is perhaps not always on the lyre, as the later passage about David's music-making communicates, because 18:10 does not mention the musical instrument. The verse only states that "David was strumming with his hand" and "the spear was in Saul's hand," and later Saul even "fell naked into a prophetic frenzy" (19:23).[42] The masturbatory scene rudely ends in verse 11 when Saul "strikes" with his spear at David and at the wall. The verb נכה, which I translate as "strike" in 18:11, also appears in the women's song in 18:7. There, too, David "strikes" (נכה) more Philistine warriors than Saul (18:7), a comparison angering Saul (18:8). In this scene, a jealously angry Saul "strikes" David with his euphemistic spear (i.e., his penis) in retaliation for David "striking" more Philistine men than he did. Saul's striking of David hints at his violent desire, growing jealousy, and murderous hatred for the man he recognizes as his successor. The emotional entanglement between the two men turns murderous after 16:23, whether or not we notice a homoerotic quality in David's calming music-making.

Stories About David's Power Struggle

The stories about David's rise to power offer convoluted and entangled routes on his path to royal power. Among the tales are David's successful escape from Saul's three murder attempts (18:10–11, 20–25; 19:10), his battles against the Philistines (23:1–14), and his two refusals to kill King Saul (24:1–7; 26). Other narratives depict David's escapes to various wilderness areas (23:15–29; 25:1) and his hiding in Philistine lands (27:1–28:2; 29; 30). The stories present David's struggles to fight his way into the graces of the Philistine king, Achish of Gath (chap. 27), and his one-on-one efforts to survive the murderous Saul (24:1–7; 26). Saul's and David's numerous monologues and dialogues (e.g., 18:21; 24:8–22) offer several pornographic, or at least sexualized, moments. For instance, Saul asks David to fight against the Philistines and bring back "a hundred foreskins of the Philistines" (18:25)

42. Bailey, "Reading Backwards," 81.

to marry his daughter, Michal. Meanwhile, Saul commands a servant (literally "slave" עבד) to tell David that "the king is delighted with you" (18:22), a phrase connoting sexual desire.[43] The text also states that "the thing" (18:22 הדבר)—collecting foreskins as a marriage gift—pleases David (18:26). Bailey wonders if "Saul knew that David was 'into' foreskins" and that "David got so excited with the activity of amassing foreskins that he couldn't stop" noticing or counting them.[44] Does David know that Saul also likes foreskins? As Stone suggests, the repeated identification of Philistine warriors by their uncircumcised penises signifies that the king understands male Philistines to be "improper examples of manhood."[45] They are like women, and so Saul offers to marry his daughter Michal to any Israelite warrior who would bring him one hundred Philistine foreskins. The verse points both at the exchangeability of women for foreskins[46] and at the implied homoeroticism among men.

Another salacious scene between David and Saul appears in the first story about David sparing Saul's life. When Saul learns that David is hiding from him in En-gedi (24:1), he marches with three thousand soldiers to find him. Going into a cave, "Saul went to relieve himself" (24:3) while David and his men hide in that same cave. The Hebrew expression is more explicit than the English translation because the Hebrew uses the idiom "Saul came to cover his feet" (ויבא שׁאול להסך את־רגליו). The Hebrew noun for *feet* is a euphemism for the male genitals (see Ruth 3:7), and the phrase "cover his feet" can also refer to urine (2 Kgs 18:27). In Judges 3:24, "covering his feet" refers to what the servants think King Eglon is doing in the "cool roof chamber,"[47] a location sometimes interpreted as a bathroom. There Ehud,

---

43. This is the convincing exegetical observation of Bailey, "Reading Backwards," 76, based on Esth 2:14, where the verb חפץ refers to the king bringing back women whom he "sexually desires."

44. Bailey, "Reading Backwards," 75.

45. Stone, "1 and 2 Samuel," 204.

46. Other biblical references illustrating this dynamic are Judg 9:54; 14:3; 15:18; see also Jobling, 1 Samuel, 216.

47. See Deryn Guest, "Judges," in *The Queer Bible Commentary*, ed. Deryn Guest, Robert E. Goss, Mona West, and Thomas Bohache (London: SCM Press, 2006), 173.

the judge, murders Eglon, which queer interpreters read as a sexually violent penetration or murderous rape.[48] Similar to Eglon's servants believing their king is urinating, King Saul does whatever he does in the cave, perhaps euphemistically urinating. Saul is doubly vulnerable there because he is alone and exposed, just like Lot living in the cave with his two daughters (see Gen 19:30: "Now Lot went up out of Zoar and settled in the hills with his two daughters, for he was afraid to stay in Zoar, so he lived in a cave with his two daughters"). Whatever Saul does in the cave, David and his men look on. Somehow David manages to cut off a corner from Saul's cloak (24:5) without Saul noticing. Van Wijk-Bos suggests Saul is asleep, like Boaz on the threshing floor in Ruth 3, when the titular heroine uncovers his "feet."[49]

At this moment David could have easily killed Saul but refrains because, in his opinion, Saul is still divinely anointed (24:6). The scene leads to a dramatic dialogue in which Saul recognizes David's moral and political superiority (24:8–22). As Alter observes, Saul is forced to admit the truth of Samuel's earlier words: "[God] has torn (קרע) the kingdom of Israel from you this very day and has given it to a neighbor of yours who is better than you" (15:28). Saul himself tears off a piece of Samuel's cloak (15:27 ויחזק בכנף־מעילו ויקרע). The action symbolizes his failing kingdom, whereas David's cutting off a piece of Saul's cloak suggests his growing power. Still, Saul remains king until he takes his own life in his losing battle against the Philistines. At this point in the narrative, David is already anointed in 16:13 and later twice more in 2 Samuel 2:4 and 5:4–5. Although David runs for his life in 1 Samuel, he is always successful and beloved by everybody, including initially by his fiercest enemy, Saul.

In sum, the beginning of the Israelite monarchy is told in individualized, homoerotic, and violent stories that recount a competitive battle between two male leaders. The stories emphasize the psychological dimensions, and so readers identify with both the rejected king and the beloved king. Yet readers are rarely asked to question the merits of the monarchical order, and so they remain fixated on the two men acting dubiously, violently, and destructively.

---

48. Guest, "Judges," 173.

49. Van Wijk-Bos, *The Road to Kingship*, 24.

Learning to Organize for Democratic Change: Concluding Comments

The stories and legends about the emergence of the monarchy in biblical Israel focus on the rise and fall of the first king, Saul, and the rise of the second king, David. The tales include both antimonarchic and promonarchic positions, as scholars have long observed.[50] The hypothesis of two or even more Deuteronomistic editions accounts for the divergent views included in 1 Samuel's thirty-one chapters. On the one hand, Samuel and God seem "hell-bound to sabotage the regime change"[51] from the system of the judges to the monarchy (see, e.g., 8:7–8; 10:18–19; 12:12, 17, 19–20; 13; 15). On the other hand, God seems to approve the people's request for a king (see, e.g., 8:9, 27; 9:15–17; 10:27; 12:14, 21–25). A conflicted position about the establishment of an Israelite monarchical system prevails in 1 Samuel, although the promonarchic position wins.

The depicted position of God in regard to the monarchy is complex. According to Serge Frolov, God changes their mind because the people want a king. Frolov states, "What is truly remarkable in Samuel 8–12 is not the apparent shift in the deity's political philosophy but rather the outcome of this shift. . . . Despite feeling undeservedly rejected yet again by the people, Yhwh unambiguously orders Samuel, not once but twice (8:9, 22), to grant their request for a king."[52] Thus, in the end, "the Torah trumps divine whims: if it says that Israel should have a king as soon as it feels the urge, that cannot be changed even if Yhwh has second thoughts."[53] Even God concurs with the monarchical system because of the people's request. The same is true for most interpreters throughout the ages. The morale of this biblical book seems to be that if even God cannot reject, and even endorses, the establishment of an Israelite monarchy, readers cannot question the merits of the monarchical system either.

---

50. See, e.g., the overview discussion in Serge Frolov, "Synchronic Readings of Joshua–Kings," in *The Oxford Handbook of the Historical Books of the Hebrew Bible*, ed. Brad E. Kelle and Brent A. Strawn (Oxford: Oxford University Press, 2020), 347–50.

51. Frolov, "Synchronic Readings," 348.

52. Frolov, "Synchronic Readings," 349.

53. Frolov, "Synchronic Readings," 350.

As this chapter maintains, the biblical depiction of Israel's first and second monarchs is not pretty. Although some of the legends share similarities in the anointment stories of the two kings and in double or even triple accounts of their competitive battles, the narratives always focus on the two male characters in an increasingly myopic fashion. Even interpreters sympathize with this or that psychological, emotional, or theological depiction. In contrast, my feminist interpretation emphasizes the sexualized and homoerotic references to the two kings, and so the interpretation exposes the individualized, sexualized, and bloody kyriarchal power struggles that many readings conceal about the early Israelite monarchy.

Most importantly, my interpretation emphasizes that 1 Samuel does not offer a blueprint for the political organization of contemporary society. Since the Bible has often been read as if it offered such a blueprint, these kinds of readings have contributed to much pain and suffering in the world. Furthermore, the reading of 1 Samuel as a prescription for monarchical systems of power also explains the existence of some monarchies across the world even today despite their largely ceremonial function and much reduced political power. Still, monarchical attitudes permeate many societies, cultures, and religions, not to mention biblical metaphors about God as king and lord. As 1 Samuel has been read to justify, endorse, or even prescribe authoritarian and nondemocratic political systems, this biblical book's interpretation history explains the lack of resistance to or rejection of monarchies. Probably non-Jewish and non-Christian monarchical traditions around the world, such as the Egyptian pharaohs or the Japanese emperors, have further reinforced a general acceptance of monarchical systems, including in 1 Samuel. While some biblical readings have also advanced civil rights and the move toward less dictatorial political infrastructures, the dangers of monarchical structures, endorsed by the Bible, persist.

A feminist commentary of 1 Samuel must thus warn against naive, literalist, or historical-theological readings that do not critically interrogate the depicted emergence of the Israelite monarchy. My interpretation stresses the problematic, contradictory, and nondemocratic dimensions of 1 Samuel. As a feminist reader, I challenge the proposition that God would sanction a monarchical system, especially given the convoluted ways in which 1 Samuel presents the initial stages of this system. Crucially, I emphasize that the tales of 1 Samuel are just that: stories told as duplicates and filled with contradictions. They focus only very marginally on the political, economic, or even theological damage inflicted on people ruled by monarchical systems of government.

In sum, my reading suggests that any interpretation, and especially a feminist one, ought to highlight that 1 Samuel presents exclusively male Israelite leaders, their thoughts, and their manifold battles with each other and with ethnonationally otherized male enemies. Accordingly, my reading—like most others—considers 1 Samuel as theopolitically tendentious literature. This biblical book illustrates political, economic, cultural, and religious assumptions, biases, and interests that are hardcore androcentric, heterosexist, ethnoreligious-centric, and kyriarchal-monarchic-centric. In my view, 1 Samuel serves as a training ground to study antidemocratic ideas prevalent even in today's world. This is the ongoing merit of reading this biblical book with a feminist hermeneutics: Readers can learn from it to recognize and expose the specter of the biblical monarchy so that they will never want to live in such an order and hopefully organize for change toward a democratic order today.

For Further Reflection

1. Marc H. Ellis, "On Samuel, God, and the Other Nations." Used by permission of the author.

   So, like all the Other Nations it was. Would be. Still is. With caveats. And a new urgency today. I read Samuel—we read Samuel—after the Holocaust and after Israel, the state, and what it has done and is doing to the Palestinian people.

   Ancient Israel wants an earthly king rather than God's rule. And gets one. With all the fixings, as Samuel warned—chariots and soldiers and taxation—thus, a certain kind of state. The whole nine yards.

   Question: Is Israel up to this different kingship? Is God?

   Samuel hesitates on earthly kingship; he knows what will transpire. As troubling is God's permission. Why does God instruct Samuel to give Israel what it wants?

   "Warn them of what will come if I'm replaced," God counsels Samuel. Samuel does as commanded. Israel still wants the deal, protection and national empowerment to end corruption and subservience. Or, perhaps, better put, a change of subservience, an earthly power over God's power.

God is so upset with Israel that God relents, almost with gusto: "Give them what they want; I know their rebellion well!"

So what kind of God is this? Has Israel's liberating God given up on Israel too early and too easily?

As if God can do without Israel.

Becoming like the Other Nations is God's big threat. Reading the text, I wonder: Is Israel as an Other Nation the Other Side of the Promised Land? Either way, God's promissory notes are heavy burdens. For there's nothing more decisive to Israel than God saying—and Israel agreeing—to be like everyone else. God forbid!

For, in truth, in Israel's long history, up to this very moment, there has never been a Jewishness that sits well with being like the Other Nations—even and especially when Israel acts as if it is.

In Israel's dialogue with God, just the anticipation of Other Nationhood is forbidding. For a good reason. It is impossible for Israel to become an Other Nation and still be Israel.

As long as Israel acts like the Other Nations, the threat remains: the loss of God's concern and guidance; Israel without direction or purpose. But, (un)raised here, is a pressing question: Who is God without Israel? Does God have a direction and purpose without Israel?

In the Bible, God and Israel are working partners, in the best of times. In the worst of times, they are codependent. Israel should take God's threats seriously but in Samuel and beyond Israel is bold. In different ways Israel holds God hostage: Who are You without Us?

Over time, the prophets arrive as mediators between God and Israel. Or perhaps, the prophets are God's and Israel's (continuing) last-ditch effort to keep their battered relationship from that ultimate divorce that render both rudderless.

The Jewish prophetic after the Holocaust and after Israel—in the face of Israel's permanent occupation of Palestine—may be another part of the discussion Samuel had with God and Israel. That discussion is being recorded right now, no doubt to be studied and thought through in another time.

2. Silvia Schroer, "About the Religious History of Astarte(s)." Used by permission of the author.

In general, biblical references depict goddesses negatively, often immersed with a polemical attitude. As the biblical authors and redactors sought to purge YHWH monotheism of any memory of a polytheistic heritage or even goddesses, biblical writers defamed goddesses and goddess worship. This attitude applies equally to Asherah and the sacred trees (*'asherim*) associated with her cult, to Astarte(s), and to the Queen of Heaven mentioned in Jeremiah. Especially formulaic phrases in the plural, such as "Baals and Astartes" or "Baals and Asherahs" (Judg 3:7), arouse suspicion that such notes are based not on historically or religious-historically reliable information but on sweeping denigration and condemnation of cults other than the cult of YHWH.

Another difficulty arises from the fact that the names of the deities are not reliable identity markers in the ancient Near East. Even when names, such as Baal, Asherah, Astarte, or Anat, appear in biblical or other ancient Near Eastern texts, such as those from Ugarit, the attributions are highly uncertain and often incomparable. For instance, the characteristics of the Ugaritic Asherah and the biblical Asherah are not identical. Thus, the same appearance of a deity in the pictorial tradition may be ascribed to different names, such as the weather god Baal, Hadad, Adad, or Teshub, or the Egyptian tree goddess Hathor, Nut, or Isis.

In 1 Samuel 7:3–4 the formulaic mention of the *'ashtarôt* (in plural) is lumped together with "foreign gods" or with "Baals." What might the writers have imagined by Astartes? Words like "remove" and "eliminate" suggest that they may represent the goddess. Luckily, many so-called pillar figures are archaeologically attested and widely known for the characteristic female figures holding up their breasts with their hands. Most likely, they depict the goddess Asherah and her cult image in the Jerusalem temple. In the blessings in

Deuteronomy 7:13; 28:4, 18, 51, the fertility of small livestock, such as their pregnant female animals, is referred to as *'ashterot so'naeka*. Thus, the Astartes (*'ashtarôt*) may be related to the large number of seals from the early Iron Age (eleventh to tenth century BCE) depicting a lactating mother animal, often a goat (see the figure). The suckling mother animal is probably a wild goat or she-goat, with the drinking cub below her. Above her back appears a scorpion, which perhaps represents the astrological constellation Scorpio due to its importance in agriculture. In front of the goat's chest is a small tree. Like the blessing formula in the biblical text, women and men are wearing the small seals around necks or wrists. The seals serve as incantations and amulets for prosperity or as a short prayer to the deity for its kindness and blessing.

Figure 3.1. Lactating mother animal. Copyright Sylvia Schroer. Used by permission.[54]

54. Othmar Keel, *Corpus der Stempelsiegel-Amulette aus Palästina/Israel: Von den Anfängen bis zur Perserzeit. Bd. 4: Von Tel Gamma bis Chirbet Husche*, Orbis Biblicus

The mention of Astarte in 1 Samuel 31:10 is one of the few biblical texts in which the name of a goddess appears not polemically but factually and with a certain focus and concreteness. The recounted looting and body snatching after the battle of Gilboa, however, is not a historically reliable context. According to the narrative, the victors return to the battlefield to take the clothes or equipment of the already beheaded leader of the defeated, perhaps as evidence or trophies. That they deposited these things in the house of Astarte, which refers to a temple, is a plausible location. The soldiers offer their booty and the defeated enemy to their goddess as a thanksgiving and votive offering. The temple itself is not localized and only mentioned in connection with the city wall of Bet-Shean. Although no archaeological evidence or other proof exists for a temple to Astarte in Bet-Shean and the city's environs, perhaps a kernel of religious history appears in Astarte's association with war, armor/weapons, and worship. Warrior goddesses are not found in the representational art of the southern Levant after the late Bronze Age, and they are already rare in the late Bronze Age. The few findings come from garrison towns where an upper class in Egyptian service combined the native goddesses with Egyptian traditions. The Near Eastern goddess Anat is associated with horses and armor in Egypt. Perhaps the population groups called "Philistines" cultivated a religious tradition of Anat. Near Bet-Shean at Tell Qarnayim, archaeologists found a clay model from the fourteenth or thirteenth century BCE. It depicts a naked goddess wearing a horned helmet frontally on a warhorse (see the figure).

---

et Orientalis, Series Archaeologica 33 (Fribourg/Göttingen: Academic Press / Vandenhoeck & Ruprecht, 2013).

Figure 3.2. Naked goddess wearing a horned helmet frontally on a warhorse. Copyright Sylvia Schroer. Used by permission.[55]

The goddess is holding flowers in her hands. Her pose corresponds to the so-called Qedeshet on the lion, which also appears on Egyptian stelae of the New Kingdom. Usually, she is depicted between an

55. Silvia Schroer, *Die Ikonographie Palästinas/Israels und der Alte Orient. Eine Religionsgeschichte in Bildern. Band 3: Die Spätbronzezeit* (Fribourg: Academic Press, 2011).

Egyptian god (Min) and a Near Eastern god (Reshef). The two flanking male gods on the clay plaque from Tell Qarnayim are not, however, clearly identifiable. The attributes of a helmet and a horse place the goddess together with her erotic aura in the realm of war. Since the object was found on the surface, we can only speculate about the meaning of the goddess. Within religious history, she stands in the midst of strong militarization typical for the late Bronze Age (fifteenth to twelfth century BCE). Symbols of militant domination become central in this period, as interest in herd animals, vegetation, and the deities responsible for them recedes into the background after such features were strongly pronounced in the middle Bronze Age (eighteenth to fifteenth century BCE). Seal representations with a riding, naked goddess date to the late Bronze Age and sporadically even to the early Iron Age (eleventh century BCE).

Pictorial evidence is indispensable for the reconstruction of the religious history of ancient Israel/Palestine. Since biblical texts are almost always tendentious, insofar as they transmit the views of certain influential circles and interests in a monotheistic portrayal of the world, extrabiblical sources such as inscriptions or miniature art open up important insights about the religious and social life of the population. The famous inscriptions of Kuntillet Ajrud, in which the goddess Asherah appears next to YHWH in blessing formulas, gave the impetus to rewrite the history of Israel's monotheism, no longer solely based on the questionable biblical descriptions about goddesses and their places in the world of the ancient Near East, including in ancient Israel/ Palestine.

3. Randall C. Bailey,"Samuel Said to Jesse, 'Are All Your Sons Here?' (1 Sam 16:11)." From "Reading Backwards: A Narrative Technique for the Queering of David, Saul, and Samuel," in *The Fate of King David: The Past and Present of a Biblical Icon*, ed. Tod Linafelt, Claudia V. Camp, and Timothy Beal, LHBOTS 500 (New York: T&T Clark, 2010), 77–78.

In 1 Samuel 16:10, however, instead of there being a sacrifice, Jesse parades, *waya'aber*, his boys one at a time before Samuel. The use of the Hiphil (i.e., causative tense) means that Jesse is supervising this activity of having his sons parade before Samuel after he has sanctified them. As Polzin states, "'to make pass, to present,' is associated with the heart of the matter."[56] One has to wonder what religious/cultic service this is describing. The narrator gives the reader a clue since, YHWH has already told Samuel to stop looking at their appearance (v. 7). Evidently Jesse, unaware of this, keeps up the parade.

As the action continues, we "observe" Samuel, who keeps "seeing," or perhaps one might say "reading," these boys. Perhaps word has reached Jesse that Samuel likes looking at boys. Samuel's response to the parade is a repetitious, *bazeh*, "in *this one*," YHWH hasn't chosen (16:8–9). This designation, *bazeh*, is fairly dehumanizing and dismissive. It is as though Samuel says, "give me some more." By the same token, the possibility of Samuel liking boys is enhanced by Samuel's question, *hatammu hanna'arim* (v. 11), literally, "Have the young boys finished?" To avoid our wondering why Samuel wants to see some more young boys, the English translators have him asking, "Are all your sons here?" Now how we got from "Have the young boys finished?" to "Are all your sons here?" is not a mystery. This is an example of what I earlier termed "cover up translation," where the translators translate in such a way to obfuscate sexual connotations to what is going on in the narrative. It does appear that Samuel is very disappointed. Is this because his mission is not accomplished, or is it that the parade has ended? While Garsiel sees Samuel's outburst as "Samuel's bewilderment . . . confounded," it could also, as I am suggesting, be seen as disappointment that the parade has ended.[57]

56. Robert Polzin, *Samuel and the Deuteronomist: A Literary Study of the Deuteronomic History: Part 2: 1 Samuel* (San Francisco: Harper & Row, 1989), 161.

57. Moshe Garsiel, *The First Book of Samuel: A Literary Study of Comparative Structures, Analogies and Parallels*, 3rd ed. (Jerusalem: Rubin Mass, 1990), 113.

4

DECOLONIZING FORESKIN TALK ABOUT THE NATION AND THE PHILISTINES

There is a refusal to recognize that, in truth, our ego has always been constituted through opposition to some Other that we have internalized—a Negro, a Jew, an Arab, a foreigner—but in a regressive way; that, at bottom, we are made up of diverse borrowings from foreign subjects and that, consequently, we have always been beings of the border—such is precisely what many refuse to admit today.

—Achille Mbembe, *Necro-Politics*

About the Philistines and Ethnonational Discourse: An Introduction

AS THIS FEMINIST interpretation explores the stories, legends, and texts of 1 Samuel, chapter 1 investigated the geopolitical locations prominent in this biblical book, chapter 2 paid attention to the various masculinities of major and minor male characters, and chapter 3 critically analyzed the antidemocratic ideology embedded in the depictions of the emerging Israelite monarchy. This fourth chapter interrogates the portrayal of the Philistines as the masculine Other nation in the land of Canaan. The Philistines are the major military opponent to be battled and defeated by the male Israelites and their male leaders. Since the ethnonational binary of the Philistines and the Israelites is always androcentric, this chapter exposes the colonizing discourse on the Philistines as a literary effort of so-called nation-building. In this discourse, the (male) Philistines are the archenemy of the Israelites.

Said differently, the Philistine-Israelite binary articulates an ethnonational identity, not in the sense of a nation-state discourse, as it has emerged since the seventeenth century CE, that combines a people (nation) with a governmental structure (state)[1] but in the sense of a group of people born into a tribe or nation that shares customs and traditions with each other. The narratives of 1 Samuel encourage listeners to identify with, give legitimacy to, and participate in the Israelite position. Importantly, the ethnonational discourse presents the Philistines as the Other, not in the sense of a historical reality of the emerging Israelite monarchy during the tenth century BCE. Rather, the literary description is part of building biblical Israel's ethnonational identity, while this portrayal distinguishes biblical Israel from the Other in past or presently shared geopolitical settings, depending on how one dates the Deuteronomistic texts. If the texts were dated into the seventh century CE, this discourse would differentiate among the various subgroups of Canaanites living in the land of Palestine. If the texts were dated into the Babylonian exile, the discourse would address an exilic community living outside the land of Palestine, far away from any formerly contested territorial realities. The literary depiction of the Philistines as the Other would then aim to strengthen the identity of the Israelite exilic community in a foreign land. In either case, the Philistine-Israelite binary is a mental-political construct, a "fantasy work,"[2] requiring careful and focused analysis in this commentary.

Feminist interpreters know that ethnonational assumptions are always also gendered, and vice versa, which means that both Israelite and Philistine women are defined and implicated by the ethnonational imaginary, though women rarely appear as characters in the stories. Moreover, feminist attention to the embedded ethnonational assumptions recognizes that there is no woman as such because women are also always positioned ethnonationally. Feminist, womanist, queer, or otherwise-gendered readers need to understand the ethnonational binary that 1 Samuel establishes, even though this binary does not explicitly refer to female characters. The mentioned Philistines and Israelites appear in male and plural grammatical forms,

1. For this and additional explanations on the historical development of the modern notion of nations, see, e.g., Michael G. Roskin, Robert L. Cord, James A. Medeiros, and Walter S. Jones, *Political Science: An Introduction*, 8th ed. (Upper Saddle River, NJ: Prentice Hall, 2003), 36–53.

2. David Jobling, *1 Samuel*, Berit Olam (Collegeville, MN: Liturgical Press, 1998), 213.

presupposing phallogocentric hegemony. Nevertheless, the ethnonational logic links tightly with the logic of gender. The questions are who the ethnonational Other is in 1 Samuel and why so many interpreters accept the othering strategy as a given.

Four sections organize the interpretation. The first section examines how various texts define the (male) Philistines on the basis of repeated references to the skin of the male reproductive organ known as the foreskin of the penis. The second section explores the Ark Narrative (1 Sam 4:1–7:1) and its presentation of the Philistines as the archenemies of the Israelites. The third section focuses on perhaps one of the most famous Philistine characters, Goliath of Gath, to elaborate on the androcentric and ethnonational dynamics in the famous warrior tale. The fourth section explores the literary function of the Philistine King Achish of Gath who serves as a stepping stone on David's path toward power and glory as the second Israelite king. A conclusion encourages the critical study of biblical texts that focus on the ethnonational binary between (male) Philistines and Israelites so that feminist and nonfeminist readers alike recognize this kind of biblical discourse in conjunction with considerations of gender.

The Sexual Objectification of the Philistines: References to the Male Foreskin[3]

Feminist theorists have long examined, deconstructed, and criticized the sexual objectification of women in patriarchal culture and society. For instance,

3. Today's masculinity scholars focus on not only the anatomical-biological features of the male foreskin but also the religious and pharmaceutical practices related to circumcision and the cut-off skin. For instance, Winston Wilde explains, "The foreskin of the male penis is also known as the prepuce, and it is homologous to the female prepuce, also known as the clitoral hood. It serves several functions, primarily to protect the glans (head) of the penis from external stimuli such as constant daily rubbing against underwear and from keratinization occurring from overexposure to light. It also provides lubrication and facilitates intromission during intercourse. The foreskin is a double-folded tissue of skin on the outside and mucosal membrane on the inside similar to eyelids or lips, and it is considered the most sensitive area of the external male genitals. . . . Most people in the world do not circumcise or cut the foreskin. Circumcision occurs most frequently among Muslims and Jews

radical feminist theorist Andrea Dworkin explains that "objectification occurs when a human being, through social means, is made less than human, turned into a thing or commodity, bought and sold."[4] Women's humanity is erased when culture and society objectify women, and thus the sexual objectification is a huge concern in feminist studies. At the same time, some feminist critics also recognize sexual objectification as a "slippery" and "multiple" concept.[5] They worry how best to define sexual objectification because it is difficult to agree on specific criteria or the conditions under which sexual objectification occurs. Feminist theorists acknowledge that sexual objectification harms because it depersonalizes and diminishes women's individuality and integrity. Feminist studies measure such harm and detail the characteristics of sexual objectification. Some liberal feminist critics want to limit the notion of sexual objectification because they fear that otherwise women are continuously defined as sexualized objects.

When the notion of sexual objectification is applied to 1 Samuel, an astute feminist reader notices the repeated mention of the male Philistines by the foreskin of their penis (ערלה). The repeated focus on the male sexual body part objectifies male Philistines and so serves as an ethnogender marker for the Philistine warriors. The Hebrew root for the foreskin as a reference to the male Philistines appears six times in 1 Samuel 14:6; 17:26, 36;

---

worldwide, as well as among Americans in general, Filipinos, and South Koreans. Most Americans and Koreans circumcise at birth, Jews at eight days, and Filipinos in adolescence; Muslims vary according to tribal traditions. In North America, circumcised foreskin waste is used for scientific biomedical research, as skin grafts, and as agents for commercial cosmetic products. Foreskin restoration techniques have also been employed for at least 2,000 years to give cut men the appearance of a foreskin." See Winston Wilde, "Foreskin," in *Cultural Encyclopedia of the Penis*, ed. Michael Kimmel, Christine Milrod, and Amanda Kennedy (Lanham, MD: Rowman and Littlefield, 2014), 72–73.

4. Andrea Dworkin, "Against the Male Flood: Censorship, Pornography, and Equality," in *Oxford Readings in Feminism: Feminism and Pornography*, ed. Drucilla Cornell, Oxford Readings in Feminism (Oxford: Oxford University Press, 2000), 30.

5. See, e.g., Martha C. Nussbaum, "Objectification," *Philosophy and Public Affairs* 24 (1995): 251. For an extensive discussion, see also Evangelia (Lina) Papadaki, "Feminist Perspectives on Objectification," *Stanford Encyclopedia of Philosophy*, March 10, 2010, https://plato.stanford.edu/entries/feminism-objectification/.

18:25, 27; 31:4. Commentators usually do not explain why this skin defines male Philistines in these verses. Johanna Van Wijk-Bos dryly notes that the mention of the Philistine foreskin is not "a complimentary label."[6] She also observes that "only Jonathan, David, and Saul refer to the Philistines" in this way.[7]

The question is what to make of this ethnogender marker. Queer interpreter Ken Stone comments that the repeated identification of the Philistines as foreskins conveys "disdain" or even "hostility" toward the Philistine men because they "were probably understood as improper examples of manhood."[8] Stone also mentions that in the ancient Near East, circumcision established manliness. Given twice, the encouragement of the male Philistines to each other to "be men" (1 Sam 4:9) indicates the significance of manliness, as well as the competitive connection between warrior success and manliness. The Philistine warriors reassure each other to be "real" men so as not to become slaves of the Israelites. Yet when Jonathan, Saul, or David refer to the Philistines by the skin of their penises, the biblical imagination reduces Philistine men to sexualized objects, perhaps in the attempt to diminish (male) Philistine battle power. Anxiety over manliness thus runs high among Israelite characters (see also 26:15), and the repeated references to Philistine foreskins provide important literary clues to highlight androcentric and ethnonational vocabulary and plot development in 1 Samuel.

Moreover, the focus on Philistine foreskins keeps the phallus in the center whenever three male Israelite characters—Jonathan, Saul, and David—talk about the ethnonational Other. Saul's final remark in 1 Samuel 31:4 is particularly pertinent. In the context of phallic vocabulary ("drawing the sword," "piercing"), Saul worries about the sexualized torture he would receive from the "foreskins" if he were to fall into their hands. The text insinuates that the Israelite king fears being gang-raped by Philistine soldiers, thus choosing suicide instead.

---

6. Johanna Van Wijk-Bos, *The Road to Kingship: 1–2 Samuel*, A People and a Land, vol. 2 (Grand Rapids, MI: Eerdmans, 2020), 104.

7. Van Wijk-Bos, *The Road to Kingship*, 133.

8. Ken Stone, "1 Samuel," in *The Queer Bible Commentary*, ed. Deryn Guest, Robert E. Goss, Mona West, and Thomas Bohache (London: SCM Press, 2006), 204.

The phallogocentric emphasis on the ethnonational Other is, however, downplayed in translations, as they avoid explicit biological-sexual vocabulary for the male sex organ's skin. Accordingly, English translations do not use the word *foreskin* but the less physically explicit adjective "uncircumcised" in 1 Samuel 14:6; 17:26, 36; 31:4. The only unavoidable exception is when Saul demands a bride price of one hundred "foreskins" (ערלות) of the Philistines in 1 Samuel 18:25 and David delivers them in verse 27. Shunning the word *foreskin* in the other four cases, translators render the Hebrew noun or adjective of the root ערל with the medicalized term *uncircumcised*, leaving far less room for the readerly imagination to recognize what body part is involved exactly. Yet in all six occurrences, the same Hebrew root for *foreskin* appears in Hebrew. For instance, in 1 Samuel 14:6, Jonathan suggests to his armor-carrying "young man" (הנער), "Let's cross over to the place of these *foreskinned* ones [הערלים; my translation]." The adjective in the masculine plural characterizes the Philistine warriors by the skins of their phalluses, which remains less explicit and more veiled in English translations. For instance, the NRSVue renders the sentence like this: "Come, let us go over to the garrison of these uncircumcised."

Yet in the Hebrew, the ethnonational otherness of the Philistine warriors is expressed in a sexualized undertone that reduces them to their genitals. Only the New Living Bible (NLB) translates the Hebrew word in a different way, abandoning the sexual objectification of the male Philistine warriors by adding a Western colonial connotation. In this translation, the Hebrew word for foreskins, ערלים, becomes "pagans," as the verse reads, "Let's go across to the outpost of those pagans." A religiously derogatory term, pagans, replaces the sexual objectification of the male Philistines to their foreskins.

The last time that the male Philistines are reduced to their foreskins occurs in 31:4. This verse demonstrates how crucial the translation of ערל as "foreskin" or as "the one with a foreskin" is in order to recognize the sexualized objectification of male Philistines as part of an ethnonational othering discourse. In this verse, Saul orders his arms-bearer to kill him so that he can avoid being "thrust . . . through" (דקר) and "made sport of" (התעלל). The two verbal roots allude to Saul's fear of being sexually assaulted. The verbal roots דקר and עלל (hitpa'el) allow for this possibility, especially in a context in which the king refers to the Philistine warriors as "the foreskins." The verbal root דקר means "to pierce through," possibly to kill, as in Numbers 25:8, where Phinehas pierces into the belly (קבה) of an Israelite man and a Midianite woman in a murderous act. The other root (עלל) can refer to sexual abuse and even gang rape in two other biblical texts. One text is about the so-called concubine (פילגש) who is gang-raped by the Benjaminite men (Judg 19:25; my translation of the Hebrew): "And they raped (וידעו) her and sexually violated (ויתעללו) her all through the night until the morning." The other text is Jeremiah 38:19, in which King Zedekiah worries of being sexually violated (התעללו בי) if handed over to the Babylonian army. In other words, King Saul's final words reduce his warring enemies to their phallic organ, as he worries about his fate if he lived. That the root בוא (to come) has sexual connotations is well established; it also appears in 31:4. The relevant part of 1 Samuel 31:4 could be translated as "Saul said to his arms-bearer: 'Draw out [שׁלף] your sword and pierce me [דקר] with it lest these foreskins come [בוא] and pierce me [דבק] and gang-rape me [התעלל] (31:4).'" This verse, like the other references to the phallic skin of male Philistines, is vulgar, violent, and filled with sexual innuendo. As usual, translators avoid such connotations here and elsewhere, so that the English text loses the Hebrew undertones.

In sum, the sexual objectification of male Philistines plays a significant role in 1 Samuel, although this literary strategy appears only six times. As the classic enemy nation, the proverbial Other, the Philistine males are classified by ethnosexual weirdness. They are unmanly, like women, and thus reduced to their genitals. This literary strategy diminishes their ethnonational status in the biblical discourse shaped by notions of hegemonic masculinity. Accordingly, the sexual objectification of the male Philistines minimizes them as powerful opponents in the literary-national biblical imagination despite their successful warrior status.

When readers understand the ethnonational, gendered discourse, the literary gravity of David's submission to one of the most powerful Philistine kings, Achish of Gath (chap. 27), becomes even more obvious. The irony of this tale consists of the fact that the Philistine commanders reportedly never trust the Israelite male. Impressed by David's military successes (21:11; 29:5), they disbelieve David's loyalty (29:9), in contrast to the Philistine king, who, foolishly, keeps trusting David (29:3, 10). Readers know the Philistine king is foolish, whereas his commanders are correct. Previously, David murders Philistine warriors, cutting off their foreskins as a bride price, and, according to the Hebrew text, even collecting double the number of foreskins requested by Saul (18:17). David also identifies the mighty warrior Goliath by his uncircumcised penis, contrasting "this foreskinned Philistine" (הפלשתי הערל הזה) to "the living God" (17:26, 36). The theological hierarchy could not be more strongly expressed than in this contrast made twice. Thus, the sexual objectification of Philistine men condemns them to the lowest status imaginable. As "foreskins," they are nothing because Israelite men do not have foreskins anymore. The sexual objectification is a powerful reminder of ethnosexual slurs serving as verbal foreplay to murderous acts of violence against the male Other. The stories about the male Philistines illustrate this dynamic.

A National Trauma of Biblical Proportions: About Philistine Military Success and Loss in the Ark Narrative (1 Sam 4:1–7:1)

Although chapter 1 of this interpretation already explored the phallic supremacist ideology articulated in various elements of the Ark Narrative (1 Sam 4:1–7:1), the tale offers additional insights into the literary-political efforts of so-called nation-building focused on the androcentric and ethnonational binary of male Philistines and Israelites. In fact, the Ark Narrative is indispensable for understanding this binary because male Philistine warriors, who already in the book of Judges (e.g., Judg 3:31; 13:1; 15; 16) appear as momentous enemies of the Israelites, succeed mightily against the Israelites in the battle at the base of a pass (near Ebenezer and Aphek; 1 Sam 4:1–2) leading up to Shiloh. The story reports the military loss of about four thousand Israelite fighters (4:2) and then, despite the presence of the ark in battle, of another thirty thousand Israelite foot soldiers (4:10), "a traumatic religious and political catastrophe," as Yehoshua Gitay puts it.[9] So profound is the Israelite military defeat that the only way of telling the story is in the

9. Yehoshua Gitay, "Reflections on the Poetics of the Samuel Narrative: The Question of the Ark Narrative," *CBQ* 54 (1992): 229.

form of satire, "a joke for the Israelites."[10] Yet source critics endlessly discuss whether the three biblical chapters of the Ark Narrative are original to the literary composition of 1 Samuel, a line of source-critical inquiry going back to the famous 1926 study by Leonhard Rost.[11]

Leonhard Rost argues that the Ark Narrative constitutes an independent text that includes 2 Samuel 6. In Rost's view, a priest wrote the Ark Narrative during David's or Solomon's rule, and the chapters were only later integrated into the Deuteronomistic History. Yet the once widely accepted notion about the literary origins and extent of the Ark Narrative has been slowly abandoned. Nowadays, many interpreters read the story within its current literary setting, propose a much later date for its composition, such as the late eighth century BCE or even the Babylonian exilic period (587–538 BCE), and offer literary readings rather than source-critical speculations.[12] In fact, a considerable number of today's interpreters regard the Ark Narrative as an "integral part of the entire plot"[13] that explains how the lineage of Eli, the priest, ended and why the ark ceased to reside in Shiloh. Often such readers emphasize that the ark's falling into Philistine hands on the battlefield was such a traumatic collective event that the Israelites coped with this trauma by remembering it as a story filled with satire. Accordingly, the story delights in the Philistine deity, Dagon, for lacking power and

---

10. Gitay, "Reflections on the Poetics," 229.

11. Leonhard Rost, *Die Überlieferung von der Thronnachfolge Davids*, BWANT 42 (Stuttgart: Kohlhammer, 1926); in English: *The Succession to the Throne of David*, trans. Michael D. Rutter and David M. Gunn, Historic Texts and Interpretations in Biblical Scholarship 1 (Sheffield: Almond Press, 1982).

12. For a review of some of these developments, see, e.g., Keith Bodner, "Ark-Eology: Shifting Emphases in 'Ark Narrative' Scholarship," *CurBR* 4 (2006): 169–197. For an eighth-century date argued on the basis of archaeology, see Israel Finkelstein and Thomas Römer, "The Historical and Archaeological Background Behind the Old Israelite Ark Narrative," *Bib* 101 (2020): 161–185. For an exilic date, see, e.g., K. A. D. Smelik, "The Ark Narrative Reconsidered," in *New Avenues in the Study of the Old Testament: A Collection of Old Testament Studies Published on the Occasion of the Fiftieth Anniversary of the Oudtestamentisch Werkgezelschap and the Retirement of Prof. Dr. M. J. Multer*, ed. A. S. van der Woode, Oudtestamentische Studiën 25 (Leiden: Brill, 1989), 128–144.

13. Gitay, "Reflections on the Poetics," 230.

seemingly prostrating (נפל לפניו) before the Israelite deity. Similar delight underlies the mention of the Philistines getting a genital disease (5:6 עפלים) that makes them send back the ark to the Israelites in Beth-Shemesh (6:2–9).

Perhaps one of the most interesting readings of the Ark Narrative comes from Walter Brueggemann, who emphasizes the centrality of the only female character, the unnamed daughter-in-law of Eli, the priest (1 Sam 4:19). Brueggemann's theological reading is unusual because source critics often ignore this tale (4:19–22) by constructing a presumably older story.[14] Eli's daughter-in-law, who is the wife of his son Phinehas, hears about the capture of the ark and the death of her father-in-law and her husband. In shock, she gives birth, names the newborn son, and then dies. Brueggemann compares this woman to Rachel, who also gives birth to a son, names him, and then dies (Gen 35:16–20). Brueggemann praises the unnamed daughter's "extraordinary piece of theology" that she articulates as she dies. She names the baby boy "Where is the glory?" (1 Sam 4:21, literally "no-glory"), and then the next verse reads, "She said, 'The Glory (כבוד) has departed (גלה) from Israel, for the ark of God has been captured" (4:22). Brueggemann explains:

> This is an extraordinary piece of theology by this dying, unnamed daughter-in-law. She has grasped the point of the capture of the ark and its nearly unutterable significance. After the accent on "save" in verse 3, we might have expected her to say that YHWH's capacity to save has gone. But no, she says "glory." She understands that the issue is not *Israel's* future, but *YHWH's* own loss. It is YHWH who has been shamed and humiliated, and who has lost credence. She is, moreover, a better Yahwistic theologian than the Philistines, for the Philistines had thought like generic theologians and had assumed that YHWH, like every God, goes from victory to victory [see 4:8]. The daughter-in-law, however, knows that this God is exposed and vulnerable, not generically sovereign, but

---

14. For instance, the story about the daughter-in-law completely disappears in the "original, pre-dtr Ark Narrative," called "an old North Israelite text," in Finkelstein and Römer, "Historical and Archaeological Background," 167.

> vulnerable to the vagaries of historical challenge. She ponders the deep disruption in the very character of YHWH, the one completely at risk in the risk of Israel.[15]

According to Brueggemann, the narrative depicts an Israelite woman as fully understanding the theological implications of the ark's capture by the Philistines, the archenemies of the Israelites. The God of Israel, the glory (כבוד) of Israel—as many other biblical texts speak of God (e.g., Exod 14:4, 17–18; Isa 26:5; Ezek 28:22; 39:13)—is now under Philistine control. She is the one recognizing the national disaster for her people, as God's glory (כבוד) "has failed, leaving a dead husband, a dead father-in-law, a routed army, a field of abandoned bodies, all topped by a humiliated God," who is "an enemy trophy" now.[16] This failed God is exiled (גלה), a more appropriate rendering than "to depart," as suggested in many English translations. Brueggemann stresses that hope disappears at this moment in the story due to the earth-shattering failure of God. As the new mother dies, God is in exile among the Philistines. The name she gives her son embraces total theo-national loss. Brueggemann spells out this moment: "Now there is only loss, shock, bewilderment, abandonment, and, finally, silence: silence all the way into the night."[17]

His interpretation centers on her pronouncement for understanding the gravity of the Israelite situation. The Philistine warriors capture the ark, in which God's presence resides and which makes the Israelites godless. Brueggemann calls the woman a "stunningly perceptive, unnamed, dying theologian"[18] because she recognizes "the truth" about God. She knows that God's "glory [is] exiled, an exile YHWH could not resist, an exile of YHWH that foreshadows the deep inheritance of exile that will mark the people of YHWH."[19] Brueggemann suggests that such a theology teaches not to live in denial and not to advance a way of life that excludes others. Yet he also recognizes that "Israel predictably became infested with violence, greed, and

15. Walter Brueggemann, "(I)chabod Departed," *PSB* 22 (2001): 121.
16. Brueggemann, "(I)chabod Departed," 121–122.
17. Brueggemann, "(I)chabod Departed," 122.
18. Brueggemann, "(I)chabod Departed," 122.
19. Brueggemann, "(I)chabod Departed," 132–133.

killing moralism," which are "the fruits of denial."[20] Unfortunately, Brueggemann's interpretation could be easily read as advancing a Christian anti-Jewish view of 1 Samuel in which Judaism is marked by theological exclusion. Although I am certain that Brueggemann would not want his reading to be understood in this way, its implicit theological stance of God having left Israel is a key theological conviction in many pre-Holocaust Christian viewpoints about Judaism.

Another observation is in order. The focus on the female character does not eliminate the major theological objection to Brueggemann's approach to 1 Samuel 4:19–22. His interpretation stands in line with biblical discourse on nationhood that others the Philistines in dramatic ways. This discourse presents even God as powerless over and against the depicted enemy. Even though the Philistines are feminized in previous tales, here they turn into successful macho warriors. Anxiety about Philistine might and power thus permeates this and the other stories. Brueggemann's reading advances the othering strategy because it does not critically interrogate the theonational ideology. Not recognizing the female character as reinforcing the androcentric and ethnonational ideology of the Deuteronomistic historians, Brueggemann's interpretation teaches truth-telling as exemplified by the final words of the dying daughter-in-law: "The ark of God has been captured" (4:11, 17, 19, 21, 22). The Philistines dominate the Israelite god, who moves into exile together with the defeated Israelites.

The othering strategy also applies to the Philistine deity, Dagon (5:1–5). Already discussed in chapter 1 of this interpretation, the Philistine deity is depicted as a theological failure decapitated and without hands lying on the ground. Also, the sexually crude and phallogocentric jokes about the Philistine health problems that characterize the result of "God's hand" as rising up against the people of Ashdod (5:6–12) reinforce colonizing discourse grounded in the androcentric and ethnonational imaginary. When the Philistines decide to get rid of the "ark of God" after seven months (6:1), the Philistine priests advise them to "return it with a guilt offering" (6:3). Then follows the androcentric and ethnonational joke about the *'opalîm* (עפלים 6:4–5, 9). Aren Maeir's interpretation that the items are phallic-shaped vessels makes sense (see chap. 1, p. 80–82).

20. Brueggemann, "(I)chabod Departed," 132–133.

Figure 4.1. Assemblage of cultic objects from cultic corner (Locus 62023), Tell eṣ-Ṣâfi/Gath, Area A, Stratum A3 (late ninth century BCE). Copyright Aren M. Maeir. Used by permission.[21]

The next story about the two young cows pulling the ark back to Beth-shemesh adds a rustic, peasant-like sense of humor filled with sexualized, ethnonational clues (6:10–12). The sages of the Talmudic era, elaborating on the two cows, describe them as singing on their way up to Beth-shemesh. One of the sages, Rabbi Meir, explains that the first verb, ישרנה, in 1 Samuel 6:12, should be understood in this way: "The Gemara asks: What is the meaning of the word *vayyisharna*? Rabbi Yoḥanan says in the name of Rabbi Meir: It means that they [the cows] recited a song [*shira*]."[22] Yet the ark does

21. Aren M. Maeir, Louise A. Hitchcock, and Liora Kolska Horwitz, "On the Constitution and Transformation of Philistine Identity," *Oxford Journal of Archaeology* 32 (2013): fig. 9, https://www.researchgate.net/figure/Assemblage-of-cultic-objects-from-cultic-corner-Locus-62023-Tell-es-Safi-Gath-Area-A_fig4_264371313.

22. Abod. Zar. 24b.

not bring joy and relief to the inhabitants of Beth-shemesh. To the contrary, the story teaches that nobody should mess with God (6:13–15, 19–21), as God kills seventy men of Beth-shemesh when the sons of Jeconiah do not rejoice about the ark's arrival (6:19). Even Israelites are not safe in this animal-singing tale. When the people of Beth-shemesh ask the people of Kiriath-jearim, all Israelites, to pick up the ark, they comply (7:1), and so the ark stays with them for twenty years (7:2). This is the end of the Ark Narrative. The next verse begins another story about Samuel. The ark reappears when King David brings it to Jerusalem in 2 Samuel 6:2.

In sum, the archenemies of the Israelites win only temporary control over the ark in a narrative filled with boorish othering humor. In the process, the andro-ethnonational tale reports both on the death of thousands of male Israelites and on the death of a new mother whose last words do not predict the outcome of the story. So-called nation-building takes a toll on all participants, female and male, human and divine.

The Son of a Gang-Raped Woman: The Story of Goliath, the Philistine Warrior Male

The story of the Philistine man, Goliath, and the famous future king, David, is iconic (1 Sam 17). It is enormously popular in children's teachings of the Bible, according to which young David is a faithful boy unafraid of the menacing Philistine soldier. In these retellings, David is a supremely faithful character who believes in God while he outfoxes the armed warrior with a stone from his little pouch. Many contemporary retellings, from children's Bibles to films to conventional expressions of underdog situations, depict David as a weaker opponent who faces and wins against a seemingly unbeatable and much stronger adversary. Such metaphorical references exist even in the Muslim tradition. The Qur'an tells a brief story about David and Jalut (جالوت Goliath) in Sure 2:247–252:[23]

23. Qur'an Sure 2:247–252. Excerpt from Muhammad Taqî-ud-Dîn Al-Hilâlî and Muhammad Muhsin Khân, *Translation of the Meanings of the Noble Qur'an in the English Language* (Madinah: King Fahd Complex for the Printing of the Holy

247. And their Prophet (Samuel) said to them, “Indeed Allah has appointed *Tâlût* (Saul) as a king over you.” They said, “How can he be a king over us when we are fitter than him for the kingdom, and he has not been given enough wealth.” He said: “Verily, Allah has chosen him above you and has increased him abundantly in knowledge and stature. And Allah grants His kingdom to whom He wills. And Allah is All-Sufficient for His creatures’ needs, All-Knower.”
248. And their Prophet (Samuel) said to them: Verily! The sign of His kingdom is that there shall come to you *At-Tâbût* (a wooden box), wherein is *Sakînah* (peace and reassurance) from your Lord and a remnant of that which Mûsâ (Moses) and Hârûn (Aaron) left behind, carried by the angels. Verily, in this is a sign for you if you are indeed believers.
249. Then when *Tâlût* (Saul) set out with the army, he said: “Verily! Allah will try you by a river. So whoever drinks thereof, he is not of me, and whoever tastes it not, he is of me, except him who takes (thereof) in the hollow of his hand.” Yet, they drank thereof, all, except a few of them. So when he had crossed it (the river), he and those who believed with him, they said: “We have no power this day against Jâlût (Goliath) and his hosts.” But those who knew with certainty that they were going to meet Allah, said: “How often a small group overcame a mighty host by Allah’s Leave?” And Allah is with *As-Sâbirûn* (the patient).
250. And when they advanced to meet Jâlût (Goliath) and his forces, they invoked: “Our Lord! Pour forth on us patience, and set firm our feet and make us victorious over the disbelieving people.”
251. So they routed them by Allah’s Leave and Dâwûd (David) killed Jâlût (Goliath), and Allah gave him [Dâwûd (David)] the kingdom [after the death of Tâlût (Saul) and Samuel] and *Al-Hikmah* (Prophethood),and taught him of that which He willed. And if Allah did not check one set of people by means of another, the earth would indeed be full of mischief. But Allâh is full of bounty to the *'Âlamîn* ([hu]mankind, jinn and all that exists).

Qur’an, n.d.), 54–56, https://www.holybooks.com/wp-content/uploads/2010/05/english-quranalhilali-khan.pdf.

252. These are the Verses of Allâh, We recite them to you (O Muhammad) in truth, and surely, you are one of the Messengers (of Allâh).

The Muslim tradition views David's battle with Goliath as a prefiguration of Muhammad's battle of Badr in March 624 CE, the first large battle between Muslims and various Arab clans living in Mecca, the holy city for Muslims.

Metaphorical references to the biblical characters are widely known in Muslim cultures. For instance, on January 7, 2009, the Indonesian newspaper *Sumut Pos* published a highly provocative image of a young man veiled with a Palestinian red *keffiyeh*, swinging a slingshot with a stone about to be shot out of it. As Ronald A. Lukens-Bull and Mark R. Woodward explain, the respected daily newspaper, published by the largest newspaper chain in Indonesia, a majority Muslim country, focuses on two themes in reports on the Gaza war of 2008 and 2009. Lukens-Bull and Woodward expound, "There were two major themes. The first was the alleged nuclear attack; the second was Palestinian fighters attacking Israeli tanks with stones and slingshots. Together they portray valiant Palestinians fighting bravely against seemingly insurmountable odds. . . . In this version of the tale, Goliath is a Jew and David is a Palestinian Arab."[24] This is a stunning twist of the dominant reading of 1 Samuel 17.

Metaphorical references to the David and Goliath story are not usually concerned with the biblical setting of the scene, as they apply to various contexts the basic idea of the underdog defeating a strongman. The narrative functions as a folktale that has a core message abstracted from the specifics. Even business and personal advice companies refer to David and Goliath as a "lesson" on how to become a successful enterprise or improve one's personal motivation.[25] In general, symbolic references to the biblical tale indicate that Goliath is a projection for all kinds of enemies, and David's killing slingshot

---

24. Ronald A. Lukens-Bull and Mark R. Woodward, "Goliath and David in Gaza: Indonesian Myth-Building and Conflict as a Cultural System," *Contemporary Islam* 5 (2011): 7.

25. See, e.g., "Small Business Lessons from 'David and Goliath,'" https://www.nzbizbuysell.co.nz/nz-business/growth/business-lessons-from-david-and-goliath#:~:text=David%20may%20not%20have%20been,do%20and%20do%20it%20well; Marcus Taylor, "David and Goliath: The Most Powerful Motivational Speech

is transferred to current situations about sociopolitical and economic corruption or even war.[26]

The male-on-male battle told in 1 Samuel 17 challenges the conventional notion about hegemonic male power as good, necessary, and effective. The story shows that a weaker man still rises to royal leadership over an entire people. No wonder this story has kindled andro-ethnonational fantasies about male national power over the centuries. Yet the ethnonational identity of Goliath as a Philistine, representing the ultimate Other in 1 Samuel, plays only a subordinate role in the highly gendered contemporary construct of hegemonic masculinity. The ease of the ethnonational reversal in the Indonesian context proves this point, as it identifies David with the Palestinians and Goliath with the Israeli Jewish state. Yet a gender reversal that would turn David into female oppressed groups, such as Afghan women fighting back against the Taliban, or Egyptian women fighting back against sexual violence and harassment by the male police,[27] or some other contemporary situation centering on women or a gender-oppressed group, seems still completely out of place. The impossibility indicates the firm hold of an androcentrically defined narrative even today. The metaphoric David, battling the metaphoric Goliath, cannot be imagined as a woman, although David has often been depicted in androgynous and gender-fluid ways.

---

of 2020 (Ft. Marcus Taylor)," *Motiversity*, November 23, 2020, YouTube Video, 10:03, https://www.youtube.com/watch?v=rWZ_y0NiJfI.

26. For a full discussion on the reception history of 1 Samuel 17, see Stefan Ark Nitsche, *David gegen Goliath: Die Geschichte der Geschichten einer Geschichte: Zur fächerübergreifenden Rezeption einer biblischen Story*, Altes Testament und Moderne 4 (Münster: Lit Verlag, 1998), esp. 312–313.

27. Emma Graham-Harrison, "Armed Afghan Women Take to Streets in Show of Defiance Against Taliban," *Guardian*, July 7, 2021, https://www.theguardian.com/world/2021/jul/07/armed-afghan-women-take-to-streets-in-show-of-defiance-against-taliban; Mona El-Naggar, Yousuf Al-Hlou, and Aliza Aufrichtig, "Stripped, Groped and Violated: Egyptian Women Describe Abuse by the State," *New York Times*, July 5, 2021, https://www.nytimes.com/interactive/2021/07/05/world/middleeast/egypt-sexual-assault-police.html.

Figure 4.2. Caravaggio, *David with the Head of Goliath* (c.1609–1610), oil on canvas, Galleria Borghese, Rome. Wikimedia Commons, https://commons.wikimedia.org/w/index.php?curid=15216629.

The androcentric persistence goes hand in hand with the ethnonational emphasis that characterizes the Philistines as the ultimate Other. My feminist reading identifies the andro-ethnonational accent, flickering throughout 1 Samuel 17, in two linguistic observations and a midrashic consideration. One linguistic observation notices that some interpreters compare the biblical tale with the shorter parallels found in 2 Samuel 21:19–22, 1 Chronicles 20:5–8, and the Septuagint, the Greek translation of the Hebrew Bible that was probably composed from the third to the first centuries BCE. Remarkably, the Hebrew text highlights the battle between the Israelites and Philistines as being over manhood, but in the Septuagint, this emphasis is absent. In 1 Samuel 17:8, Goliath challenges the Israelites when he shouts, "Why have you come out to draw up for battle? Am I not a Philistine, and are you not servants of Saul? Choose a *man* [איש] for yourselves, and let him come down to me." And again in verse 10, Goliath insists, "And give me a *man* [איש] so that we can fight together!" Gender-specific vocabulary appears not only in Goliath's calls for battle but also in the indirect and direct speeches of the Israelite men. In 1 Samuel 17:24–25, the male Israelites are classified as a single entity: "every *man* of Israel" (כל איש ישׂראל and איש ישׂראל). The Israelites are men, and so is Goliath, "the man" (האיש). This particular noun, איש, appears famously in Genesis 2:23 when the surgically transformed man exclaims his joy over the woman (אשה); the verse celebrates the heteronormative gender binary: "This at last is bone of my bones and flesh of my flesh; this one shall be called Woman, for out of Man this one was taken." The other famous passage in which the male (האיש) is placed in opposition to the divine is in Hosea 11:9c: "For I am God and no man [איש; my translation]." Similarly, the noun איש in 1 Samuel 17:24–25 refers to the specifically male gender, emphasizing the androcentric quality of the threats that Goliath and David hurl at each other.

The references to the manliness of the opponent, in conjunction with repeatedly mentioned ethnonational markers, convey the androcentric and ethnonational identities of the male Philistine and Israelite. David's twice-repeated characterization of Goliath as a "foreskin" in combination with his national identity as "this [foreskinned] Philistine" (17:26, 36) adds insult to upcoming injury and gruesome death. That Goliath is disappointed to see David as his opponent, whom he recognizes not as a man but as a boy/servant (נער) and who looks reddish and beautiful (v. 42), further reinforces the androcentric, ethnonational hostilities articulated in the narrative. Despising David, Goliath is ready to make this boy/servant his booty because the boy/servant is an unmanly opponent to the mighty warrior. The macho talk continues between the uneven fighters (vv. 43–47), and David threatens to cut off the head of "the Philistine" (v. 46), which he does in verse 51, carrying "the head of the Philistine" to Jerusalem (v. 54). The much shorter parallel in 2 Samuel 21:19–22 also includes a story about Goliath, a "giant," or about the "Rephaim" ("an old race of giants" or "ancient inhabitants of Canaan"),[28] who is killed in battle by Elhanan, son of Jair, the Bethlehemite. The tale is popular, especially when it involves the future Israelite king.

The story in 2 Samuel 21:19–22 was perhaps later transformed into a "folktale pattern of the killing of a giant or an ogre by a resourceful young man,"[29] who becomes David in 1 Samuel 17. He already acts like a king, as he wins the battle against the warrior from the Philistine town of Gath. A similar confusion appears in 1 Chronicles 20:5–8 in the short mention of two battle scenes, similar to the three different battle scenes in 2 Samuel. The Greek translation of 1 Samuel 17 is a shortened version of the David and Goliath story that excludes complicating elements. For instance, the longer version, appearing in the Hebrew text, includes a literary delay tactic in which David is selected as a fighter against the Philistine warrior only after all other Israelite warriors flee in terror from the enemy (17:12–31). The longer version also includes a fragment about Saul, who does not know David (17:55–58), although both talk with each other earlier in the story, and David even plays the harp for the depressed king in 16:14–23. The shortened version does not contain these pieces of information and reduces the story to the fight between the two men. The Septuagint also changes the sexual-ethnonational identity of Goliath from "the [foreskinned] Philistine" (17:26, 36) to "the foreigner" (ὁ ἀλλόφυλος 17:36; see also 10:5; 17:8, 10, 36, 43, 44, 48) and "this uncircumcised one" (ὁ ἀπερίτμητος 17:36, 37), yet the othering rhetoric persists.[30]

---

28. Francis Brown with S. R. Driver and Charles A. Briggs, eds., *The New Brown, Driver, and Briggs Hebrew and English Lexicon of the Old Testament* (Boston: Houghton Mifflin, 1907), 952a.

29. Robert Alter, *The Hebrew Bible: A Translation with Commentary, vol. 2: Prophets* (New York: Norton, 2019), 407.

30. For an exhaustive source-critical comparison of the Masoretic Text with the Greek translation, see Benjamin J. M. Johnson, *Reading David and Goliath in Greek and Hebrew: A Literary Approach*, Forschungen zum Alten Testament 2, Reihe 82 (Tübingen: Mohr Siebeck, 2015).

The other linguistic observation that illuminates the androcentric and ethnonational accent of 1 Samuel 17 appears in the root חרף in 1 Samuel 17:10, 25, 26, 36, 45 and in 2 Samuel 21:21. The BDB, one of the standard dictionaries of biblical Hebrew, renders the verb as "to reproach," in the sense of insulting someone, or "to taunt."[31] As a feminine noun, the word means "a reproach" or even "a scorn" but can also refer to "shame" and "disgrace" in stories of sexual violence or other forms of disapproved (violent) sexual activity, such as in Genesis 34:14; 2 Samuel 13:13; Isaiah 47:3; Ezekiel 16:57; or Proverbs 6:33. English translators render the verb in 1 Samuel 17:10, 25, 26, 36, 45 as "to defy," thus erasing any connotations about a sexualized reproach, taunt, or threat. Whether Goliath (17:10), the Israelites (17:25), or David (17:26, 36, 45) proclaim to חרף one another, the translation of this verb as "to defy" does not capture its tone in Hebrew. In contrast, English translations of 2 Samuel 21:21 use the verb "to taunt." For instance, the NRSVue reads, "When he ['a man of great size'] taunted (ויחרף) Israel." This Philistine man bullies the Israelites (i.e., he challenges the masculinity of his opponents, leading to retaliatory attacks and murder). The prominent appearance of the root חרף in 1 Samuel 17 is thus not accidental but part of a sexualized allusion haunting this tale about the future Israelite king and his Philistine warrior enemy. The gruesome end in which young David kills off the forehead-struck Philistine, cutting off his head (17:51) and carrying it to Jerusalem (17:54), communicates that this future king is a macho man. Even the archenemies of biblical Israel stand no chance against him. Eventually, he even owns Goliath's armor and sword (17:54; see also 21:9). The story teaches that nobody, not even the fiercest Philistine warrior, has a chance of beating this Israelite man.

The convergence of Goliath and David finds its culmination in a stunning midrashic tale told in a collection of stories called *The Jalkut Machiri for Psalms*, attributed to R. Machir Ben Abba Mari and published in the original Hebrew by Salomon Buber (1827–1906), a famous Jewish scholar and editor of Hebrew works and the grandfather of the even

31. *BDB* 357b.

more famous Martin Buber (1878–1965). The story about David's origin is introduced with a reference to Psalm 118:22. Here is the Hebrew text with my English translation since there is no published English translation available so far.[32]

'אבן מאסו הבונים הייתה לראש פנה'

The stone the builders rejected has become the chief cornerstone [Ps 118:22].

מדרש: הן בעוון חוללתי (תהילים נא ז), מלא כתיב בשני ווי"ן. פליגי בה תרי אמוראי במערבא. חד אמר: דוד בן אהיבה (=אהובה) היה, וחד אמר דוד בן שנואה היה.

Midrash: "Indeed I was born in iniquity" (Ps 51:7); full of [being] written with two waws. [There was a] dispute over it between two Amorai in the west. One said, "David is a son of love (= beloved)." And one said, "David is a son of hatred."

כיצד? ישי ראש לסנהדרין היה... ופירש מאשתו ג' שנים.

How? Jessi was head of the Sanhedrin . . . and withdrew from his wife for three years.

לאחר ג' שנים הייתה לו שפחה נאה ונתאווה לה. אמר לה: בתי, תקני עצמך הלילה כדי שתכנסי אלי בגט שחרור.

After three years, he had a handsome [female] slave and lusted after her. He said to her, "Daughter, fix yourself tonight so you can come to me with a divorce contract."

הלכה השפחה ואמרה לגברתה: הצילי עצמך ונפשי ואדוני מגיהנם. אמרה לה: מה טעם? שחה לה את הכל.

The [female] slave went and said to her mistress, "Save yourself and my soul and my lord from hell." She said to her, "What is the point?" She told her everything.

32. R. Machir Ben Abba Mari, *Jalkut Machiri: Sammlung halachischer und hagadischer Stellen aus Talmud und Midraschim zu den 150 Psalmen*, ed. Salomon Buber, vol. 2 (Berdychev: J. Scheftel, 1899), 214.

אמרה לה: בתי, מה אעשה שהיום ג' שנים לא נגע בי.

She said to her, "My daughter, what will I do that for three years he has not touched me?"

אמרה לה: אתן ליך (=לך) עצה, לכי תקני עצמך ואף אני כך, ולערב כשיאמר סגרי הדלת תכנסי את ואצא אני. וכך עשתה.

She said to her, "I will give you advice, go prepare yourself and I will do the same, and in the evening when he tells the door closers, go in, and I will go out." And she did so.

לערב עמדה השפחה וכבת (!) את הנר, באת לסגור את הדלת נכנסה גברתה ויצאה היא.

In the evening, the [female] slave stood and extinguished (!) the candle; she came to close the door. Her mistress came in, and she went out.

עשתה עמו כל הלילה נתעברה מדוד, ומתוך אהבתו על אותה שפחה, יצא דוד אדום מבין אחיו.

She did [it] with him all night. She became pregnant with David, and out of his love for her [female] slave, David came out red of [מבין] his brothers. . . .

לט' חדשים בקשו בניה להרגה ואת בנה דוד, כיון שראו שהוא אדום. אמר להם ישי: הניחו לו ויהיה לנו משועבד ורועה צאן.
והיה הדבר טמון עד כ"ח שנה.

For nine months, her sons asked to kill her and her son David because they saw that he was red. Yishai said to them, "Leave him, and we will have a slave and a shepherd." And it was so for up to twenty-eight years.

כיון שאמר לו הקב"ה לשמואל: 'לך אשלחך אל בית ישי הלחמי' (שמואל א, טז א), כיון שהלך הקריבו לו את אליאב... הקריב הב' והג' עד שבעת בניו.

Because God said to Samuel, "I will send you to Jesse the Beth-lehemite (Sam 1:16a)." Because he went and passed by Eliab to him. . . . He passed the second and third to his seven sons.

אמר לו שמואל לישי: 'התמו הנערים?' אמר לו: תמו.

And Samuel said unto Jesse, "Are here all your children?" And he said to him, "Finished."

אמר לו: הקב"ה אמר לו (=לי) לכה ואשלחך אל ישי ואתה אומר תמו!
אמר לו: עוד נשאר הקטן והוא רועה בצאן. אמר לו: שלח והביאהו'.
כיון שבא התחיל השמן מבצבץ ועולה.

He said to him: God told him (= me) go and I will send you to Jessi, and you said: "Finished." He said to him: "The little one is still there, and he is grazing in the flock." He said to him: "Send and bring him." As he came, the oil began to go up [on his head].

אמר לו הקב"ה לשמואל: שמואל אתה עומד ומשיחי עומד, קום משחהו כי זה הוא...
וישי ובניו היו עומדין ברתת ואימה.

The Almighty said to Samuel, "Samuel, you stand and my Messiah stands. Get up from his anointing because this is he. . . ." Jesse and his sons were standing in terror and fear.

אמרו: לא בא שמואל אלא לבזותינו ולהודיע לישראל שיש לו (=לנו) בן פסול,
ואמו של דוד שמחה מבפנים ועצבה מבחוץ. כיון שנטל כוס ישועות שמחו כלן.
עמד שמואל ונשקו על ראשו.

They said, "Samuel did not come but to despise us and inform Israel that he (= us) has an illegitimate son." And the mother of David was happy on the inside and sad on the outside. Because he took a glass of salvation, they were all happy. Samuel stood and kissed him on his head.

פתח ואמר: 'ה' אמר אלי בני אתה' (תהילים ב ז). באותה שעה אמרה אמו: 'אבן
מאסו הבונים', הבנים כתיב.

He opened and said, "*Ha-shem* said to me: 'Thou art My son' (Ps 2:7)." At that moment, his mother said, "The stone the builders [*habonim*] rejected," [but it is] written [as] the sons [*habanim*]. [Ps 118:22].

אמרה: אי בן שמאסו אותך אחיך הייתה (=היית) לראש פנה ועלית' על כלן.
אמרו לה בניה: 'מאת ה' הייתה זאת', לפיכך 'זה היום עשה ה' נגילה ונשמחה בו.

She said, "No son, you are tired, your brother was (= you were) a cornerstone [*Rosh Pena*] and you ascended above all of them." Her sons said to her, "From *ha-shem* it was." Therefore: "This is the day *ha-shem* has made; let us exalt and rejoice in it."

Importantly, the sages imagine David as a child of rape. The *Jalkut Machiri for Psalms* mentions that one group of rabbis views David as "a son of love" and that another group of rabbis sees David as "a son of hatred."[33] As an explanation for either option, the midrash continues with the following story: After Jesse, David's father, has ignored his wife for the past three years, he is lusting after a beautiful enslaved woman, asking her to dress up and see him in the evening "with a divorce contract" (גט). The enslaved woman runs to Jesse's wife for help, but the wife feels hopeless and tells the woman to go into the bedroom when he calls her. So it happens. The enslaved woman, spending the whole night with Jesse, becomes pregnant with David. Because David loves his mother, he comes out red (אדום). His brothers want to kill both the mother and David because he is red, but then they decide to make him their slave for twenty-eight years. According to this midrash, David is the result of a rape, as Jesse orders the enslaved woman to his bed; she has no choice. This story explains why David, the youngest of eight sons,[34] becomes king, showing everybody that he is a real man despite his traumatic conception story.

In yet another midrash, the Jewish sages imagine that Goliath was conceived during his mother's rape. In Midrash Rabbah Ruth 2:20, Goliath's mother is Orpah, the daughter-in-law of Naomi, who returns home and on the way is raped by "one hundred uncircumcised heathens for a whole night" (ממאה ערלות גוים שנתערו בה כל הלילה). In explaining Goliath's strange question in 1 Samuel 17:43, "Rabbi Tanchuma said: Even one dog raped her, as it is written: And the Philistine said to David, am I a dog." The same idea appears in bSota 42b, where the rabbis explain why Goliath is called a

33. R. Machir Ben Abba Mari, *Jalkut Machiri*, 214. The text is in Hebrew, and the English translation is mine.

34. Are there only four sons, as suggested by 1 Sam 17:28? Source critics observe the double introduction of David in 17:12–15, sometimes classifying the entire section of verses 12–31 as secondary because David is introduced already in 16:14–23. Various traditions combine into a seemingly coherent narrative that consists, however, of various versions about David's introduction to the king. See also the fragment in 17:57–58 that is out of place since King Saul already met David several times before.

champion (איש־הבנים) in 1 Samuel 17:4. The rabbis refer to the rape of his mother: "The word (הבנים) is related to the word *bein*, meaning between, and it means that he was born from among many, as follows: He was the son of one hundred fathers (*pappi*) and one dog (*nanai*), as his mother engaged in sexual intercourse with one-hundred men and a dog, and he was fathered from among them." In the William Davidson Talmud (Koren—Steinsaltz) of the Talmud (bSota 42b), the sages state:

> The verse recounts that he was "named Goliath, of Gath" (I Samuel 17:4). Rav Yosef taught: This is because everyone would thresh his mother by cohabiting with her like people do in a winepress [*gat*], where everyone tramples. It is written that Goliath came from "the caves [*me'arot*] of the Philistines" (I Samuel 17:23), but we read, according to the Masoretic text: He came from among "the ranks [*ma'arkhot*] of the Philistines." What is meant by the written term *me'arot*? Rav Yosef taught: The word is related to the word he'era, meaning penetrated, and implies that everyone penetrated [*he'eru*], i.e., engaged in sexual intercourse with, his mother.[35]

The sages have no sympathy for Goliath's mother. To them, being conceived during a gang rape is an insult. Even today, many children of rape feel shame and rejection from their mothers and society. Does Goliath become a mighty warrior in his quest for respect and status due to his traumatic conception story?

In sum, the folktale of David and Goliath in 1 Samuel 17 contains androcentric and ethnonational elements on the linguistic and midrashic levels. The terminology focuses on the maleness of the characters (איש), sexual innuendos are implied in the use of the verb חרף, and the ancient rabbis present Goliath and David as children of rape, thus illuminating gendered interests that intersect with ethnonational putdowns. The picture is not pretty, as the androcentric and ethnonational rhetoric of the biblical stories

35. For online access to this version of the Talmud, see https://www.sefaria.org, and more specifically for this quote: https://www.sefaria.org/Sotah.42b.6?lang=bi&with=all&lang2=en.

showcases Goliath and the Philistines as the ultimate Other of David and the Israelites.

Politically Naive, Clueless, and Ridiculous? The Stories About the Philistine King Achish of Gath

References to the ethnonational binary do not end with the defeat of the Philistine warrior Goliath. The other outstanding Philistine character that plays a prominent role in the story of David's rise to monarchical power is King Achish of Gath. He appears in 1 Samuel 21:10–15; 27:1–28:2; 29. Cynthia Edenburg describes this king's geoethnic background in this way:

> The name *'kyš* occurs as ruler (*šr*) of Ekron in a seventh century BCE dedication inscription from Ekron (Tel Miqne), and has been identified with Ikausu king of Amqar(r)una who figures in Assyrian inscriptions of Esarhaddon and Assurbanipal. . . . Therefore, I think it likely that the name of the king of Gath in 1 Samuel and 1 Kings is a reflection of the Akhayus or Ikausu of Ekron in the inscriptions. The name of the Philistine king David served may not have been preserved in the early tradition, and the compiler of the David traditions may have intended to emphasize the "otherness" of the king of Gath by borrowing the non-Semitic name of the well-known seventh-cent. king of Ekron. . . .
>
> If so, then it is possible to surmise that the stories about David's relations with the Philistines originally dealt with an anonymous king of Gath, and a subsequent seventh-century Judean scribe identified the anonymous king as Achish, since the non-Semitic name enhanced the Philistine identity of the king, or because Gath had been superseded in his day, and he wished to impart upon the king of Gath in the David stories the same standing accorded to the more recent king of Ekron.[36]

36. Cynthia Edenburg, "Notes on the Origin of the Biblical Tradition Regarding Achish King of Gath," *VT* 61 (2011): 36–37.

Few biblical scholars dispute that, first, these stories are "fictional"[37] and that, second, the archaeological site of Tel eṣ-Ṣâfi is the ancient city location of Gath, although "conclusive epigraphic evidence of the identification" has not (yet) been found.[38] The biblical narratives should therefore not be taken as memories of ancient events. The archaeological findings indicate that the biblical characterizations of the Philistines, including those in 1 Samuel, contradict the archaeological findings. They suggest that Philistine society consisted of nonconfrontational, diverse, heterogeneous, "mixed," and "entangled"[39] groups of peoples. As Daniel Pioske observes, "For a period of about three centuries we find no clear [archaeological] evidence that forces from Gath ever attacked or destroyed a single location within the neighboring regions of Israel or Judah, or, conversely, that it was attacked by individuals from these areas during this time."[40] The assessment by Aren M. Maeir, the well-known archaeologist of Tell eṣ-Ṣâfi/Gath, is unusually frank when he asserts, "Attempting to define a uniform and monolithic 'Philistine identity' is both futile—and misdirected."[41] Maeir explains why the biblical depictions of the Philistines are not historical:

> The very question of how to identify a site as being associated with the Philistine culture, and, even more basically, how the various levels of "Philistine identity" can be archaeologically defined, have been extensively discussed. Some of these attempts to differentiate between the "Philistines" and other ethnicities, based on a small set of material correlates, have led

37. See, e.g., Israel Finkelstein, "The Philistines in the Bible: A Late-Monarchic Perspective," *JSOT* 27 (2002): 131–167, esp. 133–136.

38. Yigal Levin, "Gath of the Philistines in the Bible and on the Ground: The Historical Geography of Tell eṣ-Ṣâfi/Gath," *NEA* 80 (2017): 238.

39. Aren M. Maeir, "Philistine Gath After 20 Years: Regional Perspectives on the Iron Age at Tell eṣ-Ṣâfi/Gath," in *The Shephelah During the Iron Age: Recent Archaeological Studies*, ed. Oded Lipschits and Aren M. Maeir (Winona Lake, IN: Eisenbrauns, 2017), 136, 133.

40. Daniel Pioske, "Material Culture and Making Visible: On the Portrayal of Philistine Gath in the Book of Samuel," *JSOT* 43 (2018): 7.

41. Aren M. Maeir, "Philistine and Israelite Identities: Some Comparative Thoughts," *Die Welt des Orients* 49 (2019): 152.

> to simplistic or simply mistaken differentiations. As noted in the past, many of these cultural attributes can appear on both sides of the supposed Philistine/Israelite ethnic boundaries—and even beyond. There is no doubt that the material assemblages at major sites in Iron Age Philistia are different from those of sites in regions associated with other groups (Israelite, Judahite, Phoenicians, etc.). Nonetheless, specific types of objects can be seen in many areas and used by many groups. . . . The appearance of supposedly Philistine objects should not be seen as necessarily indicating the expansion of the Philistine culture into other zones and, similarly, the appearance of Israelite/Judahite facets among the Philistines. Instead, artifact assemblages should be examined in their broader contexts in order to draw out various cultural encounters, relationships, and entanglements, as well as to elucidate new ones.[42]

Maeir cautions that biblical depictions about Philistine and Israelite encounters are not grounded in historical realities because the archaeological findings do not indicate sharp ethnonational differences between Philistine and Israelite culture. Moreover, the archaeological record gives "very little evidence of warfare-related materials in the Iron I (approximately1,200–980 BCE) Philistine culture—which belies a view of the Philistines as a conquering and dominating colonial culture."[43] The binary opposition between Philistine and Israelite group identities is thus a biblical-literary invention, and "a straightforward connection between the ideologies reflected in the biblical text and the archaeological record is problematic."[44]

Said differently, the antagonistic imaginary of 1 Samuel 21:10–15; 27:1–28:2; 29 that depicts David as fleeing twice from Saul's reach to the Philistine city-state of Gath, ruled by King Achish, is a literary-ideological plot development that is not verifiable in archaeological findings or historical

42. Maeir, "Philistine Gath After 20 Years," 134–135.
43. Maeir, "Philistine Gath After 20 Years," 136.
44. Maeir, "Philistine Gath After 20 Years," 135.

evidence.[45] Historically, all the people living in the land during Iron I were Canaanites; their cultures consisted of both imported and local elements, and so the static, monolithic, and binary group identities of the Philistines and the Israelites must be rejected. Since all of them were Canaanites, a distinction among "Philistine Canaanites," "Real Canaanites," and "Israelite Canaanites"[46] is impossible. Biblical accounts that insist on the ethnoreligious binary of Israelites and Philistines do not reflect the historical past of Iron I. As Maeir perceptively asks, "Are not the very definitions of ethnic groups presumed to appear in Iron I an ideological reflection derived from later texts?"[47] Nevertheless, the biblical stories of David's escape to the Philistine city-state of Gath have shaped postbiblical views about the Philistines and the Israelites. Fiction has made history that is still assumed, including in the androcentric and ethnonational discourse of 1 Samuel.

Two stories depict David's encounters with Achish, the only Philistine king explicitly mentioned (1 Sam 21:10–15; 27:1–28:2; 29). Only one other Philistine king, Abimelech, appears by name in Genesis 20 and 26. Historical critics submit that the accounts in 21:10–15 and 27:1–28:2; 29 go back to the same event and that the first account is "a tendentious reworking of a folk-tale."[48] Other interpreters assert that the two reports originate in repetitive events in David's life. Since none of these narratives reliably links to any historical event, literary observations produce a more interesting reading, showing a chiastic literary structure of the biblical chapters. Abigail's acknowledgment of David as the future king is the literary center of this chiasm. The female character who is already a wife and will become one of David's wives supports and enhances his role in the narrative.

---

45. Israel Finkelstein more cautiously explained twenty years ago, "The biblical references to the Philistines do not contain any memory of early Iron I (twelfth and eleventh centuries BCE) events or cultural behavior. A few texts, such as the Ark Narrative and the stories about the importance of Gath, seem to portray late Iron 1 (tenth century) and early Iron II realities." See Finkelstein, "Philistines in the Bible," 156.

46. Finkelstein, "Philistines in the Bible," 138.

47. Finkelstein, "Philistines in the Bible," 137.

48. For further details, see Edenburg, "Notes on the Origin of the Biblical Tradition," 35.

A David's encounter with the Philistine king (21:10–15)
B Singing women praise David (21:12)
C David's refusal to kill Saul (chap. 24)
D David's meeting with Abigail, who acknowledges him as the future king (chap. 25)
C' David's refusal to kill Saul (chap. 26)
B' Singing women praise David (29:5)
A' David's encounter with the Philistine king (27:1–6)

The literary analysis shows that the double reports on David's encounters with the Philistine king in 21:10–15 and 27:1–6 form the outer parts of the chiastic structure. In the center, 1 Samuel 25 reports on David's meeting with Abigail; she is the woman recognizing him as the future king. The twice-repeated phrase in 21:11 and 29:5 (the saying of the jubilantly singing women in 18:7), "Saul has killed his thousands, and David his ten thousands," further cements David as the future Israelite king, who temporarily escapes to the Philistine kingdom of Gath. The double telling of David refusing to kill Saul during his sleep in chapters 24 and 26 depicts David as more careful the second time around and as explaining why he needs to escape the jealous, furious, and murderous Saul.[49] The chiasm, in which David escapes twice to Gath, thus foreshadows his rise to the Israelite monarchy. The literary construct suggests that David is at the lowest point in his life, but from here he will rise to biblical Israel's highest office. This is literary drama at its best. The future king seemingly succumbs to Philistine authority, and so readers wonder: How can any good come out of that situation? The chiasm offers the clue: He will be the next king.

The androcentric and ethnonational depictions of eventual Philistine loss also come with a heavy dose of ridicule for the Philistine king. In both 21:10–15 and 27:1–28:2; 29, King Achish is wrong in his assessment of David. Although Achish's servants, or rather slaves (עבדים), recognize David as "the king of the land" (21:11), King Achish sees in David just another of

49. For additional details, see the analysis of Johannes Klein, "Davids Flucht zu den Philistern (1 Sam. XXI 11ff.; XXVII–XXIX)," *VT* 55 (2005): 176–184.

the many fools (21:15 משגעים) in his "house," a reference to all royal servants and family members.

The Philistine king is even more severely wrong in the second tale. This time, David arrives with six hundred men and all of their families (27:2–3), including David's two wives, Ahinoam of Jezreel and Abigail of Carmel, Nabal's widow (27:3). David requests a "place" (מקום) in one of Achish's towns, and Achish gives him a city called Ziklag (27:6), a very generous gesture. David and his men with their families live there for "one year and four months" (27:7) while they also raid "the Geshurites, the Girzites, and the Amalekites" (27:8), never leaving anybody alive, neither "man" nor "woman" (27:9). David always lies when the Philistine king asks him about the military raids. David tells him he attacked "the Negeb of Judah," "the Negeb of the Jerahmeelites," and "the Negeb of the Kenites" (27:10) because "David left neither man nor woman alive to be brought back to Gath, thinking, They might tell about us and say, David has done so and so" (27:11). Readers learn about David's true intentions, while Achish trusts him. Achish believes that David made himself so obnoxious among the Israelites that he would always be loyal to him (27:12). A foolish king, Achish falls for David's lies, and readers know it.

Achish's foolishness gets worse in the next segment of the second narrative. The king asks David to join him as his bodyguard, along with the Philistine army, in an attack on Israel (28:1–2). Achish's military commanders know better than the king. They ask him, "What are these Hebrews doing here?" (29:3). Achish's response baffles because he identifies David as "the servant of King Saul of Israel." David seems faithful to Achish, and so the king finds no fault with him for more than a year. Yet readers understand all along this king is a fool. His commanders recognize David's deceptive stance, as they insist on keeping David away from the battle. They fear David will betray them within their front lines (29:4) and quote again the saying about David's fierceness in battle: He is even more successful than King Saul (29:5). Eventually, King Achish does not withstand the objections of his commanders and confesses to David, "I have had no fault to find with you ever since you joined me, but the commanders (הסרנים) are not willing to accept you" (29:6 JPS). He also praises David to an extent that every reader knows this Philistine king is a fool. Achish praises David as "upright" (29:6 ישר) and even proclaims, "I know you are good in my eyes, like an angel [מלאך] of God, but the Philistine commanders [שׂרי פלשׁתים] said: 'He shall not go up with us to the battle'" (29:9; my translation). Achish is depicted as a weak and silly leader, but he finally listens to his commanders. He sends David and his men back to Ziklag, asking David to wait out the battle at Jezreel. This battle will kill King Saul and his sons (1 Sam 31). We cannot know what David would have done had Achish prevailed against his commanders. The question is moot because the tale affirms the androcentric and ethnonational inferiority of the Philistine king, even though he will win against Saul. Yet in the end, David will be the winner, which is the message of this tendentious story.

In short, Achish of Gath emerges as a buffoon who lacks authority among his own commanders. By repeatedly misjudging David's loyalty, he endangers himself and his soldiers. He praises David twice and is wrong each time. Meanwhile, David persistently lies to him; he is not "an angel" or a "messenger" of God (29:9). Historical critics speculate about the story's historical date, while they also acknowledge the fictional quality of the narratives. For instance, Erasmus Gass states, "It is likely that the literary fiction of an Achish of Gath makes fun of one of the [later] kings of Ekron of the same name."[50] This story is indeed fiction that does not end here. After the debacle with David, Achish disappears, and David returns to Ziklag. He finds the place devastated by the Amalekites with all the "women and all who were in it, both big [גדול] and small," taken as captives (1 Sam 30:2). He gets a priestly blessing (30:7–10), and then, with the help of an Egyptian enslaved man left behind by the Amalekite warriors (30:11–16), David and his warrior men chase down the Amalekites, kill the new enemies (30:17), and take back all captured women, men, children, and animals (30:18–20). David also rescues "his two wives" (30:18) and every daughter and son (30:19). He distributes the spoil of the battle not only among his men but also among the people in Judah, thereby currying favors among those who will later help him become Israel's second king (2 Sam 2:4).

---

50. Erasmus Gaß, "Achisch von Gat als politische Witzfigur," *TQ* 189 (2009): 237. My translation of the original German. For further details on King Achish, who ruled in Ekron during the seventh century BCE, see, e.g., Edenburg, "Notes on the Origin of the Biblical Tradition," 34–38, esp. 36–37.

In conclusion, the tales about the Philistine king and David are literary stepping stones for creating excitement and some tensions about David's unstoppable path toward royal power and glory. The androcentric and ethnonational rhetoric always sides with him, as the Philistine king is a fool, unbeknownst to him but obvious to every reader.

Telling Tales About Israelite Ethnonational Supremacy: Concluding Remarks

The interpretation of key texts in 1 Samuel demonstrates that the persistent depiction of the Philistine-Israelite binary is designed to create sympathy for the Israelites. This binary is so convincing that even contemporary readers fall prey to its rhetorical power. The ethnonational discourse does not, however, depict a historical reality. Instead, it illustrates the effort of building up biblical Israel's ethnonational identity. Scholars with different exegetical and archaeological interests propose different dates for the original writing of these texts, such as the eighth, seventh, or sixth century BCE. Regardless of the historical dating, the narratives present the (male) Philistines as the archenemies of biblical Israel in dramatic ways. Accordingly, the references to Philistine foreskins must be understood as a rhetorical strategy of sexual objectification that places Philistine warriors in the position of the sexualized Other. They are like "women" in tales filled with male anxiety over manliness. In a bizarre request, Philistine foreskins become the Israelite bride price in exchange for a royal daughter, as King Saul offers his daughter Michal to David as a wife. Contemporary English Bibles replace the physically oriented rendering of the Hebrew word *foreskin* with a medicalized term that classifies the Philistines as "uncircumcised." Sometimes the sexualized wording is completely replaced by Western colonial terminology that identifies the Philistines as "pagans." The biological gender marker, emphasizing the ethnonational difference between male Philistine warriors and male Israelites, refers to the inferior, unmanly, and thus, by extension, killable status of the male Philistines.

The literary effort of so-called nation-building that underscores the ethnonational binary between male Philistines and male Israelites also appears in the Ark Narrative (4:1–7:1). The first part of the story reports the complete Philistine military success that includes the deaths of tens of thousands of male Israelites and the capture of the ark. The defeat finds its most emotionally charged expression in the story of the unnamed wife of Eli's son Phinehas (4:10–22). Hearing about the capture of the ark and the death of her husband and father-in-law, she goes into labor. As she gives birth, she names the baby boy "no-glory" (Ichabod) and then dies. Her fate represents the fate of her male relatives. Death surrounds the birth of her male child. This narrative imagines Philistine power as all-encompassing, whereas the rest of the Ark Narrative, employing satire and comedy, recounts how the ark is returned to the Israelites. Thus, in the end, Philistine power cannot withstand the glory of the Israelite deity in the literary imagination of 1 Samuel 4:1–7:1.

The iconic story of the battle between Goliath and David is another example of hegemonic masculinity, filled with ethnonational connotations, that also lives on in contemporary sociocultural appropriations. A man, underestimated by his opponent, wins because of his brains and preparation. Accordingly, David rises to become the second king in biblical Israel. Androcentric and ethnonational accents flicker throughout 1 Samuel 17, communicating the struggle over masculinity by every man, whether he is Philistine or Israelite. Strikingly, an eighteenth-century midrash imagines both proponents, Goliath and David, as being conceived during the rape of their mothers. This convergence suggests that the rabbis observed commonalities between Goliath and David, battling so fiercely to establish their superiority over the other and within their group. Predictably, in the biblical-literary imagination, only David is poised to win, later even owning his dead opponent's armor and sword.

In short, the narratives about the future Israelite king, David, who escapes from Saul's death threats to Philistine territory and is accepted by the only named Philistine king, Achish, articulate ethnonational supremacy of biblical Israel. Yet the more than twenty years of archaeological excavations at Tel eṣ-Ṣâfi/Gath demonstrate that the biblical references to the Philistines as a warrior-prone culture are archaeologically unverifiable. The archaeological record suggests that Philistine society consisted of nonconfrontational, diverse, heterogeneous, mixed, and entangled groups of people. The binary between Israelites and Philistines, including in the stories about David's encounters with King Achish, is fictional. The literary-ideological plot development serves theopolitical interests that construct the ethnonational identity of the Philistines as inferior to the Israelites. Specifically, King Achish emerges as a Philistine buffoon who underestimates David's intentions and assists him on his relentless path toward monarchical power. Achish's military success against the first Israelite king, Saul, reinforces this plotline.

This feminist interpretation, recognizing these persistent rhetorical dynamics in 1 Samuel, highlights the androcentric and ethnonational elements in vocabulary and plot development that endorse patterns of hierarchical, unequal, and unjust patterns in the stories. Empathy with female characters, such as the unnamed daughter-in-law, is not an exegetical option because the name of her newborn son strengthens the problematic ethnonational binary between (male) Philistines and Israelites. Since the portrayal of the Philistines as war-mongering opponents of the Israelites is a biblical invention in literary service of particular theopolitical interests, commonly classified as the interests of the so-called Deuteronomistic historians, my reading exposes those interests for what they are. They are part of an anti-democratic, exclusionary, and violent ideology that serves nation-building efforts of one people over another. This kind of literary ideology requires exegetical decolonization that highlights the embedded androcentric and ethnonational dynamics. Since in this ideology, women's function is reduced to marriage and motherhood, I find it easy to resist this colonizing rhetoric and to expose the dangers of this binary strategy in 1 Samuel.

For Further Reflection

1. Robert Drews, "Canaanites and Philistines," *JSOT* 23 (1998): 49–50, n. 32.

   Our names "Philistia" and "Philistines" are unfortunate obfuscations, first introduced by the translators of the LXX and made definitive by Jerome's Vg. When turning a Hebrew text into Greek, the translators of the LXX might simply—as Josephus was later to do—have Hellenized the Hebrew פלשתים as Παλαιστίνοι and the toponym פלשת as Παλαιστίνη. Instead, they avoided the toponym altogether, turning it into an ethnonym. As for ethnonym, they chose sometimes to transliterate it (incorrectly aspirating the initial letter, perhaps to compensate for their inability to aspirate the sigma) as s Φυλιστιμ, a word that looked exotic rather than familiar, and more often translate it as αλλόφυλοι. Jerome followed the LXX's lead in eradicating the names, "Palestine" and "Palestinians," from his Old Testament, a practice adopted in most modern translations of the Bible. Jerome too eschewed the toponym, and instead of Latinizing פלשתים into *Palaestini* he either translated it into *alienigeni* or further obscured it by roughing up and then transliterating the Hebrew into *Philisthiim* (at Exod. 15:14, "the inhabitants of Palestine" become almost unintelligible as *habitatores Philisthiim*). In his *Liber Hebraicarum Quaestionum in Genesim* Jerome explained that *Palaestini* was a modern "corruption" of the ancient name "Chasloim qui deinceps appellati sunt, quos nos corrupte Palaestinos dicimus" (PL, IIXXX, col 320). But in effect Jerome's procedure reassured the Palestinian Christians of his own day that they had really no connection with the *Philisthiim* who had caused Israel so much trouble in the days of Samson and Saul.

2. Serge Frolov, "Foreskin Talk: The 'Uncircumcised' in Judges and Samuel" (Southern Methodist University, Dallas, USA). Used by permission of the author.

These days (year 2023 of the Common Era), Ukrainians rarely say "Russian." They say *katsap* (probably derived from Arabic *kassab*, "butcher"). They say *moskal'* (from "Moscow"). They say *vatnik* (a sort of cotton padded jacket worn by menial workers in cold weather). And, in a twist that tells volumes about the reach of Western mass culture, they say *orc* (Russia, accordingly, is "Mordor").

All of these are ethnic slurs par excellence. They are derisive; they are demeaning; they are hateful; they are meant to offend, to hurt. And yes, they are dehumanizing, especially "orc"— which may be one reason why it is a term of choice in official Ukrainian propaganda, media, and social networks. They make it easier to overcome natural human squeamishness and kill, especially at close quarters.

Ukrainians aren't big on political correctness. But who could blame them?

They do not hurl slurs because they want to exterminate Russians, or colonize them, or take over even a small part of their territory. They do so because Russia colonized their country for centuries—from the mid-1600s until as recently as 1991—and now wants to do it all over again, or, failing that, annex good chunks of Ukraine. They do so because Russian soldiers trample their land, killing, raping, plundering, and torturing, because Russian missiles and drones explode in their cities, night in and night out.

In addition to bullets and shells, and perhaps more potent than they could ever be, the pejorative is Ukrainians' weapon of resistance.

This is something to be kept in mind when it comes to the Hebrew Bible's only term of disparagement for a nonIsraelite population—the word *'arel*, usually translated into English as "uncircumcised," but literally meaning "one with a foreskin." Some of its thirty-five occurrences are purely technical (e.g., Josh 5:7 states matter-of-factly that after long wandering in the desert the Israelites were "foreskinned") and most of them are not associated with any particular group. In seven instances, however, the word is used specifically of the Philistines— a people that in the early first millennium BCE resided in the southwestern part of Canaan (Judg 14:3; 15:18; 1 Sam 14:6; 17:26, 36; 31:4; 2 Sam 1:20).

At one level, the term *'arel* simply registers the most obvious, and perhaps the only, visual distinction between Israelite and Philistine men: the former were (supposed to be) circumcised while the latter were not. It is for this reason that when Saul sends David to "be avenged on the king's [Philistine] enemies" in lieu of bride-price he demands foreskins as a proof of the killing (1 Sam 18:25). The distinction would be especially striking if the Philistines, who probably were originally from somewhere in the Aegean, shared the preference of Hellenic men for long, bushy foreskins.[51] The word also conveys

51. Frederick. M. Hodges, "The Ideal Prepuce in Ancient Greece and Rome: Male Genital Aesthetics and Their Relation to Lipodermos, Circumcision, Foreskin Restoration, and the Kynodesme," *Bulletin of the History of Medicine* 75 (2001): 375–405.

a sense of inferiority, however, given that the Hebrew Bible uses *'arel* to denote all sorts of physical and moral imperfection, describing a stutterer as one "of uncircumcised lips" (Exod 6:12; King James Version) and inclination to violate the divine commandments as "uncircumcised heart" (Lev 26:41). It does not quite dehumanize the Philistines, but it certainly describes them as profoundly and perhaps irredeemably flawed.

At the same time, and by no means coincidentally, the use of *'arel* of a specific ethnic group precisely coincides in the biblical narrative with the period of unrelenting Philistine aggression against Israel. They first emerge as a threat in Judges 10:7, and in Judges 13:1 God gives Israel "into the hand of the Philistines forty years" (cf. Judg 15:11). What precisely that involved is revealed in 1 Samuel 4:9: Israelites were Philistines' slaves (most English Bibles gingerly translate "servants," but the term is the one used for bondage). Samuel scores a win for Israel in 1 Samuel 7, but in 1 Samuel 9–10 it is again under Philistine occupation (in 10:5, there is a Philistine roadblock in the middle of the Israelite territory). Saul defeats the Philistine army repeatedly, thanks to his son Jonathan in 1 Samuel 13–14 and David in chapter 17, but they keep coming back, and the purpose, as clearly put by Goliath in 17:9, is Israel's re-enslavement. After Saul is defeated in 1 Samuel 31, the narrator reports that the Israelites "forsook their towns and fled, and the Philistines came and occupied them" (v. 7)—presupposing some kind of ethnic cleansing. The aggression only stops after David's back-to-back victories in 2 Samuel 5—and although the account that follows covers several centuries we do not hear about the "uncircumcised" ever again.

'Arel is an ethnic slur, to be sure, but just like with "orc" in the mouths of today's Ukrainians the context needs to be kept in view. In both cases, it is used by the oppressed against the oppressors, by the victims of an aggression against its perpetrators. It reflects a longing for freedom and motivates those who fight for it. Again, it is probably not by accident that, for the most part, the word *'arel* shows up in combat situations where Israelite warriors face seemingly impossible odds: Samson is fresh from killing a thousand enemies (Judg

15:18), Jonathan and his armor-bearer are about to attack a whole unit of Philistines (1 Sam 14:6), and David answers Goliath's challenge (1 Sam 17:26, 36). It is as though thinking, and speaking, of having too much flesh as a deficiency made it easier to confront the opponents, no matter how large they loomed.

As far as the Hebrew Bible is concerned, the sociohistorical background of the author(s) should also be taken into consideration. Although 2 Samuel 8 reports David building what amounts to a regional superpower (which Solomon ruins in 1 Kings 11), this was most likely a pipe dream. Canaan simply did not have enough population or resources for a substantial expansion, so Israelite states were always vulnerable to Mesopotamian and Egyptian conquerors and most of the time under their sway. Even if the biblical narrative, or parts of it, was written when such states existed, it was written from the position of an underdog. So much so after most of the Israelites were deported from their land (in an early rehearsal of the death marches at the final stage of the Holocaust) and then restored in it as a stateless community. For whoever wrote Judges and Samuel, emphasizing the "uncircumcised" condition of conquerors and overlords was a way of coping with constant disruption and humiliation and, in particular, with the trauma of the exile.

To be sure, dehumanization tends to become a habit, especially when practiced constantly over long periods, and there is no guarantee this habit will die quickly, or ever, when the underdog happens to gain the upper hand. In the Bible, when David conquers the Philistines in 2 Samuel 8:1 there is no indication they were mistreated, but his subsequent conquest of the Moabites in 2 Samuel 8:2 is accompanied by atrocities if not genocide. And in the case of Ukrainians, thinking and talking about Russians as "orcs" may lead to ethnic cleansing and even genocide if the country's military manages to break through into the areas where most of the population identify as Russian. Understanding the place that ethnic slurs come from does not make them completely innocent.

For two interrelated reasons, it would be advisable for well-intentioned biblical commentators to point out this dynamic nuance. First, simply decrying *'arel* as exclusive, xenophobic, and potentially colonialist would contribute to the longstanding negative stereotype of the Jews hating all the "foreskinned" Gentiles rather than those who hate and persecute them. Second, the communities that tend to identify with ancient Israel but, unlike it, wield substantial power, such as Western Christians and Israeli Jews, should be reminded that the term's biblical context—as far as both the characters and the author are concerned—is vastly different from their circumstances today. In some situations, such as that unfolding now on the blood-soaked fields of Ukraine, it can literally make a difference between life and death.

3. "A Rabbinic Interpretation of 1 Samuel 6:12" from Avodah Zarah 24b (The William Davidson Talmud). Quoted from Rabbi Adin Even-Israel Steinsaltz, *The Koren Talmud Bavli Noé*, vol. 32 (Jerusalem: Koren Publishers, 2017), https://www.sefaria.org/Avodah_Zarah.24b.17?lang=bi&with=all&lang2=en.
   The Gemara further analyzes the episode involving the cows sent by the Philistines. The verse states: "And the cattle took the straight [*vayyisharna*] way, on the way to Beit Shemesh; they went along the highway, lowing as they went" (1 Sam 6:12). The Gemara asks: What is the meaning of the word *vayyisharna*? Rabbi Yoḥanan says in the name of Rabbi Meir: It means that they recited a song [*shira*]. And Rav Zutra bar Toviyya says that Rav says: It means that they straightened [*yishru*] their faces so that they were opposite the Ark and recited a song. The Gemara asks: And what song did they recite? Rabbi Yoḥanan says in the name of Rabbi Meir: They recited the song that follows the verse: "Then sang Moses and the children of Israel this song unto the Lord" (Exodus 15:1). And Rabbi Yoḥanan himself says that it was: "And on that day shall you say: Give thanks unto the Lord, proclaim His name, declare His doings among the peoples, make mention that His name is exalted" (Isaiah 12:4). And Rabbi Shimon ben Lakish says that it was an orphaned psalm, that is, a psalm whose author and the event to which it makes reference are not specified. The psalm begins with: "A Psalm. O sing unto the Lord a new song, for He has done marvelous things; His right hand, and

His holy arm, have wrought salvation for Him" (Psalms 98:1). Rabbi Elazar says that it was the psalm beginning with: "The Lord reigns; let the peoples tremble" (Psalms 99:1). Rabbi Shmuel bar Naḥmani says that it was the Psalm beginning: "The Lord reigns; He is clothed in majesty" (Psalms 93:1). Rabbi Yitzḥak Nappaḥa says: They did not recite a verse found in the Bible, but rather, the following song: Sing, sing, acacia; ascend in all your glory; overlaid with golden embroidery, exalted by the book [*devir*] of the palace, and magnificent with jewels. The song alludes to the Ark of the Covenant, which was made of acacia wood and covered with gold. The expression: Book of the palace, is a reference to the Torah scroll that was placed in the Ark.

4. Kevin M. McGeough,[52] "David in Film" (University of Lethbridge, Canada). Used by permission of the author.
The story of David and Goliath seems perfectly suited to cinema, with its classic underdog story of a boy who confronts a legendary warrior and manages to defeat him in one-on-one combat. The story is well known but no film version has resonated much with audiences, even though many cinematic attempts have been made. The problem may be that the biblical narrative is much more complex than it first appears, as is the protagonist David, and that complexity is not easily dealt with in films based on Scripture. David's ethical failures are central to his story, which does not conform with the character arc of the stalwart heroes expected in biblical epics, the incorruptible Charlton Heston-like figures who lead their people and stand as role models of piety and devotion to the state. The choices filmmakers have made in presenting David's story on screen highlight some of the curious ways that adapting the figure of David to different movie genres transforms his characterization. Three different types of "David films" show how filmmaker choices influence the cinematic reception of the ancient king.

52. For a longer discussion on the troubles of depicting David on the silver screen, see Kevin M. McGeough, "The Problem with David: Masculinity and Morality in Biblical Cinema," *Journal of Religion and Film* 22 (2018), https://digitalcommons.unomaha.edu/jrf/vol22/iss1/33.

Arguably the most successful adaptation of the books of Samuel (at least from a commercial standpoint) is *David and Bathsheba* (1951) starring Gregory Peck and Susan Hayward as the title characters. The top-grossing film of the year, and nominated for five Academy Awards, *David and Bathsheba* involved three major "behind the screen" talents of the era: Henry King (director), Darryl F. Zanuck (producer), and Philip Dunne (screenwriter). As would be expected from the title, *David and Bathsheba* concentrates on the romance but, given the biblical account of that relationship, struggles with how to portray the heroic David audiences expect of Gregory Peck. While acknowledging his adulterous behavior, the film presents David as a veteran grappling with the traumas of his violent past, a characterization that viewers in 1951 would have been sympathetic to, still processing their own participation in World War II, a common theme in postwar biblical epic movies. This aspect of David's personality is brought out by the flashback at the end of the film to his battle with Goliath, which is depicted as David's first introduction to the complex world of international politics and courtly intrigue. Peck's David is a simple boy, manipulated by the immoral rulers who surround him, an innocent child, horrified by the blood he is forced to spill by killing another man. In the biblical passage, David's age is ambiguous, and the filmmakers portrayed him as a child, highlighting how an innocent who is forced to act violently on behalf of the state will suffer later, a sentiment that likely resonated with many veterans and their families. The flashback scene shows Peck's David gathers the emotional strength to confront his antagonists. Viewers learn that trauma after violence is to be expected (perhaps reminiscent of their own situations after World War II), but, as Peck's David does, they also learn that one can draw on memories of these experiences for strength in the present. David's moral failings are overcome by the end of the film, and he becomes a model of resilience for postwar Americans.

Ten years later, Orson Welles played King Saul in a cinematic rendition of 1 Samuel 17, *David and Goliath* (1960). Despite Welles's participation, this was not a big-budget film destined for Oscar buzz. It was a cheaply made Italian film, one of the many loosely "historical" epics to come out of Italy in the wake of the success of *Hercules* (1958) and its successors. *Hercules*, starring Steve Reeves, had suddenly made the Italian film industry very profitable due to Italy's cheap production costs and ready access to sets (Greco-Roman ruins) suitable for quasi-historical films. *David and Goliath*, though mostly filmed in Yugoslavia and not in Italy, was one of the many Hercules imitators, where King David stands in for the Greek demigod. Ivo Payer plays David (aka Ivica Pajer), a Croatian actor who spends most of the film semi-topless, showing off his muscular physique and fighting Goliath, played by Kronos, an actor who made a living as a circus giant and wrestler. Payer's version of David is akin to a bodybuilder, and David emerges as a generic ancient strongman, a slightly more literate predecessor of Conan the Barbarian. Between Orson Welles's off-script improvisations and the need to treat David as a muscular action hero, the film bears little resemblance to the story in Samuel.

Filmmakers offer similar depictions of David in Christian independent cinema of the 2000s. In *David vs. Goliath: Battle of Faith* (2016), the ancient king is a muscular soldier, trained by the warrior (not prophet) Samuel, much in the way that Rocky Balboa is coached to become the celebrated boxer in *Rocky* (1976). We see extensive sequences of physical training and body-building, culminating in a gladiator-like fight with Goliath. In this and other films, the active male body is engaged in physical fitness or combat. This is a common conceit of action films in which filmmakers display the male body without making viewers uncomfortable with overt homoeroticism. *David vs. Goliath: Battle of Faith* is an intensely violent film, with fighting sequences strung together with occasional Christian commentary. Warfare and combat skills define David's masculinity in many cinematic depictions, not just in the 2016 film. The emphasis on "working out" in this film is, however, more common in films about sports; it is an unusual theme for a film about the Bible.

Many other cinematic treatments of David exist, but most treat the character along the lines discussed here. In *The Bible: The Miniseries* (2013), produced by Roma Downey and Mark Burnett, the battle with Goliath is a transformative moment for David as it marks his metamorphoses into a skilled soldier. Timothy Chey's 2015 *David and Goliath* takes military action as a metaphor for faith. David is filled with a religious fervor to kill Goliath and demonstrate his belief in God to the rest of his companions. Richard Gere's performance in *King David* (1985) is notoriously confused, with some elements of the Bible depicted very literally (like David's dancing into Jerusalem in front of the ark), showing just how problematic the depiction of biblical otherness is in a visually realistic medium. The story of King David, despite (or because of) its quality as literature, makes for complex cinematic adaptation.

5. Harry A. Hoffner Jr., "A Hittite Analogue to the David and Goliath Contest of Champions?," *CBQ* 30 (1968): 220–222, 225. Copyright © 1968, The Catholic Biblical Association of America, Washington, DC.

One of the most fascinating and colorful aspects of the ancient epics describing warfare is the phenomenon of the contest of champions. Exciting and romantic, this practice—real and practical as it may have been in actual history—was often singled out for mention in the epic tales of antiquity. . . . Individual combat of champions was intended to obviate the necessity of a general engagement of troops which would spill more blood than necessary to resolve the dispute. . . . This kind of conflict is better described as a *duel.* The individual combat between the Egyptian Sinuhe and his Syrian antagonist (Sinuhe, lines 109ff.; ANET, 20), which has occasionally been compared with the David and Goliath contest, was also only a duel to settle a private antagonism. . . .

Recently, while I was conducting an investigation of the Hittite Apology of Ḫattušiliš III, still another possible example of such a contest of champions came to my attention. The incident arose when the Hittites sought to check an incursion of enemy troops from the land of Pišhuru formed the western boundary of the territory of the Išhupitta. Ḫattušiliš, who was at this time still not the reigning monarch of the Hittites but a general under the command of his older brother

Muwatalliš, was dispatched with 120 chariots and no infantry to meet the invading force of 800 chariots and innumerable infantry (II 34–36). Against such odds it is difficult to believe that the Hittite forces could have triumphed, since an initial victory would have been necessary to raise the Kaškaean blockade of the Hittite cities (II 41–42). It is therefore possible that Ḫattušilliš exaggerates when he describes such overwhelming odds. . . . The text which immediately concerns us (II 31–47) may be translated as follows:

> Now the Pišḫuruwian enemy came (and) made an incursion, and (the cities of) Karaḫna (and) Marišta [were] in the midst of the enemy. On that side (the city of) Takkašta was (his) boundary, and on this side (the city of) Talmaliya was (his) boundary. (His) chariotry consisted of 800 teams, whereas for (his) infantry there was no counting. Yet my brother Muwatalliš sent me (to meet him), and he gave me 120 teams of chariotry, but as to infantry not even a single man was with me. My lady Ištar, however, marched before me. At that time I personally conquered the enemy. For when I slew the man who was the *piran ḫuyanza*, the (rest of the) enemy fled. Now the cities of the land of Ḫatti which had been blockaded joined in the attack and began to defeat the enemy. So I set up a victory stela in the city of Wištawanda, for at that time the recognition of Ištar my lady had been for me. And the weapon which I had held on that occasion I devoted (?) and set up before the goddess, my lady.

The portion of this passage which bears directly upon the question of contests of champions is lines 38 to 41, where Ḫattušiliš claims that he "personally conquered the enemy" by slaying the "man who was the *piran huyanza*." The expression which I have translated as "personally" is written IŠ-NÍ.TE-YA, which would be normalized in Akkadian as *ištu ramāniya*. The Hittite phonetic normalization would *ammel tueggaz*, "from / by means of my body." From the literal and concrete sense "body" the noun *tueggaš* was extended to include the notion of "person." From this expression alone it would be impossible to decide whether *ammel tueggaz* implied only that Ḫattušiliš led the attack in person (instead of delegating this job to a subordinate officer), or that he personally was responsible for the victory through his own fighting prowess as manifested in a single combat of champions. . . .

In summary, we have here one of the closest parallels known to date to the contest of champions as seen in the Greek and Hebrew sources. The proposed parallel in the Sinuhe story (see above) is not a true contest of champions but a duel. It would appear that such contests were at home on Canaanite and Greek soil, but also in Asia Minor, where, after all, the contests of the Achaeans and Trojans have their settings. Here as in other areas it would appear that the Hittites and their Bronze Age Anatolian neighbors were true mediators in the give and take between the Greek West and the West Semitic orient.

5

DETECTING THE ERASURE OF WOMEN AND THE INSCRIPTION OF A WITCH

In my work I deconstructed "woman" as a textual site of patriarchal functions and roles and exposed the interweaving of text and ideology. I argue against the notion of the innocent literary text, seeking to demonstrate that literary aesthetic "devices" are in effect political strategies meant to construct the subjectivity of the reader. . . . My goal was not inclusion, but transformation.

—Esther Fuchs, "The Neoliberal Turn in Feminist Biblical Studies"

On the Literary Tension over the Phallogocentric Tendency to Erase Women: An Introduction

AFTER DETAILING THE geopolitics of land and gender, displaying the masculinities of major and minor male characters, determining the specter of monarchy at the end of democracy, and decolonizing Philistine foreskin talk, readers certainly wonder: Where are the women in this lengthy biblical book? As Lai Ling Elizabeth Ngan observes, the women of 1 Samuel "fit stereotypical roles" of "women in a male-dominated society as envisioned by the narrator(s)."[1] Female characters and their stories remain fragmentary, underdeveloped, and marginal, just mentioned enough to serve as foils for the male-dominated tales. Women are prototypes, featured in "auxiliary roles," whose voices are suppressed and their geopolitical, ethnic, and religious significance minimized.[2] Some feminist interpreters have approached

1. Lai Ling Elizabeth Ngan, "Class Privilege in Patriarchal Society: Women in First and Second Samuel," in *Feminist Interpretation of the Hebrew Bible in Retrospect, vol. 1: Biblical Books*, ed. Susanne Scholz, Recent Research in Biblical Studies 5 (Sheffield: Sheffield Phoenix, 2013), 110.

2. Esther Fuchs, *Sexual Politics in the Biblical Narrative: Reading the Hebrew Bible as a Woman*, JSOTSup 310 (Sheffield: Sheffield Academic, 2000), 13.

1 Samuel with the goal of reconstructing, reclaiming, or even rehabilitating the stories of the female characters as "worthy to be heard and told."[3] The tales of Hannah, Michal, and Abigail are among them. Yet countless unnamed female characters usually disappear even from feminist exegetical horizons. What is there to say about the women of 1 Samuel?

Feminist deconstructionist exegete Esther Fuchs exposes the methodological naivete of reading a text as innocent. Since the mere recovery of the formerly erased Other does not lead to full inclusion, Fuchs shows in her work on female biblical prophets that the logic of inscription entails the logic of erasure.[4] Only an exegetical hermeneutics grounded in ambiguity, uncertainty, or doubt interrupts the economy of difference that persists not only within norms of gender and heteronormativity but also in conjunction with other identity categories, such as ethnicity, race, nationality, geopolitics, class, physical ability, age, or religion. Not even a deconstructionist feminist approach is exempt from the process of inscription and erasure because interpreters are caught in binary epistemic structures. Consequently, a focus on the women of 1 Samuel participates in a "conscripted look"[5] because the female characters appear within a literary web of phallogocentric, androcentric, and heteronormative assumptions. Fuchs emphasizes that the inscription and erasure of female prophets not only expose biblical texts as inherently androcentric but also eliminate female prophets from the articulation of biblical monotheism. Fuchs's deconstructive reading thus provocatively concludes that biblical God-talk precludes female prophetic discourse.

Similarly, the women of 1 Samuel are inscribed and erased into a gendered discourse that assumes male primacy and superiority. The phallogocentric necessity for erasing female leadership and female theological equality, however, presents in a less stable articulation in the story of the woman of Endor (1 Sam 28). Despite the relentless inscription and erasure of women as male appendices in their roles as mothers, wives, daughters,

3. Fuchs, *Sexual Politics*, 111.

4. Esther Fuchs, "Prophecy and the Construction of Women: Inscription and Erasure," in *A Feminist Companion to Prophets and Daniel*, ed. Athalya Brenner, FCB 8, 2nd series (Sheffield: Sheffield Academic Press, 2001), 54–69.

5. Andrea Bachner, *The Mark of Theory: Inscriptive Figures, Poststructuralist Prehistories* (New York: Fordham University Press, 2018), 207.

and unnamed women, the erasure of the non-Israelite woman of Endor as subordinate to the militarily weakened and theologically haunted Israelite king is relatively unsuccessful. The so-called witch appears in an equal or even superior role to the king. Predictably, the conventional reading tradition views her as a theological threat to the literary mechanism of inscribing and erasing female characters. She has a strong presence in 1 Samuel 28 and in the interpretative history. The feminist question thus is whether to read 1 Samuel as a witness to the malleability of the conscripted look in which a woman's uterus is more important than her theological insight about the world. In other words, does 1 Samuel offer clues about gender equality and justice in human life, despite its overwhelming propensity toward masculine primacy and phallogocentric superiority in terms of imagined geopolitics, leadership roles and organizational structures, and ethnonational signifiers? The answer to this exegetical possibility hinges on the current separation of 1 Samuel from 2 Samuel, as additional stories about women in 2 Samuel complicate the idea of reading 1 Samuel 28 as unique evidence of a literary struggle between the phallogocentric erasure of the woman of Endor and an alternative sociotheological gender model surviving as fragmentary witness in 1 Samuel.

To consider the literary tension over the phallogocentric tendency of erasing women in 1 Samuel, this chapter focuses on female characters categorized by their inscribed phallogocentric roles. Five sections explore women's roles as mothers, wives, daughters, unnamed women, and "witch" in the culminating narrative of 1 Samuel 28. A conclusion reflects on the resulting gender dynamics of 1 Samuel.

Mothers as Pious Endorsers, Cursed Props, and Quiet Devotees of Men

The rhetoric of motherhood appears at the beginning of 1 Samuel in the famous story about Hannah, wife of Elkanah. Hannah's husband is also married to Peninnah, mother of several children. The first verse begins with Elkanah and his male lineage: "There was a certain man of Ramathaim, a Zuphite from the hill country of Ephraim, whose name was Elkanah son of Jeroham son of Elihu son of Tohu son of Zuph, an Ephraimite" (1:1). Male lineage reigns supreme, which interpreters usually take for granted.

Commentators also rarely, if ever, explicitly mention that Elkanah is a bigamist. The problem is that one of his wives, Hannah, is infertile (1:2). Motherhood is inscribed as highly desirable for women, and so even feminist interpreters stress that "women acquired honor within this system [of patrilineal kinship ideology] by their acts of deference and sexual modesty toward men and by bearing legitimate children, especially sons, for their husbands."[6] The literary problem is that female characters, yearning to become mothers, are confined to a "limited literary role" that is "largely subordinated to the biblical male protagonist."[7] They are "flat" characters lacking "literary complexity"[8] even when they communicate directly with the divinity, as Hannah does in 1:13.

That the depiction of Hannah as a woman who is desperate to have a son fits phallogocentric control of women illustrates a comment on 1 Samuel 1:12–18 made by the fourth-century CE Christian theologian John Chrysostom (347–407). He explains why he likes Hannah so much:

> I can't get this woman out of my mind, so amazed am I at her beauty of soul and charm of thought. I mean, I am attracted by her eyes weeping in prayer, always attentive, her lips and mouth not reddened with some coating but enhanced with thanksgiving to God as hers were; I admire her for her sound values, and I am more amazed that as a woman she had sound values—woman, whom many frequently criticize. . . . The reason I particularly admire her is that she escaped the charges, she put aside the accusation, that though a member of the maligned and criticized sex she repelled all the reproaches, teaching in deed the lesson that even women did not become like that by nature but by choice and their own meanspiritedness, and that it is possible for this sex to attain the heights of virtue. This creature, after all, is contentious and highly strung, and if she inclines to wickedness,

6. Gale A. Yee, "The Silenced Speak: Hannah, Mary, and Global Poverty," *Feminist Theology* 21 (2012): 43.

7. Esther Fuchs, "The Literary Characterization of Mothers and Sexual Politics in the Hebrew Bible," *Semeia* 46 (1989): 165.

8. Fuchs, "Literary Characterization," 165.

> she commits great evil; if she attains virtue, she will give up her life before forsaking her purpose.[9]

Chrysostom approves of Hannah because she seeks motherhood so single-mindedly and piously. His and similarly misogynist readings of Hannah should caution against an unequivocal embrace of her. To Chrysostom, Hannah represents ideal womanhood because she is seeking the purpose of her life in motherhood. Thus, only if we recognize in her desperate quest the high degree of "alienation" that her infertility presents to her in the thoroughly patriarchal context of the narrative, "plac[ing] a higher premium on reproduction," can we understand her struggle to overcome her infertility. In the story world, children signal "cultural success"[10] for women like Hannah.

Even further, the quest for motherhood accommodates the androcentric and heteronormative agenda when the biblical tale gives divine approval to this biblical woman: "And [YHWH] remembered her" (1 Sam 1:19). At the same time, the story depicts the two men in her life—her husband (1:8) and Eli, the priest at Shiloh (1:13)—as clueless. Acting independently and forcefully by seeking motherhood, Hannah is not described as weak, powerless, or submissive. She even makes a deal with God (1:11), talks back to the priest (1:15–16), and informs her husband about her plans for the boy (1:22). All male characters comply with her instructions that lead to the inscription of Elkanah's additional male lineage. Most famous of Hannah's children, her firstborn son, Samuel, is the last judge who installs the first Israelite king (10:1–8).

Hannah's pursuit of motherhood is so dominant in the story's beginning because it ensures the tribal-national continuation of biblical Israel. Although it is difficult to see Hannah's role as a mother erased, so renowned is her contribution to the patrilineal agenda, in the narrative her function is limited to her biological reproductive utility. As Fuchs observes about

---

9. Quoted in Robert C. Hill, "St John Chrysostom's Homilies on Hannah," *SVTQ* 45 (2001): 329–330.

10. For further details on reading biblical texts about infertility within disability studies, see, e.g., Candida R. Moss and Joel S. Baden, *Reconceiving Infertility: Biblical Perspectives on Procreation and Childlessness* (Princeton, NJ: Princeton University Press, 2015), 6, 35.

biblical motherhood in general, this mother acts contently "within the genealogical economy of patriarchy."[11] Hannah is the patriarchal dream of a woman compliant with societal expectations defined by the hegemonic ideology. She models how a "good" woman should live in the world. The other wife, Peninnah, exemplifies this role from the start, although her depiction as mean-spirited and vengeful (1:6) highlights the husband's kind portioning of food and his love for Hannah (1:5). In this phallogocentric tale, the bigamist husband holds familial power and can easily be generous, while the wife with a "successful" womb competes with the infertile wife. None of the wives are depicted as happy, whether or not they are mothers.

In contrast, Elkanah has it all: several children of one wife and another wife whom he loves. No wonder, then, that he can distribute the food according to his preferences during the family trip to the "tent of meeting" (1:9 אהל מועד), the sanctuary of Shiloh. Whether Elkanah's famous question to Hannah, "Am I not more to you than ten sons?" (1:8), indicates "narcissistic cluelessness"[12] or his "deep and solicitous love for Hannah"[13] depends on the perspective from which one reads the question. Interestingly, Hannah, the aspiring mother, does not respond to it. She proceeds with her own plans, as she leaves the bigamist family and prays to God at the doorpost of the sanctuary (1:9). Ignoring her husband, she desires motherhood as the ticket toward full acceptance in the patriarchal system in which she lives.

Hannah's compliance with the sociotheological standards of the era in which the narrative situates her goes even further. She piously submits to the divine order and divine requirements, as, for instance, when her husband has sex with her "and [YHWH] remembered her" (1:19) or when Hannah explains to Eli that her son will grow up in the sanctuary as she promised God in her earlier prayer (1:24–28). In 2:21, God even "visits" (פקד) Hannah, upon which she gets pregnant with further children, giving birth to five more: two daughters and three sons. According to the tale, God rewards her pious compliance after she hands over her firstborn son to the sanctuary.

11. Fuchs, "Literary Characterization," 151.

12. Yee, "Silenced Speak," 44.

13. Robert Alter, *The Hebrew Bible: A Translation with Commentary, vol. 2: Prophets* (New York: Norton, 2019), 178.

A song of gratitude (2:1–10) that is attributed to Hannah is famously similar to songs found in other biblical books and even in the New Testament (see Exod 15:20–21; Judg 5; Luke 1:46–56). Yet whether Hannah's song is original to the story or secondarily added like other hymns of famous women is irrelevant to a feminist exploration about the inscription and erasure of mothers in 1 Samuel. The song's reference to the children born by an infertile woman in 1 Samuel 2:5b ("the infertile [עקרה] woman gives birth to seven children, and the one of many sons languishes"[14]) does not apply to Hannah, who has become the mother of six children.

The song affirms the general notion that Hannah is a biblical character compliant with the divine order of patriarchal standards. Hannah suffers when her body does not fit into patriarchal norms and expectations for married women (1:9). Later, she praises God for turning around her fate (2:1–10). She is jubilant that even infertile women can become mothers, a phallogocentric and divinely sanctioned promise that stabilizes the phallogocentric order. The poetic insight that views infertile women as divinely protected teaches that women need to pray long and hard so that God will eventually reward them with a pregnancy. Unsurprisingly, Hannah is often cited as the prototype for infertile women everywhere.[15]

Yet after formerly infertile or fertile biblical women fulfill their patriarchal duty to support men and androcentrically defined societal expectations, they disappear from biblical narratives. Accordingly, Hannah and Peninnah vanish from the story after male lineage is secured; they are never mentioned again. One final mention of Hannah as "his wife" and "this woman" by Eli the priest occurs in 1 Samuel 2:20. Reduced to her affiliation with her husband ("wife") and her biological ability to become pregnant ("children by this woman"), she has done her job. The same is also true for her husband. He, too, disappears, being little known in the interpretation history because the story is not about him. History books are filled with unnamed or named men disappearing from patriarchal genealogies when greater men follow

---

14. My translation. That the NRSV still uses the adjective "barren" (עקרה) and not "infertile" illustrates the persistent preference for antiquarian and negatively biased vocabulary for women's bodies in many translations.

15. See, e.g., Solomon O. Ademiluka, "Hannah's Prayer for a Male Child: Interpreting 1 Samuel 1:11 in the Nigerian Context," *In die Skriflig* 55 (2021): 1–8.

them. Meanwhile, women and their daughters are rarely mentioned in the first place. In the case of 1 Samuel, the storyline continues with Hannah's firstborn son, Samuel, whose presence ensures that the phallogocentric focus of the tale continues as both his father and his mother fade away.

The deeply ingrained misogyny that inscribes and erases mothers appears three additional times in 1 Samuel. Commentators often ignore the very short references. In 1 Samuel 15:33, Samuel tells the king of the Amalekites, Agag, whom Saul previously captured (15:8), that his mother will become childless because Agag made women childless in his wars (15:33). David Jobling observes, "War also makes fathers childless," but "[a] man who became childless would probably have greater opportunity to have more children."[16] Samuel's gruesome murder and dismemberment of Agag (15:33), sometimes classified as a ritual murder because it takes place near or at the sanctuary, makes commentators shudder, although they defend the act. They remind readers that God commanded Saul to kill all Amalekites (15:3), an order Saul failed to obey (15:8). For instance, Stephen B. Chapman emphasizes that Saul's act of "mercy" toward King Agag in his refusal to perform the execution goes against "the express instruction of God."[17] Robert Alter explains that Samuel is completing what Saul failed to do and that it is Saul's failure leading to his full rejection by God.[18] Interpreters usually ignore that Samuel's murder of the enemy king entails misogynist desire centered on the hatred for mothers and specifically on the hatred for the mother of the enemy king. Samuel's remark to Agag illustrates that mothers are expedient props in men's bloody and violent struggles over power and might. If such a woman is a queen mother, I imagine her as being supportive of kyriarchal hierarchies from which she has benefited her whole life. She supports the phallogocentric order, just like the mother of Sisera, the Canaanite commander, who ponders in Judges 5:30, "Are they not finding and dividing the spoil? A woman or two for every man," as she worries about her son's fate during his most recent battle.

---

16. David Jobling, *1 Samuel*, Berit Olam (Collegeville, MN: Liturgical Press, 1998), 179.

17. Stephen B. Chapman, *1 Samuel as Christian Scripture: A Theological Commentary* (Grand Rapids, MI: Eerdmans, 2016), 145.

18. Alter, *The Hebrew Bible*, 238.

One more stunningly misogynist erasure of yet another mother emerges when King Saul discovers that his own son, Jonathan, betrays him for David. Saul shouts, "You son of a rebellious woman! Do I not know that you have chosen the son of Jesse to your own shame and to the shame of your mother's nakedness?" (20:30).

Ahinoam is Saul's wife and Jonathan's mother (14:50). Together with her husband, King Saul, she has two daughters, Merab and Michal, and two more sons, Ishvi and Malchishua (14:49). Saul disparages his wife, whom he degrades *in absentia*. This woman is a prop in the brief verbal outburst of her powerful husband. Her uterus indicates what matters most about her: She is a mother of a son who challenges the royal patrilineal system of power. A feminist interpreter could even imagine Ahinoam to have rejected her husband, the king, leaving him and later agreeing to marry David, especially since several verses mention David's wife called Ahinoam (1 Sam 25:43; 27:3; 30:5; 2 Sam 2:2; 3:2; 1 Chr 3:1). The father is ready to reject both. Perhaps Saul's vulgar reference to his wife in 1 Samuel 20:30 is also supposed to teach women that, as mothers, they must ensure to raise sons who protect the patrilineal order, or they, too, will disappear from the storyline, disowned by their own husbands. That the same fate does not necessarily await her son is illustrated in Jonathan's ongoing presence in the storyline. Jonathan dies only in 1 Samuel 31 and later remerges in David's lament in 2 Samuel 1:23, 25–27. Nor has Jonathan disappeared from the reception history, where he has enjoyed visibility throughout the centuries. For instance, in 1642 CE the famous Dutch artist Rembrandt painted the renowned artwork *David and Jonathan*.[19]

The final reference to a mother appears in 1 Samuel 22:3–4. There, David mentions both his mother and father in his request to the king of Moab to let his parents stay "until I know what God will do for me" (22:3). Ralph W. Klein casually explains that "the Moabite connections of David's ancestors" make David seek out the Moabite king, who should be recognized as an eager supporter of David because David is Saul's "rival."[20]

---

19. The famous painting can be seen online here: https://www.rembrandtpaintings.com/farewell-of-david-and-jonathan.jsp.

20. Ralph W. Klein, *1 Samuel*, WBC 10, 2nd ed. (Nashville: Thomas Nelson, 2008), 223.

David's ancestors include his great-grandmother, the Moabite woman Ruth (Ruth 1:4; 4:17), and, even further back, the first king of Moab, the son of the elder daughter who gives birth to him after the incestuous rape by her father, Lot (Gen 19:37).[21] The ethnic-gender mixture of David's ancestry, grounded in both Moabite and Israelite identities, is remarkable. Yet neither feminist nor phallogocentric interpreters dwell much on David's unusual lineage. He cares for his parents by bringing them to the Moabite king, and then the parents are never mentioned again. This understated reference to David's mother and father sharply contrasts Hannah's desperate quest for motherhood or the hateful and disparaging remarks about King Agag's and Jonathan's mothers. Is David's request to the Moabite king supposed to communicate that David will be a good king, fulfilling the fifth commandment (Exod 19:12) even when he faces dire times? Or shall readers imagine that David comfortably negotiates with the traditional enemies of Israel, including the Moabites, from whom part of his family of origin comes and whom he will defeat later (2 Sam 8:2)? David needs help from the Moabite king for his parents in 1 Samuel 22:3–4; later, he will forget about this favor and his family connections. Thus, in my view, the apparently insignificant mention of his parents hints at the callous character of David, to whom his mother and father are props in his constant struggle for power.

In sum, all four references inscribe and erase female characters as mothers. Of them, Hannah is the most well-known woman, perhaps because her intense quest for motherhood reinforces the values of patriarchy the most. Once the task is completed by being a mother and producing a son, Hannah disappears from the narrative. The other three mothers receive only one-liners, no direct speech, no names (except Ahinoam, who gets insulted), and no praise. They disappear as soon as they appear. Thus, all of these female characters reinforce the phallogocentric notion. Women are at their best when they are mothers and only important if they are mothers of famous men, even when those sons fail or get killed. In 1 Samuel, women are of little significance, except as mothers of sons, through whom they live.

---

21. For a feminist reading of this rape story, see, e.g., Katherine B. Low, "The Sexual Abuse of Lot's Daughters: Reconceptualized Kinship for the Sake of Our Daughters," *JFSR* 26 (2010): 37–54.

Wives as Incidental Embellishments of Polygynous Husbands

If the stories of mothers depict women as clamoring for sons, wives appear solely to endorse, uplift, and support their polygynous husbands. In 1 Samuel only a handful of women are wives. Among them are Peninnah and Hannah, the wives of Elkanah (chap. 1); Ahinoam, who is the daughter of Ahimaaz and Saul's wife (14:50); and the three wives of David: Michal, who loves and marries David (18:17–29) and later helps him to escape from her father (19:8–17), Abigail (25; 27:3), and Ahinoam of Jezreel (25:43; 27:3). No other women identified as wives appear in 1 Samuel, indicating the strategic mention of wives as pawns of male characters. As wives function to support, endorse, or even rescue central male leaders, the story of the bigamist wives, Hannah and Peninnah, builds the drama for the emergence of the last Israelite judge, Samuel. He will guide the transition to the monarchical system. The story of Michal illustrates the charisma, emotional coldness, and calculated manipulation of the second king, David. The story of Abigail depicts a wife escaping an unhappy marriage, possibly characterized by domestic violence, and entering a marriage with a husband who will permanently lock her in his royal home (30:2). About two wives we know nothing but their names, both called Ahinoam; they are the wives of powerful and competitive men, Saul and David. Since the specifics of both women are inconsequential to the larger narrative, their identical names hint at their exchangeability. Or perhaps David does indeed marry Saul's wife, Ahinoam, as a power move to displace Saul's kingdom, as prophet Nathan suggests in 2 Samuel 12:7–8.

The list continues with another wife, whose sole function is to showcase the power of the man she married. David's first wife, Michal, is even forced to marry Palti, the son of Laish from Gallim (25:44), although the cruel relationship between Michal and David continues in 2 Samuel 3:14–16. There David demands that Saul's surviving son, Ishbaal, send back to him his wife, Michal, who in the meantime has lived with her second husband. When she is forced to leave, Palti "went with her, weeping as he walked behind her all the way to Bahurim," until he is told to go back (2 Sam 3:16). Later, Michal despises David as she watches him dancing in the street (2 Sam 6:16). She mocks him for "uncovering himself today before the eyes of his servants' maids, as any vulgar fellow might shamelessly uncover himself" (2 Sam 6:20). Michal receives little sympathy from phallogocentric interpreters who view her as a "scorned" wife who is "sexually jealous," "resenting"[22] him politically, and ultimately remains child-free as if punished for rejecting her first husband, David. In 1 Samuel, wives serve their husbands, and if they do not, they are unworthy not only of any husband but also of motherhood. Is there a worse fate in the patriarchal imagination than being a woman without having had children?

As jealousy and emotional distress are typical responses of wives in polygamous marriages, these troubles are transparent in the wife stories of 1 Samuel. In the story of Hannah and Peninnah, the two wives compete with each other, and jealousy rules their married lives. One wife has no children, whereas the other wife has several (1:2). One wife is loved by the polygynous husband, and the other wife mocks the infertile wife (1:6). The story does not indicate whether Hannah and Peninnah agree to their husband's decision to marry two women. Meanwhile, the polygynous husband assumes innocence while standing at the center of his wives' attention, even in his own mind: "Am I not better to you than ten sons?" (1:8). As one of his wives struggles to conceive a son and so attain social status, later even giving away her firstborn son to the sanctuary, the husband complies with her wishes ("Do what seems best to you" [1:23]), like Abram, who verbally submits to Sarai's demands about Hagar (Gen 16:2, 6).

Contemporary research suggests that polygamous marriages offer complex benefits and challenges to women in such family constellations. Children may suffer from blended families, experiencing intrafamily discrimination or being sent off altogether.[23] In the biblical tale, Hannah gives away Samuel to the sanctuary of Shiloh, and so the story presents a lineage beyond the narrow confines of this specific polygamous family. The troubles of this family in which the future judge grows up are not mentioned again, and commentators do not dwell on the bigamist marriage of his parents. Still, the early verses depict the manifold tensions the wives experience and their rivalry over their husband's attention. How Peninnah's children (1:2) and Hannah's five children (2:21), including two daughters, fare in this family remains anybody's guess.

Other wives fare better in terms of being inscribed in the story, although they also do not receive male-independent attention. They, too, are erased.

---

22. See, e.g., Alter, *The Hebrew Bible*, 332.

23. Lisa Fishbayn Joffe, "What's the Harm in Polygamy? Multicultural Toleration and Women's Experience of Plural Marriage," *Journal of Law and Religion* 31 (2016): 336–353.

Their inscription, however, brings them measured fame in the interpretation history. Michal and Abigail are known biblical characters, both married to the most popular king in the Hebrew Bible. Yet ultimately, their presence only highlights David's success. They are pawns in his story that erases them as soon as they accomplish their literary purpose of advancing the hero. Even as wives of the popular king whose fame and charisma infatuate many readers, Michal and Abigail are marginal characters supporting the future king, David, over the current king, Saul, who is already rejected by God. The phallogocentric genealogies in 1 Chronicles 8:33–39; 9:39–40 omit Michal and her sister, Merab. Such is the logic of patriarchy in which even royal daughters and sisters are "bait"[24] for kings and aspiring kings alike.

One of the wives, Michal, the royal daughter, loves David from the start (18:20), although her father first offers to David her elder sister, Merab (14:49; 18:17). Since David wiggles out of the obligation in feigned humility (18:18), the king immediately marries off Merab to Adriel the Meholathite (18:19).[25] Merab and David are pawns in the mind of King Saul, who even attempts to get his young rival killed in a battle against the Philistines (18:17). Orly Keren correctly states, "Nothing in the biblical narrative can explain why Saul married Merab to Adriel or when the marriage took place."[26] Yet on the basis of some Jewish commentators, Keren also suggests a startling alternative possibility: "Can we hypothesize that it was Merab who canceled her betrothal to David?"[27] For instance, the eighteenth-century Jewish com-

24. For the notion of Merab and Michal as Saul's "bait" in his royal struggle over geopolitical power and political status, see Elke Seifert, *Töchter und Väter im Alten Testament: Eine ideologiekritische Untersuchung zur Verfügungsgewalt von Vätern über ihre Töchter*, Neukirchener theologische Dissertationen und Habilitationen 9 (Neukirchen-Vlyn: Neukirchener Verlag, 1997), 169–171.

25. The two sisters are textually confused in 2 Sam 21:8. There, Michal is reportedly the mother of five children. The attributed husband, Adriel, the son of Barzillai the Meholathite, is the husband of her sister, Merab (1 Sam 18:19). Scholars and the rabbinic tradition solve this textual problem by replacing "Michal" with "Merab" in 2 Sam 21:8. The phallogocentric genealogy ignores both sisters and any children from either woman; see the discussion later in this section.

26. Orly Keren and Harit Taragan, "Merab, Saul's Mute and Muffled Daughter," *JBL* 134 (2015): 95.

27. Keren and Taragan, "Merab," 96.

mentator David Altschuler (1687–1769) suggests this interpretation for the phrase "when the time came to give" (ויהי בעת תת) in 1 Samuel 18:19:

When the time came
to give Merab to David,
she gave herself to Adriel
and received from him the wedding contract
without the knowledge of her father.[28]

כאשר הגיעה העת
שקבע לתת את מרב לדוד,
והיא נתנה על ידי עצמה לעדריאל,
וקבלה ממנו קדושין
בלא דעת אביה

Who would have expected a protofeminist notion in this eighteenth-century Jewish commentary! Merab wants to marry another man and goes ahead without her father's permission. The unexplainable becomes suddenly explainable. David is out. As Keren asserts, "In the end, it was Merab's wishes that determined whom she wed."[29]

Then there is Merab's sister, Michal, who is said to "love" (אהב) David (18:20, 28). Her feelings are shared by many other characters, such as Jonathan (18:3; 19:14, 17), the people (18:16, 22), and even Saul (16:21). They are also the starting point for Michal's troubles in her narrated life. Saul, hearing about it and offering a wedding deal to David (18:20–27), marries Michal to him. Yet the marriage increases Saul's fear of David (18:28–29). When Michal saves her husband's life from her father's murderous plan and so, by her deceit, endangers her own life, she lies to him about David threatening to kill her (19:11–17). The power struggle between her father and her husband threatens her own life. Meanwhile, the story discloses her love for her husband, but no word explains why David marries her. J. Cheryl Exum astutely observes, "The situation is one in which the men's political considerations are paramount, while, regarding the woman, we hear only that she loves. Already the text perpetuates a familiar stereotype: men are motivated by ambition, whereas women respond on a personal level."[30]

---

28. For the online Hebrew text of Metzudat David (compiled and published between 1740–1780 CE), visit https://www.sefaria.org/Metzudat_David_on_I_Samuel.18.19.1?vhe=On_Your_Way&lang=bi&with=all&lang2=en.

29. Keren and Taragan, "Merab," 96.

30. J. Cheryl Exum, *Fragmented Women: Feminist (Sub)versions of Biblical Narratives*, Cornerstones, 2nd ed. (London: Bloomsbury T&T Clark, 2016), 6.

Figure 5.1. Marc Chagall, *David Saved by Michal*, original lithograph, 1960. © Adagp, Paris 2025. Used by permission.

Having fulfilled her function as her husband's protector, Michal disappears from the story. The next time she appears, her father removes her from her polygamous husband, who just married two other women (25:43–44). Saul gives his daughter in marriage to Palti, son of Laish, the man who will later run weeping after his beloved Michal after David takes her back (2 Sam 3:16), a heartbreaking scene. Hostage to the men in her life, Michal does not have a happy story. Perhaps she regains some agency when she despises David in 2 Samuel 6:16 (see also 1 Chr 15:29). The story reports that the queen remains child-free, enjoying bodily autonomy from the patriarchal expectation of procreation. When she is mentioned for the last time, she is no longer David's wife. She is the subject of the sentence, though identified by her father as "the daughter of Saul" (2 Sam 6:23). She does not escape patrilineal hegemony.

Interpreters disagree on the reason for Michal's child-free status. We could imagine that Michal decides to prevent pregnancy from the man who uses her on his path toward royal power. Surely, she knows about contraceptive methods and abortifacients.[31] Yet many readers do not give her this level of agency when they speculate about the reason for her child-free status. Lillian R. Klein reiterates the phallogocentric explanation according to which a woman does not have agency; she needs to submit to the male and divine authorities in her life. Klein asserts, "Michal is childless because she is depicted not as a God-fearing woman but as a woman who values her household gods and her royal status, a woman who presumes to think and act for herself."[32] Other feminist interpreters advance the notion that "the very ambiguity hints at the text's unease about locating responsibility" for Michal's child-free status.[33] Ellen White believes that perhaps the ambi-

---

31. Meir Malul, "Some Measures of Population Control in the Ancient Near East," in *Michael: Historical, Epigraphical and Biblical Studies in Honor of Prof Michael Heltzer*, ed. Yitzhak Avishur and Robert Deutsch (Jaffa: Archaeological Center Pubs, 1999), 221–236.

32. Lillian R. Klein, "Michal, the Barren Wife," in *Samuel and Kings: A Feminist Companion to the Bible*, ed. Athalya Brenner, FCB 7 (Sheffield: Sheffield Academic, 2000), 45.

33. Exum, *Fragmented Women*, 26.

guity about the cause of Michal not having any children is the narrator's way of communicating the truth of the divine promise: "No descendant of Saul would sit on the throne."[34] Under no circumstances, however, should Michal's child-free status signify that "she must be bad,"[35] in contrast to David.

Even better is a reading that views Michal as refusing to remain a doll in the androcentric game over power. Danna Nolan Fewell and David M. Gunn allow for this possibility when they ask, "Does this proud woman, a king's daughter, refuse to lend her body to any further political (ab)use? Alive to another reality than the one for whom she betrayed her father's house—she had belonged, after all, to another house and husband—does she now refuse to be further complicit in the uniting of the houses of Saul and David?"[36] Accordingly, the queen is child-free because she frees herself from male expectations and male domination, which require her to avoid pregnancy from this king. Patriarchy can do that to women and other strangers.[37] Yet perhaps 2 Samuel 21:8, according to the Masoretic Text, got it right all along: Michal (and not Merab) is the mother of five sons from the "other" husband, the one running after her, weeping, and wanting her back (see 2 Sam 3:16). No wonder Michal despises the shallow, exhibitionist king!

The other wife of the polygamous David is Abigail, the wife of Nabal (Hebrew for *fool*). After Nabal's death, the widow becomes a wife of David, the future king. Her story begins and ends in one chapter (1 Sam 25). Her goal is to rescue David, who will be king, from committing murder, as if he had not murdered tens of thousands before. She is portrayed as "clever and beautiful" and her husband, Nabal, as "difficult (קשה) and evil (רע)" (25:3; my translation). Some interpreters suggest he was physically abusive toward

---

34. Ellen White, "Michal the Misinterpreted," *JSOT* 31 (2007): 462.

35. White, "Michal the Misinterpreted," 463.

36. Danna Nolan Fewell and David M. Gunn, *Gender, Power, and Promise: The Subject of the Bible's First Story* (Nashville: Abingdon, 1993), 155.

37. See, e.g., Kathryn J. Gutzwiller and Ann Norris Michelini, "Women and Other Strangers: Feminist Perspectives in Classical Literature," in *(En)gendering Knowledge: Feminists in Academe*, ed. Joan E. Hartmand and Ellen Messer-Davidow (Knoxville: University of Tennessee Press, 1991), 66–84.

Abigail.[38] Is this the reason Nabal is identified as a "Calebite" (כלבו), perhaps in the sense of belonging to the "tribe of dogs" (כלב)[39] or as being "rough, stubborn and thoughtless,"[40] certainly a stereotypical way of thinking about dogs? He is also a wealthy man owning three thousand sheep in Carmel (25:2). He dismisses the young men (25:10–11) David sends to ask for food on his escape journey from Saul. When David receives the rejection (25:12), he prepares, together with his four hundred men, to kill Nabal (25:12–13). One young man informs Abigail about this turn of events (25:14–17), whereupon she takes a huge amount of food and "cakes of figs" (25:18–19) and rides on a donkey to bring it to David and his men, "but she did not tell her husband Nabal" (25:19). Alice Bach describes this moment in Abigail's life: "Only when she breaks free of the container of Nabal's house, does she become all-powerful, simultaneously saving and threatening the men in the story."[41] She escapes her rich husband, whom she calls a "fool" (v. 25), and makes sure to survive the fate that will befall him. Later, she marries the future king, who is impressed by her capability to recognize his abilities and promise.

Perhaps this story, then, is the phallogocentric apotheosis of wives in 1 Samuel. Surprisingly, feminist interpreter Tikva Frymer-Kensky praises Abigail for "her brilliant rhetoric" that "convinces David not to kill every male in Nabal's house."[42] To Frymer-Kensky, Abigail is "an intelligent, determined woman" who "is influential far beyond the formal confines of patriarchy."[43] This feminist reading surprises because Abigail is male-focused, submissive, and willing to call herself a "slave-woman" six times (אמה: v. 24 twice, v. 25, v. 28; שפחה: v. 27, v. 31) in contrast to the man, David, whom

---

38. Ben-Meir, "Nabal, the Villain," *JBQ* 22 (1994): 251.

39. Ellen van Wolde, "A Leader Led by a Lady: David and Abigail in 1 Samuel 25," *ZAW* 114 (2002): 356–357.

40. Hans Wilhelm Hertzberg, *I and II Samuel*, trans. J. S. Bowden, OTL (Philadelphia: Westminster, 1965), 202.

41. Alice Bach, "The Pleasure of Her Text," *USQR* 43 (1989): 49.

42. Tikva Frymer-Kensky, *Studies in Bible and Feminist Criticism*, JPS Scholar of Distinction Series (Philadelphia: The Jewish Publication Society, 2006), 166.

43. Frymer-Kensky, *Studies in Bible and Feminist Criticism*, 166.

she calls "lord" twelve times in her speech (vv. 24–31). As Esther Fuchs convincingly explains, biblical women are always "overwhelmingly" presented as "male-dependent and male-related ciphers, who appear as secondary characters in a male drama."[44] Wil Gafney also sees "an inevitable sexual undercurrent to that language" because of "the near ubiquity of sexual exploitation of enslaved women" throughout time.[45]

Should readers imagine that Abigail, trying to survive, offers her sexual service to the new and powerful man who, as she had apparently heard, will become the next king (v. 30)? Or is this wealthy wife not rather depicted according to the phallogocentric fantasy that suspects her to be ready to abandon her previous life for a rugged macho man, surrounded by his loyal warrior men, and to prostrate herself before him, "bowing to the ground. She fell at his feet" (vv. 23–24)? She pours out her heart before him while stretched out on the ground (vv. 24–31). The fugitive warrior can then be gracious to her, giving up his plan to kill every "mother's son" in Nabal's house (vv. 22, 34). He is powerful, as she lies at his feet, and grants her request to spare her husband and his property (v. 35). Then she goes home and deals with the fool, her drunken husband, who will be dead by the next day or ten days later (vv. 36–38). Thereupon David can feel self-righteous (v. 39) and marry another woman (v. 39). The wealthy woman accepts the marriage offer as she brings five young women (נערות) with her (v. 42) and probably also the rest of her property. Left to the feminist imagination is the issue about the "five young women." Why did Abigail bring them into the royal palace? Will she and they sexually serve the king, as any phallogocentric fantasy would certainly like to imagine the next scene?

Yet at that point in the storyline, Abigail has fulfilled her literary purpose. She becomes the second wife of the warrior man, who immediately adds another wife, Ahinoam of Jezreel (1 Sam 25:43), to his collection. What Abigail thinks about this turn of events is insignificant to the phallogocentric tale. None of the women speaks, although they appear by name

44. Fuchs, *Sexual Politics*, 11. Feminist Bible exegetes disagree on how to respond to this methodological tension.

45. Wilda C. Gafney, *Womanist Midrash: A Reintroduction to the Women of the Torah and the Throne* (Louisville, KY: Westminster John Knox, 2017), 206.

one last time in 1 Samuel 30:5. By then, they are stored away in David's city, Ziklag, when the Amalekites attack the town (30:1), from where David and his men will later rescue Abigail and Ahinoam (30:18–19). After this brief mention, Abigail and Ahinoam disappear from 1 Samuel because David's prowess and virility are established, as Abigail predicts in her speech (25:30). As this female figure forecasts his political success, she recognizes the male king before he himself believes it. As she becomes part of his collection of wives, she has no purpose in this phallogocentric tale other than being depicted as an obedient, submissive, and wealthy woman, wife, and widow. As Tikva Frymer-Kensky plainly states, "The story of Abigail is told because she preserved David's chances to be king."[46]

In 2 Samuel 3:2–3, both wives appear one last time, listed with their sons: First mentioned is Ahinoam of Jezreel's son, Amnon, the rapist of his half sister, Tamar (2 Sam 13); second is Abigail's son, Chileab, which means "according to his father" (see also 1 Chr 3:1). The list also includes four other sons of other wives married to the polygamist king (2 Sam 3:3–5). In 2 Samuel 11, David will see and marry yet another woman, Bathsheba, whose husband, Uriah, he will send to his death. Polygamous men, such as David, marry women to enhance their social, political, and economic standing. He does not love these wives, although one of them, Michal, loves him, at least initially. Ahinoam of Jezreel's response to David is not reported. Abigail is not said to love David either, even though David Jobling writes, "Abigail, like Michal, loves David and expresses her love in action."[47] Abigail's depiction adheres to the phallogocentric fantasy that dreams of submissive, subservient, obedient, and always willing women. At best, then, Abigail speaks to save her life, that of her servants, and her property. Afterward, she falls silent, accepting a life behind the locked doors of a palace belonging to a powerful man who keeps adding women to his growing possessions. Alice Bach notices that Abigail's story in 1 Samuel 25 is "about male authority,"[48] while the woman "deflect[s] male anger," speaks "soothing word," and

---

46. Frymer-Kensky, *Studies in Bible and Feminist Criticism*, 165.

47. Jobling, *1 Samuel*, 157–158.

48. Bach, "Pleasure of Her Text," 42.

"proffers . . . spiritual nourishment in the form of the prophecy endorsing David's destiny to reign as the chosen one of God."[49] Yet, in the end, Abigail is "shut away from the action of the story."[50]

In sum, in phallogocentric tales wives serve men, uplift them, support them, and give them children to continue the male-dominated lineage. Only Michal, who eventually sees through David's foolishness, despises him. After that moment, however, she vanishes into the silence of the text, just like the other wives. As literary embellishments, wives do not matter to the progressing phallogocentric storyline.

Named and Unnamed Daughters as Royal Bait or Phallogocentric Ciphers

The stories of 1 Samuel also mention several daughters either in passing or as playing more dominant roles as mothers or wives of this or that man. Many of the previously mentioned female characters who appear as mothers or wives also appear as daughters. The first woman, Hannah, is not identified as a daughter but gives birth to two unnamed daughters (2:21). The narrative identifies the royal daughters, Merab and Michal, as the children of Saul (18:19, 20), but Merab's significance is negligible: She disappears after the mention of her marriage to Adriel the Meholathite (18:19). Conversely, references to Michal shift between her being called "the daughter of Saul" (18:20, 28) or "his daughter" (18:27; 25:44) and "the wife of David" (19:11; 25:44). She belongs to her father or her husband, but at the story's end, she is "the daughter of Saul" (2 Sam 6:23). Daughters, appearing in gender-stereotypical roles, are also mentioned in Samuel's speech warning the people about the disadvantages of living in a monarchy: "He will take your daughters to be perfumers and cooks and bakers" (1 Sam 8:13). That the "female slaves" (שִׁפחות) Samuel mentions in 8:16 also include daughters is implied. Inscription and erasure occur simultaneously and behind the scenes. Saul's royal promise to the man who will defeat Goliath, the Philistine, includes one of the king's

49. Bach, "Pleasure of Her Text," 42–43.

50. Bach, "Pleasure of Her Text," 49.

daughters (17:25). His daughter is payment in the king's plan to eliminate the Philistine threat. Some interpreters suggest that Saul's offer of Merab to David in marriage (18:17) is his effort to fulfill the pledge. Saul's unquestioned decision to give Michal to another man at the very moment when David marries two additional women also suggests the patriarchal logic of "father knows best" (25:44).

One daughter-in-law, who is also a wife, receives attention here, although she also appears in the Ark Narrative.[51] The nameless woman is identified as the daughter-in-law of Eli, the priest, and as the wife of Phinehas, one of Eli's reprobate sons (2:12, 22, 34; 4:17, 19). The larger literary context reports on the Philistine capture of the ark. Immediately before the brief mention of the nameless daughter-in-law, Eli hears of the captured ark and the death of his sons. He falls backward with his chair, breaks his neck, and dies (4:18). The next verse reports that the pregnant daughter-in-law hears about the capture of the ark and the death of her father-in-law and her husband (in that order). Thereupon "she bowed and gave birth" (4:19). Without any further details about the birthing process, the next verse states that she is about to die (4:20). Unnamed women, midwives perhaps helping during the birthing process, advise her not to be afraid because she gave birth to a son. The woman does not respond. The next verse reports that she names the baby Ichabod, "Un-glory" or "No-glory" (4:21 אִיכָבוֹד). An explanation in the verse states that the name refers to the capture of the ark and to the deaths of her father-in-law and husband (in that order). Her final words are "The glory has departed from Israel, for the ark of God has been captured" (4:22). Yet her final words include neither Eli nor Phinehas. Jobling explains that in her mind "the only bad thing that has happened is the loss of the ark," and "she knows that they (Eli and Phinehas) were not worth much."[52]

When this daughter is viewed as a phallogocentric cipher, the brief story about this pregnant woman merely mirrors the fate of the men with whom she is associated. They die, and so she dies, even though she is giving birth while dying. In her final moments, she is depicted as naming her newborn son in the negative, "Un-glory" or "No-glory." The primal event

51. Also see the discussion on the Ark Narrative in chaps. 1 and 2 of this book.
52. Jobling, *1 Samuel*, 185.

of giving birth to new life involves death all around, including her own. Although some mothers die in childbirth, most women live. The unnamed daughter-in-law's death must thus be read as part of the larger phallogocentric viewpoint that disallows a woman and her child a future independent from the men in her life. She must die because the men in her life are also dead. Since they are gone and national disaster has befallen her people, the logic of the story requires her to die, even as she gives birth. Shall we imagine that Ichabod grows up all alone, an orphan, or was he perhaps adopted by one of the midwives? The narrative is not interested in his fate. His young life merely symbolizes the devastation befalling not only his mother and his immediate family of origin but also the people among whom he is expected to grow up. He stands for hopelessness, disaster, and the end, born to a dying mother; a dead father, who was a scoundrel anyway; a dead grandfather who failed his priestly duties; and a people deserted by God. This fragmented tale about the unnamed daughter-in-law, giving birth while dying, thus illustrates the narrated demise of Israel as a whole. Since she and her newborn son do not matter as individuals, they vanish from the scene, never to be mentioned again. This is a depressing story about an unnamed daughter with a named son.

As exegetes debate the significance of daughters in the Bible, some insist that in biblical Israel daughters enjoyed basic legal rights and legal respect of their personhood.[53] Others see in the androcentric and patriarchal depictions of daughters an indicator that they fared relatively well under the authority of their fathers; daughters suffered under male domination and power, but it was not as bad as sometimes believed.[54] The few references

---

53. See, e.g., Joseph Fleischman, *Father-Daughter Relations in Biblical Law* (Bethesda, MD: CDL Press, 2011).

54. See, e.g., Seifert, *Töchter und Väter im Alten Testament*. For an ambivalent position on the roles of daughters in the Hebrew Bible, see Johanna Stiebert, *Fathers and Daughters in the Hebrew Bible* (Oxford: Oxford University Press, 2013), who states in a crisp summary statement, "Taking all the multiple strands under investigation in this book together, the overall sense is that things are not as grim as is so widely claimed in feminist examinations of biblical fathers in relation to daughters" (214).

to named and unnamed daughters in 1 Samuel suggest that the depiction of these female characters follows the overarching phallogocentric logic. Accordingly, women support male interests in men's violent, cruel, and warring battles over status and power. Only Michal raises her voice against this display of male narcissism, and so she is promptly relegated to the narrative's shadows. Identified with her father, she loses her royal privilege. She is associated with a losing patriarch, while the man whom she comes to despise is the very man she once loved. By then, he is an admired king, and she is the daughter of a failed king.

Other daughters are pictured as physically vulnerable. One nameless daughter-in-law who is completely immersed in the phallogocentric order dies in childbirth. Her fate is worse than Michal's because she has a child while dying. In these and other stories, daughters have no story outside or next to important male characters. Sometimes daughters become wives and mothers of important men. Yet most of them immediately disappear thereafter, except for Michal, although she, too, disappears after a reference to her child-free status in 2 Samuel 6:23. Another daughter, the unnamed daughter-in-law, gets a narrative fragment but dies in childbirth. None of them is a fully developed character with her own story.

The Presence and Simultaneous Absence of Generic Unnamed Women

The inscription and erasure of women include an array of unnamed women in 1 Samuel, all of whom appear and disappear at the same time. They are and are not there. Thus, not much can be said about them, except to announce their presence and simultaneous absence. Usually, unnamed women appear in amorphous collectives, as if to provide literary color and density to the narrative. No details mark their individuality. We briefly see them, but other and more important things happen to make us forget them. For instance, there are women at the tent of the meeting reportedly getting "laid" or perhaps raped by Eli's sons (2:22). Unnamed midwives of the unnamed daughter-in-law speak encouragingly to the dying woman, telling her she gave birth to a son (4:20).

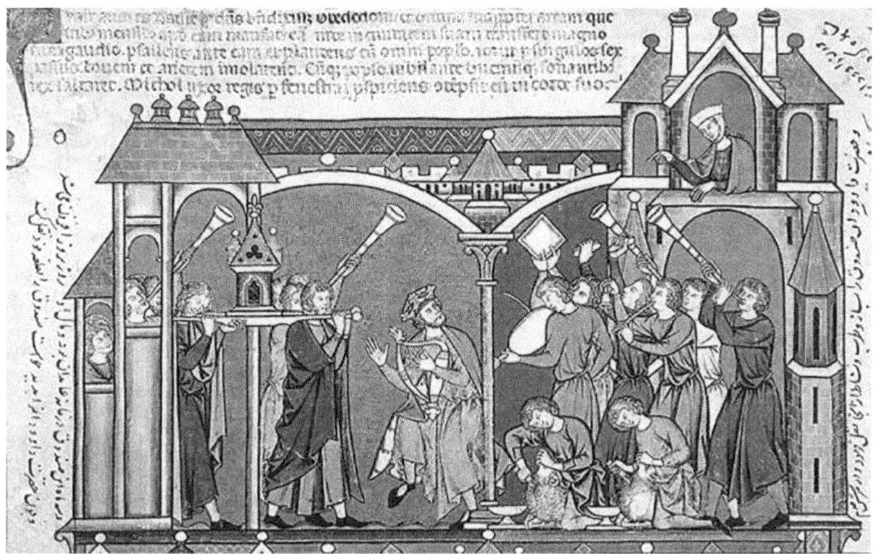

Figure 5.2. *David dances before the Ark of the Covenant and is despised by Michal* (2 Sam 6:12–16). French manuscript illumination (1250 CE). Used by permission of the Morgan Library.

Then there are female slaves (שפחות) who, with their male counterparts, will be taken by the king (8:16), as Samuel warns the people of Israel about the disadvantages of the monarchical system. When young Saul is searching for runaway donkeys, he and his male servant (נער) meet young women (נערות) at the well (9:11–13) who offer directions. When Samuel commands Saul to attack Amalek, to destroy everything, and to kill "both man and woman, child and infant, ox and sheep, camel and donkey" (15:3), Saul complies but spares King Agag (15:8). Women are thrown into the mix of people, together with animals; all of them are threatened with annihilation.

More unnamed women appear in other passages. In 1 Samuel 18:16, everybody in Israel and Judah reportedly loves David. This verse includes women, although they are not specifically mentioned. Then, in 1 Samuel 21:4–5, Abimelech the priest inquires if any of the men had sex with women, who are reduced to their sexual availability for men; David affirms that none did. In 1 Samuel 22:19, David murders everybody, including women, just as Saul did previously, and as he does again in 1 Samuel 27:9, 11, although this time he spares the animals. Later, the Amalekites capture the people of Ziklag, "the women and all who were in it, both small and great" (30:2), including David's wives Ahinoam and Abigail (30:5) and the "sons and daughters" of the Israelites (30:6). Yet David and his men rescue all of them (30:18–19). David also negotiates with his two hundred warrior men that everything, and not only the "wife and children" of each man (30:22), will be given back to those men who did not join the rescue effort.

How shall we think of this list of anonymous women sprinkled namelessly and largely voicelessly throughout 1 Samuel? It is time to go back to feminist pioneers of literary criticism and see what they said about women in phallogocentric texts. For instance, the feminist literary critic Judith Fetterley, known for her "resistant reading," claims, "The condition of woman under patriarchy is precisely that of a prince cast out. Forced in every way to identify with men, yet incessantly reminded of being woman, she undergoes a transformation into an 'it,' the dominion of personhood lost indeed."[55] When narratives depict female characters as cast out, as insignificant, as there but not there, the characters become genderless, an "it" or nonpersons, objects to be taken. This portrayal of women has an impact on readers, prompting them to identify with male characters because men have stories, and readers can learn about these men and their adventures. Even female-identified readers learn to prefer male characters because the identification with unevenly appearing groups of unnamed women is not particularly attractive or interesting.

Thus, a resistant reader like Fetterley recommends that we first define "our" loss when we read a text and then redefine "our" personhood. She made this suggestion in the 1970s when feminists did not yet theorize on the intersectionality of gender and power. In light of the anonymous women in 1 Samuel, readers of all backgrounds need to reflect on the politics of the phallogocentric logic that mentions unnamed women as collectives and as booty of men. The trouble is that so many readers still accept this kind of storytelling as "normal" because the expectation of encountering women as

55. Judith Fetterley, *The Resisting Reader: A Feminist Approach to American Fiction* (Bloomington: Indiana University Press, 1978), ix.

passive objects and enablers of men haunts not only 1 Samuel but also the contemporary world.

The Inscription of the Woman of Endor

"This woman appears to be unlike any other in the historical books," exclaims Tikva Frymer-Kensky about the female character of 1 Samuel 28. Perhaps her difference extends even far beyond the historical books of the Bible. To Frymer-Kensky, the woman of Endor is "master of an outlawed craft" and "seems so far beyond Israel's horizons as to be unable to play any part in its history."[56] Most Bible readers have heard of this female character, known as a "necromancer," a "medium," or even a "witch," conjuring up the spirit of Samuel so that fearful King Saul may know how to defeat the Philistine army (28:5). In 1 Chronicles 10:13–14, Saul's decision to "ask a ghost" (לשאול באור) is the cause for his demise in this cryptic reference in which the woman of Endor is almost absent.

The extensive narrative of 1 Samuel 28 depicts the encounter between Saul and the woman of Endor in four scenes. The first scene (vv. 3–6) reports Samuel's death, Saul's persecution of "mediums and wizards from the land" (v. 3), and Saul's impending battle against the Philistines, of which he is afraid. Although he previously "expelled the mediums and the wizards from the land" (v. 3), he does not receive a divine answer to his questions about the battle (v. 6). After his servants, or rather his slaves (עבדיו), advise him to seek out the "medium at Endor" (v. 7), he disguises himself and, with two other men, goes to "the woman [האשה] by night" (v. 8). The definite article and the noun, "the woman," emphasize her gender over her professional status as a necromancer, reminiscent of former US president Bill Clinton stating in January 1998, "I did not have sexual relations with that woman."[57]

---

56. Tikva Frymer-Kensky, *Reading the Women of the Bible: A New Interpretation of Their Stories* (New York: Schocken Books, 2002), 310.

57. For a report on this statement, see, e.g., Steven Nelson, "Bill Clinton 15 Years Ago: 'I Did Not Have Sexual Relations with That Woman,'" *US News*, January 25, 2013, https://www.usnews.com/news/blogs/press-past/2013/01/25/bill-clinton-15-years-ago-i-did-not-have-sexual-relations-with-that-woman.

The second scene (vv. 7–14) presents the encounter between Saul and "the woman," which hints at mutual respect and equality. The woman does not apologize for working in a profession forbidden by King Saul himself (v. 3). Initially, she fulfills his request willingly but cautiously. She knows fully well the king's original orders concerning "mediums and wizards" (v. 9 את האבות ואת הידעני) and is temporarily scared when she finds out that he is the very king who persecutes people like her (v. 12). Yet Saul promises he will not punish her over this matter (v. 10). He even orders her not to be afraid (v. 13). She believes him, which leads to the next scene.

The third scene (vv. 15–20) depicts the encounter between Saul and Samuel, in which Samuel almost exclusively speaks. The distressed (v. 15) "old man" (v. 14) informs Saul that nothing has changed about the king's fate (vv. 16–18). God no longer supports him because of his disobedience regarding the Amalekites (see 15:8, 17–23). Samuel announces that Saul and his sons will die in the battle against the Philistines (v. 19), and Samuel disappears thereafter. The scene ends with Saul's collapse after hearing the prediction (v. 20).

The fourth and final scene (vv. 21–25) mentions that the woman cares for Saul's physical recovery, even slaughters a calf, and prepares a meal for the king and his men. Afterward, the men leave into the night. Frymer-Kensky states that this scene portrays the woman in "an amazingly flattering" way.[58] She puts her view about the woman even more bluntly: "This is not an evil woman. Quite the contrary, the necromancer is presented as good and generous. Her ability to communicate with spirits does not make her evil. Her craft is outlawed because it is uncontrollable and ungovernable access to divine knowledge. But it is effective, and it can be benevolent."[59] Frymer-Kensky gives the woman more credit than many other interpreters. She positively compares her to "legitimate prophets" who channel "contact with divine power."[60] Frymer-Kensky also places her next to Rahab (Josh 2), Abigail, and Huldah (2 Kgs 22:14–20; 2 Chr 34:22–28), who "desire the good of the men to whom they speak." It just so happens that the woman of

58. Frymer-Kensky, *Reading the Women of the Bible*, 313.

59. Frymer-Kensky, *Reading the Women of the Bible*, 314.

60. Frymer-Kensky, *Reading the Women of the Bible*.

Endor "has the terrible task of channeling an announcement of doom but she can at least give Saul the courage and the strength to face it."[61]

Other interpreters are less generous. Stephen B. Chapman, criticizing the female character for offering physical nourishment to the king, suggests that her action "confirms her own distance from the authentic spirituality of Yahweh worship."[62] The early Jewish interpreter Pseudo-Philo rejects the idea that the woman has power over Samuel or raises him up from the dead.[63] Other Jewish interpreters of the Geonic period[64] assert that not the woman but Samuel speaks to Saul in the first place. Another interpreter, R. Samuel ben Hofni (d. 1034 CE), a Geonic thinker, doubts the existence of necromancy in general, as he asserts that the woman of Endor does not raise a dead man but says everything herself.[65] Many early Christian theologians, such as Tertullian (155–220 CE) and Jerome (342/347–430 CE), believe a demon deceives Saul, giving him a fake prophecy.[66]

Yet the third-century Christian thinker Origen makes an astounding typological move. Not only does he see in Samuel "a type of Christ," as "Samuel prophesies to Saul above" and "Christ prophesies to souls beneath,"[67] but he also identifies the "witch" as "a type of Christ." In his reading, she "has the power to bring up the inhabitants of hell, just as the Christ has the power to bring them up and through the flaming sword."[68] Patricia Cox elaborates on Origen's correlation of the woman and Christ: "The witch, however, is crucial to the completion of the typology which Origen has been constructing. She is a powerful breaker of boundaries and mediates between

61. Frymer-Kensky, *Reading the Women of the Bible*.

62. Chapman, *1 Samuel*, 206.

63. So described by K. A. D. Smelik, "The Witch of Endor: I Samuel 28 in Rabbinic and Christian Exegesis till 800 A.D.," *VC* 33 (1979): 161–162.

64. The Geonic period refers to a particular Jewish rabbinic era in Babylon that began in 589 CE and ended in 1038 CE. For more information, see, e.g., Robert Brody, *The Geonim of Babylonia and the Shaping of Medieval Jewish Culture* (New Haven, CT: Yale University Press, 2013).

65. Brody, *The Geonim*, 163.

66. Brody, *The Geonim*, 165.

67. Patricia Cox, "Origen and the Witch of Endor: Toward an Iconoclastic Typology," *AThR* 66 (1984): 143.

68. Cox, "Origen and the Witch of Endor," 144.

the underworld and another realm, just as the Christ does. Again, as with the typology of Samuel, there are curious reversals. The witch is feminine, the Christ is masculine; she calls up into the human world; he calls up into paradise. The iconoclastic force of typological juxtaposition is evident once more."[69] In contrast to the highly negative reading tradition, Origen places the woman of Endor next to Samuel. He also contrasts both of them with Christ but in theologically positive ways. This characterization of the woman as "a type of Christ" must surely be classified as one of the most unusually positive appraisals of the woman of Endor in the interpretation history of 1 Samuel 28.

The contemporary exegete David Jobling takes yet a different approach to the woman of Endor because of her "abyssal stature."[70] He criticizes the "kneejerk negative reaction" of many biblical interpreters who classify her as a "witch."[71] Proposing that "we are now open" to appreciate this female character in ways past interpreters were not, he classifies the woman of Endor as "a minister of religion, and a good one."[72] He specifies her abilities:

> She understands the need of the one who comes to her, she takes charge of the situation, she does what she can for him. In her technical capacity she efficiently performs the appropriate ceremony and gives Saul a satisfaction she realizes he must have even though it can do him no real good. In her larger capacity as minister to the whole persons he insistently gets past his self-destructiveness, making him take the sustenance that in his desperation he would forego. All this she does for her bitter enemy, the one who would expel her and her colleagues from home and livelihood—with only the lightest, faintly humorous reproach.[73]

After this encouragingly positive assessment, Jobling also notices the "objective" description in the narrative that highlights her "religious

69. Cox, "Origen and the Witch of Endor," 144.
70. Jobling, *1 Samuel*, 185.
71. Jobling, *1 Samuel*, 188.
72. Jobling, *1 Samuel*, 189.
73. Jobling, *1 Samuel*, 189.

function" and considers her "competent" in her work.[74] Jobling stresses that "this woman is no enemy to the religion of YHWH, and the religion of YHWH need not be an enemy to her. . . . If only we could persuade YHWH of it."[75] There he ends, as if insinuating that it is God's fault that interpreters have viewed the woman of Endor in mostly negative ways.

Historical critics are often baffled that the necromantic practice depicted in 1 Samuel 28 does not receive more critique or concealment within the text itself. The story presents Israel's first king as consulting a female diviner to learn from her about his fate. Her ethnic identity is not specified. In Joshua 17:11, Endor is listed as one of the Canaanite cities in the Jezreel Valley that the Israelites do not take over. Interpreters also discuss the nature of the woman of Endor's profession. For instance, Michael Kleiner notes that the narrator is convinced of the effectiveness of divination.[76] Historical critics agree that the Deuteronomistic writers consider necromancy as the epitome of Canaanite practices, thus "foreign" to Israel, and to be avoided at all costs. Historical critic Brian B. Schmidt explains that the Deuteronomistic writers retroject necromancy into the earliest literary strata of stories about Israel's monarchy. This literary strategy enables the original writers to show the depths of the age-old Israelite problem according to which even the first Israelite king intermingles with Canaanites, such as the woman of Endor, and embraces her "foreign" practice. Schmidt also explains that necromancy is a mid-first-millennial Mesopotamian practice and thus contemporary to the Deuteronomistic writers.[77] To them, the story about the woman of Endor and Saul illustrates the endemic failure of the first king, who violates central laws prohibiting paranormal rituals. Schmidt thus stresses that the biblical prohibitions are exilic or postexilic materials (e.g., Deut 18:9–12; see also Lev 19:31; 20:6, 27; 2 Kgs 21:6; 23:24; Isa 2:6). In his view, the Deuteronomistic writers retroject necromancy into the earliest

74. Jobling, *1 Samuel*, 189.

75. Jobling, *1 Samuel*, 189.

76. Michael Kleiner, *Saul in En-Dor. Wahrsagung oder Toten-beschwörung? Eine Synchrone und Diachrone Analyse von 1 Sam. 28, 3-25*, Erfurter Theologische Studien 66 (Leipzig: Benno, 1995), 225–226.

77. Schmidt, "'Witch' of En-Dor," 127–129.

Israelite past, although this practice is absent in "Levantine, Anatolian, and Egyptian magical traditions before the mid-first millennium BCE."[78]

All these efforts of historical dating, however, do not explain the astounding fact that the narrative inscribes the woman of Endor as a skilled diviner. This female character talks, decides, and knows what is going on in her world, confidently responding to the Israelite king, doing her work professionally, and even taking care of the client after he collapses. She generously offers her resources so that the king can recover before he departs. A full chapter depicts the interaction between the woman and the king. Although she is nameless in the biblical tale, Pseudo-Philo calls her "Sedecla,"[79] despite his negative assessment of her and Saul.

Yet the literary technique of inscribing the woman of Endor as a skilled diviner is ambiguous. Ann Jeffers correctly observes that phallogocentric ideology obfuscates the divinatory ritual requested by Saul and performed by the woman of Endor. Feminist interpreters, surprisingly, have not been eager to investigate this female character or her religious practice. Susan M. Pigott even suggests that "the witch of Endor is not at first an obvious protagonist" because she is "introduced as a 'witch,'" which most readers would view "in a negative light."[80] The biblical text does not call her a "witch," however, but "a woman who is a master of ghosts" (אשת בעלת אוב). Pigott also proposes to interpret the king as "wicked" because he disobeys God already in 1 Samuel 15:23 ("For rebellion is like the sin of divination"), which is "the equivalent of the sin of witchcraft."[81]

The feminist reticence has led interpreters to debate how to evaluate this female character playing such a significant role in the story of Saul. Pamela Tamarkin Reis maintains that interpreters have been "charmed" by the woman of Endor and states tongue-in-cheek, "The witch of Endor has

78. Schmidt, "'Witch' of En-Dor," 118.

79. LAB 64.3, *The Biblical Antiquities of Philo*, trans. from the Old Latin Version by M. R. James (London / New York: Society for Promoting Christian Knowledge / The Macmillan Company, 2017), 240. The text is available online at https://sacred-texts.com/bib/bap/bap78.htm.

80. Susan M. Pigott, "1 Samuel 28—Saul and the Not So Wicked Witch of Endor," *RevExp* 95 (1998): 440.

81. Pigott, "1 Samuel 28," 441.

cast a spell over biblical commentators."[82] To Reis, the woman of Endor is not particularly hospitable in 1 Samuel 28:21–22 because the woman is trying "to outwit and outmaneuver her adversary to save her own life than to try to feed him to save and fortify his."[83] As Saul just received terrible news through her process of divination and previously had persecuted people like her, "the witch" must have had enormous fear of Saul that intensified with Samuel's prophecy. Moreover, the absence of details on the meal indicates to Reis that the woman "takes the raw meat, the blood, and the sacred bread" and offers a communal meal to "seal a covenant."[84] Thus, Reis believes "the witch's meal is a blasphemous ritual," a "bloody rite," and a "heretical bargain" with Saul.[85] As he "defects from monotheism,"[86] he seals his fate on the next day. In other words, Reis views the woman not as "a generous, solicitous, and adorably illogical hostess" but as "an adroit strategist."[87]

So what is a feminist interpreter to do? Perspectives from those studying Wiccan religions and magic can help us here. For example, Nevill Drury explains that magic is unrelated to superstition because "in all phases of human history the concept of magical consciousness relates much more to the concept of *will* or *intent*—to the idea that one can bring about specific effects or changes within one's personal sphere of awareness."[88] Magic belongs within esoteric traditions that explore "hidden or unknown human potentials"[89] and require will, assertion, and mastery.[90] At the center of their own universe, magicians use particular rituals and concentrated willpower to bring forth sacred and symbolic forces or energies of the universe. Said differently, the magical arts are "means of communication with the sacred

---

82. Pamela Tamarkin Reis, "Eating the Blood: Saul and the Witch of Endor," *JSOT* 73 (1997): 3.

83. Reis, "Eating the Blood," 14.

84. Reis, "Eating the Blood," 18.

85. Reis, "Eating the Blood," 22.

86. Reis, "Eating the Blood," 21.

87. Reis, "Eating the Blood," 22.

88. Nevill Drury, *Magic and Witchcraft: From Shamanism to the Technopagans* (London: Thames & Hudson, 2003), 6.

89. Drury, *Magic and Witchcraft*, 6.

90. Drury, *Magic and Witchcraft*, 7.

powers that sustain the universe itself."[91] Mastery to access the "mysterious and unpredictable world"[92] is at the heart of this kind of spiritual practice. Since the woman of Endor is introduced as a "master" (בעל) of spirits or ghosts in 1 Samuel 28:7, she is an expert at her craft. As an intermediary between this and the other world, she does not compete with God (אלהים or יהוה) but links to the divine realm. Her divinatory ritual, bringing up the "ghost of Samuel," assists Saul in expanding his consciousness and his understanding of his life. As *The Encyclopedia of Witches, Witchcraft and Wicca* explains in the entry on "ritual," "It is a "prescribed form of ceremony to achieve a transformation of consciousness. . . . Ritual has played an important role in the development of human consciousness since the beginnings of history. . . . Ritual helps the human consciousness tap into unseen forces: forces of the inner self, forces of nature, forces of the cosmos."[93]

This is what the woman of Endor helps the king realize. She gives him the spiritual and material support to follow his path, as he comes to recognize the end of his reign and life. He leaves without any further word reported (28:25). As Ann Jeffers correctly assesses, "'Revisioning' the Woman of Endor's ritual position in ancient Israel . . . re-inscribe[s] her activities within a fluid, polemic, rhetorically loaded, and changing religious situation by recovering her role as an active agent of ritual processes."[94] The woman of Endor inscribes her agency in unexpected ways.

Female Characters as Ciphers of Phallogocentrism: Concluding Comments

The inscription and erasure of female characters in 1 Samuel follow the structure that Katy Deepwell explores in an essay on feminist interpretations of witches in contemporary art. She cautions against viewing the images

91. Drury, *Magic and Witchcraft*, 8.

92. Drury, *Magic and Witchcraft*, 9.

93. Rosemary Ellen Guiley, *The Encyclopedia of Witches, Witchcraft and Wicca*, 3rd ed. (New York: Facts on File, 2008), 288.

94. Ann Jeffers, "Forget It: The Case of Women's Rituals in Ancient Israel, or How to Remember the Woman of Endor," in *The Bible and Feminism: Remapping the Field*, ed. Yvonne Sherwood and Anna Elizabeth Fisk (Oxford: Oxford University Press, 2017), 292.

as reflections of "lived realities or as 'depictions' of real events" and instead advises viewers to recognize them as "presentations devised with imagination and fantasy which are not connected to the real."[95] The women in 1 Samuel are not "real" women to be admired or ignored but to be recognized as ciphers of phallogocentric representations of women. Each is mother, wife, daughter, unnamed or named woman, and, in one case, a witch. Does the presence of the woman of Endor satisfy yet another phallogocentric convention that mentions "witches" as "a way of adding women into the discourse, but at the cost of accepting androcentric perimeters, maintaining cultural hierarchies, and perpetuating false models of cultural evolution"?[96] The answer to this question includes the woman of Endor but also goes beyond her, as all female characters of 1 Samuel fulfill phallogocentric fantasies about "a woman's place" in a phallogocentric world.

All named or nameless women of 1 Samuel, except for one, are inscribed and erased. Remarkably, the unnamed woman of Endor is not entirely erased, unlike in 1 Chronicles 10:13–14. Her professional integrity, skill, and autonomy are inscribed in 1 Samuel 28. Although most feminist interpreters have not sought out her story, despite her subject position, she is renowned in religion, culture, and interreligious history. She is the exceptional female character of 1 Samuel, although most readers will know another woman, Hannah, better. As female characters, one located at the beginning and the other at the end of the biblical book, both stand in prominent literary positions. At least one interpreter considers both women as "literary sisters . . . mirror[ing] . . . each other."[97] Read accordingly, Hannah and the woman of Endor exemplify the "polemics and ideological structures" about women in 1 Samuel,[98] as both serve androcentric interests and needs. Not

---

95. Katy Deepwell, "Feminist Interpretation of Witches and the Witch Craze in Contemporary Art by Women," *Pomegranate* 21 (2019): 147.

96. Laurel Zwissler, "In the Study of the Witch: Women, Shadows, and the Academic Study of Religions," *Religions* 9 (2018): 13, https://www.mdpi.com/2077-1444/9/4/105/htm.

97. See, e.g., Matthew Michael, "Narrative Conjuring or the Tales of Two Sisters? The Representations of Hannah and the Witch of Endor in 1 Samuel," *JSOT* 42 (2018): 469.

98. Michael, "Narrative Conjuring," 489.

cherished for the uniqueness of their tales, these and the many other named and unnamed women fulfill literary functions that emphasize the significance and failures of male characters. Female characters serve men and are important only insofar as they contribute to the androcentric progression of the tales.

The analysis of the inscription and erasure technique produces another important feature of my reading. Not contributing to what Esther Fuchs characterizes as "an entrenchment of positivist and empiricist discourses"[99] on gender in the Bible, my interpretation interrogates and deconstructs the phallogocentric characterization of biblical women, "while at the same time providing self-presentations that are inconsistent and open-ended."[100] Although it is difficult to offer inconsistency and open-endedness, this feminist reading proffers an alternative horizon that challenges phallogocentric, heteronormative, androcentric, and misogynist reading habits.

In sum, my reading views the female characters as pious endorsers, cursed props, and quiet devotees of men. They are incidental embellishments of polygynous husbands. They do not really matter to the progression of the storyline, and only one woman emerges, nameless but independent and confident in her skills, as a competent communicator between the earthly and otherworldly realms, providing a failing king with the knowledge he requests. None of the stories in which female characters appear centers on the women. In the end, Jo Ann Hackett's assessment about women playing "a larger role in the books of Samuel than in most of the rest of the Bible"[101] is too optimistic. In 1 Samuel, female characters serve, call attention to, nurture, or validate phallogocentric goals, achievements, and failures. Women do not have their own stories in this biblical book.

---

99. Esther Fuchs, *Feminist Theory and the Bible: Interrogating the Sources* (Feminist Studies and Sacred Texts; Lanham, MD: Lexington Books, 2016), 6.

100. Fuchs, *Feminist Theory*, 8.

101. Jo Ann Hackett, "1 and 2 Samuel," in *Women's Bible Commentary*, ed. Carol A. Newsom, Sharon H. Ringe, and Jacqueline E. Lapsley, 3rd ed. (Louisville, KY: Westminster John Knox, 2012), 162.

For Further Reflection

1. David A. Schones, "Infertility/Barrenness." Used by permission of the author.

   Biblical scholarship on "barrenness" builds on pronatalist ideology that normalizes procreativity and a traditional gender binary.[102] It assumes that childlessness is inherently undesirable, something to be resolved through divine or human initiative. Researchers who refer to biblical women as "barren" often use this term innocently. They attempt to historicize the description of childlessness to convey ancient Israelite norms that value the production of offspring. Still, "barren" is not etymologically related to the Hebrew terms עקרה, רחם, or שכל but comes from the twelfth-century French word "baraigne."[103] Accordingly, "barrenness" is not more historically accurate than other descriptors for infertility in the Hebrew Bible. This term does, however, advance a negative evaluation of childlessness. For example, *The International Standard Bible Encyclopedia* states that "barrenness

---

102. Pronatalism refers to societies that strongly promote motherhood and childbirth. Often these communities create policies that encourage reproduction. Other times, they discriminate against individuals who do not reproduce, including those dealing with infertility. In antiquity, pronatalism refers to the stress placed on "the duties of marriage and procreation" by societies that required high birth rates to survive. It recognizes that pronatalist ideology stigmatizes "persons who failed to produce children [which] was incorporated into religious dogma and mythology." See Michael S. Teitelbaum, "Population: Biology and Anthropology," *Encyclopedia Britannica*, www.britannica.com/science/population-biology-and-anthropology. Antinatalism refers to societies that do not have policies promoting reproduction or discriminate against childless couples. Often these communities suffer from overpopulation or have population control measures in place such as access to birth control.

103. See, e.g., Walter W. Skeat, *An Etymological Dictionary of the English Language*, 3rd ed. (Oxford: Clarendon, 1898), 52; Walter W. Skeat, *The Concise Dictionary of English Etymology: The Pioneering Work on the Roots and Origins of the Language* (Kertfordshire: Wordsworth Editions, 1993), 30. Comparatively, infertility draws from the Latin *infertilitatem*, meaning *not fertile*. See Online Etymology Dictionary, "infertile," https://www.etymonline.com/word/infertility#etymonline_v_34830.

[sic] was a woman's and her family's greatest misfortune."[104] The *New Interpreters Dictionary of the Bible* explains that "barrenness [*sic*]—like famine, drought, and disease—was typically viewed as a sign of divine disapproval."[105] Finally, the *Encyclopaedia Judaica* succinctly states that "barrenness [*sic*] was a curse and a punishment."[106] By referring to "barrenness" as a catastrophe or punishment, biblical scholars normalize the experience of fertility and vindicate the stigmatization of infertile women. They identify childlessness as a problem that can be addressed only through procreation.

Feminist scholars in other fields regularly adopt alternatives to the term "barrenness." One example, "infertility," refers to a medical diagnosis: a "disease of the reproductive system defined by the failure to achieve a clinical pregnancy after 12 months . . . of regular unprotected sexual intercourse."[107] But while feminist researchers largely reject this definition of infertility, they reclaim use of the term as a social disability. Infertility here identifies the cultural and medical forces that lead to these women's marginalization. Other alternatives include "involuntary" and "voluntary childlessness." As Belle Boggs suggests, these phrases are a "replacement for the narrative of

---

104. Thomas Rees, "Barren," in *The International Standard Bible Encyclopedia*, ed. Geoffrey William Bromiley, vol. 1: A–D (Grand Rapids, MI: Eerdmans, 1979), 432–433.

105. Timothy Willis, "Barren, Barrenness," in *The New Interpreter's Dictionary of the Bible*, ed. Katherine Doob Sakenfeld, Samuel E. Balentine, Brian K. Blount, KahJin Jeffrey Kuan, Joel B. Green, Eileen Schuller, Pheme Perkins, Paul Franklyn, and Marianne Blickenstaff, vol. 1: A–C (Nashville: Abingdon, 2006), 400.

106. Alexander Carlebach and Judith Baskin, "Barrenness and Fertility," in *Encyclopaedia Judaica*, ed. Michael Berenbaum and Fred Skolnik, 2nd ed. (Detroit: Macmillan, 2007), 174.

107. F. Zegers-Hochschild, G. D. Adamson, J. de Mouzon, O. Ishihara, R. Mansour, K. Nygren, E. Sullivan, and S. Vanderpoel, "International Committee for Monitoring Assisted Reproductive Technology (ICMART) and the World Health Organization (WHO) Revised Glossary of ART Terminology, 2009," *Fertility and Sterility* 92 (2009): 1522.

the pitiable outsider."[108] Unlike "barrenness," involuntary and voluntary childlessness stress the choice that women (and men) make regarding their reproductive status. It recognizes that childlessness is a social, rather than a biological or medical, condition, thereby mitigating some of the gendered discrimination often associated with infertility. Additionally, these terms broaden the umbrella of those included under the childless moniker, adding partnerless individuals, men, and members of the LGBTQ community. By reconceptualizing infertility as a social rather than biological disability, feminist scholars push back against the pronatalist and heteronormative description of childlessness. Using these terms, they reject the normalization of procreativity and the stigmatization of infertile individuals.

By reframing the "barren" matriarchs as either infertile or involuntarily childless, biblical scholars can begin to challenge the pronatalist ideology underlying these texts. First Samuel 1 offers a compelling example for this type of reinterpretation. While the story reproduces the expected narrative features of biblical infertility narratives, including the description of the wife's childlessness and promise of an offspring through an intermediary, Hannah is unique in that she is never portrayed as "barren." On the contrary, the narrative simply states that she has אין ילדים, "no children" (v. 2). Hannah's procreative status immediately places her between the boundaries of voluntary and involuntary childlessness. Her characterization revolves around a choice whether to reproduce, which the narrative ties to community expectations. Although the text is ambiguous about whether Hannah wants an offspring, it clearly indicates that her childlessness places her at a social disadvantage. For example, in 1 Samuel 1:6 Peninnah adopts a pronatalist position, provoking Hannah because "[YHWH] had closed her womb." Peninnah's goading plays on reproductive norms, insulting Hannah because of her childless status. Elkanah's response is different, suggesting that Hannah does not need children. He even identifies himself as an alternative to the hypothetical ideal

108. Belle Boggs, *The Art of Waiting: On Fertility, Medicine, and Motherhood* (Minneapolis: Graywolf Press, 2016), 31.

of "ten sons" (v. 8). For some scholars, Elkanah is "far from the stereotype of patriarchy. . . . [He] cares for the wellbeing and happiness of his wife," regardless of her inability to have children.[109] His words, however, still incorporate reproductive terminology. Elkanah does not reject the normalization of motherhood so much as offer himself as a surrogate for Hannah's maternal affection. More important, Elkanah legitimizes his response by referencing the same cultural conviction as Peninnah, attributing Hannah's childlessness to God's inaction. In short, both responses to Hannah's infertility underscore her portrayal as involuntarily childless. Accordingly, Hannah's efforts to conceive are partially a reaction to this discourse around female fecundity. Still, by reframing Hannah's character as involuntarily childless, biblical scholars do not uncritically accept Peninnah's and Elkanah's assessments as fact. Rather, they can contest the pronatalist norms these characters espouse that discriminate against infertile women in this text.

2. Susanne Scholz, "Shame and Nakedness in 1 Sam. 20:30."

"You son of a rebellious woman! Do I not know that you have chosen the son of Jesse to your own shame and to the shame of your mother's nakedness [ולבשת ערות אמך]?" (1 Sam 20:30)

This verse contains two highly problematic Hebrew nouns that have contributed to misogynist views about women's sexuality. The Hebrew nouns are בשת and ערוה. The NRSVue, as well as other English translations such as the New King James Version or the New American Standard Bible, render these words as "shame" and "nakedness." The New International Version indicates the hermeneutical struggle with this sentence when it offers: "and to the shame of the mother who bore you." The combination of nouns suggests that there is something "shameful" about women and their genitals.

The first Hebrew word, בשת, is a noun in the feminine singular, translated as "shame" in all kinds of biblical settings. Only in one

109. Janice P. De-Whyte, *Wom(b)an: A Cultural-Narrative Reading of the Hebrew Bible Barrenness Narratives*, BibInt 162 (Leiden: Brill, 2018), 149.

other setting does this noun receive a sexualized meaning. In Micah 1:11, the people of Shaphir are defeated in war and leave "barefoot and naked (ערום)" in verse 8, but in verse 11 the physical lack of clothing is expressed as a sexually shameful situation. They have to go out "in nakedness shame," which in Hebrew is עריה־בשת. The noun *'eryah* is very similar to *'ervah*; instead of the waw it has a yod. The noun 'eryah also appears in Ezekiel 16:7, part of an extremely sexually violent poem. The combination of feeling shamed and sexual violence in the form of forced nakedness after military defeat has even pornographic connotations.

The second noun, ערוה, in 1 Samuel 20:30 is never translated in a sexually explicit way in English Bible versions. Translated in other biblical contexts as "nakedness," this noun refers to a person's genitals. Even the renowned biblical Hebrew-English dictionary by Brown, Driver, and Briggs openly states this fact:

> ערוה
>
> n.f. nakedness, *pudenda*. . . .[110]

In Genesis 9:22, 23, the nouns refer to Noah's genitals when he lies drunk, and Ham, the father of Canaan, sees his father's *'ervah* (v. 22) whereas his brothers, Shem and Japheth, avoid looking at their father's *'ervah* (v. 23). Leviticus 18 and 20, filled with references to the genitals ("nakedness") of female family members, prohibit male relatives to commit incestuous rape. Most biblical rape poetry contains the noun *'ervah* as a reference to a woman threatened with sexual violence. In Hosea 2:9, the divine husband imagines taking away his wife's wool and flax that covered "her nakedness" (lit. "her genitals"). The rape poem in Isaiah 47:3 refers to "daughter Babylon" as having her *'ervah* uncovered. In the rape poem of Lamentations 1:8, Jerusalem is a metaphoric woman whose *'ervah* has been seen by many. The apotheosis of biblical rape poetry is Ezekiel 16, where the divine husband fantasizes that his wife's former lovers would gang-rape her (v. 37).

110. BDB, 788–789.

In sum, Saul's curse in 1 Samuel 20:30 must be understood as an extreme expression of misogyny filled with allusions of sexual violence. The vocabulary articulates explicit hatred against his son, but the sexually violent connotations against his wife, the mother of Jonathan, should also gravely disturb feminist and nonfeminist readers alike.

3. David J. Zucker, "The Medium of Endor and Saul: Ancient and Contemporary Views," *JBQ* 48 (2020): 241–242.
Bible translations as well as scholarly articles differ on how most accurately to refer to the occupation of this woman in 1 Samuel 28:7. NJPS [New Jewish Publication Society of America Tanakh] employs the term "consults ghosts." A number of standard Bible translations such as the *New International Version* (NIV), the Roman Catholic *New American Bible* (NAB), and the Roman Catholic *Jerusalem Bible* (JB) offer explanatory descriptions prior to certain sections. All three refer to the "witch" of Endor. The word "witch" also is used in scholarly works such as in the Josephus section in the Jewish Publication Society's multi-volume, *Outside the Bible: Ancient Jewish Writings Related to Scripture*. As mentioned earlier in this article, a witch "practices black magic, that is, attempts to influence the future rather than just divine it. The [woman] of Endor is more properly a medium or necromancer (one who divines by means of the dead)." The term "witch" is used as a pejorative. Yet as noted earlier, in her role the "Medium of Endor is a minister of religion, and a good one." The editors of these various Bible translations and scholarly works felt that they had some discretion as to the wording of the titles for the subsections. In the actual text translations they were much more circumspect. NIV and NAB employ the word medium; and JB, necromancer. The *New English Bible* (NEB) translates that as a woman who has a familiar spirit (v. 7). In v. 9 when the woman herself addresses Saul she uses the term one who uses *ghosts and familiar spirits (ha-ovot v'et ha-yidoni*—NJPS). NIV has mediums and spiritists; NAB uses mediums and fortune-tellers; JB features necromancers and wizards. NEB features those who call up ghosts and spirits. NRSV translates these words as

mediums and wizards. Nowhere in the translations from the Hebrew do these sources use the word "witch."

4. "The Witch of En-Dor" by Brian B. Schmidt, from Brian B. Schmidt, "The 'Witch' of En-Dor, 1 Samuel 28, and Ancient Near Eastern Necromancy," in *Ancient Magic and Ritual Power*, ed. Marvin Meyer and Paul Mirecki, Religions in the Graeco-Roman World 129 (Leiden: Brill, 1995), 125–26.

Who then are the intended referents designated *'ĕlōhîm* in 1 Sam 28:13? One viable alternative to understanding the phrase *'ĕlōhîm . . . 'ōlîm* reflects a striking resemblance to elements attested in Mesopotamian necromancy. In the first-millennium necromantic incantation . . . , various deities including Shamash and the primordial deities of the nether-world are called upon in order to ensure the appearance of the ghost of the dead. In one such incantation, Shamash is depicted as follows: "Shamash, O Judge, you bring those from above down below, those from below up above." This role of the solar deity is also underscored in another incantation text:

> [1][. . . [2]. . .] dust of the netherworld [. . .]. [3]May he (Shamash) bring up a ghost from the darkness for me! May he (put life back) into the dead man's limbs. [4]I call (upon you), O Skull of skulls: [5]May he who is within the skull answer [me]? [6]O Shamash, who opens the darken [ss. Incantation . . .].

In view of the likelihood that the Syro-Palestinian dead were not equated with the gods, that the gods were active participants in the Mesopotamian necromancy rituals, that the text of 1 Sam 28:13–14 manifests considerable complexity in transmission, and that the biblical traditions show some acquaintance with Mesopotamian necromancy, it is our conclusion that the term *'ĕlōhîm* in 1 Sam 28:13 designates those gods known to be summoned—many from the world below—to assist the necromancer in the retrieval of a ghost. Our interpretive rendition of vv. 11–14 follows:

> 11At that, the woman said, "Whom shall I bring up for
> you?" He answered, "Bring up Samuel for me." 12When
> the woman saw Samuel, she shrieked loudly, and the
> woman said to Saul, "Why have you deceived me? You
> are Saul!" 13The king said to her, "Do not be afraid. What
> do you see?" And the woman said to Saul, "I see (chtonic)
> gods coming up from the earth." 14Then he said to her,
> "(Now) what have you perceived (cf. LXX)?" And she said
> to him, "An old/upright man coming up from the earth,
> and he is wrapped in a robe."

5. Rachel Ofer, "A Wicked Witch or a Good Psychotherapist? The Medium of Endor in Modern Hebrew Literature," *HS* 62 (2021): 193–195. Used by permission.

The story "בעלת האוב" (The Medium, 2018)[111] by Gail Hareven (b. 1959)[112] criticizes the chauvinistic social view that persecutes "witches" or "masculine" women, that is, independent women. In this story the Medium is a strong and independent woman, who earns her living from her talent *לשמוע מתים* (to hear the dead), and society persecutes her because she is considered a witch, who must be put to death. Hareven's story expresses a protest against the injustice of excluding women like the Medium, who exemplifies threatening, female "otherness."

In this story the Medium, as it were, fits the characteristics of a witch; she lives alone in a cave, outside civilization, and she is neither a mother nor a wife. She is masculine and her behavior is exceptional בעצמה נהגה בחמור ותכף כשחנרהצה רקעה ברגליה וכמו גבר דרשה ש ייקחו אותה אל הגבארים (She rode a donkey, and immediately when she stopped, jumped down, stamped her foot, and like a man demanded that they take her to the men, 57). Further on it says that she traveled the roads כלא אישה (like a non-woman, 62). However, exactly against the background of "witchlike" characteristics, the debunking of the myth stands out: the Medium is revealed as goodhearted

111. Gail Hareven, "בעלת האוב" ("The Medium"), *מיניאטורות מקראיות*, *Biblical Miniatures* (Jerusalem: Bialik Institute, 2018), 56–63.

112. See The Institute for the Translation of Hebrew Literature, http://www.ithl.org.il/page_13438.

and compassionate, who lends an ear to אנשים עצובים (sad people). According to her, she identified Saul's sadness from afar the first time she saw him, because . . . he carried his body like a foreign burden. . . . Even though she was accustomed to sad people, . . . because happy people, who are content, do not seek help through necromancy. . . . She describes Saul's sadness as exceptional: . . . you look into his eyes and it is as if you have fallen into a pit. . . .

Even though the plot of the story takes place in the biblical past (and not in modern reality), nevertheless the story distances itself from the biblical source. It includes the addition of subplots that do not appear in the biblical story and of new characters (such as the figure, [her benefactor] איש החסדה of who protected her, and his son, who continued to do so after his father's death). Hareven's story argues against the view that justifies the prophet Samuel rather than Saul (much like Tchernikovsky's ballad); Samuel is portrayed as hating Saul: גם מהקבר עולות תימרות שנאתו (even from the grave the columns of his hatred arise, 61), and Saul's madness came from his attempt to revolt against the prophet Samuel, איש שונא (a hateful person), who forced him to accept the kingship against his will (61).

The dominant feminist aspect of the story is expressed not only in the description of the Medium, but also in the description of the relations between Saul and Samuel; the Medium, about whom the narrator says היא הייתה הכמה מכל הנשים שהכיר (she was wiser than all the women he knew, 62), compares Saul's rebellion against Samuel to the rebellion of a battered wife (!), whose violent husband abuses her and she tries to rebel against him secretly. Even though he takes a second wife (an allusion to the choice of David), he continues to beat the first wife until she loses her mind:

> You know, she said, among women—there are some like him. Many. They do not dare to rise up and rebel against him, but secretly they rebel. The husband says, "cook lentils for me," and the wife serves him buckwheat . . . every time that the husband does not have his way, he beats his wife . . . until she no longer knows whether he said lentils or buckwheat . . . she became a fool . . . lost her mind . . .

The somewhat surprising comparison between Saul and a battered wife is reinforced by its allusion to the picturesque midrash that describes a wife (Rav's wife), who caused her husband grief by not cooking for him the food he wanted (lentils), but specially served him the food he did not want. Thus Saul's rebellion is compared to a typical female rebellion, characteristic of wives who are afraid of their husbands and do not dare to revolt against them openly.

6. J. Kabamba Kiboko,"A Disanga Reading of 1 Samuel 28." From J. Kabamba Kiboko, *Divining the Woman of Endor: African Culture, Postcolonial Hermeneutics, and the Politics of Biblical Translation* (LHBOTS 644; London: T&T Clark, 2017), 225–227.*
Modern Western[er]s, it seems to me, fear the departed. Death is now considered to be a failure of modern science and a separation from life. Genesis is read in a way that allows us to feel both distinct from the earth and master over it. 1 Samuel is read similarly. We call the woman, who can cross the disanga between life and the beyond, between the human and the other, between king and subject, between disempowerment and power, between fear and service, a witch. In so doing, we deny our connection to all that is. From an African perspective, we deceive ourselves and this denial does not help us. . . .

The woman of Endor is, from a Musanga perspective, made of a stronger breath than Western moderns. . . .

Our environment holds the breath of all who (and that) once lived. The woman of Endor remembers and re-members that breath. She raises it, embodies it, to communicate God's will to Saul when he is finally ready to hear. She harnesses the breath of the deceased Samuel to confront Saul with his deception of not only her, but of himself, and then comforts and strengthens Saul who must go to face his death and the defeat of his people. Can there be, I ask, a better advisor than that? Where is the evil intent? Where is the idolatry? Where is the blasphemy? It is not here, there is only the breath of Samuel. . . .

I wish I could conclude by saying that, in the Hebrew Bible, conquest theology always fails. It does not. . . . Conquest theology does not fail entirely here either. Samuel conveys that Saul lost Yhwh's favor and must die because he refused to comply with Yhwh's genocidal wishes. This cannot be easily brushed aside as some commentators have done. I think, however, we can resist this ancient understanding of God by lifting up Saul and the woman of Endor for the ways in which they both resisted empire. Saul was not perfect in this, but he paid a dear price, the ultimate price, for the resistance he did offer. These two characters are important from a postcolonial point of view. I, therefore, suggest that the well-known abbreviations used in biblical studies, "Dtr" and "DH," should not be allowed to become distorted, perhaps, hijacked, by a misreading of the biblical text:

"Dtr" should not be made to stand for *Dominatuer*, nor "DH" for the *Domination History*. The Deuteronomist permitted— maybe even orchestrated—Deut 18:10–11's voice, Samuel's voice, Saul's voice, and the woman of Endor's voice, all to sing their sometimes interdependent and sometimes contrapuntual lines. It is a song that, according to Bakhtin, resists empire. From a Musanga, feminist, postcolonial perspective, I must say that the woman of Endor has been maligned and violated consistently and undeservedly in translation and interpretation.

[*Kiboko explains on pages xiii–xiv of her book that *Disanga* has a threefold meaning among the Basanga living in the Democratic Republic of the Congo. Etymologically, the word means "to meet" and "to meet together," and thus *Disanga* refers to a crossroads or a place of gathering. Historically, the word *Disanga* refers to native people coming together with other peoples due to the land's resources. Geographically, the word *Disanga* refers to the central river in the Kasanga region running through the land and bringing two rivers together. Basically, the word refers to "living on the crossroads," whether it is between Africa and the West or between life and death.]

7. Mary Chan, "The Witch of Endor and Seventeenth-Century Propaganda," *Musica Disciplina* 34 (1980): 206–207.

At least three books of anti-Catholic propaganda whose titles refer specifically to the Witch of Endor survive from the later decades of the seventeenth century, two from the 1670s and one almost contemporary with the publication of Purcell's setting of "in guilty night."[113] In the first two of these works neither the meaning of the title is clear nor the satire specific, although each, in a general way, uses Endor and witchcraft to refer to the Roman Catholic Church. The lack of precise reference may indicate that the use of the story of Saul at Endor is simply part of the general use of biblical rhetoric at this time, to inveigh against the Roman Catholic Church;[114] it may indicate a reliance on the general, seventeenth-century, association of Roman Catholicism with witchcraft;[115] or it may suggest that the authors depended on their public's recognition of certain accepted significances for Saul, Samuel and the Witch of Endor in the context of anti-Catholicism.

The earliest of these three works, Daniel Brevint's *Saul and Samuel at Endor* (1674), seems to have been inspired by the upsurge of anti-Catholic feeling around 1675 when it was evident that James, Duke of York, had become a Catholic. Brevint's work is an invective against the beliefs and forms of the Roman Catholic Church comparing them to the enchantments of the Witch of Endor, although such comparison is implicit (from the title-page) rather than explicit in the text. Titus Oates's *The Witch of Endor* (1679) is part of the propaganda of his Popish Plot, an hysterical pamphlet against "the witchcrafts of the Roman Jesebel." Arthur Saul's *Saul at Endor* (1692) belongs in the last wave of anti-Catholic propaganda in the seventeenth century (as does Purcell's setting of Ramsey's text). Unlike the other two this is a more specific satire identifying Saul with Louis XIV, Samuel's Ghost with the Marquis de Louvois and the Witch of Endor with the old female former servant of Mme Voisin burnt for witchcraft at Louis's

113. Daniel Brevint, *Saul and Samuel at Endor* (Oxford, 1674); Titus Oates, *The Witch of Endor* (London, 1679); Arthur Saul, *Saul at Endor* (London, 1692).

114. See the examples in John Miller, *Popery and Politics in England 1660–1688* (Cambridge, 1973), 88–89.

115. See, for example, William M. Lamont, *Godly Rule: Politics and Religion 1603–1660* (London, 1969), 97–100; H. R. Trevor-Roper, "The European Witch-Craze of the Sixteenth and Seventeenth Centuries," in *Religion Reformation and Social Change* (London, 1967), 90–192.

behest. Sections of the pamphlet are devoted to discussion of Louis's protection of James II and his persecution of the "Hugonots." The whole work is a piece of pro-English propaganda, supporting William of Orange and using the Saul at Endor story only for its characters and as a satire on the means to which Catholics (Louis XIV in this case) are reduced, the Ghost finally prophesying disaster for Louis.

8. Shatha Almutawa, "The Arabic Reception of the Saul and the Medium of Endor Narrative," *HS* 62 (2021): 137–138, 142, 146, 147. Used by permission.

The tenth-century Iraqi thinkers known as Ikhwān al-Safā', or the Brethren of Purity (also known as the Sincere Brothers), include the story of Saul and the medium of Endor in their Epistle 52 on magic. This epistle is part of their larger work, *Rasā 'il Ikhwān al-Safā* (*The Epistles of the Brethren of Purity*), an encyclopedic work dedicated to the different sciences and fields of knowledge. . . .

Saul (Talūt) is a figure in the scriptures of Islam, but the biblical passage about Saul and the witch of Endor does not appear in the Qur'an. . . .

Ikhwān al-Safā''s version of the story of Saul and the Witch of Endor is quoted here in a translation by Godefroid de Callataÿ and Bruno Halflants:

> Then [there is to be found] also the Books of Annals of the Kings from the Sons of Israel, which for the Jews takes the same courses as the Torah. There it is mentioned that there was amongst them a prophet called Samuel. He was famous amongst the prophets, and there is a book about him. The Christians and the Jews admit and give credence to his prophethood and the loftiness of his power, and they possess his book. And it is reported in the book that he appointed a king for the Jews, whose name was Saul.
>
> And God Most High supported him for the killing of Amalek, and he did it, except that he disobeyed in respect of the livestock. The king was toppled from his rank, and David was anointed instead of him, on travel, and Samuel died. And Saul busied himself with killing magicians and

fortune-tellers, and amongst them was killed who was killed, and fled who fled. And he [Saul] turned to the people of the Philistines so as to fight with all the fortune-tellers amongst them. But fright pervaded him, because of the multitude of armies raised against him. And he did not find any pacifier [to respond] to his speech, as was his habit as prophet: neither magician, nor fortune-teller, nor sage. And he got anxious about this.

He said to his relatives, "Look for a magician for me; I shall ask him about the matter of my circumstances."

One suggested a sorceress to him. He had faith in her and asked her to revive a prophet he could seek [advice] from. She asked him which prophet he would choose to be revived. He chose Samuel, and she revived him. She got frightened at the sight of him and cried for help.

But Saul told her, "Do not be frightened! What did you see?"

She said, "I saw an old man, radiant like the angels of the Lord, wrapped up in a coat, as if he arose from the earth."

And Saul knew that it was Samuel. He went closer to him, and he prostrated himself in front of him.

And Samuel told him, "Why did you make me return and revive me?"

Saul said, "[This is a time] I am at a loss, because of the people of the Philistines and their fight against me, and the cessation of God's support of me, and the fact that He deprives me of clemency. I called you to consult you about my affairs."

Samuel said, "God Most High transferred the kingship to your companion. He was angry at you and at the Sons of Israel, because of what you had done regarding the livestock of Amalek. He was the one assisting the Philistines against you and [He was the one who] made them victorious. And you will proceed together with us, tomorrow, amongst the dead.

Then Saul went out and, because of this, sank to the ground unconscious. And the sorceress recognized him and came closer to him, together with those who were with him, and they did not cease to be with him until he became fit [again]. She provided hospitality to them for the night, and they departed in the morning. The fight was fierce and defeat befell the Hebrews. They [The Philistines] multiplied the killing amongst them. Three of the sons of Saul were killed, and he leant on his spear and took it out from his back. And the Sons of Israel gathered together to name David as king, and he fought whoever defied them.

All this is equally supplied by the Annals.[116]

116. Translated by Godefroid de Callataÿ and Bruno Halflants, eds., *On Magic: An Arabic Critical Edition and English Translation of EPISTLE 52a, Epistles of the Brethren of Purity* (Oxford: Oxford University Press, 2011), 112–115.

CONCLUSION

Knowing, Deconstructing, and Resisting as Feminist Exegetical Practice

We need to know how patriarchy works. We need to know how women disappear, why we are initiated into a culture where women have no visible past, and what will happen if we make that past visible and real. If the process is not to be repeated again, if we are to transmit to the next generation of women what was denied transmission to us, we need to know how to break the closed circle of male power which permits men to go on producing knowledge about themselves, pretending that we do not exist.

—Dale Spender, *Women of Ideas and What Men Have Done to Them: From Aphra Behn to Adrienne Rich*

For the master's tools will never dismantle the master's house. They may allow us temporarily to beat him at his own game, but they will never enable us to bring about genuine change. And this fact is only threatening to those women who still define the master's house as their only source of support.

—Audre Lorde, *Sister Outsider: Essays and Speeches*

THIS FEMINIST INTERPRETATION is conceptually framed around five major areas of exegetical investigation to enable an intersectional feminist, genderqueer, and masculinity-oriented interpretation of 1 Samuel. The five areas pertain to the geopolitics of land and gender (chapter 1), variously positioned male characters (chapter 2), the discourse on the emerging monarchy (chapter 3), the ethnonational stereotypes embedded in rhetorical references to the (male) Philistines (chapter 4), and the erasure of female characters (chapter 5).

This conceptual framework works particularly well because of the fragmentary, repetitive, and disjointed nature of this biblical book. As text and source critics have long observed, the thirty-one chapters, allocated to what is nowadays classified as 1 Samuel, do not constitute a linear, coherent, and chronologically sequential storyline. Textual breaks, double and even triple repetitions, sudden appearances and disappearances of characters, fragmentary tales, and literary gaps appear throughout this biblical book. Importantly, then, the conceptual framework helps readers not to get lost in the disjointed textual composition.

The five areas of exegetical investigation orient readers and accommodate biblical content, literary emphases, and theoretical challenges in the interpretation of 1 Samuel. I do not suggest that other areas would not offer valuable exegetical and hermeneutical insights for a differently conceptualized approach. But I do claim that the five selected areas move this feminist reading *beyond* an essentializing and gynocentric reading tradition that highlights female characters only. An essentializing approach that focuses exclusively on the female characters in the text was necessary, and perhaps even groundbreaking, when female characters were rarely mentioned in phallogocentric biblical scholarship. Yet this feminist interpretation appears fifty years *after* the emergence of feminist biblical scholarship in the early 1970s. By now the feminist verdict is clear: A simple recovery of female characters stabilizes kyriarchal power structures, and so more is needed than a seemingly sequential retelling of women's stories. This present feminist interpretation thus aims to expand the exegetical, hermeneutical, and methodological horizon for 1 Samuel.

The question is what we gain from this kind of approach. This is an important question for anybody reading biblical texts, but it is particularly pertinent for a reading that does not merely rehash the stories of the few female characters mentioned in 1 Samuel. The question of *cui bono*, "to whom is it a benefit," is particularly pertinent today. The question also touches on the perennial radical feminist objection to the Bible. As the founding mother of Christian feminist theologies, Mary Daly, put it so famously in 1973, "What is required of women at this point in history is a firm and deep refusal to limit our perspectives, questioning, and creativity to any of the preconceived patterns of male-dominated culture."[1] Feminists like Daly have long advised to forget about the Bible, not least about 1 Samuel, and instead to write prose and poetry disaffiliated from the troublesome, difficult, and repressive Bible-reading traditions. I do not completely agree. My interpretation demonstrates that feminist exegesis of the Bible, grounded in expansively defined notions of feminist theory that embrace genderqueer and masculinity-oriented insights, offers means to understand, deconstruct, and resist phallogocentrism in its intersectional dynamics.

Three principal reasons come to mind why feminist, as well as other cultural-studies-related reading strategies of the Bible are crucial even, or perhaps especially, today. First, biblical texts such as 1 Samuel are still being read in countless Christian and Jewish congregations and religiously affiliated institutions. Previously non-Christian communities in countries such as China have added millions of new Bible readers. In addition, most history books still describe ancient Near Eastern historiography on the basis of key events reported in the Hebrew Bible, including in 1 Samuel. Although some biblical scholars have challenged the historiographical reliability of the Bible, the Bible as a theological and historical reference point will not disappear anytime soon. Although in recent decades the geopolitical sphere of biblical influence has changed due to an increasing secularization in the Global North and an increase of Bible readers in the Global South, these shifts have not led to fewer people reading the Bible. Just the opposite. The shifts also do not mean that today's Bible readers have moved beyond literalist-antiquarian reading strategies.

Feminist approaches to the Bible in general and to 1 Samuel in particular are thus extremely important. They challenge phallogocentric, heteronormative, misogynist, and androcentric reading habits in conversation with variously defined intersectional dynamics. Since this interpretation models such an approach, the volume contributes to the effort of teaching other ways of reading the Bible in challenge to seemingly omnipresent structures of domination that centrally include gender injustice. As Elizabeth Cady Stanton observed already in 1895, "So long as tens of thousands of Bibles

---

1. Mary Daly, *Beyond God the Father: Toward a Philosophy of Women's Liberation* (Boston: Beacon, 1973), 7.

are printed every year, and circulated over the whole habitable globe, and the masses in all English-speaking nations revere it as the word of God, it is vain to belittle its influence."[2] In short, feminists and gender-justice scholars should not abandon or ignore one of the most influential religious texts of the past two thousand years.

Second, another reason explains why a feminist reading on 1 Samuel is much needed today. Since feminist and nonfeminist people alike must learn about the pervasive presence of phallogocentrism in the world, there is no better opportunity for honing our exegetical, hermeneutical, and methodological skills than a storyline that offers plenty of phallogocentric notions. Rather than reading 1 Samuel as a description, or even prescription, of kyriarchal hierarchies, this feminist interpretation teaches readers how to recognize and deconstruct those hierarchies. In my view, then, my reading offers an intellectual-hermeneutical training ground. By reading 1 Samuel, we practice to critically analyze the world. Accordingly, my approach shows readers how to correlate the study of 1 Samuel with geopolitical power dynamics, how to deconstruct assumptions about masculinity and phallogocentric power, how to recognize authoritarian-monarchical hierarchies as problematic, how to deconstruct ethnonational discourse about the "Other," and how to critique the erasure of women. In this way, feminist and nonfeminist readers alike practice their skills of identifying kyriarchal notions in and about the Bible to recognize and resist kyriarchal domination in the world. Read this way, the Bible becomes part of feminist practice that seeks to implement gender justice wherever readers are located.

Third, yet another reason should caution feminists against forsaking religious texts such as the Bible. For hundreds of years, the Bible, in its various canonical forms, has been transmitted from one generation to the next, not only endorsing and justifying monarchical and feudalist structures but also inspiring countless liberation struggles. As Elisabeth Schüssler Fiorenza eloquently states, "From the nineteenth into the twentieth and now twenty-first centuries, the Bible has been used both as a weapon against emancipatory struggles for equal citizenship in society and church and as a resource

2. Elizabeth Cady Stanton, "Introduction," in *The Woman's Bible* (Boston: Northeastern University Press, 1993), 11.

for emancipatory struggles for liberation."[3] As a complex literary text, the Bible has been there for interested readers to create biblical meanings. It is thus crucial that readers understand that they, grounded in their social locations, create biblical meanings.[4] Many readers do not recognize this crucial hermeneutical insight, perhaps having been sufficiently conditioned into the belief that the Bible says something without readers. Yet, as today's readers are living through one of the most globally dangerous moments in recent memory, with threats of nuclear war being articulated by politicians and published in mainstream newspapers, the engagement with the irrational forces that are present in the unconsciousness of people is urgently needed. A religious text such as the Bible can help in this regard. By reading the Bible, interpreters reflect on society in relation to the higher powers of the universe, even when the texts are as problematic as the narratives of 1 Samuel. What matters is to engage in a rational, intellectual discourse to hold together both the rational and the irrational and simultaneously to strive for the good, the divine. My interpretation of 1 Samuel contributes toward this goal, reasoning itself through an abundance of difficult and even fictional accounts. The volume invites readers to the arduous human task of being engaged with a theoculturally and politically significant religious text. In the process, readers ponder feminist questions of intellectual and theological importance, even though the texts under consideration contain difficult content to which feminists ought to object. The geopolitics of land and gender, the relentless focus on male characters, the implementation of a monarchical system, the characterization of male Philistines by their genitalia, and the erasure of female characters as mothers, wives, or daughters illustrate why 1 Samuel is such problematic literature for feminists. Yet the important task is to wrestle with these difficult texts because the process of wrestling connects people with their better selves. As the threat of today's sociopolitical, military-corporate, and economic-feudalistic systems becomes more obvious by the day, the present interpretation reminds readers that people are not meant to become

---

3. Elisabeth Schüssler Fiorenza, *Democratizing Biblical Studies: Toward an Emancipatory Educational Space* (Louisville, KY: Westminster John Knox, 2009), 12.

4. For further explanations, see Susanne Scholz, *The Bible as Political Artifact: On the Feminist Study of the Hebrew Bible* (Minneapolis: Fortress, 2017).

cyborgs programmed by presumably all-powerful and spectacularly wealthy technocratic oligarchs who shape societies by algorithmic digital passports or biometric social scores. Rather, people need to be agents of their own lives. They need to reflect on, engage with, and critique biblical meanings and so participate in the building of society. They need to become attentive to the needs, wishes, and dreams of all humans, animals, nature, and Planet Earth. As Herman Broch suggested in 1939, humans need to be deeply connected to the recognition that "I am the world" rather than merging into a collective mass psychosis of separation, discrimination, violence, or even war.[5] First Samuel offers countless texts to reflect on the evils of the second option. In my view, feminists should thus grab the Bible and deliberate on how to construct a just, free, and democratic society today.

In sum, this feminist reading of 1 Samuel helps readers to consider and evaluate the causes for the abundant violence and the many wars in the world. Teaching readers to recognize and deconstruct stereotypical ways of interpreting the sacred texts of the Jewish and Christian traditions, this book invites readers to reflect on their visions for humanity's future within the interrelated planetary and intergalactic ecological systems in which we live and on which we depend. Accordingly, this conceptual feminist interpretation does not engage in the widely assumed exegetical quest for biblical origins, and it does not merely rehash biblical women's stories. Rather, the volume encourages interpreters to read against the grain and correlate biblical texts to prominent issues pertaining to geopolitics and gender, various forms of masculinity, governmental systems of hierarchy and domination, ethnonational rhetoric, and the erasure of female characters. In the process, readers are invited to move their viewpoints from a hermeneutics of kyriarchal compliance to a hermeneutics of feminist resistance that always questions, contests, and deconstructs hegemonic narratives, whether they appear behind, within, or in front of biblical texts.

---

5. Herman Broch, *Massenwahntheorie: Beiträge zu einer Psychologie der Politik* (Frankfurt am Main: Suhrkamp, 1979), 18–19.

GLOSSARY

Androcentrism (adj.: androcentric): Male-centered; from the word *ἀνήρ* in Greek that means "male."

Deconstruction: A method that critically analyzes textual artifacts, broadly defined, to uncover overlooked, hidden, or otherwise concealed assumptions, viewpoints, or beliefs.

Essentializing: Restricts the idea of a person's gender to biology or an ontological quality outside of history, politics, or culture, or even as a divinely given quality of people defined as female or male only.

Ethnonational: Refers to the idea that ethnic and national concepts are interrelated and thus need to be examined together.

Feminist (adj.): An umbrella term in exegetical investigations that focus on any aspect of biblical texts and their interpretation histories related to sex and gender beyond biologically or ontologically conceptualized notions, images, metaphors, and characters in the quest of exposing, deconstructing, and reconceptualizing biblical texts and interpretation histories beyond patriarchy, androcentrism, phallogocentrism, and heteronormativity, in their intersectional dimensions

Gender: A concept recognizing biological sex differences as sociocultural, political, economic, and religious constructs that define thoughts and practices of people in any given society and that change according to place and time.

Genderqueer (or third gender): Refers to a person whose gender identity and/or expression falls between or outside of the gender binary of female and male.

Geopolitics: Describes political dynamics as they are influenced by geographical boundaries, often shaped by (neo)colonizing structures of domination.

Hebrew Bible (or Old Testament, Tanakh): Increasingly used after the Shoah/Holocaust in 1945, this term offers less negative, that is, anti-Jewish Christian, connotations than "Old Testament." The term expresses the ecumenical recognition, especially among Christian readers, that this part of the Bible is also read vigorously, and with an extensively long reading tradition, by Jews, from which the Christian tradition has emerged in various ways. In contrast, the term "Old Testament" must be understood as an exclusively Christian expression that has often viewed this part of the Christian canon as less significant than the New Testament. The term "Tanakh" is the Hebrew acronym customarily used in Judaism. The canonical order of the books is different in the Jewish and Christian canons and even within various Christian canons. The original language of the Hebrew Bible includes Aramaic in some passages, such as in the book of Daniel. The term "Hebrew Bible" is a compromise that recognizes the bireligious and complicated, if not precarious, reading traditions, especially within Christianity. Hegemonic Christianity mostly ignored, denied, or even attempted to reject this part of the canon and its original reading community of Jews, culminating in the Shoah/Holocaust.

Hegemon: A leading or major political, social, economic power (individual or collective entity such as a country).

Hegemonic masculinity: Theories and practices that construct male dominance in society and culture as superior to other gender expressions. The concept assumes the superiority of male over female, including that boys and men are physically tough, emotionally stoic, self-sufficient, and heterosexually dominant over girls and women. Any other sexual performance or orientation is strictly rejected within this mindset, although the particulars keep evolving over time and in different places.

Heterocentric (in addition to androcentric): A worldview centering on heterosexuality as the norm and the naturally given in society, often including androcentrism, that is, male-centered assumptions and practices.

Heteronormative: A stance promoting heterosexuality as the norm or preferred sexual orientation.

Heteropatriarchy: The social, political, and economic system in which heterosexual men are the dominant group in a society or culture.

Heterosexism: The sociopolitical, economic, and cultural-religious structures of oppression especially targeting queer/gay people on the assumption that heterosexuality is the norm.

Intersectionality: A concept articulating the interconnectedness of social categories, such as gender, race, and class, that create overlapping and interdependent systems of discrimination and oppression.

Iron Age I and II: The epoch starting in 1200 BCE following the Bronze Age and in ancient Near Eastern history usually divided into two major periods. Iron Age I is dated from approximately 1200 to 1000 BCE and Iron Age II from approximately 1000 to 586 BCE.

Kyriarchy (adj.: kyriarchal): A term based on the Greek terms *κύριος* ("Lord") and *ἀρχή* ("beginning," "rule," "power") and coined by feminist biblical scholar Elisabeth Schüssler Fiorenza, emphasizing two markers of sociopolitical, theocultural, and economic domination, namely, class and gender, but also referencing the many other interacting structures of power and domination. For a detailed discussion on this term and its application in biblical exegesis, see, for example, Elisabeth Schüssler Fiorenza, *Congress of Wo/men: Religion, Gender, and Kyriarchal Power* (Eugene, OR: Wipf and Stock, 2016).

Masculinity-oriented: Refers to the sociopolitical, economic, cultural, or religious expectations of being male in any given society, especially related to the roles, behaviors, and attributes considered appropriate for boys and men.

Masoretes: Jewish scholars of the sixth to tenth centuries CE contributing to the establishment of a recognized text of the Hebrew Bible and to the compilation of the Masorah.

Misogynist: The disliking of, the despising of, or being strongly prejudiced against women.

Natural knowledge: A Christian medieval concept that refers to the process of how we know what we know apart from divine revelation. In the case of "natural knowledge," the acquisition of knowledge comes from nature or the earthly realm.

Naturalized masculinity: A phrase that views masculinity as an essentialized, biological, or foundational concept in contrast to understanding masculinity (or gender in general) as a sociopolitical, cultural, economic, or theological theoretical construct that defines people's gender performance in society.

Neoliberalism (adj.: neoliberal): A political approach that favors free-market capitalism, deregulation, and reduction in government spending.

Ostracon: A piece of pottery, usually broken off from a vase or storage container, with some writing edged onto it.

Patriarchy (adj.: patriarchal): A system of society or government in which the father or eldest male is head of the family, and descent is traced through the male line.

Phallogocentrism: Focuses on the masculine (the phallus) in cultural-political theory and the practice of power.

Phallic supremacy ideology: A system of theories, ideas, and convictions leading to ways of societal organization and practices in which the phallus, and thus the male, is seen as superior.

Pithos (plural: pithoi): A Greek name for large terracotta storage containers.

Postcolonialism (adj.: postcolonial): The critical analysis of the cultural, political, economic, social, and religious legacies of Western, mostly

European, colonialism and imperialism around the globe, usually examined from the perspectives of formerly colonized peoples and their lands.

Proto-feminism: Voices of mostly female writers and thinkers in Western cultures and societies prior to the nineteenth-century movements of social change, including the suffragists and the abolitionists of slavery in the United States.

Queer: A positively reclaimed adjective from a previously pejorative term that is used particularly by younger people whose sexual orientation is not exclusively heterosexual (e.g., queer person, queer woman). More recent theorists emphasize that queer theory must resist all norms and expectations and establish new modes of living and being in society.

Subjectivities of masculinity: A phrase that emphasizes that what is perceived or understood is grounded in male-defined assumptions, emotions, thoughts, or concepts.

Tel (sometimes also spelled *tell*): Refers to an artificial topographical mound or a hill that consists of archaeological debris of consecutive settlements hidden within the soil.

WORKS CITED

Ackerman, Susan. *When Heroes Love: The Ambiguity of Eros in the Stories of Gilgamesh and David.* GTR. New York: Columbia University Press, 2005.

Ademiluka, Solomon O. "Hannah's Prayer for a Male Child: Interpreting 1 Samuel 1:11 in the Nigerian Context." *In die Skriflig* 55 (2021): 1–8.

Aguilar, Grace. *The Women of Israel.* London: R. Groombridge, 1845; New York: D. Appleton, 1872.

Ahituv, Netta. "15 Years of Separation: The Palestinians Cut Off from Jerusalem by the Wall." *Haaretz,* March 10, 2018. https://www.haaretz.com/israel-news/.premium.MAGAZINE-15-years-of-separation-palestinians-cut-off-from-jerusalem-by-a-wall-1.5888001.

Albright, William F. "The Danish Excavations at Shiloh." *BASOR* 9 (1923): 10–11.

Albright, William F. "The Danish Excavations at Seilun: A Correction." *PEQ* 59 (1927): 157–158.

Albright, William F. *Excavations and Results at Tell el-Fûl (Gibeah of Saul).* AASOR 4. New Haven, CT: Yale University Press, 1924.

Al-Hilâlî, Muhammad Taqî-ud-Dîn, and Muhammad Muhsin Khân. *Translation of the Meanings of the Noble Qur'an in the English Language.* Madinah: King Fahd Complex for the Printing of the Holy Qur'an, n.d. https://www.holybooks.com/wp-content/uploads/2010/05/english-quranalhilali-khan.pdf.

Almeghari, Rami. "Three Children Burn to Death as Candles Replace Lights in Besieged Gaza." *The Electronic Intifada,* April 10, 2012. https://electronicintifada.net/content/three-children-burn-death-candles-replace-lights-besieged-gaza/11147.

Al Mezan Center for Human Rights. "15 Years Too Long: A Factsheet on the Devastating Effects of Israel's Closure on the Gaza Strip." 2022. https://www.mezan.org/uploads/files/16551887811136.pdf.

Al-Mughrabi, Nidal. "Anger as Palestinian Authority Cuts Gaza Salaries and Pays Late." *Reuters,* May 3, 2018. https://www.reuters.com/article/us-palestinians-gaza-salaries/anger-as-palestinian-authority-cuts-gazasalaries-and-pays-late-idUSKBN1I41LM.

Almutawa, Shatha. "The Arabic Reception of the Saul and the Medium of Endor Narrative." *HS* 62 (2021): 137–155.

Alter, Robert. *Ancient Israel: The Former Prophets: Joshua, Judges, Samuel and Kings: A Translation with Commentary*. New York: Norton, 2013.

Alter, Robert. *The David Story: A Translation with Commentary of 1 and 2 Samuel*. New York: Norton, 1999.

Alter, Robert. *The Hebrew Bible: A Translation with Commentary*. Vol. 2: Prophets: Nevi'im. New York: Norton, 2019.

Anderson, Janice Capel, and Stephen D. Moore, eds. *Mark and Method: New Approaches in Biblical Studies*. 2nd ed. Minneapolis: Fortress, 2008.

Applied Research Institut in Jerusalem (ARIJ). "Qaryut Village Profile (Including Jalud Locality)." http://vprofile.arij.org/nablus/pdfs/vprofile/Qaryut_vp_en.pdf.

Bach, Alice. "The Pleasure of Her Text." *USQR* 43 (1989): 41–58.

Bach, Alice, ed. *Women in the Hebrew Bible: A Reader*. New York: Routledge, 1999.

Bachner, Andrea. *The Mark of Theory: Inscriptive Figures, Poststructuralist Prehistories*. New York: Fordham University Press, 2018.

Bail, Ulrike, Frank Crüsemann, and Marlene Crüsemann, et al., eds. *Bibel in gerechter Sprache*. 2nd ed. Gütersloh: Gütersloher Verlagshaus, 2006.

Bailey, Randall C. "Reading Backwards: A Narrative Technique for the Queering of David, Saul, and Samuel." In *The Fate of King David: The Past and Present of a Biblical Icon*, edited by Tod Linafelt, Claudia V. Camp, and Timothy Beal. LHBOTS 500. New York: T&T Clark, 2010.

Bailey, Randall C., Tat-siong Benny Liew, and Fernando F. Segovia, eds. *They Were All Together in One Place? Toward Minority Biblical Criticism*. SemeiaSt 57. Atlanta: SBL, 2009.

Bakhos, Carol, and Gerhard Langer, eds. *The Jewish Middle Ages*. BW 4.2. Atlanta: SBL, 2023.

Bal, Mieke. *Lethal Love: Feminist Literary Readings of Biblical Love Stories*. Bloomington: Indiana University Press, 1987.

Bar-Efrat, Shimon. *Das Erste Buch Samuel: Ein narratologisch-philologischer Kommentar*. Translated by Johannes Klein. BWANT 176. 9 Folge, Heft 16. Stuttgart: Verlag W. Kohlhammer, 2007.

Bashi, Sari. "Can Gaza Survive?" *Jacobin*, April 25, 2018. https://www.jacobinmag.com/2018/04/gaza-strip-palestine-israel-occupation-blockade.

Baskin, Judith R. "Women and Post-Biblical Commentary." In *The Torah: A Women's Commentary*, edited by Tamara Cohn Eskenazi and Andrea L. Weiss. New York: URJ Press and Women of Reform Judaism, The Federation of Temple Sisterhoods, 2008.

Beavis, Mary Ann, Irmtraud Fischer, Mercedes Navarro Puerto, and Adriana Valerio, eds. *The Bible and Women: An Encyclopaedia of Exegesis and Cultural History (BW)*. Atlanta: Society of Biblical Literature, 2011. https://www.bibleandwomen.org.

Ben-Meir. "Nabal, the Villain." *JBQ* 22 (1994): 249–251.

Ben Zion, Ilan. "Ancient West Bank Site Draws Christians, and Controversy." *Arab News Pakistan*, March 27, 2019. http://www.arabnews.pk/node/1473241/middle-east.

Berlin, Adele. *Poetics and Interpretation of Biblical Narrative*. Sheffield: Almond Press, 1983.

"Biblical Town of Ziklag May Have Been Discovered." *BAS*, July 27, 2019. https://www.biblicalarchaeology.org/daily/biblical-town-of-ziklag-may-have-been-discovered/.

Bird, Phyllis A. *Missing Persons and Mistaken Identities: Women and Gender in Ancient Israel*. Minneapolis: Fortress, 1997.

Blenkinsopp, Joseph. *David Remembered: Kingship and National Identity in Ancient Israel*. Grand Rapids, MI: Eerdmans, 2013.

Blenkinsopp, Joseph. *A History of Prophecy in Israel*. Rev. ed. Louisville, KY: Westminster John Knox, 1996.

"Blockade of Gaza Strip." *Britannica*. https://www.britannica.com/place/Gaza-Strip/Blockade.

Bodner, Keith. "Ark-Eology: Shifting Emphases in 'Ark Narrative' Scholarship." *CurBR* 4 (2006): 169–197.

Boggs, Belle. *The Art of Waiting: On Fertility, Medicine, and Motherhood*. Minneapolis: Graywolf Press, 2016.

Borowski, Oded. "The Biblical Identity of Tel Halif." *BA* 51 (1988): 21–27.

Børresen, Kari Elisabeth, and Adriana Valerio, eds. *The High Middle Ages*. BW 9.1. Atlanta: SBL, 2015.

Borschel-Dan, Amanda. "With Bibles and Shovels, Search for Biblical Tabernacle Gathers Pace at Shiloh." *The Times of Israel*, July 17, 2017. https://www.times ofisrael.com/with-bibles-and-shovels-a-search-for-the-biblical-tabernacle-gathers-pace-at-shiloh/.

Botterweck, G. Johannes, Helmer Ringgren, and Heinz-Josef Fabry, eds. *Theological Dictionary of the Old Testament*. Vol. 10. Translated by Douglas W. Stott. Grand Rapids, MI: Eerdmans, 1999.

Brenner, Athalya, ed. *Samuel and Kings: A Feminist Companion to the Bible*. FCB 5. Sheffield: Sheffield Academic, 1994.

Brenner, Athalya, ed. *Samuel and Kings: A Feminist Companion to the Bible*. FCB 7. 2nd ser. Sheffield: Sheffield Academic, 2000.

Bright, John. *A History of Israel.* Westminster Aids to the Study of the Scriptures. 3rd ed. Philadelphia: Westminster, 1981.

Broch, Herman. *Massenwahntheorie: Beiträge zu einer Psychologie der Politik.* His Kommentierte Werkausgabe 12. Edited by Paul Michael Lützeler. Frankfurt am Main: Suhrkamp, 1979.

Brody, Robert. *The Geonim of Babylonia and the Shaping of Medieval Jewish Culture.* New Haven, CT: Yale University Press, 2013.

Brueggemann, Walter. "(I)chabod Departed." *PSB* 22 (2001): 115–133.

Butler, Judith. *Gender Trouble: Feminism and the Subversion of Identity.* Routledge Classics. 2nd ed. New York: Routledge, 2006; originally published 1999.

Byron, Gay L., and Vanessa Lovelace. "Introduction: Methods and the Making of Womanist Biblical Hermeneutics." In *Womanist Interpretations of the Bible: Expanding the Discourse,* edited by Gay L. Byron and Vanessa Lovelace. SemeiaSt 85. Atlanta: SBL, 2016.

Caird, George B. "1 Samuel: Introduction and Exegesis." In *The Interpreter's Bible,* edited by George Arthur Buttrick. Vol. 2. New York: Abingdon, 1953.

de Callataÿ, Godefroid, and Bruno Halflants, eds. *On Magic: An Arabic Critical Edition and English Translation of EPISTLE 52a.* Epistles of the Brethren of Purity. Oxford: Oxford University Press, 2011.

Cannon, Katie Geneva. "The Emergence of Black Feminist Consciousness." In *Feminist Interpretation of the Bible,* edited by Letty M. Russell. Philadelphia: Westminster, 1985.

Carlebach, Alexander, and Judith Baskin. "Barrenness and Fertility." In *Encyclopaedia Judaica.* 2nd ed. Edited by Michael Berenbaum and Fred Skolnik. Detroit: Macmillan, 2007.

Carter, Warren. "Matthaean Christology in Roman Imperial Key: Matthew 1.1." In *The Gospel of Matthew in Its Roman Imperial Context,* edited by John Riches and David C. Sim. London: T&T Clark, 2005.

Carter, Warren. *The Roman Empire and the New Testament: An Essential Guide.* Nashville: Abingdon, 2006.

Cartledge, Tony W. *1 & 2 Samuel: Bible Commentary.* SHBC. Macon: Smyth & Helwys, 2001.

Chan, Mary. "The Witch of Endor and Seventeenth-Century Propaganda." *Musica Disciplina* 34 (1980): 205–214.

Chapman, Stephen B. *1 Samuel as Christian Scripture: A Theological Commentary.* Grand Rapids, MI: Eerdmans, 2016.

Chavel, Simeon, and Jessie DeGrado. "Text- and Source-Criticism of 1 Samuel 17–18: A Complete Account." *VT* 70 (2020): 553–580.

Claassens, L. Juliana M. "An Abigail Optic: Agency, Resistance and Discernment in 1 Samuel 25." In *Feminist Frameworks and the Bible: Power, Ambiguity, and Intersectionality*, edited by L. Juliana M. Claassens and Carolyn J. Sharp. LHBOTS 630. London: Bloomsbury T&T Clark, 2017.

Claassens, L. Juliana, and Irmtraud Fischer, eds. *Prophecy and Gender in the Hebrew Bible*. BW 1.2. Atlanta: SBL, 2021.

Claassens, L. Juliana, and Carolyn J. Sharp, eds. *Feminist Frameworks and the Bible: Power, Ambiguity, and Intersectionality*. LHBOTS 630. London: Bloomsbury T&T Clark, 2017.

Consolino, Franca Ela, and Judith Herrin, eds. *The Early Middle Ages*. BW 6.1. Atlanta: SBL, 2020.

Cox, Patricia. "Origen and the Witch of Endor: Toward an Iconoclastic Typology." *AThR* 66 (1984): 137–147.

Cross, Frank Moore. *Canaanite Myth and Hebrew Epic: Essays in the History of the Religion of Israel*. Cambridge, MA: Harvard University Press, 1973.

"Dagan." *Britannica*. https://www.britannica.com/topic/Dagan.

Daly, Mary. *Beyond God the Father: Toward a Philosophy of Women's Liberation*. Boston: Beacon, 1973, 1985.

D'Angelo, Mary Rose. "Women Partners in the New Testament." *JFSR* 6 (1990): 65–86.

Davis, Stacy. "Unapologetic Apologetics: Julius Wellhausen, Anti-Judaism, and Hebrew Bible Scholarship." *Religions* 12, no. 8 (August 2021): 1–14.

Deepwell, Katy. "Feminist Interpretation of Witches and the Witch Craze in Contemporary Art by Women." *Pomegranate* 21 (2019): 146–171.

De-Whyte, Janice P. *Wom(b)an: A Cultural-Narrative Reading of the Hebrew Bible Barrenness Narratives*. BibInt 162. Leiden: Brill, 2018.

Dinkler, Michal Beth. *Literary Theory and the New Testament*. AYBRL. New Haven, CT: Yale University Press, 2019.

Drews, Robert. "Canaanites and Philistines." *JSOT* 23 (1998): 39–61.

Drury, Nevill. *Magic and Witchcraft: From Shamanism to the Technopagans*. New York: Thames & Hudson, 2003.

Dube, Musa W. *Postcolonial Feminist Interpretation of the Bible*. St. Louis: Chalice, 2000.

Dworkin, Andrea. "Against the Male Flood: Censorship, Pornography, and Equality." In *Feminism and Pornography*, edited by Drucilla Cornell. Oxford Readings in Feminism. Oxford: Oxford University Press, 2000.

Eagleton, Terry. *Ideology: An Introduction*. London: Verso, 2007.

Eagleton, Terry. *Literary Theory: An Introduction*. 3rd ed. Minneapolis: University of Minnesota Press, 2008.

Edenburg, Cynthia. "Notes on the Origin of the Biblical Tradition Regarding Achish King of Gath." *VT* 61 (2011): 34–38.

El Baba, Eyad. "Gaza Could Become Uninhabitable in Less than Five Years Due to Ongoing 'De-development'—*UN Report*." UN News, September 1, 2015. https://news.un.org/en/story/2015/09/507762-gaza-could-become-uninhabitable-less-five-years-due-ongoing-de-development-un.

Ellis, Kirsten. *Star of the Morning: The Extraordinary Life of Lady Hester Stanhope*. New York: HarperPress, 2008.

El-Naggar, Mona, Yousur Al-Hlou, and Aliza Aufrichtig. "Stripped, Groped and Violated: Egyptian Women Describe Abuse by the State." *New York Times*, July 5, 2021. https://www.nytimes.com/interactive/2021/07/05/world/middleeast/egypt-sexual-assault-police.html.

Emanuel, Jeffrey P. "'Dagon Our God': Iron I Philistine Cult in Text and Archaeology." *JANER* 16 (2016): 22–66.

Eskenazi, Tamara Cohn, and Andrea L. Weiss, eds. *The Torah: A Women's Commentary*. New York: URJ Press and Women of Reform Judaism, The Federation of Temple Sisterhoods, 2008.

Exum, J. Cheryl. *Fragmented Women: Feminist (Sub)versions of Biblical Narratives. Cornerstones*. 2nd ed. London: Bloomsbury T&T Clark, 2016.

Exum, J. Cheryl. "Second Thoughts about Secondary Characters: Women in Exodus 1.8–2.10." In *A Feminist Companion to Exodus to Deuteronomy*, edited by Athalya Brenner. FCB 6. Sheffield: Sheffield Academic, 1994.

Exum, J. Cheryl, and David J. A. Clines, eds. *The New Literary Criticism and the Hebrew Bible*. Valley Forge, PA: Trinity Press International, 1993.

Farber, Zev. "Unspoken Hemorrhoids: Making the Torah Reading Polite." *The Torah.com*. https://www.thetorah.com/article/unspoken-hemorrhoids-making-the-torah-reading-polite.

Fell, Margaret. *Women's Speaking Justified, Proved and Allowed by the Scriptures*. London, 1666.

Fetterley, Judith. *The Resisting Reader: A Feminist Approach to American Fiction*. Bloomington: Indiana University Press, 1978.

Fewell, Danna Nolan, and David M. Gunn. *Gender, Power, and Promise: The Subject of the Bible's First Story*. Nashville: Abingdon, 1993.

Finkelstein, Israel. "The Philistines in the Bible: A Late-Monarchic Perspective." *JSOT* 27 (2002): 131–167.

Finkelstein, Israel. "Tell el-Fûl Revisited: The Assyrian and Hellenistic Periods (with a New Identification)." *PEQ* 143 (2011): 106–118.

Finkelstein, Israel, and Thomas Römer. "The Historical and Archaeological Background Behind the Old Israelite Ark Narrative." *Bib* 101 (2020): 161–185.

Finkelstein, Israel, Shlomo Bunimovitz, and Zvi Lederman, eds. *Shiloh: The Archaeology of a Biblical Site*. Monograph Series of the Institute of Archaeology Tel Aviv University 10. Tel Aviv: Institute of Archaeology of Tel Aviv University, Publications Section, 1993.

Fischer, Irmtraud, and Mercedes Navarro Puerto, with Andrea Taschl-Erber, eds. *Torah*. BW 1.1. Atlanta: SBL, 2011.

Flanagan, Alice. "Techno-Feudalism and the End of Capitalism," April 30, 2021. https://nowthenmagazine.com/articles/yanis-varoufakis-techno-feudalism-and-the-end-of-capitalism.

Fleishman, Joseph. *Father-Daughter Relations in Biblical Law*. Bethesda, MD: CDL Press, 2011.

Fritz, Volkmar. "Where Is David's Ziklag?" *BAR* 19 (1993): 58–61, 76.

Frolov, Serge. "Synchronic Readings of Joshua–Kings." In *The Oxford Handbook of the Historical Books of the Hebrew Bible*, edited by Brad E. Kelle and Brent A. Strawn. Oxford: Oxford University Press, 2020.

Frye, Northrop. *The Great Code: The Bible and Literature*, edited by Alvin A. Lee. Toronto: University of Toronto Press, 2006.

Frymer-Kensky, Tikva. *Reading the Women of the Bible: A New Interpretation of Their Stories*. New York: Schocken Books, 2002.

Frymer-Kensky, Tikva. *Studies in Bible and Feminist Criticism*. JPS Scholar of Distinction Series. Philadelphia: The Jewish Publication Society, 2006.

Fuchs, Esther. *Feminist Theory and the Bible: Interrogating the Sources*. Feminist Studies and Sacred Texts. Lanham, MD: Lexington Books, 2016.

Fuchs, Esther. "The Literary Characterization of Mothers and Sexual Politics in the Hebrew Bible." *Semeia* 46 (1989): 151–166.

Fuchs, Esther. "Prophecy and the Construction of Women: Inscription and Erasure." In *A Feminist Companion to Prophets and Daniel*, edited by Athalya Brenner. FCB 8. 2nd Series. Sheffield: Sheffield Academic, 2001.

Fuchs, Esther. *Sexual Politics in the Biblical Narrative: Reading the Hebrew Bible as a Woman*. JSOTSup 310. Sheffield: Sheffield Academic, 2000.

Gafney, Wilda C. *Womanist Midrash: A Reintroduction to the Women of the Torah and the Throne*. Louisville, KY: Westminster John Knox, 2017.

Garroway, Kristine Henriksen. "Digging Up the Past: The History of Women Archaeologists in the Society of Biblical Literature." *lectio difficilior* (January 2020). https://lectio.unibe.ch/en/archive/kristine-henriksen-garroway-digging-up-the-past-the-history-of-women-archaeologists-in-the-society-of-biblical-literature.html.

Garsiel, Moshe. *The First Book of Samuel: A Literary Study of Comparative Structures, Analogies and Parallels*. 3rd ed. Jerusalem: Rubin Mass, 1990.

Gaß, Erasmus. "Achisch von Gat als politische Witzfigur." *TQ* 189 (2009): 210–242.

"Gaza: Israel's 'Open-Air Prison' at 15: Israel, Egypt Movement Restrictions Wreak Havoc on Palestinian Lives." *Human Rights Watch*, June 14, 2022. https://www.hrw.org/news/2022/06/14/gaza-israels-open-air-prison-15.

Getty-Sullivan, Mary Ann. *Women in the New Testament*. Collegeville, MN: Liturgical Press, 2001.

Gibb, Lorna. *Lady Hester: Queen of the East*. London: Faber and Faber, 2005.

Giroux, Henry A. *Race, Politics, and Pandemic Pedagogy: Education in a Time of Crisis*. London: Bloomsbury Academic, 2021.

Gitay, Yehoshua. "Reflections on the Poetics of the Samuel Narrative: The Question of the Ark Narrative." *CBQ* 54 (1992): 221–230.

Gold, Victor Roland, Thomas L. Hoyt Jr., Sharon H. Ringe, Susan Brooks Thistlethwaite, Burton H. Throckmorton Jr., and Barbara A. Withers, eds. *The New Testament and Psalms: An Inclusive Version*. New York: Oxford University Press, 1995.

Gonzalez, Michelle A. "Latina Feminist Theology: Past, Present, and Future." *JFSR* 25 (2009): 150–155.

Good, Deirdre J. "Reading Strategies for Biblical Passages on Same-Sex Relations." *Theology and Sexuality* 7 (1997): 70–82.

Grabbe, Lester L. *Ancient Israel: What Do We Know and How Do We Know It?* Rev. ed. London: Bloomsbury T&T Clark, 2017.

Graham, John A. "Chapter 1: Previous Excavations at Tell el- Fûl; A Survey of Research and Exploration." *AASOR* 45 (1978): 1–17.

Graham-Harrison, Emma. "Armed Afghan Women Take to Streets in Show of Defiance Against Taliban." *Guardian*, July 7, 2021. https://www.theguardian.com/world/2021/jul/07/armed-afghan-women-take-to-streets-in-show-of-defiance-against-taliban.

Greco, Albert N. *The Economics of the Publishing and Information Industries: The Search for Yield in a Disintermediated World*. New York: Routledge, 2015.

Grimké, Sarah. *Letters on the Equality of the Sexes and the Condition of Woman*. Boston: Isaac Knapp, 1838.

Guest, Deryn. "Judges." In *The Queer Bible Commentary*, edited by Deryn Guest, Robert E. Goss, Mona West, and Thomas Bohache. London: SCM Press, 2006.

Guest, Deryn. *When Deborah Met Jael: Lesbian Biblical Hermeneutics*. London: SCM Press, 2005.

Guiley, Rosemary Ellen. *The Encyclopedia of Witches, Witchcraft and Wicca*. 3rd ed. New York: Facts on File, 2008.

Gutzwiller, Kathryn J., and Ann Norris Michelini. "Women and Other Strangers: Feminist Perspectives in Classical Literature." In *(En)gendering Knowledge: Feminists in Academe*, edited by Joan E. Hartmand and Ellen Messer-Davidow. Knoxville: University of Tennessee Press, 1991.

Gwertzman, Bernard. "The Tragedy of Palestinian Divisions." *Council on Foreign Relations*, October 28, 2009. https://www.cfr.org/interview/tragedy-palestinian-divisions.

Habel, Norman C., and Peter Trudinger. *Exploring Ecological Hermeneutics*. SymS 46. Atlanta: SBL, 2008.

Habermann, Abraham. "Bomberg, Daniel." In *Encyclopaedia Judaica*. 2nd ed., edited by Michael Berenbaum and Fred Skolnik. Detroit: Macmillan, 2007.

Hackett, Jo Ann. "1 and 2 Samuel." In *Women's Bible Commentary*. 3rd ed., edited by Carol A. Newsom, Sharon H. Ringe, and Jacqueline E. Lapsley. Louisville, KY: Westminster John Knox, 2012.

Hareven, Gail. "בעלת האוב" ("The Medium"). In *מקראיות מיניאטורות*. *Biblical Miniatures*. Jerusalem: Bialik Institute, 2018.

Harris, Horton. "Albright's Identification of Gibeah with Tell el-Fûl." *PEQ* 146 (2014): 17–30.

Hearon, Holly E., and Philip Ruge-Jones, eds. *The Bible in Ancient and Modern Media: Story and Performance*. Eugene, OR: Cascade Books, 2009.

Hens-Piazza, Gina. *The New Historicism*. GBS, Old Testament Series. Minneapolis: Fortress, 2002.

Hertzberg, Hans Wilhelm. *I and II Samuel*. Translated by J. S. Bowden. OTL. Philadelphia: Westminster, 1965.

Hill, Robert C. "St John Chrysostom's Homilies on Hannah." *SVTQ* 45 (2001): 319–338.

Hodges, Frederick M. "The Ideal Prepuce in Ancient Greece and Rome: Male Genital Aesthetics and Their Relation to *Lipodermos*, Circumcision, Foreskin Restoration, and the *Kynodesmē*." *Bulletin of the History of Medicine* 75 (2001): 375–405.

Hoffner, Harry A., Jr. "A Hittite Analogue to the David and Goliath Contest of Champions?" *CBQ* 30 (1968): 220–225.

Hornsby, Teresa J., and Ken Stone, eds. *Bible Trouble: Queer Reading at the Boundaries of Biblical Scholarship*. Semeia 67. Atlanta: SBL, 2011.

Horowitz, Elliott. *Reckless Rites: Purim and the Legacy of Jewish Violence.* Princeton: Princeton University Press, 2018.

Horwitz, Liora Kolska, Rona Winter-Livneh, and Aren M. Maeir. "'The Archaeological Picture Went Blank': Historical Archaeology and GIS Analysis of the Landscape of the Palestinian Village of Tell eṣ-Ṣâfi." *NEA* 81 (2018): 85–91.

Hugo, Philippe, and Adrian Schenker, eds. *Archaeology of the Books of Samuel: The Entangling of the Textual and Literary History.* VTSup 132. Leiden: Brill, 2010.

Ilan, Tal, Lorena Miralles-Maciá, and Ronit Nikolsky, eds. *Rabbinic Literature.* BW 4.1. Atlanta: SBL, 2022.

Isasi-Díaz, Ada María. *Mujerista Theology: A Theology for the Twenty-First Century.* Maryknoll, NY: Orbis Books, 1996.

Jeffers, Ann. "Forget It: The Case of Women's Rituals in Ancient Israel, or How to Remember the Woman of Endor." In *The Bible and Feminism: Remapping the Field,* edited by Yvonne Sherwood and Anna Elizabeth Fisk. Oxford: Oxford University Press, 2017.

Jennings, Theodore W., Jr. "YHWH as Erastes." In *Queer Commentary and the Hebrew Bible*, edited by Ken Stone. JSOTSup 334. Sheffield: Sheffield Academic, 2001.

Jobling, David. *1 Samuel.* Berit Olam. Collegeville, MN: Liturgical Press, 1998.

Jobling, David. *The Sense of Biblical Narrative: Three Structural Analyses in the Old Testament.* JSOTSup 7. Sheffield: University of Sheffield Press, 1978.

Jobling, David, and Tina Pippin, eds. *Ideological Criticism of Biblical Texts.* Semeia 59. Atlanta: Scholars Press, 1992.

Joffe, Lisa Fishbayn. "What's the Harm in Polygamy? Multicultural Toleration and Women's Experience of Plural Marriage." *Journal of Law and Religion* 31 (2016): 336–353.

Johnson, Benjamin J. M. *Reading David and Goliath in Greek and Hebrew: A Literary Approach.* Forschungen zum Alten Testament 2. Reihe 82. Tübingen: Mohr Siebeck, 2015.

Johnson, Elizabeth A. "God." In *Dictionary of Feminist Theologies*, edited by Letty M. Russell and J. Shannon Clarkson. Louisville, KY: Westminster John Knox, 1996.

Johnson, Elizabeth A. *She Who Is: The Mystery of God in Feminist Theological Discourse.* New York: Crossroad, 1992.

Jones, Emily. "'I Am Very Excited to Be Here': Netanyahu, Huckabee Tour Ancient Shilo." *CBNNews*, March 20, 2019. https://www1.cbn.com/cbnnews/israel/2019/march/i-am-very-excited-to-be-here-netanyahu-huckabee-tour-ancient-shilo-nbsp.

Keren, Orly, and Hagit Taragan. "Merab, Saul's Mute and Muffled Daughter." *JBL* 134 (2015): 85–103.

Kessler, Rainer. *Samuel: Priester und Richter, Königsmacher und Prophet*. Biblische Gestalten 18. Leipzig: Evangelische Verlagsanstalt, 2008.

Kiboko, J. Kabamba. *Divining the Woman of Endor: African Culture, Postcolonial Hermeneutics, and the Politics of Biblical Translation*. LHBOTS 644. London: T&T Clark, 2017.

Kim, Jong-Hoon. *Die hebräischen und griechischen Textformen der Samuel- und Königebücher: Studien zur Textgeschichte ausgehen von 2 Sam 15, 1–19, 9*. BZAW 394. Berlin: De Gruyter, 2009.

Kinglake, A. W. *Eothen, Or Traces of Travel Brought Home from the East*. London: John Ollivier, 1844.

Kitzberger, Ingrid Rosa, ed. *Autobiographical Biblical Criticism: Between Text and Self*. Leiden: Deo, 2002.

Klein, Johannes. "Davids Flucht zu den Philistern (1 Sam. XXI 11ff.; XXVII– XXIX)." *VT* 55 (2005): 176–184.

Klein, Lillian R. "Michal, the Barren Wife." In *Samuel and Kings: A Feminist Companion to the Bible*, edited by Athalya Brenner, 37–46. FCB 7. 2nd Series. Sheffield: Sheffield Academic, 2000.

Klein, Ralph W. *1 Samuel*. 2nd ed. WBC 10. Nashville: Thomas Nelson, 2008.

Kleiner, Michael. *Saul in En-Dor. Wahrsagung oder Toten-beschwörung? Eine Synchrone und Diachrone Analyse von 1 Sam. 28, 3-25*. Erfurter Theologische Studien 66. Leipzig: Benno, 1995.

Kochavi, Moshe. "An Ostracon of the Period of the Judges from 'Izbet Sartah." *Tel Aviv: Journal of the Institute of Archaeology of Tel Aviv University* 4 (1977): 1–13.

Kraemer, Ross Shepard, and Mary Rose D'Angelo, eds. *Women and Christian Origins*. New York: Oxford University Press, 1999.

LaCugna, Catherine Mowry. *God for Us: The Trinity and Christian Life*. San Francisco: HarperCollins, 1991.

Lapp, Nancy L. "The Third Campaign at Tell el-Fûl: The Excavations of 1964." *AASOR* 45 (1978): i–313.

Lanard, Noah. "The Dangerous History Behind Netanyahu's Amalek Rhetoric." *Mother Jones*, November 3, 2023. https://www.motherjones.com/politics/2023/11/benjamin-netanyahu-amalek-israel-palestine-gaza-saul-samuel-old-testament/.

Lehmann, Hartmut. "Pietism and Nationalism: The Relationship Between Protestant Revivalism and National Renewal in Nineteenth-Century Germany." *CH* 51 (1982): 39–53.

Lehtipuu, Outi, and Silke Petersen, eds. *Ancient Christian Apocrypha*. BW 3.2. Atlanta: SBL, 2022.

Lemche, Niels Peter. *Ancient Israel: A New History of Israel.* Cornerstones. 2nd ed. London: T&T Clark, 2015.

Lemche, Niels Peter. *Back to Reason: Minimalism in Biblical Studies.* Discourses in Ancient Near Eastern and Biblical Studies. Sheffield: Equinox, 2022.

Leneman, Helen. *Love, Lust, and Lunacy: The Stories of Saul and David in Music.* Bible in the Modern World 29. Sheffield: Sheffield Phoenix, 2010.

Lerner, Gerda. "One Thousand Years of Feminist Bible Criticism." In *Creation of Feminist Consciousness: From the Middle Ages to Eighteen-Seventy.* New York: Oxford University Press, 1993.

Leuchter, Mark. *Samuel and the Shaping of Tradition.* Biblical Refigurations. Oxford: Oxford University Press, 2013.

Levenson, Alan T. "Was the Documentary Hypothesis Tainted by Wellhausen's Antisemitism?" *TheTorah.com*, 2021. https://thetorah.com/article/was-the-documentary-hypothesis-tainted-by-wellhausens-antisemitism.

Levin, Yigal. "Gath of the Philistines in the Bible and on the Ground: The Historical Geography of Tell eṣ-Ṣâfi/Gath." *NEA* 80 (2017): 232–240.

Lewis, Rona S. Avissar, and Aren M. Maeir. "New Insights into Bliss and Macalister's Excavations at Tell eṣ-Ṣâfi/Gath." *NEA* 80 (2017): 241–243.

Liew, Tat-siong Benny, and Fernando F. Segovia, eds. *Reading Biblical Texts Together: Pursuing Minoritized Biblical Criticism.* SemeiaSt 98. Atlanta: SBL, 2022.

Lorde, Audre. *Sister Outsider: Essays and Speeches.* Trumansburg, NY: Crossing Press, 1984.

Low, Katherine B. "The Sexual Abuse of Lot's Daughters: Reconceptualizing Kinship for the Sake of Our Daughters." *JFSR* 26 (2010): 37–54.

Lukens-Bull, Ronald A., and Mark R. Woodward. "Goliath and David in Gaza: Indonesian Myth-Building and Conflict as a Cultural System." *Contemporary Islam* 5 (2011): 1–17.

Lynk, Michael. "How Gaza Was Made into an Unlivable Place." *Al Jazeera*, July 24, 2017. https://www.aljazeera.com/indepth/opinion/2017/07/gaza-unlivable-place-170723091946355.html.

Maeir, Aren M. "A New Interpretation of the Term *ʿopalim* (עפלים) in the Light of Recent Archaeological Finds from Philistia." *JSOT* 32 (2007): 23–40.

Maeir, Aren M. "Philistine and Israelite Identities: Some Comparative Thoughts." *Die Welt des Orients* 49 (2019): 151–160.

Maeir, Aren M. "Philistine Gath after 20 Years: Regional Perspectives on the Iron Age at Tell eṣ-Ṣâfi/Gath." In *The Shephelah During the Iron Age: Recent Archaeological Studies*, edited by Oded Lipschits and Aren M. Maeir. Winona Lake, IN: Eisenbrauns, 2017.

Maeir, Aren M., ed. *Tel eṣ-Ṣâfi/Gath I: The 1996–2005 Seasons*. Vol. 1: *Text*. Vol. 2: *Plates*. Ägypten und Altes Testament 69. Wiesbaden: Harrassowitz, 2012.

Maeir, Aren M. "The Tell eṣ-Ṣâfi/Gath Archaeological Project: Overview." *NEA* 80 (2017): 212–231.

Maier, Christl M., and Nuria Calduch-Benages, eds. *The Writings and Later Wisdom Books*. BW 1.3. Atlanta: SBL, 2014.

Maeir, Aren M., Louise A. Hitchcock, and Liora Kolska Horwitz. "On the Constitution and Transformation of Philistine Identity." *Oxford Journal of Archaeology* 32 (2013): 1–38.

Maier, Christl M., and Carolyn J. Sharp. *Prophecy and Power: Jeremiah in Feminist and Postcolonial Perspective*. London: Bloomsbury, 2013.

Malbon, Elizabeth Struthers, and Edgar V. McKnight, eds. *The New Literary Criticism and the New Testament*. Valley Forge, PA: Trinity Press International, 1994.

Malul, Meir. "Some Measures of Population Control in the Ancient Near East." In *Michael: Historical, Epigraphical and Biblical Studies in Honor of Prof Michael Heltzer*, edited by Yitzhak Avishur and Robert Deutsch. Jaffa: Archaeological Center Pubs, 1999.

Marble, Annie Russell. *Women of the Bible: Their Services in Home and State*. New York: The Century Co., 1923.

Marchal, Joseph A. "Queer Studies and Critical Masculinity Studies in Feminist Biblical Studies." In *Feminist Biblical Studies in the Twentieth Century: Scholarship and Movement*, edited by Elisabeth Schüssler Fiorenza. BW 9.1. Atlanta: SBL, 2014.

Mari, R. Machir Ben Abba. *Jalkut Machiri: Sammlung halachischer und hagadischer Stellen aus Talmud und Midraschim zu den 150 Psalmen*, edited by Salomon Buber. Vol. 2. Berdychev: J. Scheftel, 1899.

Mbembe, Achille. *Necro-Politics*. Translated by Steven Corcoran. Theory in Forms. Durham, NC: Duke University Press, 2019.

McFague, Sallie. *Models of God: Theology for an Ecological, Nuclear Age*. Philadelphia: Fortress, 1987.

McGeough, Kevin M. *The Ancient Near East in the Nineteenth Century: Appreciations and Appropriations*. Vol. 1: *Claiming and Conquering*. Hebrew Bible Monographs 67. Sheffield: Sheffield Phoenix, 2015.

McGeough, Kevin M. "The Problem with David: Masculinity and Morality in Biblical Cinema." *Journal of Religion and Film* 22 (2018). https://digitalcommons.unomaha.edu/jrf/vol22/iss1/33.

McKinlay, Judith E. *Reframing Her: Biblical Women in Postcolonial Focus*. Sheffield: Sheffield Phoenix, 2004.

Meryon, Charles Lewis. *Travels of Lady Hester [Lucy] Stanhope Forming the Completion of Her Memoirs, Narrated by Her Physician*. 3 vols. London: Henry Colburn, 1846.

Metzger, Bruce M. "To the Reader." In *The Holy Bible Containing the Old and New Testaments with the Apocryphal/Deuterocanonical Books: New Revised Standard Version*. New York: Oxford University Press, 1989.

Meyers, Carol L. *Rediscovering Eve: Ancient Israelite Women in Context*. New York: Oxford University Press, 2013.

Meyers, Carol, Toni Craven, and Ross S. Kraemer, eds. *Women in Scripture: A Dictionary of Named and Unnamed Women in the Hebrew Bible, the Apocryphal/ Deuterocanonical Books, and the New Testament*. Boston: Houghton Mifflin, 2000 / Grand Rapids, MI: Eerdmans, 2001.

Michael, Matthew. "Narrative Conjuring or the Tales of Two Sisters? The Representations of Hannah and the Witch of Endor in 1 Samuel." *JSOT* 42 (2018): 469–489.

Moore, Stephen D. *The Bible in Theory: Critical and Postcritical Essays*. Atlanta: SBL, 2010.

Moore, Stephen D. *Poststructuralism and the New Testament: Derrida and Foucault at the Foot of the Cross*. Minneapolis: Fortress, 1994.

Moss, Candida R., and Joel S. Baden. *Reconceiving Infertility: Biblical Perspectives on Procreation and Childlessness*. Princeton: Princeton University Press, 2015.

Munro, Ealasaid. "Feminism: A Fourth Wave?" *Political Insight* (September 2013). https://journals.sagepub.com/doi/pdf/10.1111/2041-9066.12021.

Mykytiuk, Lawrence J. "Is Hophni in the 'Izbet Sartah Ostracon?" *AUSS* 36 (1998): 69–80.

Nelson, Steven. "Bill Clinton 15 Years Ago: 'I Did Not Have Sexual Relations with That Woman.'" *US News*, January 25, 2013. https://www.usnews.com/news/ blogs/press-past/2013/01/25/bill-clinton-15-years-ago-i-did-not-have-sexual-relations-with-that-woman.

"Netanyahu's References to Violent Biblical Passages Raise Alarm Among Critics." *npr*, November 7, 2023. https://www.npr.org/2023/11/07/1211133201/netanyahus-references-to-violent-biblical-passages-raise-alarm-among-critics.

Ngan, Lai Ling Elizabeth. "Class Privilege in Patriarchal Society: Women in First and Second Samuel." In *Feminist Interpretation of the Hebrew Bible in Retrospect: Biblical Books (Vol. 1)*, edited by Susanne Scholz. Recent Research in Biblical Studies 5. Sheffield: Sheffield Phoenix, 2013.

Niditch, Susan. *"My Brother Esau Is a Hairy Man": Hair and Identity in Ancient Israel.* New York: Oxford University Press, 2008.

Nitsche, Stefan Ark. *David gegen Goliath: Die Geschichte der Geschichten einer Geschichte: Zur fächerübergreifenden Reyeption einer biblischen Story*. Altes Testament und Moderne 4. Münster: Lit Verlag, 1998.

Noth, Martin. *The Deuteronomistic History*. JSOTSup 15. Sheffield: JSOT, 1981.

Noth, Martin. *The History of Israel.* Translated by P. R. Ackroyd. 2nd ed. Harper Theological Library. New York: Harper & Row, 1960.

Noth, Martin. *Überlieferungsgeschichtliche Studien: Die sammelnden und bearbeitenden Geschichtswerke im Alten Testament.* 2nd ed. Tübingen: Max Niemeyer Verlag, 1957.

Nowell, Irene. *Women in the Old Testament.* Collegeville, MN: Liturgical Press, 1997.

Nussbaum, Martha C. "Objectification." *Philosophy and Public Affairs* 24 (1995): 249–291.

OCHA. "The Humanitarian Impact of the Internal Palestinian Divide on the Gaza Strip," June 23, 2017. https://www.ochaopt.org/content/humanitarian-impact-internal-palestinian-divide-gaza-strip-june-2017.

Ofer, Rachel. "A Wicked Witch or a Good Psychotherapist? The Medium of Endor in Modern Hebrew Literature." *HS* 62 (2021): 181–205.

Oren, Eliezer. "Ziglag: A Biblical City on the Edge of the Negev." *BA* 45 (1982): 155–166.

Papadaki, Evangelia (Lina). "Feminist Perspectives on Objectification." *Stanford Encyclopedia of Philosophy*, March 10, 2010. https://plato.stanford.edu/entries/feminism-objectification/.

Peleg, Yaron. "Love at First Sight? David, Jonathan, and the Biblical Politics of Gender." *JSOT* 30 (2005): 171–189.

Penchansky, David. "Deconstruction." In *The Oxford Encyclopedia of Biblical Interpretation*, edited by Steven McKenzie. New York: Oxford University Press, 2013.

Petersen, Alan. "Research on Men and Masculinities: Some Implications of Recent Theory for Future Work." *Men and Masculinities* 6 (2003): 54–69.

Peterson, Brian Neil. *The Authors of the Deuteronomistic History: Locating a Tradition in Ancient Israel.* Minneapolis: Fortress, 2014.

Pigott, Susan M. "1 Samuel 28—Saul and the *Not* So Wicked Witch of Endor." *RevExp* 95 (1998): 435–444.

Pini, Barbara, and Bob Pease. "Gendering Methodologies in the Study of Men and Masculinities." In *Men, Masculinities and Methodologies*, edited by Barbara Pini and Bob Pease. Genders and Sexualities in the Social Sciences. Houndmills: Palgrave Macmillan, 2013.

Pioske, Daniel. "Material Culture and Making Visible: On the Portrayal of Philistine Gath in the Book of Samuel." *JSOT* 43 (2018): 3–27.

Polzin, Robert. *Samuel and the Deuteronomist: A Literary Study of the Deuteronomic History: Part 2: 1 Samuel*. San Francisco: Harper and Row, 1989.

Posadas, Jeremy D. "Teaching the Cause of Rape Culture: Toxic Masculinity." *JFSR* 33 (2017): 177–179.

Priests for Equality. *The Inclusive Bible: The First Egalitarian Translation*. Lanham, MD: Rowman and Littlefield, 2007.

Rampton, Martha. "Four Waves of Feminism." October 25, 2015. https://www.pacificu.edu/magazine/four-waves-feminism.

Rees, Thomas. "Barren." In *The International Standard Bible Encyclopedia (Vol. 1: A–D)*, edited by Geoffrey William Bromiley. Grand Rapids, MI: Eerdmans, 1979.

Ress, Mary Judith. *Ecofeminism in Latin America*. Women from the Margins. Maryknoll, NY: Orbis Books, 2006.

Reis, Pamela Tamarkin. "Eating the Blood: Saul and the Witch of Endor." *JSOT* 22 (1997): 3–23.

Ringe, Sharon H. "When Women Interpret the Bible." In *Women's Bible Commentary*, edited by Carol A. Newsom, Sharon H. Ringe, and Jacqueline E. Lapsley. 3rd ed. Louisville, KY: Westminster John Knox, 2012.

Robinson, Edward. *Biblical Researches in Palestine, and in the Adjacent Regions*. Vol. 1: *Journal of Travels in the Year 1838*. Boston: Crocker and Brewster, 1856.

Ronen, Gil. "Digging Up Shiloh." *Israel National News*, July 28, 2010. http:// www.israelnationalnews.com/News/News.aspx/138836.

Roskin, Michael G., Robert L. Cord, James A. Medeiros, and Walter S. Jones. *Political Science: An Introduction*. 8th ed. Upper Saddle River, NJ: Prentice Hall, 2002.

Rost, Leonhard. *Die Überlieferung von der Thronnachfolge Davids*. BWANT 42. Stuttgart: Kohlhammer, 1926.

Rost, Leonhard. *The Succession to the Throne of David*. Translated by Michael D. Rutter and David M. Gunn. Historic Texts and Interpreters in Biblical Scholarship 1. Sheffield: Almond Press, 1982.

Ruether, Rosemary Radford. *Sexism and God-Talk: Toward a Feminist Theology*. Boston: Beacon, 1993.

Rutledge, David. *Reading Marginally: Feminism, Deconstruction and the Bible*. BibInt 21. Leiden: Brill, 1996.

Said, Edward. "Identity, Authority, and Freedom: The Potentate and the Traveler." *Boundary* 2 21 (1994): 1–18.

Said, Edward W. *Orientalism*. New York: Vintage Books, 1978.

Sakenfeld, Katharine Doob. *Just Wives? Stories of Power and Survival in the Old Testament and Today*. Louisville, KY: Westminster John Knox, 2003.

Sass, Benjamin. *The Genesis of the Alphabet and Its Development in the Second Millennium B.C.* Ägypten und Altes Testament 13. Wiesbaden: Harrassowitz, 1988.

Schlein, Lisa. "UN Says Gaza Could Become Uninhabitable by 2020." *Voice of America*, September 13, 2018. https://www.voanews.com/a/un-says-gaza-could-become-uninhabitable-by-2020/4569898.html.

Schley, Donald G. *Shiloh: A Biblical City in Tradition and History*. JSOTSup 63. Sheffield: JSOT Press, 1989.

Schmid, Konrad. "The Interpretation of Second Temple Judaism as 'Spätjudentum' in Christian Biblical Scholarship." In *Confronting Antisemitism from the Perspectives of Christianity, Islam, and Judaism (An End to Antisemitism! Vol. 2)*, edited by Armin Lange, Kerstin Mayerhofer, Dina Porat, and Lawrence H. Schiffman. Berlin: De Gruyter, 2020.

Schmidt, Brian B. "The 'Witch' of En-Dor, 1 Samuel 28, and Ancient Near Eastern Necromancy." In *Ancient Magic and Ritual Power*, edited by Marvin Meyer and Paul Mirecki. Religions in the Graeco-Roman World 129. Leiden: Brill, 1995.

Schneiders, Sandra M. *The Revelatory Text: Interpreting the New Testament as Sacred Scripture*. Rev. ed. Collegeville, MN: Liturgical Press, 1999.

Scholz, Susanne. *The Bible as Political Artifact: On the Feminist Study of the Hebrew Bible*. Minneapolis: Fortress, 2017.

Scholz, Susanne. "Concubine." *Bible Odyssey*. https://www.bibleodyssey.org/people /related-articles/concubine/.

Scholz, Susanne. "The Disneyfication of Shiloh: Biblical Historiography and Archaeology as Methodological Regimes of Military Occupation." *SJOT* 36 (2022): 112–137.

Scholz, Susanne, ed. *Feminist Interpretation of the Hebrew Bible in Retrospect*. Recent Research in Biblical Studies 7, 8, 9. Sheffield: Sheffield Phoenix, 2013, 2014, 2016.

Scholz, Susanne. *Introducing the Women's Hebrew Bible: Feminism, Gender Justice, and the Study of the Old Testament.* 2nd ed. New York: Bloomsbury, 2017.

Scholz, Susanne. "Postcolonial Biblical Criticism and Feminist Studies." In *The Oxford Handbook of Postcolonial Biblical Criticism*, edited by R. S. Sugirtharajah. Oxford Handbooks. Oxford: Oxford University Press, 2023.

Scholz, Susanne. "Tracing Difference, Power, and the Discourse of Gender: Deconstruction in Feminist Hebrew Bible Studies." In *Feminist Interpretation of the Hebrew Bible in Retrospect (Methods: Vol. 3)*, edited by Susanne Scholz. Sheffield: Sheffield Phoenix, 2016.

Schottroff, Luise, and Marie-Theres Wacker, eds. *Feminist Biblical Interpretation: A Compendium of Critical Commentary on the Books of the Bible and Related Literature*. Translated by Lisa E. Dahill, Everett R. Kalin, Nancy Lukens, Linda M. Maloney, Barbara Rumscheidt, Martin Rumscheidt, and Tina Steiner. Grand Rapids, MI: Eerdmans, 2012.

Schottroff, Luise, and Marie-Theres Wacker, eds. *Kompendium Feministische Bibelauslegung*. Gütersloh: Chr. Kaiser/Gütersloher Verlagshaus, 1998.

Schroeder, Joy A., and Marion Ann Taylor. *Voices Long Silenced: Women Biblical Interpreters Through the Centuries*. Louisville, KY: Westminster John Knox, 2022.

Schroer, Silvia. *Die Samuelbücher*. NSKAT 7. Stuttgart: Verlag Katholisches Bibelwerk, 1992.

Schuller, Eileen, and Marie-Theres Wacker, eds. *Early Jewish Writings*. BW 3.1. Atlanta: SBL, 2017.

Schuller, Kyla. *The Trouble with White Women: A Counterhistory of Feminism*. New York: Bold Type Books, 2021.

Schüngel-Straumann, Helen. "God as Mother in Hosea 11." In *A Feminist Companion to the Latter Prophets*, edited by Athalya Brenner. FCB 8. London: T&T Clark, 2004.

Schüssler Fiorenza, Elisabeth. *Democratizing Biblical Studies: Toward an Emancipatory Educational Space*. Louisville, KY: Westminster John Knox, 2009.

Schuster, Ruth, and Nir Hasson. "Biblical City of Ziklag Where Philistines Gave Refuge to David Found, Researchers Claim." *Haaretz* (July 8, 2019). https://www.haaretz.com/archaeology/.premium.MAGAZINE-biblical-city-where-philistines-gave-refuge-to-david-found-researchers-claim-1.7455800.

Schutte, P. J. W. "When *They*, *We*, and the *Passive* Become *I*—Introducing Autobiographical Biblical Criticism." *HTS Teologiese Studies / Theological Studies* 61 (2005): 401–416.

Segovia, Fernando F. "Criticism in Critical Times: Reflections on Vision and Task." *JBL* 134 (2015): 6–29.

Seifert, Elke. *Töchter und Väter im Alten Testament: Eine ideologiekritische Untersuchung zur Verfügungsgewalt von Vätern über ihre Töchter*. Neukirchener theologische Dissertationen und Habilitationen 9. Neukirchen-Vlyn: Neukirchener Verlag, 1997.

Shanks, Hershel. "A 'Centrist' at the Center of Controversy: BAR Interviews Israel Finkelstein." *BAR* 28 (November/December 2002). https://library.biblicalarchaeology.org/article/a-centrist-at-the-center-of-controversy/.

Shea, William H. "The 'Izbet Ṣarṭah Ostracon." *AUSS* 28 (1990): 59–86.

Sherwood, Yvonne. *A Biblical Text and Its Afterlives: The Survival of Jonah in Western Culture*. Cambridge: Cambridge University Press, 2000.

Sherwood, Yvonne. "Introduction." In *The Bible and Feminism: Remapping the Field*, edited by Yvonne Sherwood with the assistance of Anna Fisk. New York: Oxford University Press, 2017.

Silberman, Neil Asher. *Digging for God and Country: Exploration, Archeology, and the Secret Struggle for the Holy Land, 1799–1917*. New York: Knopf, 1982.

Silberman, Neil Asher. "Restoring the Reputation of Lady Hester Lucy Stanhope: A Little-Known Episode in the Beginnings of Archaeology in the Holy Land." *BAR* 10 (1984): 68–75.

Skeat, Walter W. *An Etymological Dictionary of the English Language*. 3rd ed. Oxford: Clarendon, 1898.

Skeat, Walter W. *The Concise Dictionary of English Etymology: The Pioneering Work on the Roots and Origins of the Language*. Kertfordshire: Wordsworth Editions, 1993.

"Small Business Lessons from 'David and Goliath.'" *Insightsquared*. https://www.nzbizbuysell.co.nz/nz-business/growth/business-lessons-from-david-and-goliath#:~:text=David%20may%20not%20have%20been,do%20and%20do%20it%20well.

Smelik, K. A. D. "The Ark Narrative Reconsidered." In *New Avenues in the Study of the Old Testament: A Collection of Old Testament Studies Published on the Occasion of the Fiftieth Anniversary of the Oudtestamentisch Werkgezelschap and the Retirement of Prof. Dr. M. J. Mulder*, edited by A. S. van der Woude. Oudtestamentische Studiën 25. Leiden: Brill, 1989.

Smelik, K. A. D. "The Witch of Endor: I Samuel 28 in Rabbinic and Christian Exegesis till 800 A.D." *VC* 33 (1979): 160–179.

Sojourner Truth. "Ain't I a Woman?" Modern History Sourcebook. https://sourcebooks.fordham.edu/mod/sojtruth-woman.asp.

Spender, Dale. *Women of Ideas and What Men Have Done to Them: From Aphra Behn to Adrienne Rich*. London: Routledge and Kegan Paul, 1982.

Stahl, Ziv. Emek Shaveh, and Yesh Din. "Appropriating the Past: Israel's Archaeological Practices in the West Bank," December 2017, 1–40. https://emekshaveh.org/en/wp-content/uploads/2017/12/Menachsim-Eng-Web.pdf.

Stanton, Elizabeth Cady. "Introduction." In *The Woman's Bible*. Boston: Northeastern University Press, 1993.

Steinsaltz, Rabbi Adin Even-Israel. *The Koren Talmud Bavli Noé: Avoda Zara Horayot*. Vol. 32. Jerusalem: Koren Publishers, 2017.

Steussy, Marti J. *Samuel and His God*. Studies on Personalities of the Old Testament. Columbia: University of South Carolina Press, 2010.

Stiebert, Johanna. *Fathers and Daughters in the Hebrew Bible*. Oxford: Oxford University Press, 2013.

Stone, Ken. "1 and 2 Samuel." In *The Queer Bible Commentary*, edited by Deryn Guest, Robert E. Goss, Mona West, and Thomas Bohache. London: SCM, 2006.

Stuckey, Johanna H. "The Great Goddesses of the Levant." *Journal of the Society for the Study of Egyptian Antiquities* 30 (2003): 127–157.

Sugirtharajah, R. S., ed. *The Oxford Handbook of Postcolonial Biblical Criticism*. Oxford Handbooks. Oxford: Oxford University Press, 2023.

Taitz, Emily, Sondra Henry, and Cheryl Tallan. *The JPS Guide to Jewish Women 600 B.C.E.–1900 C.E.* Philadelphia: JPS, 2003.

Taylor, Marcus. "David and Goliath: The Most Powerful Motivational Speech of 2020 (Ft. Marcus Taylor)." Motiversity, November 23, 2020. YouTube Video, 10:03. https://www.youtube.com/watch?v=rWZ_y0NiJfI.

Taylor, Marion Ann, and Agnes Choi, eds. *Handbook of Women Biblical Interpreters: A Historical and Biographical Guide*. Grand Rapids, MI: Baker Academic, 2012.

Teitelbaum, Michael S. "Population: Biology and Anthropology." *Encyclopedia Britannica*. https://www.britannica.com/science/population-biology-and-anthropology.

Thornton, Stuart. "Tell eṣ-Ṣâfi/Gath Excavations." *National Geographic Society*, May 20, 2022. https://education.nationalgeographic.org/resource/case-study-tell-es-safigath-excavations.

Tuchman, Barbara W. *Bible and Sword: England and Palestine from the Bronze Age to Balfour*. New York: Ballantine Books, 1984.

United Nations Country Team in Palestine. "Gaza in 2020—A Liveable Place?" August 27, 2012. https://reliefweb.int/report/occupied-palestinian-territory/gaza-2020-liveable-place.

Vander Stichele, Caroline, and Todd C. Penner, eds. *Her Master's Tools? Feminist and Postcolonial Engagements of Historical-Critical Discourse*. Global Perspectives on Biblical Scholarship 9. Atlanta: SBL, 2005.

Van Wijk-Bos, Johanna W. H. *The Road to Kingship: 1–2 Samuel*. A People and a Land. Vol. 2. Grand Rapids, MI: Eerdmans, 2020.

Varoufakis, Yanis. *Another Now: Dispatches from an Alternative Present*. London: Bodley Head, 2020.

Varoufakis, Yanis. "Capitalism Has Become 'Techno-Feudalism.'" *Al Jazeera*, February 19, 2021. https://www.aljazeera.com/program/upfront/2021/2/19/yanis-varoufakis-capitalism-has-become-techno.

Varousfakis, Yanis. *Technofeudalism: What Killed Capitalism*. Brooklyn, NY: Melville House, 2024.

Varoufakis, Yanis. "Techno-Feudalism Is Taking Over." *Project Syndicate*, June 28, 2021. https://www.project-syndicate.org/commentary/techno-feudalism-replacing-market-capitalism-by-yanis-varoufakis-2021-06.

Walker, Alice. *In Search of Our Mothers' Gardens: Womanist Prose*. New York: Harcourt Brace Jovanovich, 1967, 1983.

Wellhausen, Julius. *Geschichte Israels*. Berlin: G. Reimer, 1878.

White, Ellen. "Michal the Misinterpreted." *JSOT* 31 (2007): 451–464.

White, Ethan Doyle. "Wicca." *Encyclopedia Britannica*. https://www.britannica.com/topic/Wicca.

Wiese, Christian. *Challenging Colonial Discourse: Jewish Studies and Protestant Theology in Wilhelmine Germany*. Translated by Barbara Harshav and Christian Wiese. Studies in European Judaism 10. Leiden: Brill, 2005.

Wilde, Winston. "Foreskin." In *Cultural Encyclopedia of the Penis*, edited by Michael Kimmel, Christine Milrod, and Amanda Kennedy. Lanham, MD: Rowman and Littlefield, 2014.

Wilkins, Brett. "Netanyahu Accused of 'Genocidal Intentions' in Gaza After 'Holy Mission' Speech." *Common Dreams*, October 30, 2023. https://www.commondreams.org/news/netanyahu-genocide.

Williams, Delores S. *Sisters in the Wilderness: The Challenge of Womanist God-Talk*. Maryknoll, NY: Orbis Books, 1993.

Willis, Timothy. "Barren, Barrenness." In *The New Interpreter's Dictionary of the Bible*. Vol. 1: A–C, edited by Katherine Doob Sakenfeld, Samuel E. Balentine, Brian K. Blount, Kah-Jin Jeffrey Kuan, Joel B. Green, Eileen Schuller, Pheme Perkins, Paul Franklyn, and Marianne Blickenstaff. Nashville: Abingdon, 2006.

Wimbush, Vincent L. *Scripturalectics: The Management of Meaning*. New York: Oxford University Press, 2017.

Wolde, Ellen van. "A Leader Led by a Lady: David and Abigail in 1 Samuel 25." *ZAW* 114 (2002): 355–375.

Wolin, Sheldon S. *Democracy Incorporated: Managed Democracy and the Specter of Inverted Totalitarianism.* Princeton: Princeton University Press, 2008.

Yee, Gale A. "The Silenced Speak: Hannah, Mary, and Global Poverty." *Feminist Theology* 21 (2012): 40–57.

Yee, Gale A. "Yin/Yang Is Not Me: An Exploration into an Asian American Biblical Hermeneutics." In *Ways of Being, Ways of Reading: Asian American Biblical Interpretation*, edited by Mary F. Foskett and Jeffrey Kah-Jin Kuan. St. Louis: Chalice, 2006.

Zegers-Hochschild, F., G. D. Adamson, J. de Mouzon, O. Ishihara, R. Mansour, K. Nygren, E. Sullivan, and S. Vanderpoel. "International Committee for Monitoring Assisted Reproductive Technology (ICMART) and the World Health Organization (WHO) Revised Glossary of ART Terminology, 2009." *Fertility and Sterility* 92 (2009): 1520–1524.

Zucker, David J. "The Medium of Endor and Saul: Ancient and Contemporary Views." *JBQ* 48 (2020): 235–244.

Zwissler, Laurel. "In the Study of the Witch: Women, Shadows, and the Academic Study of Religions." *Religions* 9 (2018): 1–18.

INDEX OF BIBLICAL AND RELATED TEXTS

INDEX OF AUTHORS